SELECT DISCOURSES

OF

SERENO EDWARDS DWIGHT, D. D.,

PASTOR OF PARK STREET CHURCH, BOSTON; AND PRESIDENT OF HAMILTON COLLEGE, IN NEW YORK.

WITH A

MEMOIR OF HIS LIFE,

BY

WILLIAM T. DWIGHT, D. D.

PASTOR OF THE THIRD CONGREGATIONAL CHURCH, PORTLAND.

BOSTON:
PUBLISHED BY CROCKER AND BREWSTER,
47, Washington-street.
1851.

INTRODUCTION.

THE Discourses, entitled, "The Death of Christ," which extend through the first 168 pages following the Memoir, were delivered in the month of January, 1826, and were published the same year. They have been for many years entirely out of print, and as the discussion of the great question there presented has been thought very able and satisfactory, their republication in this volume, it is believed, will be welcomed by various readers.

In the selection of the Discourses which occupy the remainder of the volume, the Editor could not, of course, aim at any thing like system. Yet, if he mistakes not, a certain sequence and order will be observed. In the first Discourse, entitled, "God's constant trial of man," the hearer, or man universally, is contemplated as the subject of a probation appointed by his Creator. In the second,—"There is no Difference," the results of this probation are distinctly exhibited. In the third,—"Make you a new heart," man, the sinner, is required at once to return in penitence to the holy service of God.—This, which is his most reasonable service, he is immovably disinclined to do: and, therefore, in the fourth Discourse,—"Regeneration, a sovereign work," the Divine Agency which overcomes this hostility, is presented as God's sovereign exercise of grace. In the fifth,—"The Church," as an Association instituted by Christ, and including those who have been professedly regenerated, is considered. In the sixth,—"Why many Christians mistake their own characters," a question affecting the relative usefulness and happiness of many belonging to the Church, is satisfactorily discussed. The seventh,—"Everlasting Life, already begun in the believer," illustrates the greatness of the change of state which has taken place in all the regenerated, or in every Christian. The eighth,—"Fellowship with the Father and the Son," contemplates, in a somewhat different manner, the exalted privileges of which the mature Christian is possessed, while here on earth. In the ninth,—"Heaven," or the final and blissful abode of the Christian, is vividly exhibited. In the tenth,—"Mutual Recognition in Heaven," or the renovation of that acquaintance and intercourse in Heaven which has existed between Christians on earth, is the subject last in order.

To these Discourses is appended an Address on the Greek Revolution. It was originally delivered as a Discourse on the text, "Thou shalt love thy neighbor as thyself;" and was subsequently repeated and then published in its present form, at the request of "the Greek Committee" in Boston, in 1824. It is here republished, as a specimen of the Author's manner, when treating such a subject.

CONTENTS.

MEMOIR.

The Author of these Discourses was extensively known. Although he was compelled by disease to withdraw for the last fifteen years from every kind of active life, few persons, while his health continued, mingled in a larger circle of acquaintances, or made more numerous or warmer friends. His death was truly mourned, and his memory will be cherished by those friends, who have survived him. To such, it is believed, the following Memoir will be acceptable. By others it will, I trust, be deemed sufficient for me to say, that the state of retirement and almost seclusion in which his latter years were passed, and which was strongly contrasted with the stations of public usefulness which he had previously occupied, has seemed to call for some such notice as that which is here given.

Sereno Edwards Dwight was born in Greenfield, a beautiful village in the town of Fairfield, Connecticut, May 18, 1786. He was the fifth son and child of Rev. Timothy Dwight, D. D., LL. D., President of Yale College. His mother, Mrs. Mary Dwight, was the second daughter of Benjamin Woolsey, Esq., of Dosoris, Long Island.

His baptismal name, Sereno Edwards, was given in remembrance of an uncle, the brother of his father, and the next in seniority among a numerous family. This uncle, after having attained to maturity and married, entered the medical profession ; but was lost at sea not far from Nova Scotia, at no distant period before the birth of the nephew. The latter part of the name, Edwards, was given to the uncle in memory of his maternal grandfather, the first President Edwards. The former part, Sereno, was not given as a name of fancy merely, but I have been unable to discover its immediate origin. Its remote source is probably Italian. Its articulate sounds are unusually musical, but the name itself, until within the last thirty years, has been very rare. Whether the surprise which the announcement of a name so uncommon often occasioned, or some other consideration, rendered it unwelcome, to the nephew, is uncertain ; but, from early life, probably, he became dissatisfied with it, and occasionally contemplated either his own silent disuse of it, or its being changed by a legislative act. On the title page of some of his publications he chose that his name should appear, as S. Edwards. His personal dislike to the name, Sereno, has not, however, been entertained by all, as it has been frequently given to various individuals in immediate remembrance of himself.

Young Dwight was, almost from his birth, a child of no ordinary promise. He very early manifested great quickness of apprehension, mastering with ease the usual lessons of children of his own age. His bodily conformation was corresponding. Few who subsequently saw him when he had reached full manhood, or had attained to forty years of age, at either of which periods he was deemed one of the handsomest men of his time, would doubt that, when a little child or an active lad, he must have given promise of the man. In these early years his health was very good, his spirit was uncommonly cheerful and hopeful, and with his active frame and quick intellect he thus presented to his parents and other friends that most attractive spectacle—a bright and ardent boy, on whom life's morning is rising without a cloud, and before whose path the flowers and foliage of May are every where expanding. This development of character and temperament was, in his case, aided by various circumstances. His village birthplace, Greenfield, has been ever indeed a peculiarly secluded spot, but its natural attractions have been rarely equalled. It forms the summit of an elevated hill, whose front looks down on the shores of Long Island Sound at three miles distance, and which recedes inland so as to constitute an extended area. The prospect thus afforded of the surrounding country, and of the inland sea that washes its shore, is noble: hill and valley, widening plains and scattered villages, with the magnificent expanse of the Sound, greeting the eye. On this beautiful spot, and in the midst of a quiet but flourishing village, whose locality secured for its inhabitants a pure and healthy atmosphere, young Dwight was born; and there his childhood and early youth were passed. He was thus nurtured and trained absolutely at home. Unlike many who, in later years, were his classmates at Yale College, unlike thousands of youths who are now in constant training for admission to our literary institutions generally, he was never withdrawn from the guardianship of parental vigilance and affection. Of the fidelity of that guardianship it is unnecessary here to speak. Under its eye, and as the youngest son of the family until he had attained to nine years of age, he grew up through infancy and childhood—not as a sickly hot-house plant, whose artificial richness is the omen of its speedy decay; but a healthy, vigorous shoot, branching forth in natural but not wild luxuriance. His social, intellectual, and moral character was thus formed from the commencement. His father, during the entire residence of the family at Greenfield, taught an academy for pupils of both sexes, which he had himself instituted at the commencement of his pastoral labors. This school soon became celebrated, so that fifty or sixty pupils were annually drawn to the village, a portion of whom became inmates of his own family. This, his then youngest son, became himself one of these pupils as soon as his early years would permit. While his intellect was thus cultivated by his father at the school, and while a less formal but not less valuable mental training was imparted to him by both his parents at home, he was familiarly introduced—even as a child—into polished and intelligent society. His father's house had then become, scarcely less than it was subsequently at New Haven, the centre of a most desirable circle of friends and strangers. Young Sereno's intellect was thus gradually, but rapidly, unfolded, from year to year; while the godly instructions, and example, and prayers of his father constituted the suitable training of his heart. And few pious fathers, it may be here properly said, even among eminent ministers, have been able so to present to their children the character and government of God as constituting the motives to a life of holiness and faith, as was ever done by President Dwight in the bosom of his own family. The result, through the divine blessing was, what may be anticipated in every such case—that this son grew up from the earliest childhood, to "fear God and keep his commandments." Happily preserved as he was from contact with vicious companions in these early years, through the vigilance of parental fidelity and also from the secluded position of the village itself, he then formed the moral habits which were conspicuous to those best acquainted with him in later years. Among these were a deep respect and love for his parents, purity of conversation and feeling, a marked dislike of whatever is mean and grovelling, generosity of spirit, and a conscientious reverence for sacred things.

When Sereno was seven or eight years of age, he was severely attacked by the scarlet fever. The disease took its usual course, and the boy, as was supposed, had recovered; when, in consequence of his playing in the open air in a raw spring day, he caught a bad cold, which was speedily followed by what is called,—the secondary stage of the disease. He was then seized with convulsion fits, of which he had more than thirty, and was brought very near to death. While he was in this state and scarce a hope remained of his recovery, his father, whose parental attachments were very strong, was deeply distressed at the prospect of his death; and as all mortal efforts were evidently powerless, he was led with the greater earnestness to try the efficacy of prayer. While thus interceding for the life of the child, he felt himself prompted to stipulate,—to vow, may be the more accurate language—that, if God would spare the child and restore him to health, he would himself employ all his own influence in training him up for the ministry of the gospel. The state of mind which gave rise to such a vow, or covenant, on the part of the father, will be perfectly intelligible to some who may read this narrative. The true disciple is invited to approach the throne of grace with just such a filial freedom and boldness, in his time of need. He may address Him who is invisible as unreservedly, as confidently, as did ever the father of the faithful, or the lawgiver of Israel,—talking with Him, pleading with Him, covenanting with Him, "as a man talks with his friend." The child was spared to the supplications of the father, and in subsequent years, after having finished his course of study at Yale College and a course of instruction of equal length as an officer in the same institution, he entered on the profession of the law, which he pursued for six years with good success. At that period the vow which the father had made in the son's extremity, and the influence which the father had exercised in successive years, were, through divine grace, made effectual in the choice of the ministry by the son as his future sphere of duty. Anticipating here for a moment what will be more fully specified hereafter, I would add, that the first discourse of the son which was also preached in the presence of the father, was from the passage: " For this child I prayed; and the Lord hath given me my petition which I asked of him. Therefore also I have lent him to the Lord; as long as he liveth he shall be lent to the Lord."

In December, 1795, young Dwight, when between nine and ten years of age, was removed with the other members of the family to New Haven, his father having then entered on the presidency of Yale College. His transfer from the secluded village of Greenfield to the beautiful town, which, for the next twenty-one years, was to be his residence, was doubtless only favorable to himself. Here, as previously, living ever under the parental roof and guided by the same watchfulness and affection, the influence of a literary institution which now began indirectly to affect him, must have tended the more rapidly to form his studious habits, and to develope his mental powers universally. Whether he had commenced the study of the classics while at Greenfield, I have no means of ascertaining; but he entered on such studies immediately after his removal to New Haven, and pursued them diligently until his admission into Yale College in 1799. He passed a portion, perhaps the whole, of this period of his pupilage, under the successive masters of the Hopkins' Grammar school,—an institution, whose origin under a more imposing title dates as far back as 1658, if not earlier. Two of these masters, Stephen Twining, Esq., of the class of 1795, and John Hart Lynde, Esq., of the class of 1796, have been long deceased: a third, the venerable Dr. Murdock, the very learned annotator of Mosheim, still lives in the vicinity of the institution from whose walls he went forth fifty years since. Upon soliciting information from him respecting the scholarship of the subject of this Notice, its writer received the following reply:

"New Haven, March 19, 1851.

Rev. and Dear Sir:—

Your late excellent Brother, the Rev. Sereno E. Dwight, D. D., was under my instruction in the Hopkins' Grammar School at New Haven, during one or two quarters in the year 1798: and he was not only the best scholar in that school, but the best ever under my instruction any where. His progress was so rapid, that he could not be kept in any class more than a few days. He so soon mastered the Greek of Homer, that he took the whole 3d Book of the Iliad (a short Book, indeed) for a single lesson. Besides Greek, he studied Hebrew under me for a time. His conduct in school was a perfect pattern of suavity, docility, and obedience to good order.

I rejoice to hear that you are about to publish a volume of Sermons, selected from those which he left in manuscript, with a memoir of his Life prefixed. It will, I have no doubt, do honor to his memory.

With high esteem,

Dear Sir, yours,

JAS. MURDOCK."

As has been already noticed, young Dwight became a member of Yale College in 1799, when he had somewhat more than completed his thirteenth year. The letter of Dr. Murdock is an assurance that he must have been fully qualified for admission to that seminary: indeed, it is not improbable that, among a class of about seventy, not one of its members was better fitted than himself. A youth, nay, a child—as he may be almost termed, who, while at school, so speedily distanced every class in which he was placed that it became necessary to permit him to study alone, and who could master the third Book of the Iliad at a single lesson, could undoubtedly have been prepared for admission into the same Seminary with honor to himself, had the qualifications for membership in 1799 been the same as they now are in 1851. Still, his age was premature for an entrance upon a college life. Such was, no doubt, the opinion of his Father. But the son had already made so rapid progress, that it would have been very difficult to have confined him for two or three additional years to the walls of a grammar school, especially as he could appeal to the father's example,—the latter having become a member of the Freshman class in the same institution in 1765, at the age of thirteen. Happily, as we shall soon see, young Dwight surmounted every difficulty, and escaped every temptation to which the student at College, and especially the boyish student, is exposed. But the writer would again express his conviction, and it is one in which the officers of the New England colleges will, probably, universally concur, that the admission of youths at the age of thirteen or fourteen is to be deprecated. Such indeed has been in later years the advance in the qualifications for admission, and such the corresponding advance of the whole collegiate course, that a youth of fifteen is now relatively but little older than was the youth of thirteen, fifty years since. But aside from the present demand for more mature powers of mind to grapple with and master the difficulties of the existing course of collegiate studies, a similar advance is needed in moral discrimination and firmness of principle. The temptations besetting the young student, have been greatly increased within the last thirty years,—temptations, if not, as is often the case, to gross sensual indulgence, yet to neglect of study for other objects. Secret societies have during this period been largely multiplied within these seminaries, whose influence, as a whole, has been injurious to scholarship and to morality. The youth is not only, as Wordsworth affirms, "father of the man;" but our literary institutions have become so thoroughly republican, that the youth at college as well as elsewhere is not slow to discover that he is "the man" himself. The parent who would not, probably, be saddened by the career of a son whose intellect and whose morals may be both found wanting in his course of trial, should not send him to the halls of a college before he has attained to sixteen, or, what is better, seventeen years.

The subject of this Memoir, as has been intimated, was the cause of no such parental suffering. Having been exceedingly well fitted, he took at once an honorable position among his classmates, and this position he never subsequently lost. Of about seventy, he was the youngest but two, if not literally the youngest. Many of these were young men, as will be readily believed by those who read over the names of the class of 1803, of vigorous minds,—an equality with whom could be scarcely maintained during successive years of study by one so much younger than themselves. And where in such cases the race is maintained by the stripling *pari passu*, until its very termination, not rarely are his overtasked powers enfeebled for future effort, even if they are not all buried in a premature grave. Young Dwight, possessed, however, too much vigor of body and mind to permit him, either soon to be left behind, or to sink from exhaustion at the honorable termination of the four years' struggle. His scholarship was such, that he received for the Junior year the "Salutary Oration"—a very unusual distinction for a youth of sixteen. When he was graduated at the close of the subsequent college year, at the age of seventeen, he delivered an oration on "Divorces,"—a subject, that seems foreign to the taste or the studies of one still so young, but indicating at the same time, the settled moral principles which he had already adopted. The legislation of Connecticut was even then, as it has continued to be ever since, stained by a law authorizing divorces for other grounds than that which has been established by Him who instituted marriage, and who has never commissioned individuals or legislators to lessen its original sanctity. Young Dwight selected this subject as his theme, and fearlessly maintained the scriptural standard to be the sovereign law.

His moral habits, while a member of the college, as might be presumed from what has been just remarked, were only praiseworthy. It is not intended that he had already become a true disciple of Him, whose gospel he delighted in subsequent years to preach; although many Christians undoubtedly are habitually less exemplary than he was during this period. Neither is it intended, that just such youths apparently as was the subject of this Memoir, are not, and perhaps frequently, the subjects of evangelical piety; although themselves may disclaim the possession of such a character. The child who is born and nurtured within a pious atmosphere, whose first recollections are thus associated with the inculcation of the fear of God, the preciousness of the Saviour, and a conscientious performance of daily duties, and who beholds in the parent's life the bright exemplification of these instructions, may be truly converted long before he himself imagines it. In such cases the outward change—which is the only evidence of the indwelling grace, is often, for a considerable period, scarcely perceptible. Indeed, happier were it for our churches generally, happier for Christian parents and for their children, were the training to be ever steadily directed to just such anticipated results. The family would then, as it were, universally become as it is yet destined to become, the nursery of the Church, and the great primary design of its institution be visibly accomplished. But without affirming that young Dwight was at this season a true Christian, his conduct while in college was truly exemplary. His habits as a private pupil, which, as we have already seen, were those of "suavity, docility, and obedience to good order," were but strengthened while an academical student. His father was at the same time the head of the College ; and while he was a most tender parent, and a kind instructor and counsellor of the young men under his care, he was also a thorough disciplinarian. The son followed the teachings of the father in both these relations, and whether as an individual simply or as a student, was without reproach. These four years were doubtless, in many respects, the happiest period in his life. Such, indeed, would be a true affirmation of most of the Alumni of our colleges. Were they questioned as to those golden years when hope was brightest, and forebodings of the unknown future were all but unknown ; when the days rose and set with scarcely a cloud, because the pulse of health beat full, the toils were light and the intercourse with their fellows was fraternal and joyous;—how many would instantly recur to their college days, and sigh for "joys departed, never to return!" Emphatically might this be asserted of him whose course we have traced thus far. Then in the glow of youth and health, a stranger personally to the ills of life and to that constitutional gloom which is often their precursor, distinguished for his talents and scholarship, his domestic and social relations generally such as many would deem enviable, the months and years of but few could have passed more happily away.

Immediately after his thus leaving college, he accompanied his father, with several other graduates, in one of those journeys through New England, the description of which was ultimately given to the public in the four volumes of President Dwight's Travels. These excursions were made from year to year, during the six weeks' vacation following the annual commencement; and were always most pleasant and profitable, as well to the younger friends who were associated with him as to the author of that work. In those days, when rail-roads had not made travelling a mere matter of swift locomotion, and when half the population of our villages even were not apparently to be found everywhere present except at home, the daily progress of the traveller on horseback or in the chaise along the valley of the Connecticut or from town to town upon the line of sea coast, alternated occasionally by one or more days' resting amid the hospitalities of intelligent and polished families, was a source of pleasure and of health, to which our present system of noise and crowding and whirling onward, which is called,—travelling, varied as it is by a brief abode at some watering place or in a thronged city hotel, can make no pretensions. From one of these most pleasurable excursions, the narrative of which will be found in one of the volumes of the Travels, young Dwight returned homeward after a few weeks' absence, to enter upon what was to him the new business of instruction.

This was as an Assistant in an Academy, which had been established in the village of South Farms, a parish of the beautiful town of Litchfield. The principal was James Morris, Esq., a graduate of Yale College—at this time of more than thirty years' standing, and a man of uncommon worth. He was a student at Yale while President Dwight was a tutor, and their acquaintance subsequently ripened into a friendship which continued through life. The influence of this gentleman upon the intellectual and religious character of the inhabitants of this village was so happy and so long continued, that it was said, and no doubt justly, that "the people of South Farms had grown handsomer in 'Squire Morris's time.'" Our young Alumnus, now but seventeen and a half years of age, passed the coming year as the Assistant of this gentleman, and resided during that period in his family. The pupils were of both sexes, and they came thither from remote states, as well as from the neighboring towns. The studies were classical and miscellaneous, and not a few of the young men were considerably more advanced in age than the Assistant. But his influence as an instructor and as an individual was, apparently, not lessened by the circumstance of his youth. He had now attained to manly stature, his face was bright with intelligence, and his manner was already dignified as well as courteous. His intercourse with Mr. Morris and his worthy family was pleasurable only, the pupils were docile and respectful, and thus the year passed pleasantly away.

Returning to New Haven, he passed the succeeding year as an amanuensis of his father. President Dwight, as is known to the readers of the introductory Memoir of his life in his Systematic Theology, was afflicted from early life, with an extreme weakness of the eyes,—occasioned by their premature use after his recovery from the measles. This weakness was so great that, while he resided in Greenfield, he was compelled to preach habitually from brief notes—being wholly disqualified from writing out his discourses. The same practice was necessarily continued for a number of years after his entrance on the presidency; but as his salary was increased during the latter half of his tenure of the office, he was then enabled to offer a compensation—a most inadequate one indeed,—each year, to an amanuensis. Small as was the stipend, however, the employment was coveted; and fourteen young men, graduates of the college, occupied it during as many successive years till his decease. His System of Theology was thus principally dictated by him during the first four years, to the first four amanuenses, of whom his son, Sereno, was the first. About the first forty discourses of the System were thus written by the subject of this Memoir, as it was the practice of his father, unless when peculiarly interrupted, to dictate a new discourse every week. During the same period also he thus wrote, under the same dictation, various miscellaneous discourses, and certain portions, it is probable, of the Travels. The Theological Sermon was usually dictated, and then written down, during the first two days, when its author was not interrupted by visitors: the remainder of the week was employed in dictating and in writing down other discourses, or miscellaneous compositions. Had not this process been thus pursued, none of President Dwight's Works, some of his occasional discourses excepted, would have ever appeared. In this employment the son was a useful auxiliary to the father.

His intelligence was such, as to require no second utterance of the sentence which had been previously unheard or misunderstood; and his handwriting, though not graceful, was uncommonly legible, and rapidly executed. His own knowledge of Theology as a science, must have been much increased by such an employment. Inquisitive and active as his mind ever was, he could be permitted to propose inquiries and suggest difficulties, and thus become instructed by luminous explanations from his father, which few of those who succeeded him would have deemed allowable to themselves. Possibly had this year not been thus occupied, he might not have ultimately entered the ministry.

The ensuing year, the third after his leaving college, and which also immediately preceded his entrance on the office of Tutor, was devoted, as is supposed, to a course of study more or less general. No reference to this period of his life has been found among his manuscript papers, and the writer of this brief Memoir was then a child, and residing at some distance from New Haven at a classical school, so that his own recollections are here wholly at fault. What this course of study was, and how great the progress made, is matter only for conjecture. His thirst for knowledge, and his more than ordinary facility of acquisition, are assurances that the year must have been profitable.

At the commencement of the college year of 1806, Mr. Dwight became a tutor in Yale College—an office, which he retained for the four succeeding years. This portion of his life, it will be perceived, was of the same duration as his previous course of academical study, and was, perhaps, not less important in the formation of his mind and character. The class of which he took the supervision, in company with his fellow tutor, Mr. Mills Day, (a gentleman, whose premature death was deeply mourned by all acquainted with his modest but uncommon worth,) had been just admitted; so that one half of the class which was specially commited to his instructions, was to continue under his almost exclusive guidance for the three following years. This circumstance was equally favorable to the teacher and to his pupils. He was not thus constrained to build on another's foundation, to make over again what another had previously marred, to subject himself to the invidious comparisons of students who preferred a former teacher's instructions, or discipline, or demeanor. The young men were to be moulded by him solely, so far as the circumstance of his being their only instructor could invest him with such a power; for the present system of appointing tutors to specific departments of instruction is, comparatively, of recent date. The character of the class, and particularly of his own division, was also desirable. It is the class of 1810 in the Triennial Catalogue, and the names there enrolled of many since become eminent in the various walks of life assure us, that there was no ordinary amount of talents then placed under the supervision of a single instructor. The letter of Rev. Dr. Goodrich, which appears below, himself one of the pupils of Mr. Dwight, informs us that the tutor was fully adquate to every demand which was thus made on him, and that throughout the entire course he secured the respect and confidence of these young men. Whatever the branch of study, whether the classics or mathematics or rhetoric, he was at home in them all; and his aptitude to impart instruction—by no means a uniform attendant on thorough scholarship in the teacher—was corresponding. Where discipline in its different forms was needed, he hesitated not to enforce it; while his frank and friendly demeanor secured general good will. His fine personal appearance, to which previous allusion has been made, undoubtedly increased his influence as an instructor. His height exceeded six feet, his person was symmetrical, he was perfectly erect and graceful in his movements, his forehead was uncommonly broad and lofty, his countenance full of intelligence, and his general air for so young a man that of uncommon dignity. Not a few of his division of the class were considerably older than himself, but they manifested the same respect for him in the daily intercourse of the recitation room as their youngest associates. That this account is not hyperbolical, the letter already referred to is sufficient authority.

"Yale College, May 16th, 1851.

Rev. and Dear Sir:—

Your brother, the Rev. Sereno E. Dwight, D. D., was tutor of the class to which I belonged in College. I was under his instruction three years; and in compliance with your request, I will mention what occurs to me, respecting his character and habits as an instructor.

Few men ever entered on the tutorship at so early an age. He was, I believe, but little more than twenty. Many of his pupils were older than himself, and none of them were more than four years younger. Yet he commanded the entire respect of the class; and I believe there was not one of us who did uot consider it a privilege to be under his instruction. There was so much animation in his character and mode of teaching, that he made the recitation room a lively and cheerful place. He was then in high health; the disease, which afterwards preyed so long upon his constitution, had not yet commenced; and the alacrity with which he performed every duty, seemed to diffuse itself among his pupils, so that most of us felt our studies as thus conducted, to be rather a pleasure than a task. He was thorough and exact in every branch of instruction, but the classics were his favorite study. The translations which he gave from time to time, were uncommonly close and elegant. He entered fully into the spirit of the author, and endeavored to make the recitations not a mere exercise in grammatical analysis, but a means of refining the taste of his pupils and enriching their minds with elevated sentiments or useful knowledge. He bestowed much attention upon English composition. His criticisms were kind but rigid; and when he saw talents for writing that might be developed, he took great pains to draw them forth by encouraging the timid and quickening the indolent. His whole course of instruction pointed remarkably to the duties of a public life. He was himself preparing for those duties, and such was the cast of his character, that he identified, to an uncommon degree, his own pursuits with those of his pupils. Hence, he spared no pains to make them able writers and speakers. He encouraged extemporaneous debate. He gave great attention to the disputes of the Junior year. He seemed determined, in short, to carry us along with him, as far as possible, in the course of training which he had marked out for himself; and the obligations under which he laid us, have been felt by many with increasing force in the advance of years.

I am very truly,
And with much respect,
CHAUNCEY A. GOODRICH."

It has been said that the four years which Mr. Dwight passed as a student, were in many respects the happiest part of his life. Yet it is doubtful, whether his subsequent four years as a tutor were less pleasurable. The buoyancy of youth is indeed more free from care and foreboding, and is therefore more light hearted, but the quality of its pleasures is inferior to those of early manhood. The draught of the latter is deeper, its taste is keener and more discriminating. The young man of twenty-two and twenty-four is far more intellectual than the youth of eighteen; his plans and hopes, instead of the flight of the vagrant bird, have begun to circle around some valued object; and life has become to him far more of a distinct and prized reality. Such discriminations might be justly made in his particular case. He had, indeed, finally separated from the society of most of his classmates, but the mature friendships which he was now forming were more than a compensation. His associates in the instruction and government of the college, both the permanent and the temporary officers, were men whose society was in itself equally pleasant and profitable. The President was his father. Two of the three professors, the same whose respected names have long been first in seniority, were not many years older than himself; and the third somewhat older still, is now the honored ex-President. With each of these his associations were familiar and friendly. His fellow tutors were also all men of personal worth and intelligence, so that rarely indeed could the office which he filled present equal attractions to another.

While he was a tutor, he commenced the study of Law. He had been informed by his father, and doubtless long anterior to this period, of his own desperate sickness when a little child; of the prayer which was then offered, and of the promise then made, by that father. But while revering that parent as few sons ever do revere a father, he could only reply that he did not deem himself a renewed man; and that he could not, therefore, conscientiously, commence a course of study for the ministry. That prayer and that promise, however, were yet to receive their full answer of fulfilment, although neither the father nor the son may have anticipated it at the time. Sovereign influences were no doubt even then directing the way, however litttle they were seen. But with such views of his own character, Mr. Dwight could make no other decision, and he entered accordingly on a course of legal study. His first instructor was the Hon. Charles Chauncey of New Haven, who had been for many years a Justice of the Superior Court of that state, but who had retired from the bench. Under the direction of this gentleman, he and one or more associates pursued the study of the elementary principles of the profession ; and when it became necessary for him to acquire a knowledge of its practice, he then became a student in the office of Nathan Smith, Esq., then, and for many years, one of the most eminent lawyers in the state. His course of study under Judge Chauncey he was able to pursue without iufringing upon the claims of his office as a tutor; neither did his subsequent preparation apparently interfere with these duties, as he was admitted to the bar soon after his resignation of that office.

After Mr. Dwight had completed the first three years of his tutorship, the class, of one half of which he had been the instructor, entered on the studies of the fourth year under the direction of the President. He commenced, accordingly, the instruction of one division of the class which was admitted in 1809, and was graduated in 1813. With these young men he remained one year, commanding similar respect and confidence to those which he had received from his senior pupils.

He was admitted to the bar of New Haven County in

November, 1810,—two months after his connection with the college had terminated, and he now entered at once with his characteristic ardor upon the life of a lawyer. In many respects he was peculiarly fitted for ultimate success and distinction in his profession. His talents were superior, his previous acquisitions could be all rendered auxiliary, the nice logical distinctions of law—as a science—he relished and readily comprehended, he was sufficiently fluent, and his character was unblemished. His ardent temperament, to which allusion has been just made, was somewhat of a disadvantage; for the lawyer, whether giving counsel in his office or conducting the cause of his client in court, should of all men be self-collected and cool. Imperturbableness not unfrequently gains the mastery, whether amid the strifes of the forum or the debates of the senate chamber, over a superior intellect which is easily moved from its balance. It is not intended that Mr. Dwight was hot headed or passionate, few men were less so; but that his natural ardor was such as to require watchfulness and restraint, when amid exciting scenes. Thus it is wisely ordered. Where the endowments and acquisitions are enviable, there will be found some drawback, some infirmity, making a compensation, as it were, to those who might otherwise repine at the superiority to which they cannot attain. Had his subsequent life been wholly given to the law, he would have doubtless completely overcome, as he did in a good degree actually overcome, this excitability. Expediency and philosophy, not to speak of higher principles, are usually efficient teachers in such cases.

As Mr. Dwight, like almost all other lawyers, was constrained to make his way to success by his own efforts, he had sufficient leisure for legal study for a considerable period. This absence of active business, so often dreaded by the young lawyer, is in most cases indispensable to ultimate distinction. Law, like many other sciences, is to be fully mastered only after long years of patient application. Where clients crowd upon the lawyer of but three or five years' standing, so that his time is principally spent at court, he may become prompt, fluent, confident, and for a time rapidly grow in repute ; but the thorough student will at length overtake him, and then leave him far behind. The subject of this Memoir preferred the latter species of eminence, and his diligence in study was corresponding. His habits of application would authorize such an affirmation here, could there be no reference to living testimony, for he who has been ever characteristically studious, will least of all intermit his application when once entered on a permanent profession. Such testimony, however, is not wanting. A gentleman, who was then and for a number of subsequent years among the foremost in the profession at New Haven, and who in later years has been one of the most eminent of the Bar of New York, informs me that, brief as was his legal career, he was deemed a "learned lawyer."

In August, 1811, Mr. Dwight was married to Miss Susan Edwards Daggett, the eldest daughter of Hon. David Daggett, who was then at the head of the legal profession in the State, and who was in later years Chief Justice of its highest court. This lady was possessed of a vigorous and cultivated mind, and of a refined taste, and at the time of their marriage she had been for several years a professed disciple of the Saviour. Their union continued for twenty-eight years, and it was distinguished for the steadfastness and strength of their mutual affection.

They had but one child, a daughter, who died in the earliest infancy.

While Mr. Dwight was slowly making progress at the bar, he found some leisure, as other lawyers have done who have finally reached a high eminence, for the labors of an author. He had been for some time preparing the materials for a work on Geography, which he would have completed, and then published in his own name. This being in some manner made known to Rev. Dr. Morse of Charlestown, Mass., whose own work on geography had been printed in successive editions, he proposed to Mr. Dwight that the materials thus collected, with some others also which himself should furnish, should be moulded into a new edition which should still bear his own name. The work was thus ultimately written, much after the plan of the geography of Pinkerton; and when published, it bore the name of Dr. Morse. Mr. Dwight, it is supposed, was substantially the author of the work, although the writer is unable to speak with precision as to the relative claims of the two gentlemen. The knowledge of geography which he thus personally acquired, was comprehensive and accurate to an extent rarely equalled.

While at the bar, he also wrote another work, which was not published until a number of years after his entrance into the ministry. This was a treatise on that still vexed question,—the lawfulness of marrying a wife's sister. He espoused the negative, and in an elaborate dessertation, in which the argument from the Scriptures is exegetically examined at great length, considered the whole subject rather in the style of a lawyer than of a divine. When the volume, a duodecimo of near two hundred pages, was at length published at New York in 1836, he referred in the preface to its composition in such a manner, that a reader unacquainted with the author's personal history, might suppose him to have never left his original profession. This was not, of course, intended to mislead any one; but as no allusion was then made to his ministerial character, and none indeed was called for, the mistake might have been naturally made. The work was subsequently republished in Great Britain, with a highly commendatory introduction, by Rev. Dr. Wardlaw of Glasgow. The reasoning of Mr. Dwight has been deemed by some readers unanswerable; but the question, after all that has been written on it, and after all the enactments of parliaments and votes of kirks and general assemblies, seems to have come no nearer to a generally satisfactory decision.

Neither of these works was permitted to interfere with the legitimate claims of his profession. The cases in which he was employed and which were gradually and surely increasing, received his full attention; in the language of the gentleman to whom reference has been already made, "he prepared them well, and argued them ably." As his own standing at the bar continued to be but recent until his abandonment of it for the ministry, he could be but rarely employed as the senior counsel; but I am informed from the same quarter, that "it was deemed an advantage to have him as an assistant in a case, because it was known that he would be thorough in the preparation." This was his general characteristic, whatever the subject of investigation: thoroughness. He would fully ascertain the facts, on which the merits of the case rested; and he would then soundly apply the principles of law. To adopt once more the language of the same gentleman, when generally describing Mr. Dwight's professional position: "he was a faithful, able, and learned lawyer." Such a character he could not have possessed, it should be here said, had he not been strongly attached to the profession itself. The lawyer may occasionally acquire wealth, or he may render his profession the handmaid to his ambition, while in either case it is disrelished for itself alone : but he who would attain to its legitimate honors, must seek them because they accord with his own tastes. Such indeed is obviously the case in every walk of life, especially in those which are highly intellectual or moral. Like " the prize of the high calling of God in Christ Jesus," incomparably nobler than them all, they must be sought with the heart, if they are to be ever attained. It should then be said here that, when Mr. Dwight, after six years' practice at the bar resolved to change his profession, it was not from any previous disrelish for its studies or its other duties, nor from any scruples as to its being consistently pursued by a Christian man. Many years afterwards, when the writer of this Memoir, having in contemplation a similar change in his own case from the Law to the Ministry, consulted his Brother as to its expediency, the answer was given in the negative.

His health which had been uninterrupted for many years, was weakened nearly two years after his admission to the bar by a lingering fever. While thus unwell, a dose of mercury was prescribed among other remedies by the physician ; but instead of the ordinary healthful action of the medicine, its influence was most noxious. A fiery eruption soon extended over different portions of the bodily frame, the irritation of which was most distressing, and which no applications could effectually remove. Of this malady a more particular account will be given hereafter.

It has been already said that Mr. Dwight, when the ministry had been named to him as a profession by his father, had replied that he did not deem himself a renewed man. It has been also observed, that his life had been irreproachable. In his domestic and social relations, he had been, to the external eye, one who apparently feared God and kept his commandments. None were more constant in the public exercises of religion : he had maintained family prayer from the commencement, nor is there reason to doubt that he was regular in his private devotions. Many would have named him as an example to not a few professed Christians, and he himself could have truly said—" All these things have I kept from my youth up." Whether, while he thus disclaimed the character of personal piety, he was expecting to secure in time the requisite evidence of possessing it by his continuance in this course of blameless living, or whether he was waiting for some peculiar intervention of divine grace to remove every obstacle, cannot be asserted. It is not improbable that he was resting to some extent on both of these anticipations. But the time at length arrived, when he was to rest on other hopes than these.

At this season, in the summer of 1815, a revival of religion had been making some progress in the First Congregational Church, of which Rev. Dr. Taylor, now Professor of Didactic Theology in Yale College, was then the Pastor. On some one Sabbath at this time a sermon was preached by the Pastor on the subject of prayer, with a special reference to the prayers of unconverted persons,—the preacher affirming that all prayer, to be acceptable to God, must be offered in true penitence and faith, or, in other words, by a holy heart. Mr. Dwight, who was then a parishioner, heard this discourse, and was much dissatisfied with its strain. In describing it to others he stated, and no doubt sincerely, that Mr. T. had virtually preached, if he had not directly said, that it is sinful for impenitent men to pray. The latter gentleman was informed respecting Mr. Dwight's complaints of the sermon, and on the following Sabbath he pursued the subject at greater length, and especially as a reply to such objections,—using in his arguments the most familiar and direct style. The truth thus presented was accompanied with other power than that of the preacher. He for whom it was peculiarly intended, when entering, as was his wont, on the evening devotions of the family, was soon compelled to desist,—his deep emotion preventing him from proceeding. The next morning he called at the house of his pastor, and after conversing for a moment on indifferent topics, the tears began to run down his face, and he then without delay told Mr. Taylor that he had come to converse with him respecting his own salvation. All timidity and hesitation were at once dismissed, his objections to the sentiment respecting the nature of the prayers of impenitent persons were abandoned, and he became at once absorbed in the great question of his own reconciliation to his Maker. His convictions, as Dr. T. informs me, from whom I have received this narrative, were very deep and thorough; and within a few days he began to be conscious of a new and sacred peace. O blessed change, when man thus becomes "a new creature!"

Some readers of these pages may look with incredulity or wonder at this stage of the narrative, assigning either no explanation of the issue as it became now apparent in Mr. Dwight, or ascribing it to mere fanaticism, or enthusiasm. But such a solution will not answer. The previous Memoir assures us that he possessed neither of these temperaments, neither did they control him at any portion of his subsequent life. Though of ardent temperament, this had been a characteristic from boyhood, it was not now first developed. He was too intelligent, too rational, to be led away by religious delusions; nor had his previous career been stained by any of those flagrant or secret crimes, the remembrance of which sometimes overwhelmns their subject with remorse. Reasoning directly from the effect to its adequate cause, we can assign none—if we profess to credit the revelations of the New Testament—but the truth made efficacious by the Holy Spirit's grace.

The change in Mr. Dwight was so marked, as immediately to be visible. He had no false shame to deter him from openly glorying in the Cross, and he began at once to act, as one who had consecrated himself without reserve to the service of Christ. In the public and private duties of religion, and in familiar conversation, he was now evidently swayed by a new spirit. He also began, in company with two other gentlemen who had been long professed disciples, to conduct social religious meetings in various private families. So evident indeed was the change, that the opinion was soon entertained among his friends that he would speedily relinquish the law for the ministry. Such was indeed his early formed purpose, which he communicated at the time to his pastor, and doubtless also to his wife and his father; but, which, for obvious reasons, was then made known to but few others. What were the chief considerations which thus swayed him, the writer is ignorant. Every such case must be, necessarily, determined by its own peculiar relations. He was, probably, conscious of a far stronger desire for the ministry than for the law,—nay, the latter profession had not, improbably, become distasteful to him; his anticipated usefulness, as he must have decided, would be greater; and then his father's prayer and vow, though not prescribing for him the rule of duty, must have been seriously pondered. He had no misgivings as to the decision; and as soon as the proper time had come for action, he acted accordingly.

Every such case, it has been just said, has its own characteristic features, so that no one can become a precedent for others. Unquestionably, Christian men are as truly needed at the bar as in the ministry. A pious lawyer or a pious physician, may, each, not less signally honor the gospel during a useful life, than a preacher of righteousness. In many cases, perhaps in most, if the newly converted lawyer still retains his relish for his profession, it would be unwise in him to forsake it for the pulpit. If his desire for the self-denying duties of the ministry is so strong as with difficulty to be resisted, then, if possessed of the appropriate mental training, and if neither his age nor circumstances dissuade him, he may properly yield to that desire.

His purposed change of profession, as has been said, was not immediately announced. He was to adjust his professional business, which had been gradually augmenting, and this required considerable time. He was also to become himself possessed of that preliminary state of thought and feeling, of purpose and conversation generally, which should render the change, when publicly announced, familiar instead of strange to himself; and this demanded much time for reading, for reflection, for conversation with wise counsellors. Pursuing the order of dates, it may be here observed, that he made a public profession of his faith, in the First Congregational Church of New Haven, Oct. 29, 1815. That he was received, and probably in the early part of the following year, under the care of the Association which subsequently licensed him to preach, can scarcely be doubted, as the latter measure is regularly a consequent upon the former in such bodies; but of the time when he was thus received, I have no knowledge. He was licensed by the West Association of New Haven County, Oct. 8, 1816.

Soon afterwards he preached his first sermon. The text, as has been observed on one of the earliest of these pages, was :—" For this child I prayed, &c." His father, as it has been also said, was a hearer. What reflections, what emotions, must have crowded upon both ! In the afternoon of the same day, the father preached in the same pulpit, that of the First Congregational Church. As the latter was then sinking under the disease which proved fatal in the succeeding winter, this discourse was, in the providence of God, the last which he delivered. The last discourse of the father, and the first discourse of the son, delivered on the same Sabbath and in the same pulpit,—and of a son who had been thus restored from that desperate sickness of childhood, and whose life had now all converged, as it were, to this very issue ;—this was a rare coincidence !

A few weeks subsequent, Mr. Dwight was chosen by the Senate of the United States their Chaplain for the session of 1816–17, and accompanied by Mrs. Dwight, he proceeded to Washington, where he passed the winter. His official duties were far from being burdensome ; he formed some pleasant acquaintances and renewed others, and the session passed away for him not unprofitably. While he was thus occupied, he henrd the tidings of his father's decease at New Haven, and he was overborne with grief. His filial affection and reverence had been always signal, and this event, which he had not anticipated, required the exercise of all his submission. His meeting again for the first time, on his return, his mother and a younger brother, who had been present with his father during the last sickness, was but the irrepressible exhibition of his emotions.

Well does the writer remember the hurried entrance, and then the repeated convulsive bursts of anguish, and then the bending down upon a table for support under the shock that was all but rending his frame!

In the summer of 1817 he was unanimously invited by the Park Street Church and congregation in Boston, to become their pastor. This invitation he accepted, and he was ordained Sept. 3, 1817. The discourse on the occasion was preached by Dr. Beecher, then pastor of the church in Litchfield, Conn., from Psalm xix. 7—10. Its title, as subsequently printed, was, "The Bible, a Code of Laws." On the same occasion were ordained several missionaries, who were soon to proceed to other countries under the control of the American Board.

Mr. Dwight was more generally known as the Pastor of the Park Street Church than in any other relation. The years thus passed, were his years of greatest usefulness. It will be obviously proper, accordingly, that a somewhat more extended account should be given of this portion of his life. That this may be properly done, it will be necessary to allude to the original formation of the church itself.

Soon after the commencement of the present century, it began to be extensively known that the preaching of the ministers then occupying the Congregational churches in Boston, had become widely different in its doctrinal character from that of their earlier predecessors. What are usually termed, the doctrines of grace, or what has been distinctively called, the Orthodox system of faith, had been gradually relinquished; and what is now familiarly termed, liberal Christianity, had been made the substitute. It is unnecessary to inquire as to the cause, or the progress, of this change: the fact, with which alone we are concerned here, is now universally admitted. So gradual however had it become, that, at the period just named, but one church,—"the Old South,"—was considered as in any measure retaining the primitive faith of New England; and in even this church that faith was almost struggling for existence.

Some few of the members of this church who deeply deplored this departure from the belief of their ancestors, began at this time occasionally to meet each other for fraternal communion and conversation; and these meetings, in conjunction with those of a circle of pious females which were similar, continued for several years. They were then induced to attempt to build a house of worship, and to form a church,—the creed of which was prepared for the occasion, and was distinctively orthodox. Their new sanctuary was dedicated in January, 1810; and in July, 1811, Dr. Griffin, then a professor in the Theological Seminary at Andover, was installed as the first pastor. He was dismissed in May, 1815.

From this statement, purposely made as concise as possible, it will be seen that the position now occupied by Mr. Dwight was peculiar. The enterprise, as it may be termed, of the little band which had resulted in the formation of the Park Street Church and congregation, had been viewed with general jealousy from the beginning; the new sanctuary had involved them largely in debt; and the style of preaching of the first Pastor, (of which the Park Street Lectures are a specimen,) powerful as it was admitted to be, had but augmented the prevalent disfavor towards the new Society. Their numbers also were comparatively few. With the state of things, as it has been now described, their new pastor was fully acquainted.

He entered with his whole heart upon this difficult sphere of duty. His constitutional ardor was now regulated by

Christian principle, but its energy was not lessened. His conversion had been attended, as we have seen, by a process of thorough conviction; and the first features of this vital change often continue to be characteristic through life. They evidently pervaded his entire ministry. He had abandoned his previous profession and renounced all that the world could offer him in prospect, because he had become conscious that he was "not his own;" and as the servant of his Divine Master, he proceeded with more than ordinary fidelity and self-denial to do his appointed work. In his different departments of labor, the church were prepared to give him the requisite co-operation, and he found among them many efficient "fellow-helpers to the truth."

His primary sphere of labor and of usefulness he rightly deemed to be, the pulpit. He was to preach the pure gospel. This was the cardinal object for which he had been invited thither by those, who wished that the truth as it is in Jesus might be once more proclaimed throughout that city of the Pilgrims as in former days, for the edification of the saints and for the conversion of sinners. He began, with such views, to address his discourses directly to the conscience. His preaching, from the very commencement, was so strongly characterized by directness and pointedness, that he might be described as one who, in the best sense of the language, was always aiming at a revival of religion either among his unrenewed or his believing hearers. As the sermons which he left behind him, and of which an unusually large number have been completed, considering the comparatively brief period of his ministry, are examined in their chronological order, it is surprising to note how constantly such is the strain. Whatever the leading subject, whether it related to men as renewed or unconverted, or simply as moral agents, whether doctrinal or preceptive, whether intended for instruction or impression, the discourse is rarely closed without addresses to one class, and ordinarily to both classes, of the most searching character. There is no harshness of language nor of sentiment. There is no accumulation of fearful scriptural terms and images, as if a mere repetition of horrors were the chief employment of the preacher. There is no self-righteousness, no assumed air of a judge calmly sentencing a criminal, either of which evinces that the preacher is a stranger to the meekness and compassion of the Saviour. But there are constantly found a directness and a closeness of application, both to the worldling and the Christian, which evince that, forgotten as such preaching had been until within the past few years, he meant to declare to them the whole counsel of God. As auxiliary to this result, Mr. Dwight adopted from the commencement the most simple and familiar phraseology. His own taste, as we have seen, was highly cultivated ; his conceptions were often poetical ; and had he coveted, as do many, a repute for pulpit eloquence, few, it is believed, would have surpassed him. But as if such objects were unthought of, he has adopted in his ordinary discourses a phraseology so plain as to be intelligible to the most illiterate and obtuse ear. The reader of the polished pages of some of our modern classics would have pronounced much of Mr. Dwight's preaching distasteful for this reason, had he not been too much impressed by its directness and energy to permit him to be critical. As illustrations of this characteristic, I would refer to the first four Discourses of this volume which follow the Discourses on the Death of Christ; and also to the Discourse on the subject—Why many Christians mistake their own characters. It is believed that but few published American sermons are more pointed, more fitted to convince the conscience, than these, while few are so absolutely inartificial and plain in their style.

The subjects of his discourses were habitually selected on the same principle: all were directly aimed at the promotion of holiness. Had his ministerial course extended through twenty instead of eight years, his range of subjects would have been doubtless much more comprehensive; but during its brief continuance he seemed incapable, as it were, of contemplating but two objects,—the immediate conversion of the sinner, and the constant growth of the believer, as the results of his preaching. His sermons were accordingly to an unusual degree the exposition and illustration of such themes as, the sinfulness of unrenewed men in their relations to the law, the providence and the grace of God, the duty of immediate repentance, the sinner's fixed disinclination to return to God the only inability, the fulness of grace and salvation in the Saviour, the sincerity of the divine invitations, the necessity of regeneration, the duty of constant growth in holiness, the future glory of the church—now rapidly approaching, and the blessedness of the heavenly state. With these were associated among other topics three to which he gave a special prominence, the Christian training of children by their parents, revivals of religion, and the errors of the system which had been so widely substituted in that city for the doctrine of grace. While there is scarce a subject which has not been treated in some form or other, for of him it may be truly affirmed that he purposely kept back nothing, these were the themes to the enforcement of which his own conversion in its characteristic features had inclined him, these constituted the staple of his preaching. And these, as has been just remarked, were ever presented with a directness so personal, the hearer, instead of being permitted to conjecture whether another might not be intended instead of himself, or of pausing to criticise the preacher's oratory, was constrained so anxiously to look within his own heart, that it is matter of wonder how speedily popular Mr. Dwight became, and how steadily he retained this popularity.

In addition to the labors of the pulpit, there were various other modes in which, as would be expected, he habitually sought access to his people for their benefit. Besides a third and familiar meeting on Sabbath evening, he conducted a regular meeting on the week, in each of which a similar earnestness and solemnity attended his ministrations. But he should be specially noticed for his deep interest, as a preacher and pastor, in the young. His frequent discoursing on the duty of parents to train up their children religiously, has been just mentioned. Though himself the parent of but one child, and of which he was almost immediately bereft, no father of a large family seemed to be more fully pervaded by a sense of the obligations thus originated; none could raise the standard of duty higher, or more feelingly urge its claims. One of his discourses on this subject, which was preached in various places, was at a subsequent period considerably enlarged, and was printed in New York, in 1838, as an 18 mo. of 82 pages, with the title of "Forbid them Not: or the Hindrances, which prevent little children from coming to Christ." Few of the same nature are better fitted to be useful, and had not the copyright been sold, it might have appeared in this volume. With the same object in view he established a Pastor's Bible Class for the younger members of the congregation, including those principally who were above fourteen years of age. This is supposed to have been the first such class ever established in Boston, or in the churches in that vicinity. Its number was at first less than forty, but was soon increased so as to crowd the room. To use the words of one describing it,—"There the descent of the Divine Spirit was early manifested. The lucid exposition and faithful application of Scripture truths caused many a suppressed sigh to be heard, many a silent tear to fall, and many an anxious soul mentally to inquire—'What shall I do to be saved?'" Mrs. Dwight was accustomed to be present with her husband at the meetings of this Bible Class, when she occupied a particular seat; and a small picture, subsequently engraved, was executed, representing Mr. Dwight in the attitude of addressing the Class which surrounded him, while his wife is seated in her usual position by his side.

His pastoral visits were made an important means of usefulness. His multiplied duties did not permit him to make such visits frequent, neither is it supposed that, except in peculiar cases, they can be repeated often to advantage; but when he was able from time to time thus to call on his people, his evident design was the promotion of their eternal welfare. On such occasions he conversed with the members of the family and the domestics, as a pastor who sought familiarly to apply the instructions of the pulpit, and then closed the interview with prayer. His deep feeling and solemnity steadily tended to strengthen every good impression. Similar to such visits were those which he was accustomed to make to little associations of ladies, who held meetings among themselves for their religious improvement.

His efforts for the prosperity of the foreign missionary enterprise were conspicuous. At the time of his ordination the American Board had been in existence but seven years, and its sphere of operations, as well as its resources, was narrow; but among its many friends who have beheld its rapid enlargement in later seasons, none have been more zealous than was then Mr. Dwight. He personally introduced the observance of the Monthly Concert into the Park Street Church, and into the Congregational churches of Boston, and the system of contributions which has subsequently been there maintained. At these meetings he was accustomed to communicate such religious intelligence as was new and important, and also to describe geographically the missionary stations and the surrounding regions of country. His extraordinary knowledge of geography was here peculiarly serviceable, and as the general subject itself habitually awakened his lively interest, and as but few persons could more command the attention of auditors either in conversation or when speaking alone, it will not be doubted, as some of those who were then his parishioners have recently stated to me, that these concerts possessed an extraordinary attraction. It may be also observed here that the mission of the American Board which was established at Jerusalem, was first suggested, as is believed, by Mr. Dwight.

The preaching of Mr. Dwight, as has been previously said, seemed to be constantly directed, as it were, towards one great object,—a revival of religion among his church and congregation ; and some of the additional means which he adopted in more familiar intercourse, have been also noticed. As has been already implied, the seasons when these visitations of salvation were frequently known among the Congregational churches in Boston had long since disappeared, so that "a captivity," as it has been termed, of more than "seventy years" had now elapsed. But the day for their return had now at length come. In the summer and autumn of 1822 the commencement of a revival was apparent in the Park Street

Church, which soon after extended to the two other orthodox churches in that city. Its subjects were speedily so numerous, that from three to four hundred persons assembled in a common public room for the purpose of inquiry and counsel from their pastors. The revival continued through the following winter, and the labors of Mr. Dwight, as well as of the other pastors, were multiplied and constant. They were aided by the co-operation of their respective churches, and the results were evidently most auspicious. When the spring had come, the same demand still existing for ministerial effort, several of the most experienced and distinguished ministers from the churches in New England were sent for to assist the wearied pastors of the churches in Boston. This relief had become indispensable to the subject of this Memoir, who had become exhausted for the time by the incessant demands on his bodily and mental powers, so that he was constrained to travel for a season for rest and recruiting. But the ultimate results, as just observed, were most auspicious. Large accessions were made to these respective churches, the number in Park Street, where the revival commenced, being the largest. The preliminary work of conviction was also peculiarly thorough, so that the changes were more than ordinarily enduring. The influence on that church, particularly, has been visible until the present time. This, their first season of refreshing from above, has been also, as I am informed, the most signal. How much of the subsequent growth of Christ's kingdom which has been apparent in the multiplication of orthodox churches in Boston and in their existing efficiency, is to be directly ascribed to this first and great revival, it is difficult indeed to conjecture. The immediate influence of these scenes on Mr. Dwight was such as would have been anticipated from his temperament and character. An unusual mellowness of feeling pervaded his conversation, and the tear was ever ready to flow, so that those who sought his counsels were assured of what is so needful at such a time,—their pastor's deep sympathy. As the result, the converts loved him with an unusual affection. Few pastors indeed have equally possessed, what the apostle Paul valued so highly,—the love of their spiritual children. He merited this as truly by his faithfulness as by his tender sympathies, for while he anxiously sought to strengthen the weak and to guide the doubting, none dreaded more than he to encourage a fallacious hope.

While Mr. Dwight was thus laboring in his Master's service and at length reaping the abundant harvest, it will be supposed that he must have become extensively known to those who desired the progress of evangelical religion in Boston. His house had thus become the resort of many visitors from different portions of the country, who were cordially welcomed, for, like his father, he was "given to hospitality." The courtesy which he was thus showing under his own roof, he persuaded the families of the congregation, it may be proper here to observe, to show publicly on a conspicuous occasion. The evangelical Congregational ministers of the state were not accustomed at this time, to visit Boston in the month of May, as at the present day. It was at his suggestion, that the hospitality of his own people (and perhaps, also, of the other kindred churches in the city) was tendered to these ministers throughout the commonwealth, in anticipation of the then approaching season of May. The tender was accepted; and, as the result, a similar yearly attendance has been secured each succeeding anniversary.

The fruit of his labors had now become apparent in the

enlargement of the society, not less than in the growth of vital holiness. At his ordination, their numbers were few and their strength was feeble; but at the close of the revival just noticed, they had become numerous and powerful. Many young men, a most desirable element to every religious congregation, were first drawn by his reputation to become his hearers; and when converted, as many of them were, they added strength to the growing body. But while prosperity of every kind was thus attendant, the pastor, to whose indefatigable labors it was so largely owing, had been for some time paying the tax so frequently demanded in such cases, in his impaired health and vigor. His recruiting during a brief interval of rest after the revival, was but temporary, and in the summer of 1824 it was evident that a protracted season of relaxation had become indispensable. It was therefore unanimously voted by the church, that he might be absent from his pastoral duties for a year, with the design that he should visit Europe; they also voted that his salary should be continued, and that the pulpit should be supplied at their expense, during this period. Mr. Dwight accordingly soon set sail from New York for Europe in the month of August, and after a voyage in which he suffered much from sickness, he landed on the continent.

His absence continued through the allotted term, he having returned in August, 1825. He visited France, Switzerland, and Italy, which was his eastern terminus; and retraced his way on the continent through Austria and Germany, after which he arrived at London in the anniversary week of May, 1825. His continental journeys were very pleasant and salutary to his health, and as he presented himself as a delegate from one or more of our national societies at the anniversaries in London, he was introduced at once, without using one of his letters, to a large circle of desirable acquaintances. So constant was the demand upon him as a speaker, that he spoke ten different times in about eleven days,—the call being often first made as he sat on the platform, and with an earnestness which constrained him, however reluctant, to yield. A more extended notice would be given of this tour, including some very interesting incidents, had not a packet of his letters containing the only account been unfortunately destroyed.

On his return Mr. Dwight was cordially welcomed by his people, and he resumed his official duties with apparently recruited health. His labors were continued with no serious embarrassment till the close of January, 1826, when, in consequence of unusual exertions in speaking in the pulpit, he perceived his voice to be much injured, so that every subsequent effort to speak was attended with great difficulty. This evil he ascribed, and probably correctly, to the unusual dimensions of the church in which he preached, its area then being very large and its elevation uncommonly great. Neither did he possess, as do many public speakers, that skill in adapting the voice to the structure of the room that is to be filled, which is indispensable to the health and comfort of the preacher. Unlike most persons, he had not what is called—a musical ear; he could not discriminate between the different notes of the octave; so that, although his voice was uncommonly pleasant in conversation, he seemed unable to regulate it when its tones were elevated. His difficulty in speaking was at times excessive, and apparently from this cause only. Much indeed of his previous ill health, which had occasioned his European excursion, had been thus originated. He became accordingly convinced that a disability, occurring so soon after his return, and from a cause which was irremovable—as a change in the dimensions of the building seemed to be altogether inexpedient, when contemplated in connection with his many pastoral duties, rendered his dismission necessary both for the people and himself. He came to this conclusion with extreme regret, for the union had been most happy; but his opinion having become fixed, he urged the necessity of his dismission so strongly that the congregation could only comply. He was dismissed April 10, 1826, both the people and the council bearing honorable attestation to his fidelity and usefulness.

That he was sincere in these convictions, is not to be doubted: yet it is questionable whether he did not act precipitately. So great had been his usefulness, so harmonious the connection, that it s severance—whatever the occasion—was to be exceedingly deprecated. No pastoral station could have been selected for him in New England that was more desirable. At this very time his prospects of a long ministerial career, steadily brightening with good to men and with honor to God, were never more distinct. Had he made a longer experiment of his power of speaking, or resorted to a temporary cessation from the effort, the difficulty might, perhaps, have been overcome. Without questioning the entire sincerity of his brother's course in this matter, the writer has ever regretted the decision.

Soon after his dismission Mr. Dwight returned to New Haven, in which city and its vicinity he resided the seven succeeding years. During the earlier portion of this time he preached occasionally in various pulpits, and might have again assumed the pastoral office, had he favored the application. Perhaps the only reason why he was not speedily resettled, was his commencement of an important and arduous enterprise—that of writing an extended Life of the first President Edwards, and of editing a new and enlarged edition of his works. This work had been recommended to him, nay, it may be said, urged upon him, by his father in preceding years; it was a work also of which he had never lost sight while in Boston, but for the execution of which he was then disabled by his uninterrupted ministerial duties. He had however, even then, been diligently collecting the materials. At New Haven, and while residing also occasionally, for the sake of the needed retirement, in some of the neighboring villages, he possessed adequate leisure; and then entering on the work, he prosecuted it with more or less rapidity for a number of the following years. This edition of Edward's Works was ultimately published at New York, in 1829, in ten octavo volumes, of which the first volume contains the Life. This constitutes a very large octavo of 766 pages, and indicates on every page the fidelity and unwearied research of its author. All previous biographies of President Edwards are little more than a brief succession of annals, compared with this. The introductory account of his childhood; the narrative of his ministry at Northampton, and especially of the events ending in his dismission; his personal history, while at Stockbridge, with the account of the machinations of his persecutors at that time; and much also of the subsequent part of the volume; are, in many portions, entirely new, and in others are so largely amplified, that no additional biography will, probably, be hereafter deemed necessary. In the English reprint of this edition of Edwards' Works, this Life is styled by Henry Rogers, (the associate Editor of the Edinburgh Review, and the writer of the article on Faith and Revelation in one of its late numbers) in an introductory Essay, "the admirable Life of Edwards." The additions to the Worcester edition of Edwards' Works, which were made in Mr. Dwight's edition, consist of the Life, just mentioned—in itself a very large volume; of the Life and Diary of Brainerd, which, in addition to the very brief account in the Worcester Edition, occupies almost a volume; of Miscellaneous Observations of President Edwards; of Types of the Messiah; of Notes on the Bible; and of many Occasional Sermons.

Early in 1828, Mr. Dwight commenced, in conjunction with his youngest brother, Henry, a large school for boys in New Haven, which was modelled on the plan of the German Gymnasiums, and which during its continuance was familiarly called by that name. The design was, to furnish a thorough classical education; and for such lads as were not to be trained for college, the best preliminary instruction for active life. A succession of first rate teachers was employed for the various departments, and in addition, the two principals themselves gave instruction in certain branches, while exercising a general superintendence. The system was so complete that, while the school continued—which was more than three years—no college in New England could probably afford superior advantages to those pursuing the same branches of study. Boys and young men were sent thither from every part of the country, the number for a season exceeding one hundred, and for a considerable part of the time being very large. Towards the close the number was much diminished. The health of the younger Mr. Dwight, long imperfect, became still feebler; while that of the elder brother, which had been long affected by the malady already briefly noticed, was gradually unfitting him for the toilsome duties of such a station. The Gymnasium was discontinued in the summer, or fall, of 1831.

A more distinct notice must be here taken of this malady. Previous to its commencement, Mr. Dwight possessed a remarably vigorous constitution, and enjoyed as uniform health and cheerfulness as are almost ever allotted to man. It commenced in 1812, about two years after his admission to the bar. In consequence of a sudden change of temperature succeeding in the evening of a very warm day in October, he became exceedingly chilled, and before the next morning he was seized with a violent lung fever. To arrest this fever at the commencement a large dose of calomel was prescribed, which produced a more distressing salivation, as the subject of it long afterwards remarked, than any other case which he had ever seen, except one in the general hospital of Paris. His confinement to his bed continued for five weeks, and during this period measures were adopted to promote a constant perspiration, which—whatever may have been its effect on the fever—carried the mercury to the third skin, where it lodged, and immediately produced a mercurial sub-fever. These particulars and others which follow are taken from a description of the malady, given by himself in a letter to another, which was written twenty-five years after its commencement. This description is so minute and accurate, as to furnish important hints to a skilful physician respecting so peculiar a complaint; while it exhibits a case of physical suffering so aggravated and long continued, as to occasion wonder that health had not been long previously completely destroyed, and reason often driven from its throne. The details of this letter cannot, of course, be here given. The disease first manifested itself in a fiery irritation over the crown of the head, and thence extended from the neck over the upper half of the front of the body, as well as locally on the back; occasioning in various places an almost leprous incrustation of the skin, from which, when broken, a caustic, poisonous ichor would issue. Other localities of the body were similarly affected, in which the disease ultimately became seated, occasioning often great suffering during the day but almost intolerable anguish at night. The sufferer was then compelled to pass regularly through a process of measures to secure relief, which seemed only less painful than the torment of the disease itself. Without these, to sleep was impossible; and when using them, sleep was scarcely ever secured—as he says in this description—until two in the morning, and usually not until three. These particulars are here given, as without them no just conception can be formed of the habitual sufferings of Mr. Dwight during a large portion of the last three-fifths of his life. A further but brief notice of the same disease will be also necessary on a subsequent page. No other reference will be here made to it than to say, that, after having endured the distress which it occasioned him for twenty-five successive years, he thus describes it at the close of the letter:—"If there be in the present life any cup of unmixed and double distilled misery—it is this."

Mr. Dwight continued to reside at New Haven from the closing of the Gymnasium-school in 1831, until the spring of 1833. In March of that year he was chosen President of Hamilton College in New York, by the Trustees of that institution, and in April he signified his acceptance of the appointment. He was inducted into office on the second Wednesday of August. In September, he received the honorary degree of *Doctor of Divinity* from Yale College.

The institution over which he now began to preside, was at this time in a most unprosperous condition. From various causes which had been for some time operating, the number of students had been greatly reduced, and the college itself had become deeply in debt. An attempt had been made to raise by subscription from its friends a sum sufficient to discharge these debts: this had proved however, an almost entire failure, and was soon abandoned. Dr. Dwight was but imperfectly acquainted with this state of the college, when he accepted the appointment.

To save the institution from ruin it was indispensable that a large sum of money should be raised, and the new President, at the meeting of the Trustees, when its acceptance was made known, was appointed "an Agent to raise funds which would place that College on a permanent footing." The sum of fifty thousand dollars, to be invested as a permanent fund, was deemed necessary for this object, and not less necessary were deemed the personal efforts of Dr. Dwight to secure it. Had he foreseen the burden which he was thus called to assume, it is not improbable that he would have declined accepting his office. His proper duties were a general superintendence of the institution, and the personal instruction of the senior class. To relinquish these for a large portion of the year, that he might publicly present the wants of the college at meetings in the different towns which were to be visited, and then personally solicit subscriptions from various individuals, was an exchange little expected and less welcome. But having accepted the office, and perceiving that the efforts contemplated were indispensable to save the college, he entered on his self-denying work with great zeal and energy. Accompanied by one of the Trustees, who had been appointed his associate, he travelled extensively over various portions of the state, making public addresses in the larger towns, and obtaining subscriptions from a great number of individuals. Five months, if not a larger part, of the college year of 1833–4 were thus occupied, and including a large sum which was obtained by one of the professors who also labored for the same object, the subscription of fifty thousand dollars was completed, by the following June.

Dr. Dwight instructed the senior class of the year just specified during the whole period, except while absent on this unofficial course of duty. He also instructed the class immediately succeeding throughout the entire year. The text books were Locke, Paley's Moral Philosophy, Say's Political Economy, and Butler's Analogy. In his instructions he made the specific lesson, whatever it may have been, simply the text for the elucidation and inculcation of his own views, assenting to the author or differing from him, as his own independent course of study and thought inclined him. This, as one of his pupils informs me, generally, he was accustomed to do with an amplitude of discussion and illustration which stimulated the young men themselves to the proper mental efforts—both as students, and at the recitation. Such, it needs not be here observed, is the only mode of teaching, which deserves to be called instruction. The teacher, whatever his department, and whether in a college or theological seminary—whether in a school of law or medicine, if he would not merely quicken the memory of the students at the expense of dulling their intellects, will do something more than inculcate implicit deference for the text-book and its author, and then bestow the largest praise on him who most correctly repeats the lesson. Aside from the exact sciences, there is but one book which is to be thus treated; and its expounders and commentators, from Augustin down to Edwards, and to the present hour, can claim as little the unqualified assent of the youthful student as any other writer. Dr. Dwight, while presiding at Hamilton, as while a tutor at Yale, taught the young men to think for themselves, and, as inseparable from this, to call no man master. Brief as was his connection with the college, he succeeded in imparting to his immediate pupils much of the same spirit. In such instructions he was peculiarly aided, both by his ardent temperament, and by his uncommon powers of address. None who have listened to him, whether as the preacher, or instructor, or in familiar conversation, ever questioned his sincerity or his earnestness, when speaking on an important subject; and the favorable impression thus made, was deepened among his pupils and in the familiar circle by his copiousness of thought and language, and by his brilliant imagination. His presidency continued but little more than two years, so that his talents for instruction were but partially displayed. As an evidence of the respect and confidence which he acquired, however, it may be added, that one long conversant with the institution indirectly informs me, that "he never heard a syllable of complaint lisped against him as a teacher." Another, the pupil already referred to, describes him as "a very superior teacher." A third, who is also an alumnus of the college, and who has been long an Editor of a very widely circulated religious newspaper in the city of New York, thus speaks of his presidency generally. "The students were exceedingly charmed with his style of instructions; and to this day, now seventeen years since, I remember it to have been very quickening, suggestive and brilliant. His departure was much regretted by the students, especially those of the more advanced classes. His whole general influence on them as a teacher, a disciplinarian and a man, was such as to wake them up from the sluggish, inefficient, inactive state of mind into which they had settled, and to make them feel that they had something to do in the world—to make them work like men." This last informant mentions him, as "the *one teacher*, who did more than all the other teachers combined, whose instructions he had himself ever enjoyed," to stir him up to a proper conception of his duties and privileges as a student and a man.

Allusion is made by this gentleman to Dr. Dwight's course as a disciplinarian. I learn from still another source, that "he was decided in discipline; but that he endeavored to anticipate the necessity for its exercise, by giving to the students, both in his own class room and in the general meetings of the whole body, sound and wholesome instruction and advice." As a matter of fact, no difficulties in the government of the college occurred during his presidency.

In Sept., 1835, Dr. Dwight deemed it his duty to resign the presidency of Hamilton College. His reasons, as specified in his letter of resignation, were these: "That the College was much more deeply in debt than he had anticipated on his acceptance; that, although after a year of unceasing toil, mortification and self-denial, he and others had succeeded in raising a fund of $50,000, the college had still a debt of $15,000 or more without means of payment; that, although since his accession, the number of students had been steadily increasing, yet there was no prospect that the College would attain a permanently prosperous footing on its present location; that he had, therefore advocated its removal to Utica, which project the Trustees had refused to countenance; and that he, therefore, felt it his duty to resign." How far these reasons should have availed with him, the writer feels incompetent to decide. The college which has subsequently received important aid from the state, and from private donors, has been for some years very flourishing. That the president was sincere in his convictions, is undoubted. Still, it is to be regretted, that he did not remain longer at his post, and patiently exert the influence which he was widely acquiring for the removal of existing evils—whatever they were. It is scarcely to be doubted that, at no distant season, most of them would have disappeared.

After his resignation Dr. Dwight returned to New Haven, where he resided, though often absent, until the fall of 1838. During this period he spent a few months in presenting the subject of African Colonization to public audiences, in its immediate connection with the Pennsylvania Colonization Society. Had he possessed full health, none of our great philanthropic institutions could have more worthily commanded his best services; for the ultimate object of many of its warmest friends (whatever may have been the original design of its founders) is the civilization and evangelization of Western and Central Africa,—a result inseparably connected with the final triumphs of the Redeemer's kingdom.

His malady still continued to distress him. Indeed, the letter describing it must have been written during the preceding year. In addition to the sufferings already mentioned which had now become seemingly inveterate, it had also produced dyspepsia in some of its worst forms. Twice was he thus apparently brought to the verge of dissolution. He had from time to time tried the prescriptions of various physicians, during its successive stages; but as the benefit, if received, was temporary only, he began at length to distrust all such remedies, and to try those recommended by more questionable authority. Some of these, as is not unfrequently the case, were apparently salutary for the season, and he was thus led to the use of them more frequently and occasionally in large quantities. The general effect in all such cases is injurious, and in his own case it was very injurious; yet not let others censure nor wonder, until they have passed through a similar furnace. Sufferings such as he has depicted, endured—with frequent mitigations, no doubt—for ten, twenty, and twenty-five years, will at length prompt their subject to resort to any remedies, any measures, commended by credulous hope. The mind is no less affected by such a disease than the body, for the whole nervous system is made to enter from the commencement into the closest sympathy. Such was signally and unhappily the state of Dr. Dwight. His mind, like his bodily frame, became constantly excited and often chafed. He made scarcely a mental effort but under the pressure of this iron weight; if he resorted to relaxation, his disease, like a haunting spectre, was still present; if, like others when in sore trouble, he anticipated final relief and cure, that hope, so often false, would soon yield to despondency. It would have been strange indeed if his demeanor toward others, nay, if his character in its outward aspect, had not been thus affected. Difficulties which but rouse a man in health to efforts that ensure success, soon intimidate the nervous invalid. Opposition to his own plans or opinions is often misconstrued; his extreme sensitiveness renders him unconsciously irritable; where he cannot convince nor persuade, his very earnestness may make him dogmatical, and a speedy retreat from trouble or continued labor seems a duty where others would patiently "stand in their lot." Such has been the gradual change in many others,—such had for many years been gradually becoming the change in the subject of this Memoir; and in a still more marked degree was this apparent after his removal to the city of New York, in the fall of 1838. He was accompanied by Mrs. Dwight, who had ever been a most affectionate wife, sharing with him every trial, and cheering him in his darkest hours. As their only child, who was born a few years after their marriage, had soon died, their mutual affection, which, as has been previously observed, was peculiarly strong, had gradually acquired a corresponding singleness and devotedness. But he was soon to be deprived of her sustaining presence, as her health, which had been for some time feeble, gave way entirely in the following summer; at the close of which she died, at the house of her father in New Haven. Her husband returned to New York, a solitary man, uncertain as to the future, disabled, in his own view by his disease, from pursuing the ministry or any literary employment, and constrained—for the time at least—to suffer each day to pass away as innocently and, in one sense, as inactively as it might.

Weeks, months, years, slowly lapsed, and he continued thus to live. At the beginning of what thus proved the last stage of his life, he firmly cherished the hope that he should be speedily relieved from his disease, so far at least as to permit his resumption of the pastoral office or an entrance on some other course of active duty. To become cured, in whole or in part; to become daily comfortable, instead of suffering ceaseless anguish;—this was his constant object. For its attainment he not only continued to consult and to reconsult physicians, and to try the efficacy of successive remedies which skill or empiricism recommended, but he also ceaselessly sought, as he had ever done, the intervention of the Great Physician. To the urgency, the intenseness of the supplications, in seasons of social devotion, others, besides the writer might here bear witness. To a still greater importunity in his hours of secret communion, his Bible bears moving attestation.

Others who cannot enter into the feelings of a Brother, when seeing these mementos of a fainting spirit that still clung to a covenant God, may here peruse passage after passage, which the owner of the volume had specially selected and marked out as fountains of consolation and hope; and these all refer to *waiting on God.* One of these,—the close of the 27th Psalm, and it is from the book of Psalms pre-eminently that this store-house of encouragement was drawn, is here cited as an example. "Wait on the Lord; be of good courage, and he shall strengthen thine heart; wait, I say, on the Lord." This is underscored, as if every word had been pondered and treasured up, and the entire verse is also connected in a similar manner with the preceding one so truly descriptive of the sufferer's own feelings:—"I had fainted, unless I had believed to see the goodness of the Lord in the land of the living."

While the early part of these his last years was thus insensibly passing away, his mind continued active. He did not enter on any extended course of literary or scientific research, desirable as it would have been for himself and others, for this demanded more health, more firmness of purpose than what he deemed himself now to possess; but he satisfied his characteristic thirst for knowledge by reading, and also at intervals by investigating some specific subject which interested him for the time. In this he was very kindly aided by the partners of a large bookselling house, Messrs. Bartlett and Welford, who gave him free access for many years to the valuable works with which their shelves were constantly filled. Here he might be often found, either engaged in intelligent conversation, or absorbed in reading some newly imported work. He could thus keep pace with the publications of the season, at home and abroad, while his mind was for the time healthfully refreshed. Could he have investigated several subjects successively with the acuteness displayed in the "Hebrew Wife," which had been lately published, although originally written when he was a lawyer, he might have made important additions to the general stock of knowledge, and perhaps effectually resisted his own increasing tendencies to disease and extreme depression. But while unfitted, as he thought, for such efforts, his mind was kept constantly active. Strangers or former acquaintances, when in conversation, ever found him to be well informed on literary subjects, ready at any moment to sustain his own part in a courteous discussion, and evincing, unless overborne by debility, his characteristic ardor.

After his residence in New York had commenced, he rarely, if ever, entered the pulpit. From every such effort his feeble health, as he was satisfied, precluded him. He experienced, however, a very high gratification in listening to the preaching of several of the ministers of that city. Having no family, and feeling disinclined, as a minister himself, to become connected with any particular church, he was accustomed to attend, in an irregular alternation, on the preaching of four or five ministers whom he peculiarly preferred. In describing them respectively, he would commend each for the mental vigor which, as a hearer, he found necessary to secure his own undiverted attention: but he would more earnestly commend the deep-toned spirituality and the searching exhibition of truth, which also drew him to each as a frequent auditor. Where these were divorced, no pulpit oratory, no stores of learning nor doctrinal acuteness, could have ever made him a hearer. When mentioning some impressive discourse to which he had been thus listening, his change of voice and countenance and manner would usually almost at once reveal his own deep interest in the subject; and he would thus unconsciously assure the friend whom he was addressing, that he prized none the less than when at Park Street Church, the fundamental doctrines of the gospel.

I have said, that years thus passed away. He not unfrequently visited New Haven while his mother, whom till her last hours he treated with rare filial reverence and affection, continued to live. It is believed that he also visited one or more of the springs famed for benefiting cases resembling his own; and that he may have passed portions of several summers in quiet villages, as a temporary retreat from the heated city. He was also accustomed for a number of years, as the warm season drew nigh, to form indefinite plans of travelling to some distant, secluded spot, and of there passing the summer months—solely occupied in applying remedies for the cure of his disease. Such projects, though scarce ever carried into effect, gave occupation and excitement for the time to his thoughts, and were thus salutary. There were also intervals when he appeared to be sensibly mending, and when the long absent friend would have pronounced him at the first interview to be as cheerful, if not also as healthy, as when he was residing in Boston. Had his income, which for one living in New York was very limited, permitted him to travel again, and for several years, in Europe, in company with a suitable friend, his health might possibly have been still recruited. But confined as he had thus become to the city, with the habitual persuasion that his disease was incurable, his depression of spirits gradually withdrew him from society, and his health became more and more feeble. To a few friends he still clung, but he was too much of a sufferer, too constantly sad, for any other intercourse. Indeed, for many years before his decease, his mind, when occupied with the subject of his malady, was evidently unhealthily affected. On all other subjects, even to the last, his intellect retained its undiminished vigor, and his feelings were in accordance. But when conversing about his feeble health, a morbid excitability, in which his opinions were evidently swayed by his habitual and often intense despondency, betrayed itself. In this respect his state of mind strongly resembled that of the poet, Cowper, with this diversity,—that the mind of the latter was the primary seat of disease, while that of the former suffered but in sympathy with the body. Few of those who knew him best, could know what constant and exhausting demands were for almost forty years made on that sympathy; how the poisonous disease of the skin, the fevered irritation of the nerves, with accompanying dyspepsia in some of its worst forms, and all acting on a brain long since made unnaturally sensitive and constantly denied for hours at night the soothing restorative of sleep, may chafe even the pious spirit, and render life a pilgrimage of gloom. One of his Christian friends, in speaking of his condition, remarked, that "nothing but the influence of religion had preserved Dr. Dwight from insanity:" and another deliberately said, that "nothing besides could have restrained him from suicide."

But he was graciously preserved from both. He, who had most mysteriously but wisely appointed it for him so long to suffer, enabled him also to endure unto the end. In the spring of 1850, the writer saw his brother for the last time in the city of New York. He had then but partially rallied from a severe attack, closely connected with his disease, which had confined him for a month; and his unusual debility was apparent to the little circle of family friends with whom, during their brief sojourn in the city, he passed much of the time. But when warmed in conversation, he forgot for the season his sufferings, and conversed with an enthusiasm and eloquence on various subjects characteristic of his happiest days. The effect on two strangers who happened to be present a part of the time, was, to rivet them to their seats; where, as if spell bound, they listened in mute admiration until the lateness of the hour caused him to withdraw.

In the early part of the following October he visited Philadelphia, with the purpose of trying the efficacy of hydropathy. His physician, to whom he had been specially recommended, perceiving his great debility, had but moderately subjected him to the usual regimen, when, after a few weeks, which were pleasantly spent, he was suddenly seized with chills and fever, and the attack soon extended to the brain. One of the most eminent physicians of the city was called in consultation, who pronounced the symptoms to be those of a softening of the brain,—a disease, to which intellectual men are more subject than others, and which has been lately increasing in this country. The writer was speedily summoned by telegraph from Portland to Philadelphia, and on entering the chamber was familiarly recognized by his brother. The memory of the latter, however, once so tenacious, was almost gone. During the first half of the week that followed, he would often commence replying to questions addressed to him, and after uttering a few words with difficulty, would then stop, and place his hand on his head as if overborne with pain; then, after a pause, he would either complete the sentence, or, what was perhaps more frequently the case, sink into entire unconsciousness. Twice, and twice only, through the week, did he address the writer, except when thus replying; in the last of which instances, he uttered a brief law maxim in Latin, for the purpose of qualifying his refusal to a request just made. Once, when the danger of his case was intimated, he immediately closed his eyes and appeared to be engaged in prayer; but after the briefest reply to a second and then a third suggestion, he sunk at once into insensibility. At no one moment was he fully aware of his state, nor after the first day or two was he capable of comprehending it. The last day and night were passed in seeming unconsciousness of every object around him, and in this state he departed early in the morning of Saturday, November 30, 1850:—welcomed, it is humbly trusted, among the first to greet him, by those whom he had ever most filially revered and those most fondly loved, to that world where "there shall be no more death, neither sorrow nor crying, neither shall there be any more pain;" and where "God shall wipe away all tears from the eyes."

His remains were conveyed, early on the ensuing week, to New Haven, where, after appropriate funeral solemnities, they were deposited by those of his wife, within the beautiful cemetery of that city, which also contains the ashes of his parents, and of two of his brothers. His grave is designated by a marble monument, which bears the following inscription:

SERENO EDWARDS DWIGHT, D. D.,

Second Pastor of Park Street Church, Boston; and third President of Hamilton College, in New York.

A Scholar, a faithful Pastor, a truly able and eloquent Preacher; and destined, having "turned many to righteousness," to "shine as the stars forever and ever."

Born May 18, 1786.

Died November 30, 1850.

Æ. 64.

As an appropriate close of this Memoir, the following letter, addressed to the writer, and signed by the Pastor, Rev. Mr. Stone, and Rev. Louis Dwight, as a Committee of the Church, is here introduced.

"Boston, Dec. 6th, 1850.

Dear Sir:—

The Park Street Church desires to express its sympathy with you, and other relatives and friends, on occasion of the death of your brother, Rev. Sereno E. Dwight, and to assure you that his character as former pastor of this church is held in affectionate remembrance. Many surviving members of the Church testify their strong appreciation of his services. They well remember his faithful preaching; his affectionate and heavenly conversation; his most acceptable and useful pastoral visits; his earnest personal private appeals to their hearts and consciences; and his successful labors as a minister of Christ. Especially do they remember, and often speak of, his comprehensive views, his animating addresses, and his earnest prayers at the Monthly Concert for the conversion of the world; and his most effective services in revivals of Religion.

His person and manners, his intercourse in general society, and his extensive knowledge made him very pleasant to many people in Boston, as well as to the religious society with which he was more immediately connected.

Many members of this church, now living, have thought much of him, during the long years of his absence and sickness, and gladly, at any time, would, if they could, have alleviated his sufferings.

We have often heard with deep sympathy, how much he suffered from his protracted and unmitigated disease, which laid him aside from pastoral duty and public usefulness.

There is a singular coincidence of circumstances illustrating the kind of affectionate remembrance in which he was held. At a Union Meeting for Prayer in the Old South vestry in Boston, on Friday morning, Nov. 29th, 1850, it only having been heard by report that Mr. Dwight was sick in Philadelphia, his name was mentioned, as an esteemed Christian minister, and once a Pastor of Park Street Church ; and prayers were solicited in his behalf. In a few hours after, on Saturday morning, Nov. 30th, we trust his departed spirit was glorified with his father and with Christ, where there is no more pain.

Most affectionately your friends in the fellowship of the gospel."

Yes. Were it not for the hope of a speedy recognition and union in that world of purity and joy between those whom death has severed, how often would the hearts of survivors die within them! That hope now lessens the sorrow of A BROTHER.

Portland, July, 1851.

DISCOURSES.

DISCOURSES ON THE DEATH OF CHRIST.

LUKE XXIII. 33.

AND WHEN THEY WERE COME TO THE PLACE WHICH IS CALLED CALVARY, THERE THEY CRUCIFIED HIM.

THE Death of Jesus Christ, whether we regard him as *a mere man*, as *a superangelic being*, or as "*God manifest in the flesh*," was a wonderful event in the government of a righteous God. As such it is everywhere represented in the Scriptures; and as such it has been uniformly regarded by the church, in every country and in every age.

That the Scriptures actually point out the Great End for which it took place, is admitted by all; yet the various theories devised to account for it differ as widely from each other, as they could have done, if their several authors, instead of looking to the Scriptures for an explanation of this most singular event, had resorted merely to conjecture. These theories, though numerous, may all be reduced to two classes:—those which *deny*,—and those which *admit*,—that the Death of Christ was an ATONEMENT FOR THE SINS OF THE WORLD. They who regard it as an Atonement, insist that, without it, mankind could not have been pardoned nor saved; while those who deny that it was an Atonement, I believe without an exception, deny also those, which have been regarded by the great body of the church in every age, as the Fundamental Doctrines of

Christianity.* Probably, therefore, it will be admitted on both sides, that no question can be more important or more deeply interesting to man, than the question, WHY DID JESUS, THE MESSIAH, DIE UPON THE CROSS?

As this is a point of mere revelation, it can be determined only by a reference to the Scriptures; and he, who examines them attentively for this purpose, will perceive that the sacred writers have adopted two different modes of presenting the subject to the mind. They have recorded a series of *facts* relative to the Death of Christ, which no believer in the scriptures can controvert. They have also, in various *forms of phraseology*, directly declared the great end for which he died. It will be admitted that these facts, and these forms of phraseology rightly interpreted, are perfectly consistent *with each other;* and that no explanation of this event, which is not consistent *with both*, can be true. In attempting to answer this question, it is my design therefore, to detail the facts connected with it at some length; to recite also the forms of expression referred to, with the view of determining their true scriptural import; and then to inquire how far the various Theories devised to account for the Death of Christ are consistent with these facts, and with the plain declarations of the Scriptures. It was the rule of Newton, in his philosophical researches, to reject every explanation of an event inconsistent with the phenomena that attended it; and, to adopt the same rule on the present occasion, will probably be regarded by every mind as at once fair and safe.

THE FACTS relative to the Death of Christ, which I propose to recite, are the following:

1. It was not *the result of Accident.*

* Particularly, the Depravity of Man, the Deity of Christ, the Reality and Necessity of Regeneration, the Personality and Agency of the Holy Spirit, Justification by faith, and Eternal punishment.

It is obviously true that no event, so far as relates to God, is the result of accident; for "known unto God are all his works from the beginning of the world." And with regard to the death of Christ, Peter said to the Jews, on the day of Pentecost, "Him, being delivered by the determinate counsel and foreknowledge of God, ye have taken, and with wicked hands have crucified and slain."* And the whole company of apostles and disciples say, in their united prayer, "Of a truth against thy holy child Jesus, both Herod and Pontius Pilate, with the Gentiles and people of Israel, were gathered together, to do whatsoever thy hand and thy counsel determined before to be done."† The sufferings and death of Christ were not therefore the result simply of popular tumult, or of the machinations of Herod and the Sanhedrim, but are to be referred, originally, to the determinate counsel of God.

2. It was *the subject of Prophecy.*

This fact is often asserted in the New Testament. Peter declared to the Jews, that "God before had showed by the mouth of all his prophets that the Christ should suffer;"‡ and in his first epistle, he says that "the prophets inquired and searched diligently, what, or what manner of time the Spirit of Christ, which was in them did signify, when he testified beforehand the sufferings of Christ, and the glory which should follow."§ Luke also tells us that our Lord, in one of his last interviews with his disciples, showed them from Moses, the Prophets and the Psalms, that the Christ must suffer and rise from the dead.‖ And Peter on the day of Pentecost declares to the Jews, that the passage in the 16th Psalm, "Thou wilt not leave my soul in Hades,

* Acts, ii. 23.
† Acts, iv. 27. 28.
‡ Acts, iii. 18.
§ 1 Peter, i. 10—12.
‖ Luke, xxiv. 44—46.

neither wilt thou suffer thine Holy One to see corruption,"* refers—not to David, but—certainly to Christ.

This fact is also evident from the prophecies themselves. Every one who admits with John that the serpent, who tempted and deceived our first parents, and who said unto them, "Ye shall not surely die," was not simply and merely a serpent or snake, but "that old serpent, the Devil and Satan," who was "a liar from the beginning," who "deceives the nations;" and that the seed of the Woman was the seed of the Virgin; will of course admit that the prophecy communicated to "the Tempter" in Paradise,—The Seed of the Woman "shall bruise thy head; and thou shalt bruise his heel," refers directly to the death of Christ. In addition to this, and the passage just cited from the 16th Psalm, I shall mention but two of the predictions of this event in the Old Testament. The first of these, in the 53d chapter of Isaiah, is so minute and exact an account of the death and burial of Christ, that it seems far more like a history, than a prophecy. It exhibits him as "the Man of Sorrows," as "wounded for our transgressions," as "led like a lamb to the slaughter," as "numbered with the transgressors," and as having "his tomb with the rich man;" and it is accordingly often quoted as referring to this event by the apostles. I will refer you to a single instance to prove this point. The Ethiopian treasurer was reading this chapter of Isaiah when Philip joined him in his chariot. The Treasurer then asked Philip, "Of whom speaketh the prophet this—of himself, or of some other man? Then Philip opened his mouth, and began at the same scripture, and preached unto him Jesus."†

The other prediction from Daniel concludes in the following manner: "And after threescore and two weeks

* Acts ii. 29—31.

† Acts viii. 32—35.

from the going forth of the commandment to restore and rebuild Jerusalem shall Messiah be cut off, but not for himself.*

3. The Death of Christ was *absolutely necessary.*

In his conversation with Nicodemus, our Lord tells him, "As Moses lifted up the serpent in the wilderness, even so *must* (οὕτως ὑψωθῆναι δεῖ —even so is it *necessary* that) the Son of man be lifted up, that whosoever believeth on him might not perish, but might have everlasting life."† How momentous the necessity here mentioned, when the everlasting life or perdition of all who believe, i. e. all who are actually saved, turns on the fact of his Death! In his prayer to the Father, he says,—"I know that thou hearest me always;"—yet amid the sorrows of Gethsemane, we are told that he went a little further from his disciples, and prayed, "O my Father!—if it be possible,—let this cup pass from me!" The cup was his approaching death upon the Cross. Of course, if the end of his Death was to be answered, it was not possible, that the cup should pass from him, or that he should not suffer death. After his resurrection he said to the two disciples, on the way to Emmaus, "Ought not the Christ,"—(οὐχὶ ταυτα ἔδει παθεῖν τον Χριστον, *Was it not necessary* for the Christ)—"to suffer these things?"

This necessity did not arise either from the fact that the event had been predicted; or from the arbitrary appointment of God. God does not first lay himself under unwise or unnecessary obligations, by predicting events not proper in themselves; and then justify himself, on the ground that he has pledged his word to bring them to pass. —"He sees the end from the beginning."—Neither is he more arbitrary in his appointments, than in his dispensa-

* Daniel, ix. 25, 26.

† John, iii. 14, 15.

tions. The death of Christ was predicted, only because it was appointed; and it was appointed in the beginning, not arbitrarily or without reason, but under as clear a view of the reasons which rendered it necessary, as if it had not been resolved on until the morning of the crucifixion. The necessity existed therefore independently both of the appointment, and of the prediction; and was in the order of nature the cause of both. It was appointed, merely because it was necessary to accomplish the End for which it took place; and that this necessity was absolute, we learn from the occurrences in the garden of Gethsemane. There was therefore from eternity an invincible necessity that the Son of God should die, if the end actually brought to pass by his death was to be accomplished.

4. It has excited a very deep interest *in the heavenly world.*

Peter, after declaring that the Holy Spirit, who was in the prophets, predicted " the sufferings of Christ, and the glory which should follow," subjoins, " which things the angels desire to look into;" or more literally, " into which things, the angels bending over earnestly, desire to look."* These sufferings therefore, and the glory that should follow, had been early revealed in heaven, and had occupied the deeply interested attention of its exalted inhabitants.—On the Mount of Transfiguration, when the face of Christ did shine as the sun, and his raiment was white as the light; when a voice came forth from the cloud of glory,—" This is my beloved Son, hear ye him;"—and when Moses and Elijah appeared in glory, conversing with him; the subject of their conversation was " his decease, which he should accomplish at Jerusalem."—An angel came from heaven to comfort him in the garden, when in

* 1 Peter, i. 10—12.

the view of his approaching sufferings, his soul was "exceeding sorrowful even unto death."

This interest of the heavenly world in the Death of Christ has not diminished since it took place. An angel descended and rolled away the stone from the mouth of his sepulchre. Two angels were in the sepulchre, to announce to his disciples his Resurrection. His death has changed the worship of heaven, and put a new song into the mouths both of saints and angels. "And I beheld," says John, "in the midst of the throne, a LAMB, as it had been slain. And they sang a new song, saying, "Thou art worthy; for thou wast slain, and hast redeemed us to God by thy blood, out of every kindred and tongue, and people and nation. And I beheld and I heard the voice of many angels round about the throne, and the four living ones, and the four and twenty elders; and the number of them was ten thousand times ten thousand and thousands of thousands; saying with a loud voice, 'Worthy is the Lamb that was slain to receive power, and riches, and wisdom, and might, and honor, and glory and blessing.' "*

To understand fully the importance thus given to the Death of Christ, we must recollect that the songs of heaven had been previously occupied in praising God for the display of his perfections in Creation and Providence; and that, on the occurrence of this event, the whole population of the upper world learned A NEW SONG—an ascription of blessing and praise to the Lamb that was slain. No other event in the universe has produced such a change in the praises of heaven. If then the heavenly hosts were not mistaken in their views of this event; no other event in the universe is comparable to it in importance.

* Rev. v. 6—12.

5. A similar degree of importance is attached to this event by the writers of the sacred volume.

It is spoken of as the great manifestation of the love of God:—"God commandeth his love toward us, in that, while we were yet sinners, Christ died for us." "Herein is love; not that we loved God, but that he loved us, and sent his son to be the propitiation for our sins." It is mentioned as the highest possible evidence of the willingness of God to bless mankind. "He that spared not his own Son, but delivered him up for us all, how shall he not with him also freely give us all things." It is mentioned as the sum and substance of the Gospel, which the Apostles preached: "We preach Christ crucified, unto the Jews a stumbling-block, and unto the Greeks foolishness, but unto them which are saved the power of God." "I am determined to know nothing among you, but Jesus Christ and him crucified." It is described as the only thing in which an Apostle could glory: "God forbid that I should glory, save in the Cross of our Lord Jesus Christ; by which the world is crucified unto me, and I unto the world."

Thus, there is a perfect harmony in the interest felt in this event, and in the views entertained of its importance, by inspired men on earth, and by the holy inhabitants of heaven.

6. Various *Titles* were given to Christ with reference to his Death, which are given to no other person. By John the Baptist, he was publicly announced to the Jewish nation, on the banks of the Jordan, in the following manner, "Behold the Lamb of God who taketh away the sin of the world." He is called by Peter "a Lamb without blemish and without spot;" and by John, "the Lamb," "the Lamb that was slain," and "the Lamb slain from the

foundation of the world." He is called the Redeemer; and the reason is given by the saints in heaven, "Thou art worthy, for thou wast slain and hast redeemed us to God by thy blood;" as well as by Paul—"We have redemption through his blood, even the forgiveness of sins." He is called "the Saviour of the world;" and the reason assigned is because "he shall save his people from their sins;" and of this language two explanations are given, both connected with his death. The first is, that he saves us from the wrath of God or the punishment of sin: "God commendeth his love toward us in that while we were yet sinners, Christ died for us; much more then, being now justified by his blood, we shall be saved from wrath through him." The second is, that he saves us from the power of sin: "Who gave himself for us, that he might purify unto himself a peculiar people zealous of good works." He is called the Deliverer; because, in the language of Paul, "he delivered us from the wrath to come." He is also called a Ransom; because he "came to give his life a ransom for many." These titles are given to no other individual.

7. Great multitudes who lived and died before his death, were possessed of *real piety, and went to heaven;* and of these, numbers were men of pre-eminent piety. This was true of Abel, Enoch, and many others before the Deluge; of Noah, and Melchizedeck, of Abraham, Isaac and Job, of Jacob, Joseph, and still greater numbers in Patriarchal times; of Moses and Joshua, of Samuel, Elijah, and the prophets, and far greater multitudes under the Levitical economy. As they all died before the death of Christ, they knew nothing of that event, unless it was typified in sacrifices, or unless they were acquainted with and fully understood the prophecies in which it is predicted." That

they had some indistinct apprehensions of the subject, some assurance of "the bringing in of a better hope" than sacrifices presented, we, who believe that sacrifices were merely types of the Great Sacrifice, most fully admit. That their views were exceedingly imperfect, we know from two facts. "No prophecy of Scripture is of its own interpretation,—(its own interpreter;) or is adequately understood until it is fulfilled. The Disciples also, with all the helps derived from sacrifices, from prophecy, from the repeated and most explicit annunciations of the event by Christ himself, and from witnessing the Sacramental Supper, could say, after the event had taken place, "We trusted that it should have been he, which should have redeemed Israel;" and could render it necessary for Christ to say to them,—"O fools, and slow of heart to believe all that the prophets have spoken! Ought not the Christ to have suffered these things, and to enter into his glory?" By the great body of those that died before him, we have reason therefore to suppose that his death was, to say the least, very imperfectly understood.

8. Those who died and went to heaven before his coming, for some reason or other, felt a deep personal interest in his death. Our Lord himself informs us that the patriarchs and prophets foresaw his coming, and rejoiced in their anticipations of the event: "Your father Abraham rejoiced to see my day, and he saw it and was glad." "For I tell you that many prophets and kings have desired to see those things which ye see, and have not seen them; and to hear those things which ye hear, and have not heard them." This interest, we are told by Peter, was excited by the Death of Christ: "Of which salvation (that of the soul) the prophets have inquired and searched diligently, who prophesied of the grace that

should come unto you; searching what, or what manner of time the spirit of Christ which was in them did signify, when he testified beforehand the sufferings of Christ, and the glory that should follow." Those, who thus died in faith before the coming of Christ constitute one common family with those, who have possessed the same character since his death: "Of whom the whole family in heaven and earth is named." They are styled one "general assembly and church of the first-born." This union of the righteous of all generations into one family is not merely said to be accomplished by Christ, but by his blood: "In whom we have redemption, through his blood, even the forgiveness of sins, according to the riches of his grace;—having made known unto us the mystery of his will, according to his good pleasure which he hath purposed in himself; that in the dispensation of the fulness of time he might gather together in one all things in Christ, both which are in heaven and which are on earth, even in him." When this one family arrive in heaven, whether they lived before or after the appearance of Christ on earth, they feel, for some reason or other, one common obligation to Christ, and express their thanks in one common song; and that song is an acknowledgment of one common benefit conferred on each, the benefit of redemption: "And they sung a new song, saying, Thou art worthy—for thou wast slain, and hast redeemed us to God by thy blood, out of every kindred, and tongue, and people and nation." There is no diversity of feeling here. The acknowledgment made, by such of the redeemed as died before the coming of Christ, is not merely, like that of the angels, founded on the pleasure which they take in the happiness of *others;* it is founded on a *personal* benefit conferred on *themselves.*

2

They do not merely say with the angels—" Worthy is the Lamb that was slain;" but as a part of " the general assembly and church of the first-born," they unite in a still deeper expression of gratitude,—" Thou hast redeemed us to God by thy blood."

9. Christ *knew* that he was to suffer death. He knew kimself to be the Messiah ; and he had read the numerous prophecies, which announced his death as certain. At the commencement of his ministry, he said to Nicodemus,—" As Moses lifted up the serpent in the wilderness, even so *must* the Son of Man be lifted up." On Mount Tabor, Moses and Elijah conversed with him on his own approaching death. On his last journey to the scene of his sufferings, he said to his Disciples,—" Behold we are going up to Jerusalem ; and the Son of Man shall be betrayed unto the chief priests and unto the scribes ; and they shall condemn him to death, and shall deliver him to the Gentiles to mock, and to scourge and to crucify him." The evening before his crucifixion, he announced his death to his disciples, pointed out Judas as his betrayer, instituted the sacramental supper for its commemoration, and in the full view of its approach endured the agony of the garden. The certainty of his Death on the Cross was, therefore, a subject of frequent and familiar contemplation, throughout every part of his public ministry.

10. Christ did not die, *because he deserved death.*

The conduct of his enemies throughout his life proved that they were convinced of his innocence. He was often in their power, and was the object of their violent hatred and unceasing persecution. Had they believed that he deserved to die, they would have arrested him, and brought him to an open and fair trial, that they might at once justify themselves and destroy his influence ; yet, though they often sought to kill him, it was always either secretly, or by violence, and never by proving him worthy of death before a lawful tribunal. The fact, too, that at last they subjected him to a mock trial; and even on such a trial, thought it necessary to suborn false witnesses against him; proves conclusively that, in their view, a fair trial must have resulted in his acquittal.

That he did not deserve death *under the Levitical Law*, is easily evinced from his examination before the High Priest. Caiaphas commenced the examination in his own house, during the night, by asking him of his disciples, and of his doctrine. Jesus answered, "I spake openly before the world; I ever taught in the synagogue, and in the temple, whither the Jews always resort, and in secret have I said nothing. Why askest thou me? ask them which heard me, what I have said unto them; behold, they know what I said." The first charge related to what he said respecting the temple: "Destroy this temple, and in three days I will build it again;"—Referring to the temple of his body. One set of witnesses testified, "This fellow said, I am able to destroy the temple of God, and to build it in three days." Another set declared, "We heard him say, I will destroy this temple that is made with hands, and within three days I will build another made without hands." In their testimony they neither agreed with each other, nor with the fact; and the charge was so frivolous, that the High Priest himself paid it no attention. When it was day, the Sanhedrim, the chief priest and scribes, led him into the council-room: and finding no other charge, on which they could try him under their Law, the High Priest at length adjured him by the living God to tell them,—"Whether he was Christ, the Son of the blessed God?" He then replied, "I am." "Then the High

Priest rent his clothes, saying, He hath spoken blasphemy; what farther need have we of witnesses? Then the whole Council exclaimed, He is deserving of death;" and they all pronounced him "guilty of death." The fact that he called himself the Son of God, he admitted; the blasphemy, he denied, on the ground that he actually was the Son of God, and had also proved it by the highest possible evidence. These were the only two charges alleged against him while he was in the power of the High Priest; and on both his perfect innocence is apparent.

He did not deserve death *at the hand of the government.* This is conclusively proved by the subsequent occurrences of his trial. Pilate and Herod, who were his judges, were both false and bloody men; and the Sanhedrim, who accused him, were the most sagacious and malignant of mankind. Their first charge was,—"We found this fellow perverting the nation," but of this, they could specify no instance, and produce no evidence. They then accused him of forbidding to pay tribute to Cæsar; when he actually directed the payment of it, as well as paid it himself. They next charged him with treason, in usurping royal authority to himself, "He said that he himself is Christ, a king;" but this they could not substantiate. The truth was, that, when the people came by force to make him a king, he refused the offer; and it was his own most explicit declaration, "My kingdom is not of this world." Pilate then went out to the Jews, and said, "I find no fault at all in this man." On hearing this, they were still more fierce, and, as their last charge, accused him of stirring up a sedition in Galilee. Pilate, finding him to be a Galilean, sent him to Herod, as Galilee was his province; but Herod, after trying in vain to convict him of the charge, and treating him with the utmost contempt, sent him back to Pilate. Then Pilate, calling together the chief priests, and the rulers and the people, said unto them, " Ye have brought this man unto me as one that perverteth the people ; and behold, I have examined him before you, and I have found no fault in this man, touching those things whereof ye accuse him. No ; nor yet Herod ; for I sent you to him ; and lo, nothing worthy of death has been done by him ; I will therefore chastise him, and release him." And when they were clamorous for his crucifixion, he called for water, and washing his hands said to them, " I am innocent of the blood of this righteous person."*

He did not deserve death nor suffering *at the hand of God.* Suffering is inflicted for sin, and for sin only ; and is intended either to punish, or to reform. But Christ was absolutely free from sin ; and therefore neither deserved punishment, nor needed reformation. Of this we have the most decisive evidence. To establish it, we can appeal to his enemies. They were always watching his words and conduct, and he boldly challenged them,—" Which of you convinceth me of sin ?" Yet, when put to the proof on his trial, they could substantiate no charge against him. Pilate and Herod likewise pronounced him innocent ; and Judas, returning the thirty pieces of silver, said to the chief priest,—" I have sinned, in that I have betrayed the innocent blood :"—a fact which they also admitted in their reply,—" What is that to us ; see thou to that." " Here then is the testimony of his accusers, of his judges, and of his betrayer.

We can appeal to his friends ; and they wrote as they were moved by the Holy Ghost. Paul declares to the

* See Doddridge's Expositor for a full and connected account of the Trial of our Lord.

Hebrews, that he was "holy, harmless, undefiled and separate from sinners;" and that "he was in all points tempted as we, and yet without sin:"—and to the Corinthians, that "God made him to be sin for us, who knew no sin." Peter informs us, that "he did no sin, neither was guile found in his lips;"—and John that "in him was no sin." The eleven also, after the best opportunity of observing the most secret actions of his life, were led, from a thorough conviction of the perfect purity of his character, to renounce all that they valued in the present world, and to devote themselves to suffering and death.—We can also appeal to God the Father. He twice declared concerning him, with an audible voice, "This is my beloved Son, in whom I am well pleased." In raising him from the dead, likewise, he gave the most public testimony of his perfect approbation.

11. His Death, on his own part, *was Voluntary.*

His consent to die was solely owing to the consequences of his death; for merely in itself considered, he was utterly unwilling to die. When the Jews sought to kill him, as they often did before he had fully manifested to the nation and to the world that he was the Messiah the Son of God, he took effectual care, knowing their wicked designs, to save his life; and repeatedly escaped from their hands. The reason assigned is, that his hour was not yet come. In the garden, his agony and bloody sweat, and his prayer thrice repeated with his face to the ground, "O my Father, if it be possible, let this cup pass from me!" furnish the highest conceivable evidence that, if it had been possible, he wished to avoid his approaching sufferings. Yet we have seen that he perfectly knew when, where, by whom, and in what manner, he was to suffer death. That he also voluntarily consented to die, he himself declares in the most explicit manner,—"I lay down my life for the sheep. No one taketh it from me, but I lay it down of myself. I have power to lay it down, and I have power to take it again." In Galilee, he told his disciples, that he was going up to Jerusalem to be crucified; he might therefore have remained in Galilee, and not have gone up to the Passover. After his arrival, his opportunities to escape were abundant. He might have left Jerusalem when Judas left the upper chamber; but instead of that he said to him,—"What thou doest do quickly." As he was now fully revealed as the Messiah, though he knew all the machinations of Judas and the priests, he chose not to avoid them; because as it is said, "he knew that his hour was now fully come." In the garden, when the Roman guard approached, and inquired for Jesus of Nazareth, he said unto them,—"I am he;"—and "they drew backward, and fell to the ground."—One word from his lips prostrated them in the dust. And when Peter, drawing his sword, cut off the ear of the High Priest's servant, he said to him,—"Thinkest thou that I cannot now pray to my Father, and he shall presently give me more than twelve legions of angels?" Certain it is, therefore, that Jesus, instead of being surprised by his enemies, had his whole life to deliberate whether he would be crucified or not; and that there never was a moment, when he might not, if he had pleased, have avoided that ignominious death.

12. It occurred *very early after the commencement of his public ministry.*

He entered on his ministry after he was thirty years of age. The previous part of his life was passed in such absolute obscurity at Nazareth, a village in the remote parts of Galilee, that, notwithstanding the remarkable scenes of his infancy—the annunciation to the shepherds, the offerings of the magi, the prophecies of Simeon and Anna, the murder of the infants, and the conversation with the doctors in the temple—he lived there all this time unknown and unsuspected as the Messiah: so absolutely unknown, that John the Baptist his kinsman, who knew himself to be the forerunner of the Messiah, and who knew that the Messiah was actually come, assured the Jews, at his baptism, that until he saw the Holy Ghost descend in a bodily shape like a dove, and rest upon him, he did not know what individual was the Messiah.* Then, for the first time, was it said to the Jews—"Behold the Lamb of God, who taketh away the sin of the world!" So unsuspected had his character as the Messiah been, that his acquaintance in Nazareth, when they saw him after his baptism stand up in the synagogue and read the Scriptures, asked instinctively, "How knoweth this man letters, having never learned?" His public ministry continued but three years and a half, or at most but four years. His death occurred at the most important and eventful period of his life. He had all the activity and ardor of youth, combined with the full vigor of manhood. He had become extensively known, and had gained a high character as a holy man, as an eminent prophet, and worker of miracles. His fame and influence were continually extending, and the number of his disciples regularly increasing. The apostles were wholly unprepared for his death. When he was apprehended, they all forsook him and fled; and, when he was crucified, their faith in him as the Messiah entirely failed. When he died not a word of the New Testament

* The reason of this was, that John had lived previous to his entrance on his ministry near Hebron, in the *South* of Judea; while our Lord had lived during the same period in the *North*, at Nazareth.

was written, and but a small part of the instructions necessary to compose it were given. The Church too was not yet organized, and no permanent order of ministers appointed. His followers were very few, feeble, and timid, and they were so fully convinced that he was to be a reigning temporal Messiah, that, when they saw him crucified, they were utterly confounded and disheartened.

13. The Sacramental Supper was instituted as *a perpetual commemoration of his Death*. "For as often as ye eat this bread, and drink this cup, ye do show the Lord's death until he come." Except his resurrection,* which was a consequence, and in him as the Messiah the Son of God, obviously a necessary consequence, of his death; no other occurrence of his life,—not even his birth, is thus commemorated. To the day, or the week, or the month, in which he was born, there is not an allusion in the New Testament; and even to the year, the allusion is so indistinct, as not only to have occasioned a long and yet unsettled controversy, but to have led those who fixed the Christian Era into a mistake as to the true year of the Nativity. As this commemoration of his death is divinely appointed; and as no other event of his life, not even his birth, is thus commemorated; it is obvious that his death was the event of prime importance in his life; that, which especially occasioned his Incarnation, that peculiarly, which called forth the song of the angels at Bethlehem.

14. His Death, both as it was appointed by God, and as it actually took place, was violent and ignominious. Peter, as we have already seen, declares that Herod and Pontius Pilate, with the Gentiles and the people of Israel, did only "what the hand and counsel of God had determined before to be done." The night before his crucifix-

* In the Christian Sabbath.

ion, he was arrested as a criminal. In the council-room of the Sanhedrim the men who held him, mocked him, spit in his face, buffeted him, smote him, blindfolded him, and struck him in the face with the palms of their hands. In the palace of Herod, he was mocked, insulted, and arrayed in a gorgeous robe. In the hall of Pilate he was scourged, crowned with thorns, spit upon, smitten on the head, and mocked with pretended homage. On Calvary, he was nailed to the cross, and there, between two thieves who suffered with him, and amid the taunts and insults of the surrounding populace, he expired.

15. His Sufferings were *inconceivably intense and distressing*. The scene in the garden of Gethsemane was all owing to the fact, that in the most lively and realizing manner he anticipated the events of the following day. In the commencement of it we are told that, taking Peter, James and John, "he began to be in great dejection, amazement and anguish of mind." Then he said to them, "My soul is exceedingly sorrowful, even unto death; tarry ye here, and watch with me." Then he went forward, and kneeled down, and fell on his face, and prayed that, if it were possible, the hour might pass from him. "And he said, O my Father! all things are possible unto thee; if it be possible, let this cup pass from me; nevertheless, not what I will, but what thou wilt!" And he returned, and found them sleeping. And again he went away the second time, and prayed, saying, "O my Father! if this cup may not pass away from me, except I drink it, thy will be done!" And he returned, and found them asleep again. And he went away the third time, and prayed, saying the same words. And there appeared an angel from heaven, strengthening him. And being in an agony, he prayed yet more earnestly; and his sweat was as it were great

drops of blood, falling to the ground." If this overwhelming agony arose from the bare expectation of his sufferings on the morrow, how beyond conception dreadful must have been the actual endurance of those sufferings; when crowned with thorns, and nailed to the cross, and subjected to the triumph of the powers of darkness, he cried out with a loud voice, "My God, my God, why hast thou forsaken me!"

16. He endured sufferings far more intense than those of mere crucifixion—sufferings *inflicted on him by God*—sufferings not of *the body*, but of *the mind*. Isaiah announced that this would be the case. He says "We esteemed him smitten of God, and afflicted." He calls his sufferings, "the travail of his soul;"* as if, in comparison with his mental sufferings, those of his body did not deserve to be mentioned. He declares that "the Lord laid on him the iniquities of us all." He also predicted, that he should "make his soul* an offering for sin;" as though the mere sufferings of his body would have been wholly inefficacious.

Christ himself taught his followers not to be afraid of a violent death;—"Fear not them which kill the body; and after that have nothing more that they can do;"—and doubtless he had sufficient firmness and consistency to do that himself, which he enjoined as a duty on others.

The scene in the garden is wholly inexplicable, if it was occasioned by the anticipation of mere *bodily* suffering. Paul knew that himself was to be crucified, and that his time was drawing near. Yet he said, in the full and sol-

* The idea that נֶפֶשׁ signifies merely the *body*, or the *animal life*, and never *the soul*, *the spirit*, is perfectly unfounded. See Gesenius' Lexicon on this word; and among other passages, Deut. xxvi. 16.—Cant. i. 7.—1 Sam. i. 15.—and Ex. xxiii. 9; in each of which as well as in many other places it denotes *the spirit*, *the seat of the thoughts*, *volitions*, *and affections*.

emn anticipation of that event,—" I am ready to be offered, and the time of my departure is at hand;"—and Peter, when the hour of his crucifixion had arrived, requested that he might be crucified with his head downward, as unworthy to suffer in the same attitude with his Master. They felt no shrinking, no withdrawing from the dreadful conflict; and thousands of martyrs,—many of them in feeble health, many of them nearly exhausted by previous tortures, many of them youths, and many of them females, have approached the cross or the faggot, not only without agony or extreme agitation, but with alacrity, and even with triumph. Yet Christ, under the bare expectation of his sufferings on the following day, being " in great dejection, amazement and anguish of mind," thrice prostrated himself to the ground, offering that most earnest prayer—" O my Father, if it be possible, let this cup pass from me!" and then he prayed still more earnestly, and being in an agony, " his sweat was as it were great drops of blood falling to the ground." Why then this amazing difference? If Christ was *a Super-angelic being;* this conduct of his, on the supposition that he anticipated no sufferings but those of *the body*, indicates a want of fortitude, a weakness of nerve and of resolution, utterly inconsistent with his exalted character, and lowering him down below the level of Paul, and Peter, and multitudes of others, even of youths and helpless females. If you doubt on this point, read any history of Martyrdom, and you will doubt no more. And if Peter or Paul had discovered similar terror on the near approach of crucifixion, we should have regarded it as decisive evidence of the want of resolution. If Christ was *a mere Man;* yet he was a perfect man, and fully conscious of the entire approbation and love of God, and knew that he did not die for his own sins. What unspeakable supports are these under sufferings and death! Why then this amazement, this agony, this sweat of blood flowing to the ground! Will it be said—pardon me the question, it has been said—that this was owing "to the peculiar tenderness of his feelings," and to "the delicate susceptibility of his nervous system?" If by this phraseology is intended, his *lively sympathy for the distresses of others*,—that indeed is a virtue; but it has nothing to do with the case. If by it he intended, *a peculiar susceptibility of pain, and a peculiar dread of enduring it;* it is a mere imperfection, a weakness, for which in every other case we have no respect—a want of that fortitude and tranquillity of mind, which great multitudes of women, and they, too, imperfect and sinful, have exhibited in full view of the faggot and the cross. Will it be said, that his apprehensions of the approaching scene were peculiarly clear and distinct? They could not be more so than the apprehensions of those, who are brought to the very edge of that fire in which they are to be burned, or to the very foot of that cross to which they are about to be nailed. Will it be said that his anticipations of suffering were peculiarly realizing? Yet Paul had been in deaths often, and thrice stoned, and once left for dead; but he said, "None of these things move me, neither count I my life dear unto me. I am ready to be offered, and the time of my departure is at hand." The anticipations surely were not more realizing than the reality; he was not falsely alarmed, and in that way deceived with regard to the magnitude of his sufferings; yet the two malefactors, under the actual endurance of these sufferings, and with nothing from within or from above to sustain their minds, appear to have undergone them, and for a longer period, without a complaint.

The bodily sufferings of many of the martyrs appear to have been far greater than the sufferings of the cross. Many of them were roasted by a slow fire; many were broken on the wheel, and left to expire under long protracted agonies; while others had their flesh torn off by red-hot pincers. Any one compelled to make his choice, would prefer the death of the cross to either of these, or to many other modes of destroying life under long-continued tortures. Many also endured the cross itself. Multitudes of those martyrs did not merely endure their sufferings without a groan; they sang Hosannas to a crucified Redeemer, while in the very agonies of death.

The scene witnessed on Calvary establishes the same point. Christ certainly knew what his chief sufferings were; yet he does not allude to his bodily sufferings, when his agony on the cross became overwhelming. He makes no mention of the wounds in his hands or his feet, or of the racking of his frame. His only cry was, "My God, my God, why hast thou forsaken me!"—and this most bitter cry announced that, when Jehovah withdrew his face, his soul was in a far deeper darkness than that in which the veiling of the sun involved the outward world.

On no supposition therefore, which does not bring on Christ the charge of a weakness and irresolution passing that of multitudes of women, can we explain the phenomena of Gethsemane and Calvary, except on the single supposition that Isaiah was in the right, when he said that he was "smitten of God," that "it pleased Jehovah to bruise him," that the Lord laid on him "the iniquity of us all," that he suffered "the travail of his soul," and made his soul an offering for sin;" and that he himself was right in supposing that his great sufferings, those in comparison with which the sufferings of his body were forgotten, arose from the fact that he was forsaken of God.

17. Very remarkable events *preceded, attended, and followed, his Death.*

What a most surprising meeting was that on Mount Tabor. There went up to the holy mount, Jesus the Mediator, and the three chief apostles; Peter, James and John; and there came down from heaven to meet them, not merely Elijah the chief of the prophets, and Moses the lawgiver of Israel, but God the Father, revealing himself in the voice, and in the cloud of glory which overshadowed the mount; and the subject of their conversation was his approaching DEATH.

Scarcely less remarkable was the scene witnessed at his Crucifixion. When he bowed his head and gave up the ghost, the sun was darkened; and the veil of the temple was rent in twain from the top to the bottom; the earth did quake, and the rocks rent; the graves were opened, and many bodies of the saints which slept arose and appeared unto many. At his resurrection, also, "behold there was a great earthquake; for the angel of the Lord descended from heaven, and came, and rolled back the stone from the door of his sepulchre, and sat upon it. His countenance was like lightning, and his raiment white as snow; and for fear of him, the keepers did shake and became as dead men."

What other event, let me ask, ever summoned such a conclave of Earth and Heaven; or covered the noonday sun with an untimely veil; or waked up from their long sleep the lifeless tenants of the grave?

18. The sufferings and death of CHRIST, considered merely *in themselves, and unconnected with their consequences*, were a very great evil.

The death of any living man, considered in itself, and apart from the consequences which may attend it, is mere ly, so much suffering for nothing. But the sufferings of Christ were beyond conception intense and dreadful, and considered in themselves were an incalculable evil. Of his own opinion on this point, the scene in Gethsemane is a most emphatical expression.

The character of Christ enhances this consideration to an inconceivable degree. He arose on this world as the Sun of righteousness, to diffuse a heavenly light and warmth and life over the realms of darkness and of death. "I," said he, "am the Light of the world; he that followeth me shall not walk in darkness, but shall have the light of life." He was the great Prophet of mankind; teaching what they needed to know concerning God, their present character, and their own everlasting happiness and virtue. His example was a perfect exhibition of piety to God, and of benevolence to man. One stroke of the pencil of Peter has depicted his whole life—"Jesus of Nazareth, the man who went about doing good." His miraculous power was exerted continually in healing the sick; in restoring the maimed; in causing the lame to walk, the blind to see, the deaf to hear, and the dumb to sing; in giving reason to the lunatic, in casting out demons, and in bringing back the dead to life. He was the great friend and benefactor of the human race. Unless his death accomplished some end of inconceivable importance, how undesirable was it that he should die at all? How vast an amount of good would have flowed from his example, from his instructions, from his miracles, from his prayers, had his life been protracted only to seventy years; how incalculable this amount of good had it been prolonged to the end of the world! Were he now on earth, and after the lapse of eighteen centuries, only more vigorous in health, and wisdom and beneficence; with what eagerness should we repair to the country where he resided, to the place in which he dwelt, to the house which he inhabited, that we might even once "*behold the Man.*" How enviable would be the privilege to sit at Jesus' feet, to listen to his counsels, to unite in his prayers and his praises, to follow his example, to share in his beneficence, and to receive his blessing! How astonishing the fact, unless his death accomplished an amount of good beyond all conception great, that he should have been cut off from the land of the living, in three years and a half from the time that he was first made known to mankind!

19. The Death of Christ, *in itself considered*, was only calculated *to prevent the progress of his religion.* It disappointed the hopes of his friends, and left them in almost absolute despair. It also sated the malice of his enemies. The ignominy of his death as a public malefactor was a constant theme of reproach. Paul informs us that the Cross was everywhere an offence, and that the preaching of the Cross was to them who perish foolishness. He declares that it was one principal hindrance to the progress of Christianity. "We preach Christ crucified, to the Jews a stumbling-block, and to the Greeks foolishness." The Jews in their writings, particularly in the "Toldoth Jesu," or, The Generations of Jesus, familiarly ridicule Christianity as "The Religion of him who was hanged;" and this is the language in which it has been described to their children in every age. I need not add that the same fact has often been urged by infidels as the opprobrium of Christianity; and if the reasons, which we can assign for his Death, do not adequately show *Why Jesus the Messiah should die upon the Cross;* the objection is one that cannot be answered.

20. After his Resurrection, Christ *was seen but rarely by his Disciples*, and *was actually seen by no one else.*

His first appearance after his resurrection, was to Mary Magdalen alone ; the second, to her and the other Mary ; the third, to Peter alone ; the fourth, to the two disciples, Cleopas and his companion, on the way to Emmaus ; and the fifth, to the eleven, as they sat at meat. All these occurred on the day of his Resurrection. The sixth was to the eleven, at Jerusalem ; the seventh, to the eleven, at the Sea of Tiberias ; the eighth, to the disciples on a mountain in Galilee, which was beyond a doubt the appearance mentioned by Paul to more than five hundred at once ;* the ninth, to James alone ; and the tenth, to the eleven, and probably others of the disciples, on Mount Olivet at the time of his Ascension.†

HAVING thus stated the principal Facts relative to the Death of Christ, which are recorded in the Scriptures ; I shall now proceed, in the second place, to examine the Forms of phraseology, in which the Great End accomplished by his death is there directly explained. These are various, and well deserve our most particular attention.

1. It is said that he died *for mankind.*

To die for another, is phraseology susceptible, in itself, of different meanings. This is owing to the fact that the preposition, *for*, sometimes denotes merely, *because of*,

* If this was not so, then the appearance on the mountain in Galilee was only *to the eleven ;* and that *to more than five hundred* was *the ninth ;* but where it took place we do not in that case know. There is no reason to doubt, however, that they were one and the same appearance.

† See Archbishop Newcome's Harmony of the Gospels, in the Notes to Sections 147—156 inclusive.

and sometimes, *for the sake of*, i. e. *for the benefit of*. *To die for*, is once used in the Scriptures in the former sense. When Abimelech said to Isaac, " How saidst thou, she (Rebekah) is my sister ?" Isaac replied, " Because I said, Lest I die *for her ;* which is precisely equivalent to, Lest they kill me in order to obtain her. Here, if Abimelech had put Isaac to death, in order to obtain Rebekah, the latter would have died—not for her sake, i. e. not to relieve her from any evil, or to do her any positive good ; and of course in no sense for her benefit ; but—for the sake of Abimelech himself, for the gratification of his passion. The exact version of the passage would have been therefore, Lest I die—not *for her*, but—*because of* her.

But wherever *to die for another*, denotes to die *for his sake ;* i. e. where the end to be accomplished by the death terminates in the individual for whom it takes place ; as is the fact in every other case where this language is used in the Scriptures, there is not a solitary instance in which it denotes to die *as an example to him*, or *to furnish him with evidence*, or *to promote his moral improvement*. When David says, " Would to God I had died for thee, O Absalom, my son, my son !"*—he plainly intends—" that I had died in thy stead." So when it is said—" The fathers shall not die for the children, but every man shall die for his own sins ;"†—it clearly denotes either dying instead of the children, or, as a manifestation of anger for their sins. So when John tells us, that Caiaphas said, " It is expedient that one man die for the people, and that the whole nation perish not ; and this spake he, not of himself ; but, being high-priest that year, he prophesied

* 2 Sam. xiii 33.

† Deut. xxiv. 16 ; and 2 Kings xiv. 6 ; and 2 Chron. xxv. 4.

that Jesus should die for that nation, and not for that nation only, but that also he should gather together in one the children of God that were scattered abroad;"*—he not only informs us that the phrase, to die for the nation, means, instead of the nation, i. e. in order to prevent them from perishing; but that for Jesus to die for the nation, is the same thing as for Jesus to die instead of the nation. And when the Apostle declares, "Scarcely for a righteous man, will one die; yet peradventure for a good man, some one would even dare to die;"† by *for*, he obviously means, in both cases, *instead of*.

We then ask, Do the Scriptures declare, that Christ died for men?—The angel Gabriel announced to Daniel, "In threescore and two weeks, the Messiah shall be cut off, but not for himself;"‡ and every passage of Scripture, which explains his death, confirms this declaration. Christ told his disciples, "I lay down my life for the sheep;"§ and subsequently, "This is my body, which is broken for you;"|| "This is my blood, which is shed for many."¶ Paul informs the christians at Rome, that "God spared not his own Son, but delivered him up for us all."** He asks those at Corinth, "Was Paul crucified for you?"†† intimating that Christ was; warns them to do nothing by which a weak brother should perish, "for whom Christ died;"‡‡ and tells them that "one died for all."§§ John also declares, "He laid down his life for us."||||

These passages, it is universally admitted, teach us that Christ died—not simply because of men, as Isaac feared

* John xi 50, 51.
† Rom v. 7.
‡ Daniel ix. 26.
§ John x. 15.
|| Luke xxii. 19. and 1 Cor. xi. 24.
¶ Mark xiv. 24. and Luke xxii. 20.
** Rom. viii. 32.
†† 1 Cor i 13.
‡‡ 1 Cor. viii. 11.
§§ 2 Cor. v. 14.
|||| 1 John iii. 16.

that he might die because of Rebekah; but—for the sake of men, for their benefit. While, therefore, it is conceded that the phrase, to die for another, might have had a more loose and indefinite meaning; its actual meaning in the Scriptures is clearly defined, and denotes when applied to the death of Christ, that he *died instead of mankind*.*

2. It is said that he died *for our* sins.

To die for sin, has but one meaning in the scriptures. In the case of *the sinner himself*, to die *for his own sins*, uniformly denotes, *to suffer death as the punishment of his sins*. "But every one," says Jeremiah, "shall die for his own iniquity; every man that eateth the sour grape, his teeth shall be set on edge."†

To die for the sin of another, also, in no solitary instance which I can find denotes, *to suffer death as an example to him*, or *for his reformation*, or *moral improvement;* but in every case, either *to suffer death as a manifestation of the displeasure due to his sins*, or *to die instead of the sinner*. Thus in Ezekiel, "The son hath walked in my statutes, he shall not die for the iniquity of his father."‡ So also in the inquiry of Balak, "Shall I give my first-born for my transgression, the fruit of my body for the sin of my soul?"§ As these are all the passages in which these two phrases are found, except those which relate to Christ; it is certain that the phrase to die for the sin of another, never denotes to die for his reformation, but to suffer death as the manifestation of anger due to his sin.

That Christ died for our sins, is taught in the most explicit manner. It was predicted by Isaiah, "He was

* For the Scriptural references in this and several of the following heads, am chiefly indebted to Taylor on the Atonement.

† Jer. xxxi. 30; and Ezekiel xviii. 26. ‡ Ezek. xviii. 17.

§ Mic. vi. 7.

wounded for our transgressions, he was bruised for our iniquities." "The Lord hath laid on him the iniquities of us all." "For the transgression of my people was he stricken.*" It is declared with equal plainness in the New Testament. Paul says to the christians at Rome, "He was delivered for our offences;"†—and again,—"While we were yet sinners, Christ died for us;‡—to the Corinthians, "Christ died for our sins, according to the Scriptures:"§—and to the Galatians, "He gave himself for our sins;"‖—while Peter declares "Christ also hath once suffered for sin, the Just for the unjust."¶

From the uniform meaning of the phrase to die for sin, it is therefore clear, that Christ's dying for our sins denotes,—not his suffering death for our reformation, but his suffering it, as the manifestation of the anger of God due to our sins.

3. It is said that he died *for the forgiveness* or *pardon* of our sins.

Forgiveness is *remission of punishment;* and punishment is *the manifestation of displeasure,* on the part of a ruler *against sin.* That such is the scriptural use of these terms, the following passages will prove. Joshua said to the Israelites, "The Lord will not forgive your transgressions; if ye forsake him, he will do you hurt, and consume you."** The consequence of God's not forgiving their sins, was his consuming them. "The Lord," says the sacred historian, "sent the bands of the Chaldeans against Judah, to destroy them, for the innocent blood, which Manassah shed, which the Lord would not pardon;"†† so that God's refusing to pardon the sin of Judah,

* Is. liii. 5, 6. 8. † Rom. iv. 25. ‡ Rom. v. 8.
§ 1 Cor. xv. 3. ‖ Gal. i. 4. ¶ 1 Pet. i. 18.
** Josh. xxiv. 19, 20. †† 2 Kings xxiv. 4.

was the cause of their destruction. "Thou hast forgiven the iniquity of thy people," says David, "thou hast turned from the fierceness of thine anger."* "He that shall blaspheme against the Holy Ghost," says our Lord, "hath never forgiveness; but is in danger of (Gr. ἔνοχος; *obnoxius; qui tenetur quasi vinctus et obstrictus; doomed to*) eternal damnation."† Never to have forgiveness, is therefore the same thing, as to be doomed to eternal damnation.

The forgiveness of our sins, denotes therefore the remission of their punishment; and *to die for the forgiveness of our sins*, is the same thing as *to die, that we may be delivered from the punishment of our sins.* But did Christ die for the forgiveness or remission of our sins? At the institution of the Sacramental Supper, he gave an official and public explanation of the design of his death: "This is my blood of the New Testament, which is shed for many, for the remission of sins."‡ To the disciples after his resurrection he said, "Thus it was necessary that the Christ should suffer, and rise from the dead, and that repentance and remission of sins should be preached in his name among all nations."§ Paul often uses similar language. To the Romans he writes, "Whom God hath set forth to be a propitiation, through faith in his blood, to declare his righteousness for the remission of sins that are

* Ps. lxxxv. 1, 2.

† Mark iii. 29. See also Ps. lxxviii. 38.—Lam. iii. 42, 43.—Heb. x. 26, 27. -as well as the prayer of Solomon, 1 Kings viii. 33, 34, 35, 36, 37, 38, 39, rhere in every instance *to forgive the sins* of Israel, is explained *to remove* ›me *evil brought on them for sin;* in other words, *to avert punishment.*—ee also Ex. x. 17.—Is. lv. 7.—Jer. v. 7. 9, and xviii. 23, and xxxvi. 3.—Mic. i. 18.—Matt. xii. 31.—Luke xii. 10.—Acts viii. 22, 24.—Heb. x. 17, 18. 28, ›, 30.

‡ Matt. xxvi. 28.

§ Luke xxiv. 46, 47. (*ουτος εδει παθειν τον Χριστον.*)

past, through the forbearance of God;"* and both to the Ephesians and Colossians, "In whom we have redemption through his blood, even the forgiveness of sins."† As therefore Christ died for the forgiveness of our sins, as forgiveness is the remission of punishment, and as punishment is the manifestation of the anger of God due to our sins; it follows, that Christ died, in order that we might be saved from the punishment of our sins, or from that manifestation of the Divine displeasure, which they deserve. But if this be true, then, if he had not died we must have received the punishment due to our sins. Of course his sufferings are the reason why we do not suffer; in other words they are *vicarious*, or *a substitute for our punishment.*

4. It is said that he died as *a sin-offering*, and as *a sacrifice for our sins.*

We need not here enter at large into the subject of sacrifice; nor inquire what the Heathens meant, by the sacrifices offered to their deities. Neither is it necessary to investigate the design of all the various kinds of sacrifices, prescribed in the ceremonial law. Our attention will be confined to *sacrifices for sin*, or as they are usually called *sin-offerings*, and *trespass offerings;* and the design of these we shall learn from the Scriptures themselves:— "To the Law and to the Testimony."

A sacrifice for sin was an animal slain, and offered to God, in behalf of the sinner; and the design of it is thus explained by the Lawgiver who prescribed it: "If the whole congregation sin through ignorance, they shall offer a young bullock for the sin, and the bullock shall be killed before the Lord; and the priest shall make atonement for

* Rom. iii 25.

† Eph. i. 7. and Col. i. 14.—See also 2 Cor. v. 19, 21. and Heb. x. 17, 18.

them, and it shall be forgiven them."* "If a soul sin, and commit a trespass against the Lord; he shall bring a ram without blemish for a trespass-offering, and it shall be forgiven him."†

By the very terms of the institution, therefore, *a sin-offering*, or *a trespass-offering*, was offered in sacrifice in order *that the sins of the offerer might be forgiven;* in other words, *that he might be delivered from the punishment of his sins.*

That the writers of the New Testament understood the subject in this manner, is certain. We are told in the epistle to the Hebrews—"By the Law, almost all things are purged with blood; and without shedding of blood is no remission;"‡ i. e. no deliverance from the punishment of sin. The Apostle, in this passage, not only declares that sacrifices were offered for the pardon of sin; but that there was no pardon, no remission of punishment, without the shedding of blood. In the following chapter he declares, "Now where remission of these (of sins and iniquities) is, there is no more offering for sin;"§—in other words, where the sins of the worshipper are remitted, he needs offer no farther sacrifice on account of them:—showing most conclusively, that if his sins had not been forgiven, he must have offered sacrifice in order that they might be forgiven; and that his offering, or his not offering, a sacrifice for sin, was the turning point of his pardon, or his punishment. Again he says, "If we sin wilfully, after we have come to the knowledge of the truth, there remaineth no more sacrifice for sin, but a certain fearful looking-for of judgment and fiery

* Lev. iv. 13—20.

† Lev. vi. 1. 5, 6. and many other passages in the Pentateuch.

‡ Heb. ix. 22.

§ Heb. x. 18.

indignation:"*—in other words, if a sinner has gone so far in provoking God, that no more sacrifice for his sins can be accepted, then he has nothing before him but fiery indignation; i. e. his sins cannot be forgiven, nor their punishment be remitted. The design of sin offerings or sacrifices for sin, was therefore to procure the forgiveness of sin, or the remission of its punishment.

But was Christ a Sacrifice for sin, or a Sin-Offering? Isaiah predicted that he should be: "Thou shalt make his soul an offering for sin."† To the Corinthians, Paul writes, "He hath made him to be sin (ἁμαρτίαν, a sin-offering‡) for us, who knew no sin:"§ and to the Ephesians, "Christ also hath loved us, and given himself for us, an offering and a sacrifice to God for a sweet-smelling savour."|| To the Hebrews he often declares this truth—"Christ needeth not daily, as those high priests, to offer up sacrifice first for his own sins and then for the people's, for this he did once, when he offered up himself."¶ "Now once in the end of the world, hath he appeared to put away sin, by the sacrifice of himself."** Christ was once offered, "to bear the sins of many."††—"This man, after he had offered one sacrifice for sin, forever sat down on the right hand of God."‡‡

* Heb. x. 26, 27.

† Is. liii. 10. נשא, the customary Hebrew word for *trespass-offering*.

‡ The word Αμαρτία, in the Greek of the Septuagint, in at least 114 instances, denotes *a sin offering;* and is the customary rendering of חוא the Hebrew word for *sin-offering*. As likewise, Christ *knew no sin*, he was not made *to be sin for us*, unless in one of these three senses, either, 1. That our sins were so *transferred* to him that he became guilty of them; which will not be admitted; or 2. That he became *an offering for sin;* or 3. That God *treated him as a sinner* for us. The two last meanings are substantially the same.

§ 2 Cor. v. 21. || Eph. v. 2. ¶ Heb. vii. 27.

** Heb. ix. 26. †† Heb. ix. 28. ‡‡ Heb. x. 12.

As therefore Christ died as a *Sacrifice for the sins of men*, or as *a Sin-offering for us ;* and as the design of sacrifices for sin or sin-offerings, was to procure *the forgiveness of sins*, or *the remission of their punishment ;* it follows that the design of Christ's death was *to procure the forgiveness of our sins*, or *the remission of their punishment.*

This truth is strikingly illustrated and enforced by Paul, when he calls Christ, " Our Passover." The word פֶּסַח (Πασχα, Passover,) denotes both the day, on which the feast was celebrated ; and the lamb, sacrificed at the feast. The latter is obviously its meaning, wherever mention is made of killing the passover ;* of sacrificing the passover ;† of roasting the passover ;‡ and of eating the passover.§ As here applied to Christ, it will be admitted to have the latter meaning ; the allusion being most certainly not to the day of the feast, but to the lamb, that was sacrificed for it.

To understand this allusion, we must remember that, on the evening of that night, in which God was to manifest the fierceness of his anger against the Egyptians,—the night preceding the departure and deliverance of the Israelites—they were directed in every house to sacrifice a lamb, and sprinkle its blood upon the door-posts ; that wherever the blood of the paschal lamb—the passover—was thus sprinkled, God passed over those houses and their inhabitants, and did not visit them with his vengeance ; while on those Israelites, whose houses were not thus sprinkled, his vengeance fell, as it did on the Egyptians.

* As in Ex. xii. 21 ; 2 Chron. xxx. 15. 17 ; xxxv. 1. 11 ; Ezra vi. 20 ; Mark xiv. 12, and Luke xxii. 7.

† Ex. xii. 27 ; xxiii. 18 ; xxxiv. 25 ; Deut. xvi. 2. 4, 5, 6 ; and 1 Cor. v. 7.

‡ 2 Chron. xxxv. 13.

§ Ex. xii. 11 ; 2 Chron. xxx. 18 ; Matt. xxvi. 17 ; Mark xiv. 12 ; Luke xxii. 8. 11. 15, and John xviii. 28. In all *twenty-five* instances.

The blood of the passover, (the paschal lamb) was therefore shed, that those who were sprinkled with it might be passed over in the hour of vengeance, or might be delivered from the anger of God.

As the deliverance of Israel from the bondage of Egypt, and their settlement in the land of promise, represented the deliverance of the church of God from sin, and their establishment in "a better country, even a heavenly;" we can easily understand the Apostle when he calls the blood of Christ "The blood of sprinkling;" and when he says, "Christ our passover (our paschal lamb) was sacrificed for us."* The true "Israel of God," those who are sprinkled with "the blood of sprinkling,"†—the blood of Christ "our paschal lamb," "the Lamb of God, who taketh away the sin of the world"—will be passed over, or be saved from the vengeance of God, when it shall fall on the world of the ungodly.

It is said that the passover, or paschal lamb, was not a sacrifice. When, however, we remember that it was a lamb, slain, and offered to God; that the sacred writers speak familiarly of sacrificing the passover;‡ and that the Apostle, in this very passage, says "Christ, our Passover, was sacrificed, ἐτυθη § for us; we cannot be at a loss on this point. It is also said that if the paschal lamb was a sacrifice, it was not a sacrifice for sin, or a sin-offering. To this it is sufficient to reply, 1. That although it is not expressly called a sacrifice *for sin* in its institution, yet it is declared to have had the same efficacy,—that of saving him who offered it from the wrath of God:—"And the blood shall be to you for a token upon the houses where ye

* 1 Cor. v. 7. † Heb. xii. 24.

‡ Ex. xii. 27; xxiii. 18; xxxiv. 25; Deut. xvi. 2. 4, 5, 6; 1 Cor. v. 7.

§ Θύω is the appropriate Greek verb for, *to sacrifice*.

are; and when I see the blood, I will pass over you, and the plague shall not be upon you to destroy you."*—2. That we prove Christ to have been a Sacrifice for sin, or a Sin-offering,—not because he is called our passover, but—because, in numerous passages, it is expressly said, that he was a sacrifice for sin and a sin-offering.†

5. It is said that the Death of Christ was *an Atonement for the sins of men.*

The word To Atone, is in the Hebrew כִּפֵּר; and signifies, 1. *To cover, to overlay.* This is probably its original meaning.‡ And because sins are metaphorically *covered* or *hidden from the sight*, when they are *forgiven*, it denotes, 2. *To forgive, to be merciful to.*§ Hence, as a causative verb, it denotes, 3. *To procure forgiveness, to expiate, to make atonement;* and is the word, in the original of the old Testament, uniformly answering to the phrase, *to make atonement.*‖

* Lev. xii. 13.

† See the passages referred to in pp. 29, 30.

‡ In this sense it occurs Gen. vi. 14, "thou shalt *pitch (cover) it;*" and, *as a noun*, in the same sense denotes *pitch*, "so called from its use for *smearing, covering.*" (*Gesenius.*)—In a similar sense in Is. xxviii. 18. Your covenant shall be *disannulled*, "*blotted out, obliterated*, because a writing was thus *covered* by drawing *the style* over it" (Gesenius.) In a similar sense, *as a noun*, it denotes *a village*, in 1 Chron. xxvii. 25. Cant. vii. 11. Neh. vi. 2; and Ezek. xxxviii. 13, became *obscure, hidden:—Snow* and *hoar-frost*, as *covering* the ground, in Ex. xvi. 14; Job xxxviii. 29; Ps. cxlvii. 16:—*The alhenna* in Cant. vii. 11. (Gr. κυπρος, Eng. Tr. *camphor*, or *cypress-tree*:) and *a bribe* in 1 Sam. xii. 3.—Amos v. 12, because a bribe *covers* the eyes.

§ As denoting *to forgive*, it is used in Deut. xxi. 8, 8; xxxii. 43.; 2 Chron. xxx. 18; Ps. lxv. 3; lxxviii. 38; lxxix. 9; Prov. xvi. 6; Is. vi. 7; xxiv. 14; xxvii. 9; and Jer. xviii. 23. In several of these passages it is rendered *purge* and *cleanse.*

‖ *To make atonement, to expiate*, is its customary meaning. As *a verb*, in the following passages, it is translated *to make atonement.* Ex. xxix. 33. 36, 37; xxx. 10, 10. 15, 16; xxxii. 30; Lev. i. 4; iv. 20. 26. 31. 35; v. 6. 10. 13. 6. 18; vi. 7; vii. 7; viii. 34; ix. 7. 7; x. 17; xii. 7, 8; xiv. 18, 19, 20, 21,

The *Offerings*, mentioned as presented for *atonement*, were different in different cases.

1. When an ox gored a man to death, if the owner knew that he was wont to push in times past; the general law required him to be put to death; but there were circumstances in which he might pay a sum of money "for the ransom of his life."* If the person gored were a freeman, the amount to be paid was to be determined by the ordinary tribunals; but in the case of a servant it was regularly thirty shekels of silver. As the mulct in the

29. 31. 53; xv. 15. 30; xvi. 6. 10, 11. 16, 17, 17, 18. 24. 27. 30. 32, 33, 33, 33, 34; xvii. 11. 11; xix 22.—Num. v. 8; vi 11; viii. 12. 19. 21; xv. 25. 28, 28; xvi. 46, 47; xxv. 13; xxviii. 22 30; xxix. 5; xxxi. 50; 2 Sam. xxi. 3; 1 Chron. vi. 49; 2 Chron. xxix. 24; Neh. x. 33.

As *a noun*, it is rendered *Atonement* in Ex. xxix. 36; xxx. 10. 16; Lev. xxiii. 27, 28; xxv. 9; Num. v. 8; xxix. 11.

As *a verb*, it is used in *a similar sense*, in Num. xxxv. 33; 1 Sam. iii. 14; Ez. xliii. 20. 26. where it is translated *to purge*, *to cleanse:* in Lev. vi. 30; viii. 15; xvi. 20; Ez. xlv. 15. 17. 20; Dan. ix. 24, where it is rendered *to reconcile*, *to make reconciliation*, and should be rendered *to make atonement:* —in Gen. xxxii. 20; Prov. xvi. 14; Ezek. xvi, 63, where it is rendered *to pacify*, *to appease*, because an atonement, an expiation procures *forgiveness*, or *pacifies anger*.

As *a noun*, it is used *in a similar sense*, in Num. xxxv. 31, 32. where it is rendered *satisfaction:*—in Ex. xxi. 30. where it is rendered a *sum of money*, i. e. *a fine* as giving satisfaction for an injury:—in Ex. xxx. 12; Job xxxiii. 24; xxxvi. 18; Ps. xlix. 7; Prov. vi. 35; xiii. 8; xxi. 18; Is. xliii. 3. where it is rendered *a ransom*, and in all but the two last denotes *a ransom for the life*, because an atonement *released* or *ransomed* from punishment:—in Ex. xxv. 17, 18, 19, 20, 20, 20. 22; xxx. 6; xxxi. 7; xxxv. 11; xxxvii. 6, 7, 8, 9, 9; xxxix. 35; xl. 18; Lev. xvi. 2, 2. 13, 14, 15, 15; Num. vii. 89; where it is rendered (Sept. ιλαστηριον) *mercy-seat*, i. e. *the place of expiation*, or o *receiving pardon:*—and in Amos ix. 1. (כפתר, by mistake for כפרת) where i is rendered *altar*, or *that on which the atoning sacrifice is offered.*

Thus of the 154 instances, in which the word occurs, 13 appear to refe directly to its original meaning, *to cover;* 12 to the second meaning, *to for give;* and 129 to the third, *to make atonement.* Of these last 80 are rendere *Atonement* in our version, and 49 by nouns or verbs of a cognate signi cation.

* Ex. xxi. 28—30.

case of a servant went to his master, it is probable that in the case of a freeman it went to the surviving relatives.

2. Whenever a census was taken of the children of Israel, every man of twenty years and upwards, was required to bring half a shekel to the priests "for the service of the tabernacle of the congregation."* The service of the tabernacle of the congregation required, every day, the offering of a lamb of the first year every morning for a burnt-offering, and of another every evening; and with each lamb a tenth deal of flour, mingled with a fourth part of a hin of beaten oil, and the fourth part of an hin of wine;† and in addition to these, there were very expensive weekly, monthly, and yearly sacrifices for the whole congregation. The money given for this service was called "the atonement-money of the children of Israel;"‡ and was "given by every man unto the Lord for the ransom of his life, when thus numbered, that there might be no plague among them, when they were numbered."§ As it went to the service of the tabernacle, and thus furnished the sin-offerings and burnt-offerings which made atonement for the whole people; it might well be called "the atonement-money of the children of Israel."

3. An individual, for the following offences—for not disclosing the truth, when adjured as a witness; for touching a carcass; for touching an unclean person; and for unintentionally neglecting to do what he had sworn;—if he was so poor that he could not bring a lamb, nor even two turtle-doves, nor two young pigeons;—was directed to bring the tenth part of an ephah of fine flour for a sin-

* Ex xxx. 12—16. and Numbers xxxi. 48—54.

† Ex. xxix. 38—42.

‡ Ex. xxx. 16.

§ Ex. xxx. 12. See Selden, *De Jure Nat. et. Gent. Lib* ii. c. 8.

offering; and the priest took a handful of it, and burnt it on the altar, as a sin offering, and the priest made an atonement for him as touching his sin; and it was forgiven him.* Had he been able to bring a lamb, he would have been required to offer it as a sin-offering to make an atonement; or could he have brought the two doves, or pigeons, one would have been offered as a sin-offering, and the other as a burnt-offering, to make atonement.† As he could do neither, the flour, on account of his extreme poverty, was accepted, instead of the regular sin-offering—a mere substitute for the animal sacrifice which he otherwise must have offered for his sins. But, because God accepts the solitary prayer of the sick man on his bed, as his worship on the Sabbath; does it therefore follow, that solitary worship, and not the worship of the sanctuary, is the worship of the Sabbath? If not, neither can it be alleged from this exception in an extreme case that atonement could be made without sacrifice.

4. In the revolt of Korah the congregation had united, the anger of God was kindled, and the people were falling dead before it. In this emergency Moses said to Aaron, "Take a censer, and put fire therein from off the altar, and put on incense, and go quickly unto the congregation, and make an atonement for them; for wrath is gone out from the Lord; the plague is begun!" Aaron did so, "and he put on incense, and made an atonement, and stood between the living and the dead; and the plague was stayed."‡ Had there been time, Aaron was required to bring the two goats for a sin-offering, and a ram for a burnt offering to the door of the tabernacle, and kill one of the goats, and the ram: and to take a censer full of

* Lev. v. 11—14. † Lev. v. 6 7. ‡ Numbers xvi. 41—50.

coals from off the altar, and put the incense on the fire, that the cloud of incense might cover the mercy-seat; and then to take the blood of the goat, and sprinkle it with his finger on the altar, and then to confess the sins of the people on the head of the other goat, and send him away into the wilderness.* All this required time, and supposed the high priest to have leisure to do it. But, in the existing emergency, when the people were dying by thousands, Moses, being divinely instructed for the given case, and believing that God will have mercy and not sacrifice, and that God requireth of a man, according to what he hath, and not according to what he hath not, very wisely directed Aaron to omit what he could not do, towards making the atonement for the people—the sacrifice of the ram and of one goat, the sprinkling with its blood, and the sending forth of the other; and to do what he could do—to take the censer, and the holy fire, and to burn the sweet incense, that God might accept it for an atonement. But can this case of awful necessity, when, and that too within the space of a few moments, fourteen thousand seven hundred were dead, before Aaron could finish doing what he did do by way of atonement;—can it prove that the regular Levitical atonement was made merely by incense, or that the victims, the sacrificed goat and ram, both prescribed as an essential part of the atonement in the same law which prescribed the censer, the fire, and the incense, did not constitute a part of the atonement? Because Christ did not direct the thief on the cross to be baptized, when he professed his faith in him; does it therefore follow that it is not our duty to be baptized, as well as to believe?

The three last are all the instances which I have been

* Lev. xvi. 5—22.

able to find, in which it can be even supposed that an atonement was made to God, without the sacrifice of life. In the first, the money thus paid by the whole nation, bought the animals for the service of the tabernacle; which, when sacrificed, made an atonement. Of course, though it was called the atonement-money, yet the atonement was not made without the sacrifice of life. And when the individual, as he paid it to procure the burnt-offering and the sin offering, to make atonement, was told that it was "for the ransom of his life," he was most affectingly reminded, that his life was forfeit, and that the life of the animal was sacrificed instead of his own. In the second, the individual was told that the law required a lamb, for a sin-offering to make an atonement for him, but that on account of his utter inability to furnish it, or even two doves, God was pleased to accept the fine flour as a sin-offering. On the third I need make no comments. These cases, I think, will satisfy no one that the Levitical atonement did not imply the substitution of a life; as that of the man gored by an ox was not an example of an atonement made to God, but a mere pecuniary satisfaction to the survivors; while of the three last the first was a case of money paid to procure the sacrifices which made atonement; and the second and third were cases, in which sacrifices were expressly required for sin-offerings to make atonement, but, owing to extreme necessity, could not be procured.

5. In two instances atonement is represented as made by the sacrifice of human life. When the people began to commit whoredom with the women of Moab, and the fierce anger of the Lord was kindled against Israel, and the plague was begun; Zimri, a prince of Simeon, brought

his Midianitish woman into the midst of the camp before Moses and the people, as they were assembled to weep and to humble themselves at the door of the tabernacle, on account of this very sin. And when Moses called on the judges to slay every one his man of them that were thus guilty, Phinehas, the grandson of Aaron, rose up, and took his javelin, and thrust both of them through; and the plague was stayed, after twenty-four thousand had died. And God blessed him, "because he was zealous for his God, and made an atonement for the children of Israel."* Here *the life of the guilty persons* was the atonement. The anger of God was really manifested against them, instead of being manifested, as it usually was typically, against the life of the animal offered as a sacrifice for sin.

The other case was the following. The Israelites had sworn to the Gibeonites, by Joshua, to preserve them; yet "Saul and his bloody house" in their zeal for Israel had slain them. For this, God sent a famine on Israel; and David, on inquiring the reason of the Lord, was answered, "It is for Saul and his bloody house, because he slew the Gibeonites." He then assembled the Gibeonites, and asked them, "What shall I do for you and wherewithal shall I make the atonement, that ye may bless the inheritance of the Lord. And the Gibeonites said 'Let seven men of the sons of him, who plotted against us to destroy us, be delivered unto us; and we will hang them up unto the Lord in Gibeah of Saul.† The atonement here spoken of was made by the sacrifice of the life of seven of the guilty family; but it was an atonement to the Gibeonites; a satisfaction for the murders inflicted on them by Saul and his bloody house; just as every criminal makes an atonement,

* Numbers xxv. 1—13.

† 2 Sam. xxi. 1—9.

a satisfaction to the violated laws of his country when he suffers their penalty.

These two cases however, although they explain the general nature of Atonement, yet exhibit the word rather in the way of accommodation, than in its strict Levitical import. But we are now prepared to learn its *official* appropriate meaning, when used to explain the actual efficacy of the sacrifices appointed in the ceremonial code of the Israelites.

Here it may be proper to inquire, when an animal was sacrificed to make atonement, *in what* did the atonement, consist ? This question is directly and formally answered in the law itself: " *The life* of the flesh is in *the blood;* and I have given it you upon the altar *to make an atonement*, for your souls ; (*lives* נַפְשֹׁתֵיכֶם ;) for it is THE BLOOD, *that maketh an atonement* for the *life*."* Here it is expressly said that the blood maketh the atonement, because THE LIFE is in the blood. The atonement therefore consists in the shedding of the blood, as the seat of the life ; in other words, it consists in the cutting off of life, or the infliction of death.

The Levitical law gave directions with regard to sacrifices for atonement in the following cases :

1. In the case of *Diseases*. (1.) For recovery from leprosy. The priest taking two birds, was to sacrifice one, and sprinkle the leper with blood, and let the other bird loose. And the priest was to offer three lambs, for a trespass-offering, a sin-offering, and a burnt-offering ; and sprinkle the blood of the first on the leper, and make an atonement.† (2.) For recovery from a running issue, the priest was to offer one turtle-dove or pigeon for a sin-offer-

* Lev. xvii. 11.

† Lev. xiv. 4—7, 10—20.

ing, and another for a burnt offering.* (3.) In the case of puerpery. The priest was to bring a lamb for a burnt-offering, and a pigeon, or turtle-dove for a sin-offering to the door of the tabernacle, and sacrifice them and make atonement; and the mother was cleansed.† (4.) For a house infected with leprosy. The priest taking two birds was to sacrifice one, and sprinkle the house with its blood, and let the other loose.‡ The very language of the law, in these cases, led the diseased person to regard *diseases* as the fruit of sin; and, in those which were peculiarly painful and defiling, God required him when recovered, not only to present a thank-offering, but by a sacrifice for sin to make an atonement for his sins, of which he had thus been most affectingly and solemnly reminded, and thus distinctly to acknowledge, what was most true, that he *deserved death* at the hands of God. That the Jews regarded the subject in this light, is obvious not only from the language of scripture, but from the uniform testimony of their distinguished writers.§

2. In cases of *Ceremonial Uncleanness*, (1.) Touch-

* Lev. xv. 14, 15. 29, 30. † Lev. xii 6, 7. ‡ Lev. xiv. 51—53.

§ "In the opinion of all the Jewish writers of eminence even those cases of defilement which were *involuntary*, such as leprosy, child-bearing, &c. uniformly implied an idea of guilt. Thus Abarbanel, speaking of the case of puerpery in the 12th of Leviticus, says that "*without committing sin, no one is ever exposed to suffering*; that it is a principle with the Jewish Doctors that *there is no pain without crime*; and that *therefore*, the woman who had endured the pains of child-birth was required to offer *a piacular sacrifice*." In the case of the leper in Lev. xiv. he remarks that the sin-offering was enjoined, "because the whole of the Mosaic religion being founded on this principle that *whatever befals any human creature is the result of providential appointment*, the leper must consider his malady as *a judicial infliction for some transgression*." Magee on Atonement and Sacrifice, N. Y. Ed. p. 154.—That this principle is correct and scriptural is certain; for although we cannot learn the comparative sins of men from the dispensations of the present life, nor conclude that the afflicted are greater sinners than the prosperous, as the Jews did, with regard to those who were crushed by the

5

ing the carcass of an unclean beast.* (2.) Touching the uncleanness of men.† These persons need only wash to be clean, unless they entered the sanctuary;‡ but, in that case, were required to offer *a lamb* for a sin-offering, to make atonement. The reason given for this was, that the sanctuary was most holy, that no one who was impure could enter it without profaning it, and that every one who thus entered it was sentenced "to be cut off from among his people," unless he offered a sin-offering to make an atonement.§ (3.) In the case of the Nazarite.‖ A Nazarite was bound by a vow, during the days of his separation, 1. To abstain wholly from wine and the fruit of the vine.¶ 2. Not to shave his head.** 3. Not to come near any dead body, even that of his father or mother, or any other thing that might communicate ceremonial uncleanness.††—If he was present with a dead body, even by accident, as in the case of sudden death; it was regarded as sin and he was required after seven days' cleansing to offer two turtle doves, one for a sin-offering, and one for a burnt-offering, to make atonement for him, for that he sinned by the dead.‡‡ He was then to shave his head and commence his days of separation anew. To be present with a dead body, was a ceremonial sin, and therefore to be thus purged. And the reason of this precept, says *Abarbanel*, (Preface to the book of Leviticus, chap. xiv.,)

tower of Siloam; yet nothing is more certain than that we are taught in the Scriptures to regard every species of suffering as *the legitimate fruit of sin;* to view the sufferings which we ourselves endure as *chastisements for our personal sins;* and to acknowledge that we have *merited* far more than we *receive.* See Ontram on Sacrifices, Eng. Tr. D. I. C. 12. §§ 6, 7.

* Lev. v. 2. † Lev. v. 3.

‡ Lev. xi. 28. 40, and Num. xix. 13. 19, 20.

§ Lev. vii. 20, 21, and Num. xix. 13. 20.

‖ Num. vi. ¶ Num. vi. 3, 4. ** Num. vi. 5.

†† Num. vi. 6, 7. ‡‡ Num. vi. 9—12.

was "to make men very cautious how they contracted any defilement."

3. In the case of *Consecrations*. (1) Of the *priests*. To consecrate Aaron and his sons, Moses offered a bullock for a sin-offering, and two rams for a burnt-offering; putting the blood of the bullock on the horns of the altar, sprinkling the blood of one of the rams round about the altar, and that of the other on the persons and garments of Aaron and his sons, to make atonement for them.* (2.) Of the *altar* and the *tabernacle*. Moses was directed to sacrifice a bullock every day for seven days to make atonement upon the altar.†

4. For *sins of ignorance*.‡ (1.) Of the *priests*. (2.) Of the whole *congregation*. In each of these cases a bullock for a sin-offering, to make atonement.§ (3.) Of a ruler. (4.) Of one of the common people:—for each a kid of the goats for a sin-offering for his sin, to make atonement.|| (5.) For a sin of ignorance in the holy things of the Lord, a ram for a trespass-offering to make atonement.¶

These sins were not those in which *the ignorance* was invincible, and where the law of God in the given case could not be known; but the ignorance was voluntary and therefore criminal.** The language of the Law proves this. "If any one sin through ignorance, while he doeth

* Ex. xxix. 10—33.

† Ex. xxix. 36, 37, and xxx. 10, and Lev. xvi. 15—19.

‡ Lev. iv. and Num. xv. 27—29.

§ Lev. iv. 3. 13. 20. || Lev. iv. 22. 26, 27. 35. ¶ Lev v. 15, 16.

** They were sins committed *in ignorance*, just in the same manner as the Jews are represented, in Acts iii. 17, to have crucified Christ κατα αγνοιαν, *through ignorance*; just as Paul ascribes all the wickedness of the heathens to *the ignorance* that was in them (δια την αγνοιαν) because of the hardness of their hearts; and as Peter calls their *sinful lusts*, εν αγνοια επιθυμιαις, *lusts in ignorance*. Magee on At. and Sac. 192.

somewhat against any of the commandments of the Lord, which ought not to be done, and is guilty."* They were opposed to presumptuous sins, and were committed involuntarily, imprudently or by mistake.† Three things were necessary to constitute the sin; 1. It was something prohibited, and not a sin of omission. The language is "concerning things which ought not to be done." 2. It was done not wilfully. 3. It was not for transgression in thought, but in *external act;* "and shall do against any of them."‡

5. For *individual sins of greater aggravation.* (1.) For a witness to keep back the truth, when the judge adjured him by an oath to disclose it. He was to bring a lamb for a trespass-offering to make atonement.§—(2.) For *fraud, breach of trust, lying, false-swearing,* and *fraudulent detention of the property of others.* The offender was not only to make restitution, and add a fifth; but to bring a ram for a trespass-offering to make atonement.||—(3.) For sinfully neglecting to perform, what he had bound himself by an oath to perform. He was to bring a lamb for a trespass-offering, to make atonement.¶—(4.) For impurity with a woman betrothed. He was to bring a ram for a trespass-offering, to make an atonement.**

6. For the sins of the Priests, on the day of Atonement. A young bullock was offered for a sin-offering, and a ram for a burnt-offering; the blood being sprinkled on, and before, the mercy seat to make atonement for them.

7. For the sins of the congregation at large. (1.) On the day of Atonement. The Great day of Atonement was

* Lev. iv. 27.

† Schleusner. Thesau. in LXX. ακουσιως, *non sponte, imprudenter, per errorem.*

‡ Lev. iv. 27.

§ Lev. v. 1.

|| Lev. vi. 1—7.

¶ Lev. v. 4.

** Lev. xix. 20—23.

an annual celebration ; a day of humiliation appointed on the tenth day of the seventh month. It was " for all the iniquities of the children of Israel and all their transgressions in all their sins, to make atonement for them." The high priest was directed to take a ram for a burnt offering, and two kids of the goats for a sin-offering, to present them to the Lord before the door of the tabernacle ; to take a censer full of fire from the altar, and put sweet incense upon it within the veil, that the cloud of incense might cover the mercy-seat ; to sacrifice the ram and one of the goats, and sprinkle the altar and make atonement, to confess the sins of the people on the head of the other, and then send him away loaded with the sins of the people into the wilderness.—(2.) In the cases of the rebellion of Korah, and of the sin of the people with the women of Moab, atonement was made for the people. These cases have been already sufficiently examined.

There were various sins, for which no sin-offering was pointed out ; and for which no atonement could be made, but by *the destruction of the sinner's life.* The law pointed out no atonement for murder, adultery, incest and various other species of impurity, filial impiety, or idolatry. In the case of murder, it is expressly said, " Moreover ye shall take no *atonement* (כֹּפֶר) for the life of a murderer, who is guilty of death ; for blood it defileth the land ; and to the land no atonement shall be made, (וְלָאָרֶץ לֹא־יְכֻפַּר) for the blood that is shed therein, but by the blood of him that shed it."*—In the case also of the children of Eli, it is said, " The iniquity of Eli's house shall never be atoned for, (יִתְכַּפֵּר) by sacrifice or offering."

What then was *the efficacy* of an Atonement.

* Numbers xxxv. 31, 33.

The owner of the unruly ox, paid a sum of money as a civil penalty "for the ransom of his life." In the case of numbering the people it was atonement-money paid, by each man, "for the ransom of his life." In the case of the Gibeonites, the anger of God was turned away, and the famine prevented. In the various cases of recovery from disease, the sins of the individual were forgiven. In the cases of ceremonial uncleanness, the ceremonial sins of the individual were pardoned; and without making the prescribed atonement, it is expressly said that the individual "shall be cut off from Israel." In the case of consecrations, it procured the pardon of the priests and the Levites. In every case of a sin of ignorance, where atonement was made, as well as in every case of more aggravated sins, the sin was forgiven. On the great day of Atonement it procured the forgiveness of "all the iniquities, and all the transgressions in all the sins" of both priests and people, for the preceding year. This language is universal, including every offence which was capable of expiation. In the case of Korah, as soon as Aaron had made atonement; as well as in that of the Moabitish women, when Phinehas had made atonement; the plague was stayed, and the people ceased to die; and in the latter God said of Phinehas, "He hath turned my wrath away from the children of Israel, that I consumed them not—he was zealous for his God and made an atonement for the children of Israel." In addition to this it is said, in the official explanation of the nature and design of the Atonement, "For the life of the flesh is in the blood, and I have given it to you upon the altar, to make an atonement for your lives; for it is the blood, that maketh atonement for the life." If then, by the phrase *vicarious suffering*, we denote *any evil inflicted on one being, to expiate the sin of another*, that is, *to save the other from punishment, and procure the pardon of his sins;* then it is certain, that the sufferings and death of the animals, sacrificed to make atonement under the Levitical Dispensation, were in the strictest sense *vicarious.* In other words, in the sufferings inflicted on the animal in taking away his life, there was a typical manifestation of the anger of God, which was instead of the real manifestation of it in the punishment of the sinner; and the former was accepted by God in lieu of the latter.

But is it declared in the Scriptures, that the DEATH OF CHRIST WAS AN ATONEMENT FOR THE SINS OF MEN? The assertion, that this is no where said, has been often made; and with a rashness, which can be excused on no other supposition, than that those who make it, have looked no farther than to the words of the English Version.

It is here distinctly admitted, that the word *Atonement*, is found but once in the English New Testament,—Rom. v. 11, "By whom we have now received *the atonement;*— and that the original, την καταλλαγην, ought not to have been rendered *the atonement*, but *reconciliation.* Let us then examine whether it is not asserted, in both Testaments, that the death of Christ was an atonement for sin.

In the vision of Daniel, relating to the kingdom of the Messiah, the angel Gabriel informs him, "Seventy weeks are determined upon thy people, and upon thy holy city,— to finish the transgressions, and to make an end of sins, and to make reconciliation for iniquity, (in the Hebrew, וּלְכַפֵּר עָוֹן *and to make atonement* for iniquity,) and to bring in everlasting righteousness." To whom this refers, the following verses explain: "Know therefore and understand, that, from the going forth of the commandment to restore and to rebuild Jerusalem, unto THE MESSIAH the

Prince, shall be seven weeks, and threescore and two weeks; and after the threescore and two weeks shall the MESSIAH be cut off, but not for himself; and he shall confirm the covenant with many for one week; and in the midst of the week, the sacrifice and the oblation shall cease." Here then it is expressly asserted that, when the Messiah shall be cut off, but not for himself, he shall *make Atonement for iniquity.*

We will now examine the state of the fact with regard to the Old Testament. The word כָּפַר we have seen, occurs in the Old Testament in 154 instances; 13 of which refer to its original meaning, *to cover;* 12 to its second meaning, *to forgive;* and 129 to its usual meaning, *to make atonement*, of which 80 are rendered *atonement*, or *to make atonement* in our version, and 49 by nouns or verbs of a cognate signification. In the Greek of the Septuagint כָּפַר is rendered by the verbs ιλασκομαι, and εξιλασκομαι, both meaning, *to make atonement, to propitiate*, in 81 instances; and by their derivative nouns in 39 more;* and by the words, λυτρον and εισφορα, both denoting *atonement, ransom*, and αλλαγμα *substitute* in 10:†—in all 130. These

* Εξιλασκομαι, *to make atonement*, occurs in 78 instances: Gen. xxxii 20; Ex. xxx 10. 15, 16; xxxii. 29; Lev. 1. 4; iv. 20. 26. 31. 35; v. 6. 10. 13. 16. 18; vi. 6. 30. 37; viii. 15. 34; ix. 7, 7; x. 17; xii. 7, 8; xiv. 18, 19, 21. 29. 31. 53; xv. 15. 29; xvi. 6. 10, 11. 16, 17, 17, 18. 20. 24 27. 30. 32, 33, 33, 33, 34; xvii 11, 11; xix. 22; xxiii. 28; Num. v. 8; vi. 11; viii. 13. 19. 21; xv. 23. 26, 26; xvi. 46, 47; xxv 13. 31. 50; xxxv. 33; Deut. xxi. 8; 1 Kings iii. 14; 2 Kings xxi. 3; 1 Chron. vi. 49; 2 Chron. xxix. 24; xxx. 19; Neh. x. 33; Prov. xvi 15; Ezek. xvi. 62; xliii. 20. 26; xlv. 15. 17. 20; Dan. ix. 24.—Εξιλασις, *Atonement*, occurs in Num. xxix 11.—Εξιλασμα, *Atonement*, in 1 Kings xii. 3, and Ps. xlviii. 7; Εξιλασμος, *Atonement*, in Ex. xxx. 10; Lev. xxiii. 27, 28; xxv. 9, and 1 Chron. xxviii. 11.

Ιλασκομαι, *To make Atonement*, occurs in *three* instances. Ps. lxiv. 3; lxxvii. 42; lxxviii. 9. Ιλασμος, *Atonement*, in Numbers v. 8, and ιλαστηριον, *mercy-seat*, in the 25 already recited in a preceding note.

† Λυτρον occurs in Ex xxi 30; xxx. 12; Num. xxxv. 31, 32; Prov. vi. 35; xiii. 8. Εισφορα in Ex. xxx. 16. Αλλαγμα in Is. xliii 3, and Amos v. 12.

facts are sufficient to prove that the words ιλασκομαι and εξιλασκομαι, as *verbs*, and their derivatives ιλασμος, εξιλασμος &c. as *nouns*, are the appropriate words in the Greek for rendering the word כָּפַר *To make Atonement*, from the Hebrew.

But, on opening the New Testament, we find that the Apostle to the Hebrews says of Christ, " It behoved him to be made like unto his brethren ; that he might be a merciful and faithful high priest, εις το ἱλασκεσθαι τας ἁμαρτίας του λαου, *to make atonement for the sins of the people*."* John too declares, " And he is the Ιλασμος, *Atonement for our sins ;* and not for ours only, but *for the sins of the whole world*.† In a subsequent chapter he tells us, " Herein is love, not that we loved God but that he loved us, and sent his Son to be the Ιλασμον, *atonement for our sins*.‡ And the Apostle to the Romans declares, " Whom God hath set forth to be ιλαστηριον, *an atonement* through faith in his blood, to declare his righteousness for the remission of sins that are past."§ It is said that, Ιλαστηριον, though denoting etymologically, *the place of atonement* or *propitiation*, always denotes in the Septuagint *the mercy-seat*, and therefore does not denote *an atonement* here. What then I ask was the mercy-seat ? It was the

It is rendered by Αθωοω *to forgive* in Jer. xviii. 23. by Αγιαζω *to purify*, in Ex. xxix. 33. 36 ; by Αφαιρεω, *to put away* (sin,) in Is. xxvii. 9, and xxviii. 18 ; by Αφιημι *to put away* in Is xxii. 14 ; by εκκαθαριζω *to purify*, in Deut xxxii. 43 ; by καθαριζω to purify in Ex. xxix. 37, and xxx. 20 ; by καθαρισμος *purification*, in Ex. xxix. 36, and xxx. 10 ; by καθαρος γινομαι, *I become pure*, in Is. i. 16.

It is rendered by Κωμη *a village*, in 1 Chron. xxvii. 25 ; Neh. vi. 2 ; Cant. vii. 11, Ezek. xxxviii. 13 : by ομιχλη a cloud, Ps. cxlvii 11 ; by παγος and παχνη *snow, hoarfrost*, in Ex. xvi. 14. and Job xxxviii. 29 ; by Ασφαλτοω *to smear*. and Ασφαλτος *pitch*, in Gen. vi. 14 ; by κυπρος the cypress, in Cant. i. 13, and by κατεπετασμα, *a veil*, in Ex. xxvi. 34, and xxx. 16.

* Heb. ii. 17. † 1 John ii. 2. ‡ 1 John iv. 10. § Romans iii. 25.

golden cover of the ark, with a golden cherub at each end, made out of it, and overshadowing it with his wings. On it and before it, the blood of Atonement, was sprinkled, and the atonement for sin made. Surely then the Apostle did not intend to be understood *literally*, that Christ was the golden cover of the ark. In the very passage, he speaks of the blood of Christ, as procuring for us the forgiveness of sins, and Moses tells us that the blood of the sin-offering, continually sprinkled *on* and *before* the ιλαστηριον, made atonement, and procured the forgiveness of sin. This of itself would be sufficient to prove that the Apostle when he calls Christ the ιλαστηριον intends, not the mercy-seat itself, but either *the atonement* which the blood of Christ made, or *the victim, the atoning sacrifice*, whose blood made the atonement. But when too we find him using a similar figure in two other cases—" We have an altar, θυσιαστηριον, of which they have no right to eat who serve the tabernacle ;" i. e. *an offering, a sacrifice ;* and again, " They who minister at the altar ought to be partakers of the altar—not surely of the altar itself—a mere heap of stones, but—of the sacrifices offered upon it ; when also we find him in the passage just quoted, expressly declaring that Christ made atonement for the sins of the people ; when likewise we find Josephus, an Hellenistic Jew as well as Paul, and his contemporary, also using the word, ιλαστηριον not to denote the mercy seat, but in such a manner that it can only be rendered atonement ;* and when Chrysostom uses it as a

* " Michaelis says (Marsh's Mich. i. 187,) Josephus having previously observed that the blood of the martyrs had made atonement for their countrymen, and that they were ωσπερ αντιψυχον, (*victima substituta*) της του εθνους αμαρτιας (*a victim substituted for the sin of the nation*,) continues as follows, και δια του αιματος ευσεβων εκεινων, και του ΙΛΑΣΤΕΡΙΟΥ του θανατου αυτων, η θεια προνοια τον Ισραελ διασωσε, (Quoted from Magee, p 134) The literal English of this passage is, " And by the blood of these devout men, and *the atonement of their death*, Divine providence saved Israel."

propitiatory gift;* we feel assured that Paul meant in this passage to declare, "Whom God hath set forth to be *an atonement*—or a propitiatory sacrifice—for *the remission of sins.*"

Here then, without alluding to the word Λυτρον, another of the words employed to render כָּפַר, and used with its derivatives in no less than nine instances to point out the design of Christ's death; without referring again to the numerous passages, in which he is declared a sin-offering, the appropriate design of which was *to make atonement;* we find *one* express declaration in the Old Testament, and *four* in the New, that the Death of Christ was *an atonement* for the sins of mankind. But we have seen that when an animal was sacrificed to make atonement for sin, the suffering of death was inflicted on him, or his life was taken away, *to save him, for whose sins the atonement was made, from the punishment of his sins*, or *to procure their pardon.* The Death of Christ therefore was inflicted to save men from the punishment of their sins or to procure their pardon. God "laid on him the iniquities of us all," or manifested his anger against our sins in his sufferings and death, that he might not manifest it in our punishment. His sufferings therefore were *a substitute* for the punishment of our sins.

6. It is said that he died *to reconcile us* to God.

The reconciliation of two individuals implies previous enmity, or alienation *in one*, or *in both.* It is contended, however, that *our reconciliation to God*, by the death of Christ denotes—not *that God ceases to manifest his anger towards us*, but—*that we cease from our enmity towards God.* On this point the Scriptures shall speak for themselves.

* The language of Chrysostom is, Ιλαστηριον 'Αχαιοι τη Αθηνα τη 'Ιλιαδι. The Greeks sent *a propitiatory gift* to the Trojan Minerva."

In the law of the sin-offering it is said, "The blood of the sin-offering is brought into the tabernacle of the congregation, to reconcile withal in the holy place."* But, as the blood of the sin-offering was shed, that the sins of the offerer might be forgiven, or that God might not manifest his anger against him; The reconciliation here effected by the blood, denotes—not the offerer's laying aside his enmity, but—*God's forgiving the sins of the offerer*, or not manifesting his anger against him. The Philistines said to Achish, "Wherewith shall David reconcile himself (Sept. διαλλαγήσεται, be reconciled) to his master; shall it not be with the heads of these men?"† As the anger was on the side of Saul, David's being reconciled to Saul, denoted not the laying aside of David's, but of Saul's, anger.—"If thou bring thy gift to the altar" says our Lord, "and there remember that thy brother hath aught against thee; first be reconciled to thy brother, and then come and offer thy gift."‡ As my brother is here the offended party; for me to be reconciled to my brother, is therefore—not to lay aside my own anger, but—to persuade my brother to lay aside his anger, and forgive me. Another passage from the New Testament not only shows the meaning of the language generally, but the precise meaning of the phrase, *to be reconciled to God:* "God hath given to us the ministry of reconciliation, viz. that God is in Christ reconciling the world unto himself, not imputing their trespasses unto them."|| For God *to reconcile the world unto himself*, is therefore the same thing as for God *not to impute their trespasses unto them.* But what is it for God not to impute to any one his trespasses, or sins?—It does not denote, *to reform him*, to *sanctify him:* no such use of the

* Lev. vi. 30. † 1 Sam. xxix. 4. ‡ Matt. v. 24. § 2 Cor. v. 19.

phrase can be found. Its meaning is defined with exact precision by David, " Blessed is he, whose transgression is forgiven, whose sin is covered; blessed is the man unto whom the Lord imputeth not iniquity."* It is therefore to forgive his sins; in other words to remit the punishment which they deserve."† The phrase, God's reconciling the world unto himself, through Jesus Christ, denotes therefore his forgiving the sins of the world through Jesus Christ, or *his remitting the punishment* of their sins.

But do the Scriptures assert that the Death of Christ is the means of our reconciliation to God? They shall answer for themselves. The Apostle to the Gentiles writes to the Romans, " If, when we were enemies, we were reconciled to God by the death of his Son; much more, being reconciled, we shall be saved by his life;"‡—to the Ephesians, " Christ hath reconciled both Jews and Gentiles unto God in one body by the cross;"§—to the Corinthians, " God hath reconciled us to himself by Jesus Christ—For he hath made him to be sin (to be a sin-offering) for us, who knew no sin, that we might be made the righteousness of God in him:"||—to the Colossians, " For it pleased the Father, having made peace by the blood of his cross, by him to reconcile all things unto himself; and you that were some time alienated, and enemies in your mind by wicked works, yet now hath he reconciled in the body of his flesh, through death, to present you holy, and unblamable and unreprovable in his sight.¶

* Ps. xxxii. 1, 2.

† Those, who wish to know how the phrase *to impute trespasses* or *sins*. is used in the Scriptures, may examine Lev. xvii. 4; 2 Sam. xix. 19, and Rom. v. 13; and indeed all the passages, in which it is found. It has but one meaning.

‡ Rom. v. 10. § Eph. ii. 16. || 2 Cor. v. 18. 21.

¶ Col. iv. 20—22. See also 1 Pet. iii. 18.

The Death of Christ is therefore the means of reconciling mankind to God; and that reconciliation consists in God's "not imputing their trespasses unto them;" i. e. in his *forgiving their sins*, or remitting the punishment which they deserve.

7. It is said that Christ, in his sufferings and death, *bare our sins*, or *iniquities*.

The phrase, *to bear sin*, or, as it is sometimes rendered, *to take away sin*, needs explanation. In the Hebrew, we find two different verbs, סָבַל and נָשָׂא, both signifying *to bear*, connected with חַטָּאָה, *sin*, עָוֹן, *iniquity;* and פֶּשַׁע, *trespass* or *transgression*.

To the phrase *to bear sin*, two very different meanings have been attached: 1. That of *bearing them away*, in the sense of *removing them;* and 2. That of *bearing them as a burden*, in the sense of *bearing with them*, or *enduring them*, on the part of him who is offended, and of *bearing or enduring their punishment*, on the part of the offender, or of a third party who takes his place, or suffers on his account.

In investigating this point, it may be proper to ask, What is meant by the phrase to remove our sins, or to remove our iniquities?—Does it mean, to annihilate our sins? That, in the very nature of things is impossible. A sin is a fact,—a transgression actually committed:—and to annihilate a fact,—to bring it to pass, after a sin is once committed, that it shall not have been committed,—is not within the reach even of Omnipotence.—Does it mean to annihilate the guilt of our sins? That is equally impossible. As it must forever be a fact, that a given sin now past was committed; so it must forever be a fact, that he who committed it is guilty of its commission. The guilt is equally a fact with the sin itself. Does it mean, to transfer our sins to another? That also is physically impossible. A given sin when committed, is an act, past, and irrevocable: an act, concerning which it must forever be true, that it was performed by the sinner himself, and not by another. Does it mean, to transfer the guilt of our sins to another? This is no less an impossibility. Guilt is inseparably connected with sin; and as it never can be true, with regard to a given sin, that any one but the sinner, committed it, so it never can be true, that any one else is guilty of its commission. Will it be said that it denotes to remove our sinfulness? I ask again, What is the meaning of the phrase, to remove our sinfulness? Does sinfulness here mean guilt? But to remove the guilt of sin, we have just seen is impossible. Does it mean, to remove our sinful dispositions?—our propensities to sin? and thus to reform us, or sanctify us? After a careful examination, I have not been able to find a passage in the sacred volume, in which either of the verbs translated, to bear, is connected with a word, the appropriate or customary meaning of which is sinfulness, sinful dispositions, or propensities to sin:—not a passage in which it is not connected with sin, or transgression, as a fact, an act committed; or with iniquity, as guilt actually incurred by such an act. To explain it by the phrase, to remove our sins, in the sense of removing our sinful inclinations, is therefore to take for granted the point in debate, and that too in direct opposition to the uniform language of the Scriptures; and to explain it by the phrase, to remove our sins, in the sense of causing them to cease to exist, i. e. of annihilating them, implies as we have seen a direct absurdity.

We will now endeavor to determine the meaning of the phraseology in question, by a reference to the passages in which it is found. The meaning of the Hebrew verb, סָבַל, as given by Gesenius,* is "*to bear*, particularly *a heavy load*;" and this is the only meaning, which it has itself, or which it has communicated to any of its derivatives.†

The verb נָשָׂא, according to Gesenius, denotes, 1. "*to lift*, or *raise up*"—2. "*to bear*," and under this meaning, (1.) "*to bear away*," as a dead body is borne, Judges xvi. 31—(2.) "*to suffer, endure*;"—(3.) "*to bear the guilt of any one, to suffer for it*."—3. "*to take*," and under this *to take* or *carry away*.

The word סָבַל as connected with *sin, iniquity*, is used in only two instances. Our fathers have sinned, and are

* Gibbs' Gesenius.

† As this is a point of consequence, I have collected all the passages, in which the verb or its derivatives are used.

In the following seven passages *the verb itself* is thus translated, Gen. xlix. 15,—"he bowed his shoulder *to bear*," i. e. as *a burden*. Ezra vi. 4, as a participal noun, "*foundation*," or that which *bears* or *sustains* the building. Ps. cxliv. 14, rendered "*strong to labour*," by Gesenius, "*loaded*, hence *prolific*." Eccl. xii. 6, "and the grasshopper shall be *a burden*." Is. xlvi. 4, in two instances, "I *will carry* you," i. e. as *a burden* is carried. In Isaiah liii. 4, it also occurs as a verb: "Surely, חלינו הוא נשא, he hath taken away *our sicknesses*, and *carried our sorrows*, ומכאבינו סבלם. For a very acute and satisfactory critique on this passage see Magee on Atonement, pp. 229—240, N. Y. ed. in which the following points are established: 1. That חלינו, in the first clause denotes not *griefs* but *sicknesses* or *bodily infirmities*; 2. That, מכאבינו, in the second, denotes *sorrows*, or *torments of the mind*; and 3. That, סבל, here, as well as every where else, means, *to bear as a burden*. These are the only places where *the verb* is found except the two mentioned in the Text.

Its *derivative nouns* are thus rendered; סבל, 1 Kings xi. 28, "*the charge*," and in the marginal reference "*Heb. the burden*, of the house;" Neh. iv. 17, "*burdens*;" and Ps. lxxxi. 6, "*burden*,"—סבל, 1 Kings v. 15—"*that bare burdens*;" 2 Chron. ii. 2 and 18. "*to bear burdens*,"—and xxxiv. 13, "*bearers of burdens*;"—and Neh. iv. 10, "*bearers of burdens*;"—סבל, "*a burden*," in Isaiah ix. 4, and x. 27, and xiv. 25.—סבלה, "*a burden*," Ex. i. 11, and ii. 11, and v. 4, 5, and vi. 6, 7.—These *twenty-five* instances are all in which the word occurs, except those mentioned in the text; and in each of these the allusion is *to bearing, as a burden*, and in no one *to bearing away*, in the sense of *annihilating*, or *bringing to an end*.

not, and we have *borne their iniquities ;** i. e. we are suffering evils inflicted on account of their iniquities, as is obvious from the preceding verses, " Our necks are under persecution, we labour and have no rest," &c.—The other passage relates to the Death of Christ, " For he shall bear their iniquities."† וַעֲוֹנֹתָם הוּא יִסְבֹּל As these are the only two passages, in which the phrase, סָבַל עָוֹן, *to bear iniquity*, is found ; it is certain, both from the uniform meaning of סָבַל, and from the force of the phrase in the passage first quoted, that when Isaiah says of Christ, " He shall *bear their iniquities*," the phrase denotes—not that he *removed the iniquities* of men, *by annihilating* either their *sins*, or their *guilt*, or their *sinfulness ;* but—that he *bare their sins as a burden, by enduring sufferings inflicted on account of them.*

The word נָשָׂא, as connected with sin and iniquity, is of frequent occurrence, and is applied to various classes of individuals :

1. *To the party offended ;* and in this application it always denotes *to bear with, to forgive, to pardon, to remit the punishment of a sin*, or to refrain from manifesting displeasure on account of it :—" Yet now, if thou wilt, forgive (תִּשָּׂא, αφες, *bear with*) their sin."‡ In the same sense it is applied *to the Angel*, who was to go before the Israelites : " He will not pardon (יִשָּׂא) your transgressions."§—*to Joseph ;*||—*to Moses and Aaron ;*¶—*to Samuel ;***—*and to David :*†† in each, denoting, and being rendered, *to forgive*, or *pardon.*

* Lam. iii. 7, comp. Jer. xxxi. 29, and Ezek. xviii. 2. † Is. liii. 11.

‡ Ex. xxxii. 22. See also the following passages in each of which it is applied to God, and denotes *to forgive ;* viz. Ex. xxxiv. 7 ; Num. xiv. 18 ; Josh. xxiv. 19 ; Job vii. 20 ; Ps. xxv. 18 ; xxxii. 1. 5 ; lxxxv. 2 ; Is. xxxiii. 24 ; Hos. xiv. 2 ; Mic. xvii. 18.

§ Ex. xxiii. 21. || Gen. l. 17, in two instances. ¶ Ex. x. 17.

** 1 Sam. xv. 25. †† 1 Sam. xxv. 28.

But what is it to forgive a sin? It is not to take away, to remove the sin, or its guilt, or to cause either to cease to exist;—That, we have seen, is physically impossible: nor is it to remove the sinfulness of the sinner; had Moses and Aaron forgiven the sin of Pharaoh, it would in no degree have implied, that he had ceased to be sinful:—it is to take away the punishment due to it; or to endure, to bear with the sinner, notwithstanding his sin. Here therefore the phrase, *to bear sin*, denotes—not *to remove*, *to annihilate*, but, *to bear as a burden.*

2. *To the offender;* and, in this application, it uniformly denotes *to bear the punishment* due to sin. Thus, "That they bear not iniquity, and die."* Here, also, the phrase *to bear sin*, denotes, *to bear as a burden.*

3. *To a third party.* It is thus applied

(1.) To *Aaron, the priests and levites*, with reference to the iniquity of *the sanctuary*, of *the priesthood*, and of *the congregation.* This subject may be thus explained. The people had been forbidden to profane the sanctuary by entering it in their uncleanness, under the penalty of death. They complained to Moses, that on this footing they should all be consumed;† in consequence of which, God announces to Aaron and the priests that, if through their negligence, the sanctuary was thus profaned they should bear the iniquity, or suffer the punishment; and therefore directs them "to keep the charge of the sanctuary, that there be no wrath any more upon the children of Israel." The obvious meaning therefore is, that if any

* Ex. xxiii. 43. See also Lev. v. 1. 17; vii. 18; xvii. 16; xix. 8. 17; xx. 17. 19, 20; xxii. 9. 16; xxiv. 15; Num. v. 31; ix. 13; xiv. 13; xviii. 1. 22, 23, 32; xxx. 15; Ezech. xvi. 58; xxiii. 35. 49; xxxix. 26; and xliv. 10. 12, 13. These twenty-eight instances are all in which the phrase occurs in this application; and in each one it denotes, *to suffer the punishment* of sin.

† Numbers xvii. 12, 13, and xviii. 1.

legal defilement should profane the sacred things, the priests should bear the punishment, or make atonement for such profanation.

It is also said of Aaron, with reference to the *ceremonial* iniquity of the holy things, "That Aaron may bear the iniquity of the holy things which the children of Israel may hallow in all their holy gifts." This language supposes a defect or profanation on the part of the offerers, which would be pardoned in consequence of the gifts being presented by Aaron and his sons in their consecrated vestments. Aaron's bearing the iniquity of the holy things offered to God, was therefore his procuring pardon for the iniquity of those who offered them.

(2.) *To the prophet Ezekiel.* "Lie thou also on thy right side, and lay the iniquity of the house of Israel upon it; according to the number of the days that thou shalt lie upon it, thou shalt bear their iniquity. For I have laid upon thee the years of their iniquity, according to the number of the days three hundred and ninety days; so shalt thou bear the iniquity of the house of Israel. And when thou hast accomplished them, lie again on thy right side, and thou shalt bear the iniquity of the house of Judah, forty days; I have appointed a day for a year." While in this posture, the prophet is directed to eat the vilest food, and that in the least quantities, to typify to the people the punishment which God would bring upon them in the destruction of Jerusalem. For Ezekiel to bear the iniquity of the people in this manner, was therefore the same thing as, typically, to suffer their punishment; or, by a lively type, to represent to them the punishment which they were to suffer.

(3.) *To the goat of the sin-offering.* "And Aaron took the goat, which was the sin-offering for the people, and slew it, and offered it for sin. And Moses diligently sought the goat of the sin-offering, and behold it was burnt; and he said to the sons of Aaron, "Wherefore have ye not eaten the sin-offering in the holy place, seeing it is most holy, and God hath given it you to bear the iniquity of the congregation, to make atonement for them before the Lord."* The sin-offering we have already seen was sacrificed, that the sins of the congregation might be forgiven, or that the congregation might not receive the punishment of their sins. Here also it is said to bear the iniquity of the congregation, and to make atonement for them. For the goat thus sacrificed to bear the iniquity of the congregation, is the same thing, therefore, as for the goat to be sacrificed *to procure the forgiveness of their sins*, or *to take away*, *to remove*—not *their sins*,—that was a physical impossibility; but—*the punishment* of their sins.

(4.) To the *goats* offered on the great day of Atonement. On these two goats, lots were to be cast; one lot for the Lord, and one lot for the scape-goat, and while the goat on which the first lot fell, was to be sacrificed, the other was kept alive

* Lev. ix 15, and x. 16, 17. It has been urged that, *to bear the iniquity*, here refers to *you*, (*the sons of Aaron*,) and not to *it*, (*the goat of the sin-offering*,) because *you* is *nearer* than *it*, in the arrangement of the sentence. The original is as follows, ואתה נתן לכם לשאת את־עון העדה לכפר עליהם "And he hath given it you *in order to bear* the iniquity of the congregation, *in order to make atonement* for them."—This passage is precisely parallel in its construction with the following, ואני נתתיו לכם על־המזבח לכפר על נפשתיכם. "And I have given it you upon the altar *to make an atonement* for your souls." Here, according to the proposed rule of construction, *to make atonement* must refer to *you*, (*the sons of Aaron*) and not to *it*, (*the blood of the sin-offering*.) Let us then read the whole passage, "For the life of the flesh is *in the blood*, and I have given *it* you to make an atonement for your souls; for it is *the blood, that maketh an atonement* for the soul." As therefore *to make atonement*, in the latter passage, refers to *it*, (*the blood of the sin-offering*,) so does *to bear the iniquity*, in the former, refer to *it*, (*the goat of the sin-offering*,) and as additional evidence of this fact, it is said in the former passage, "he hath given it you to bear iniquity, *to make atonement*."

as a scape-goat, and led into the wilderness. With regard to the offering of these two goats the following things deserve our notice: 1. The sins to be atoned for, on the great day of Atonement, were all the sins of the nation for the preceding year.* 2. The two goats are called one sin-offering: "Thou shalt take one ram for a burnt-offering, and two kids of the goats for a sin offering."† 3. The scape-goat was *offered to God*, though not *sacrificed*. "The scape-goat shall be presented alive before the Lord, at the door of the tabernacle of the congregation."‡ 4. The Atonement for the people was made by both. "And he shall kill the goat of the sin-offering, and sprinkle his blood on the mercy-seat, and make atonement because of the transgressions of the children of Israel in all their sins."§ "But the scape-goat shall be presented alive before the Lord to make an atonement with him."‖ 5. The two goats, as one *sin-offering* for the sins of the people, and *as making one atonement*, were offered that the sins of the people might be *forgiven*."¶ 6. Aaron was directed *to put* all the iniquities, transgressions and sins of the children of Israel *upon the head* of the goat. "And Aaron shall confess over him all the iniquities of the children of Israel, and all their transgressions in all their sins, putting them upon the head of the goat."** 7. It is said, "the goat shall *bear upon him* (עָלָיו) all their iniquities unto a land not inhabited."†† 8. Although it is not expressly said of the other goat, that which was sacrificed, that he also *bare the sins* of the people; yet, as it is said that he was sacrificed as a sin-offering, and to make atonement for their sins; as it is also said in the official explanation of the

* Lev. xvi. 21. † Lev. xvi. 5. ‡ Lev. xvi. 29.
§ Lev. xvi. 15, 16. ‖ Lev. xvi. 9, 10. ¶ Lev. xvi. 5. 9. 15. 21. 22.
** Lev. xvi. 21. †† Lev. xvi. 22.

sin-offering, " God hath given you the goat of the sin-offering, to bear the iniquity of the congregation, to make atonement for them before the Lord ;"* and as it is said that the two goats were one sin-offering, and both made atonement for sin ; it is obvious that by both, as one sin-offering, offered for the forgiveness of sins, the sins of the congregation were borne : the suffering for these sins falling on the goat that was sacrificed ; while the leading away of the other goat, loaded with these sins, as with a burden, only represented in a lively manner the effect of that sacrifice. We cannot then be at a loss as to the phrase, he shall bear the iniquities of the congregation ? The language itself " he shall bear them upon him," shows that they were laid on him as a burden. And what was the effect of this offering of the two goats,—the sacrifice of one, and the leading away of the other,—with regard to the " iniquities, transgressions, and sins" of the people? Did it take away in the sense of removing or annihilating, or transferring to another, either the sins themselves, or the guilt of them? To do either of these was physically impossible. Did it remove the sinfulness, the sinful propensities,—of the congregation? The language is not sinfulness or sinful propensities ; it is " their sins and transgressions" of the preceding year, i. e. positive acts of sin, and not sinful propensities ; and, in point of fact, we find from the history that their sinful propensities did not go off with the scape-goat into the wilderness, but remained behind in all their number and all their strength. Was it then a type of the removal, the annihilation, of the actual sins of all Israel for one year ? If it was, it was a type of an utter impossibility—a mere absurdity—the supposition of which implies that the wheels of duration can

* Lev. ix. 15.

roll backward, and make past moments again present. Moses, however, has not taxed our faith with the admission of this absurdity. When he tells us that the two goats were a sin-offering, and made atonement for actual sins, and that the design of every sin offering was to bear sin, to make atonement, and to procure the forgiveness of the offender; he teaches us most conclusively that the goats bare the actual sins of the people in the sense of taking away their punishment; in other words that God was pleased in consequence of *the sacrifice for sin* (either from regard to "*the blood of bulls and of goats*" merely, or from immediate reference to A NOBLER SACRIFICE,) to treat the Israelites, as if the sins hand never been committed.

(5.) *To one man, as enduring sufferings, inflicted for the sins of another.*

"And your children shall wander in the wilderness forty years, and bear your whoredoms"* i. e. endure sufferings inflicted in consequence of them. "If he beget a son, that hath walked in my statutes, he shall not die for the iniquity of his father, he shall surely live."—"Yet ye say, Doth not the son bear the iniquity of his father?" "The soul that sinneth, it shall die; the son shall not bear the iniquity of the father, neither shall the father bear the iniquity of the son; the righteousness of the righteous shall be upon him, and the wickedness of the wicked shall be upon him."† Here the prophet gives us a definition of this language, and teaches us that, *to bear iniquity*, either *one's own* or *that of another* is not, *to remove*, or *annihilate it*, but *to undergo suffering inflicted on account of it.*

As the result of this inquiry it is clear, when the verb, נָשָׂא is joined with sin, or iniquity that, as applied to the

* Num. xiv. 33. † Ez. xviii. 14. 17, 18, 19, 20.

party offended, it uniformly denotes, to forgive; to remit deserved punishment, to bear with the sinner; as applied to the offender, it uniformly denotes, to bear, or suffer the punishment of sin; and as applied to a third party, it denotes in all cases, to bear sin as a burden, to be responsible for it, and where suffering is actually endured,* to endure suffering as an infliction for that sin.

When therefore Isaiah tells us, that Christ in his crucifixion "bare (נָשָׂא) the sins of many;"† we are sure that he means just what he meant in the preceding verse—"he shall bear (יִסְבֹּל) their iniquities;" i. e.—not, he shall bear them away, in the sense of removing them, or annihilating them; but—he shall bear them as a סָבַל a burden, he shall endure sufferings inflicted on account of those sins. And when he also tells us, "It pleased Jehovah to bruise him;" "Jehovah hath laid on him the iniquity of us all;" "And with his stripes we are healed;" we cannot but see that, on account of our sins, God inflicted those sufferings on Christ that we ourselves might be exempted from their punishment.

To bear sin, in the New Testament has precisely the same meaning; and the sacred writers employ those Greek verbs to express this idea, which the translators of the Septuagint had before employed to render סָבַל and נָשָׂא. They uniformly apply this language to Christ as *a sufferer*, as *dying on the Cross for our sins;* and never as *a teacher*, or as *an example*. "Who his own self bare our sins in his own body, on the tree."‡ The Apostle, by here using αναφερω, *to bear*, the identical word employed in the Septuagint to translate both סָבַל and נָשָׂא in Isaiah liii. 11, and 12; and by adding, "by whose stripes ye were healed;"

* Where not actually endured, it was endured typically.

† Is. liii. 12.

‡ 1 Pet. ii. 24.

shows us that he only quotes the prophet, and uses the phraseology in a similar manner. Paul employs the same language :—" So Christ was once offered, to bear(ανενεγκειν) the sins of many ;" which, only changing the future tense to the past, is a translation of Isaiah liii. 11, " And he shall bear," יִסְבֹּל ανοισει, " the sins of many."

John the Baptist uses similar language in announcing Jesus as the Saviour of mankind : " Behold the Lamb of God, who taketh away, αιρων, Marg. Ref. "*beareth*," the sin of the world."* The verb, αιρω, as connected with την αμαρτιαν, is in every instance except this, both in the Septuagint and the New Testament, applied to *the party offended*, and denotes *to forgive sin, to bear with the sinner.* Here it is applied to Christ in his mediation for the world. That it denotes—not to remove the sinfulness, the sinful propensities of the world, but—*to bear*, i. e. *suffer for* the sins of the world in order that those sins might be forgiven, will be obvious from the following considerations. 1. The similar verbs εξαιρω and αφαιρεω, in the Septuagint, when thus connected, denote *to make atonement for*, i. e. *to procure the forgiveness of*, sin. 2. Christ is here said to take away sin as *a Lamb*, and not as *an Example*, or *an Instructer*. 3. Isaiah, from whom the epithet as applied to Christ is borrowed, when he says, " He is brought as a lamb to the slaughter," takes care to introduce it with " The Lord hath laid on him the iniquity of us all ;" and to subjoin, " He shall bear the iniquities of many ;" and again " He bare the sin of many." 4. The evangelist John, who records this annunciation, calls Christ the lamb slain, and the lamb, whose blood had redeemed men to God out of every kindred, and nation, and people and tongue. 5. The same evangelist tells us that Christ is " an Atonement,

* John i. 29.

ἱλασμος, for the sins of the whole world." These considerations fully prove that the phraseology has here the same meaning, as in every part of the Old Testament, and in every other part of the New; and that the Lamb takes away the sin of the world, not as a teacher, but as the ἱλασμος for our sins.

8. We are said to be *redeemed* and *ransomed* by the death of Christ.

To redeem, and *to ransom*, are used interchangeably to translate the same words from the Hebrew and the Greek, and convey the idea of deliverance from evil: of a deliverance effected by some species of loss or sacrifice sustained on the part of the deliverer; which is accepted as an equivalent for the evil, from which the person redeemed is delivered. The Scriptures speak of the redemption of land from mortgages, of a slave from bondage, and of property from a vow, all by the payment of money; and of the first-born of men and of unclean beasts from sacrifice, by a substituted sacrifice. They also speak of redemption from iniquity, from death, from the grave and from the punishment of sin.

This language is applied to Christ in a manner which it is not easy to mistake. He says of himself, "Even so the Son of Man came—to give his life, a ransom for many." It has been contended that the ransom here spoken of is a ransom from *the power*, and not from *the punishment*, of sin. Salvation from the power of sin, is regarded by those who receive the doctrine of an Atonement, not only as a part of the salvation effected by Christ, but as a part so essential, that without it no salvation could exist. The question in this case is not, therefore, Whether Christ came to deliver his people from the power of sin;—that is admitted on all hands;—but, Whether he died to save them from the punishment of sin. When therefore we find him saying that he came "to give his life, a ransom for many," we turn to another passage in which he himself interprets this language: "This is my blood of the New Testament," διαθηκης, *Dispensation*) which is shed for many, for *the forgiveness of sins.*" But to forgive sin, on the part of God, we have seen is *to remit merited punishment.* Christ then being his own interpreter; he gave his life as a ransom for many to deliver them from the punishment to which they were doomed. Paul, in two of his epistles, speaking of the Death of Christ, explains this language in a manner equally unequivocal: "In whom we have redemption through his blood, even the forgiveness of sins."* The redemption which Christ's blood accomplished for us was, therefore, the forgiveness of our sins, i. e. exemption from their punishment. In another passage, his language is if possible still more incapable of being misunderstood: "Christ hath redeemed us from the curse of the law, being made a curse for us; for it is written, Cursed is every one who hangeth on a tree."† The *curse of the law* is not *the transgression of the law.* The law does not say in pronouncing its curse on the sinner, If you transgress once, you shall continue to transgress. No law was ever written in this manner. It says, "The soul that sinneth, it shall die." The curse of the law is *its penalty*, the punishment which it threatens to inflict on the transgressor. The evil then from which Christ is here said to redeem us, is that manifestation of the anger of God to which we were doomed by the condemning sentence of his law. But when did he thus redeem us?—The Apostle replies, When he died on the tree.—And in what way?—He again answers, By being made *a curse* for us: i. e.

* Eph. i. 7. and Col. i. 14. † Gal. iii. 13.

by enduring sufferings and death, as an infliction for our sins. But how came he to be nailed to the tree? The whole company of the Apostles inform us that he was delivered by the determinate counsel and foreknowledge of God; and from Isaiah we learn that "it pleased Jehovah to bruise him, and put him to grief;" and that "Jehovah laid on him the iniquities of us all." It was Jehovah then who inflicted upon him sufferings and death as a curse, that we might be redeemed from the curse of the law, the punishment to which we were doomed in consequence of our sins. If then Christ had not been made a curse for us, we must have endured the punishment due to our sins. His sufferings were therefore *in the stead* of the punishment of our sins.

Various other forms of expression, all of the same general import, are adopted by the scriptural writers to point out the end accomplished by the death of Christ; and of these I can mention only one. "But God commendeth his love toward us, in that while we were yet sinners, Christ died for us. Much more then being now justified by his blood, we shall be saved from wrath through him." To justify, as a legal phrase, is the opposite of to convict, or to condemn. Under a dispensation of law, it denotes, to pronounce innocent; and under a dispensation of grace, to pronounce not liable to punishment. In this passage therefore the apostle declares that the death of Christ is the means of exempting us from punishment; and then repeats the idea in different language by asserting, that *by his blood* we are saved from *the wrath* of God.

The length and minuteness of this part of the inquiry perhaps deserve an apology. The design has been to settle the meaning of each of the principal forms of expression adopted by the sacred writers to point out the end actually accomplished by the death of Christ. The evidence adduced in each case has been wholly from the Scriptures themselves; and if I am not deceived, it has been proved that those numerous forms of expression have one uniform meaning, concerning which even "the wayfaring man" need not err.

THESE are some of the *facts*, recorded in the Scriptures as connected with the death of Christ; and some of the *forms of phraseology*, by which they point out why this remarkable event took place. Having detailed the former, and recited and explained the latter, in the manner originally proposed; it remains in the third place, to inquire, How far the various theories devised to account for his death are consistent *with both?* These, you may recollect, are reducible to two classes: those which deny, and those which admit, that his death was an atonement for the sins of the world. Of the former class there are no less than six, to which I now propose to direct your attention. Each of these, we will compare both with the facts, and with the forms of phraseology in which the event is explained; and when this has been done, we will subject the theory, which regards it as an Atonement, to a similar scrutiny.

Before we commence this examination, in the progress of which we shall attempt to answer the question, *What was the Great End accomplished by the Death of Christ?* —it may not be improper to make the following remarks.

1. Several ends are often accomplished by a single event.

2. Of two or more ends accomplished by a single event, one may be the chief end of that event; and the others

only subordinate ends. Thus, to give light to living creatures was the chief end of the creation of light; while, to paint the clouds, or the rain-bow, was only a subordinate end.

3. An end accomplished by a given event may be merely incidental; necessarily growing out of the existing circumstances of the case, but being in no respect the great end, the final cause, for which the event took place. Thus: it was necessary that Christ should die; and it was also necessary that he should be raised from the dead. But, to rise from the dead, is a miracle; and a miracle furnishes evidence that the instructions of him who works it are true, and his mission divine. Christ's resurrection therefore, like every other miracle, furnished this evidence. Yet, as "it was not possible, that the Son of God should be holden of death" for thousands of years, his resurrection necessarily grew out of his death, and the evidence thus furnished necessarily grew out of his resurrection. This evidence was therefore an incidental end accompanied by his death—necessarily growing out of the circumstances attending it. The fact that his death furnishes the evidence in question, is no proof, then, that to furnish evidence was the great end of his death. But our present inquiry is not, Whether a given end was actually accomplished by his death? That numerous ends were accomplished by it, is certain. Our inquiry is, What was the Great End of Christ's Death—that which made it absolutely necessary; that which rendered it so surprising, so interesting an event, both on earth and in heaven.

The various explanations of this event, which deny that it was an Atonement for the sins of the world, will now be examined.

I. It is said that the Great End of Christ's Death was, *to prove his Sincerity.*

That the death of every martyr, and that of Christ as truly as that of every other, does prove him to have been sincerely devoted to the cause for which he died, is unquestionable. Still, if I mistake not, this scheme is attended with insurmountable objections.

1. The Scriptures no where mention this, as the great end of his Death.

2. He might have proved his sincerity without dying. Abraham did this ; and so did Moses, and Elijah. Who doubts the sincerity of John ? Who, that now believes in the sincerity of Christ, would have doubted it, if he had not suffered a violent death ? It is but a poor respect that we pay to the character of the Son of God, to say that he could not establish a reputation for sincerity without being crucified.

3. To go of set purpose and devote one's self to death, when one can avoid it, merely to prove one's sincerity ; is at the best an act of very doubtful morality. To die as a martyr, a witness to the truth of God, when his enemies have us in their power, and will put us to death if we do not renounce it,—is one thing ; but voluntarily to place ourselves in their power when we certainly know that they will put us to death, merely to gain a reputation for sincerity,—is another. Paul, when Aretas, King of Damascus, sought to put him to death as a Christian, instead of voluntarily suffering death to prove his sincerity, took care to be let down through a window in a basket, and so escaped from his hands. Again ; when forty men had bound themselves by oath, that they would not eat nor drink until they had killed Paul, this zealous apostle, instead of embracing so fair an opportunity of proving his sincerity, sent his nephew to Claudius Lysias the Roman Governor, for a powerful body-guard to resist them, and conduct him in

safety to Cesarea. Christ, too, at an earlier period of his ministry, "walked in Galilee; for he would not walk in Jewry, because the Jews sought to kill him." Often also he escaped from his enemies, when they were bent on putting him to death, because his hour was not yet come, although his death would have furnished as much evidence of his sincerity, as at the time when it actually occurred.

4. On this scheme, Christ's death was altogether premature and untimely. If he could not sufficiently establish a reputation for sincerity, by a ministry of three years and a half, he should have lived thirty or forty years longer. In that lapse of time he doubtless might have succeeded; or if not, he might at least have blessed mankind with his instructions, his example and his miracles; and then if it had been necessary, might have devoted himself to death.

5. Why, in this case, is the death of Christ represented as an event of so much importance? What possible explanation can we give of the scene on Mount Tabor? The well known rule of Horace,

> "Nec Deus intersit, nisi Dignus vindice nodus
> Inciderit"—

"Let not the Deity interpose, unless the occasion is one which demands his interposition," is as sound a rule of common sense in the events of Providence, as in the plan of a dramatic poem. Why then does Jehovah descend from heaven, with Moses and Elijah, to meet Jesus and the three disciples on the holy mount?—To converse with him about the mode in which he was to prove his sincerity?—Why too that change in the worship of the upper world? Did the countless myriads of angels forget all the other glories of Jehovah, and commence a new song that is to be sung forever and ever, because Jesus had furnished evidence to mankind that he was sincere; and are the words of the song, in which the redeemed respond to the angelic choir, " Thou art worthy, for thou wast slain, and hast redeemed us to God by proving thy sincerity ?" Had Paul no other subject of preaching, that he could declare " I am determined to know nothing among you, but the fact that Jesus Christ has proved his sincerity ?"—Was there nothing in heaven, or in God, to glory in, that he could say, " God forbid that I should glory save in the evidence of the sincerity of Christ ;" or did he indeed tell the Galatians, " Christ hath redeemed us from the curse of the law by dying to prove his sincerity ?"

6. How in this way shall we satisfactorily explain the circumstances of his death ? Had he so little firmness, that the mere dread of bodily suffering would lead him not only to fall three times prostrate with his face to the earth, and to cry out with inconceivable amazement and anguish of mind, " O, my Father, if it be possible, let me not die to prove my sincerity ?" Why too that travail of the soul, that offering of the soul a sacrifice, that bruising from Jehovah, that overwhelming agony which caused his sweat to become as it were great drops of blood ? Why that horror of deep darkness which forced from him the expiring cry, " My God, my God, why hast thou forsaken me ?"—Did Jehovah forsake him, because he was proving his sincerity ?—Why too that sympathy of the surrounding Universe, as he bowed his head, and gave up the ghost ? If a stranger had been at Jerusalem, at that Passover, and, seeing the singular and melancholy procession moving onward to Calvary, had followed Jesus thither ; and as he expired had witnessed the darkness, and the earthquake, and the rending rocks, and the opening graves, and had asked one of the many dead who came forth, " What mean these convulsions of nature ! Why does yonder sun veil his face in

sackcloth? Why do these solid pillars tremble, and give way? Why are the slumbers of the tomb disturbed; and what has called you forth from your silent mansions?"—would the answer have been—"The son of Joseph and Mary is dying, to prove his sincerity?"

7. This theory contravenes the whole language of Scripture. Christ, when he explains the design of his own death in the Eucharist, tells us "This is my blood, which is shed," not to prove that I am sincere; but—"for the remission of sins." No sophistry can make Christ's dying to prove his sincerity, the same thing with his bearing our sins in his own body on the tree, with his being made a sin-offering for us, with his giving himself a ransom for us, with his redeeming us from the curse of the law by being made a curse for us, and with our having redemption through his blood, even the forgiveness of our sins.

8. If this theory be true, all the martyrs deserve the title of Redeemers, Saviours and Mediators, as truly as Christ; for they proved their sincerity as fully, and in the same manner. Is it then true that Paul died for us; that he died for our sins; that he died for the forgiveness of our sins; that he "became a sin-offering for us;" that his death was an atonement for our sins; that he bare our sins in his own body on the tree; that he hath redeemed us from the curse of the law, being made a curse for us; and that by his death we are reconciled to God? Do the Scriptures say this of Paul?—But why not?—The death of Jesus merely proved his sincerity, and the death of Paul proved his; and both were preachers of the same Gospel. If then the phrases, bearing our sins, being made a curse for us, and others like them, when applied to Christ, mean nothing but his dying to prove his sincerity; they are just as applicable to any other martyr, as to Jesus; and

Paul is, in the same sense of the word with Jesus, the Saviour of the world, and the Redeemer of mankind. Then too we may lawfully say, " I am determined to know nothing among you save Paul and him crucified." " We preach Paul crucified, unto the Jews a stumbling-block and unto the Greeks foolishness, but unto them who are saved the power of God."

II. It is said to have been the Great End of Christ's death, *to set us an Example of Fortitude.*

To this theory there are several invincible objections.

1. Though the patience of Christ under sufferings is frequently mentioned in the Scriptures, and mentioned as an example for our imitation ; yet it is no where spoken of as the great end of his death.

2. If this was the great end of his sufferings, why did he die so early after his ministry began ? If the world could safely wait more than four thousand years for such an example, it might well have waited a few years more. Why then was not his life prolonged, and he permitted to instruct and bless mankind for forty years instead of three and a half ? He could have exhibited as much fortitude at the age of seventy as at the age of thirty-five ;—and in addition to this, he might have completed and published the New Testament, established the christian church, and witnessed the triumphs of his religion. Why, too, if he must die at this early age, did he begin his ministry so late in life ; why not be baptized at twenty-one instead of thirty-one ? It was not owing to any immaturity of knowledge, or wisdom ; for at the age of twelve he was able to confound the whole body of the rabbis in the temple. Why then were these precious ten years spent by him in working under his supposed father Joseph, at the trade of a car-

penter, in the obscure village of Nazareth, instead of being occupied in healing, and enlightening, and reforming mankind ?

3. The lawfulness of devoting one's self to death, merely to set an example of fortitude, is at the best exceedingly doubtful. The savages of the west, indeed, sometimes do this ; but a Christian with the scriptures before him may fairly question the propriety of the conduct. Is it lawful for me to leap into a furnace, in order to shew how well I can endure pain ? If John Rogers had thrown himself on the burning faggots to prove his fortitude, would he not have been a suicide rather than a martyr ? But Christ's death was voluntary and deliberate. He went purposely to Jerusalem to die ; he also remained there to die ; and he said to Judas as he went out to betray him, " What thou doest, do quickly."

4. The fortitude of Christ, viewed as an example for our imitation, is not perfectly appropriate. If Christ was a super-angelic being, it can scarcely be regarded as an example at all. The desponding christian, whom you should urge to copy it, might well reply, " True, the Saviour submitted to his sufferings with fortitude and resignation ; and well he might, for he was a super-angelic being, and had inconceivable energy and resolution. Give me the same ; nay give me even those of an angel ; let me also have been in heaven, and know as well what heaven is, and that it is my home ; let me have the full assurance of the love of God ; and let me know that at the close of this short life I shall ascend to pre-eminent honour and glory ; and I too will bear any affliction without a murmur."

If Christ was a mere man, still there were several important points of difference between him and other men. He was without sin ; the Spirit was given him without measure ; he had peculiar intelligence, wisdom, and energy of character; in him dwelt all the fulness of the Godhead bodily; he was pre-eminently the object of the Father's love ; he could look to him for support and strength under every trial ; and he was soon to set down with him on his throne on high. If then some one was to die to set an example of fortitude, which we could fairly be called on to imitate, it should not have been one of a character and in circumstances so perfectly unlike ours, it should have been a man in all respects like ourselves. If you urge the christian, who is sinking under his sufferings, to imitate the example of Jesus, he may well answer you, " True indeed he set an illustrious example of patience and resignation under suffering ; but then he had great helps which I have not. Give me the same support, let me also be without sin, give me the Spirit without measure, endow me with his strength of understanding, shed abroad upon me such a measure of the Father's love, furnish me with the same divine support, let all the fulness of the Godhead dwell in me bodily, and let me have the same glorious prospects, and I will imitate his example, and will sustain with filial resignation every trial which God in his providence calls me to endure."

5. Why on this supposition, was there this imperative necessity of Christ's death :—a necessity so stern and inflexible, that the thrice repeated prostration in the garden, accompanied by the thrice repeated prayer, " O my Father, if it be possible, let this cup pass from me !" and followed by the agony and the sweat of blood, could not bend it :—a necessity so absolute, that, unless the death of Christ took place, the wheels of providence must stop, and the gracious purposes of God towards man all be defeated. Is a single example of fortitude the great hinge of the gov-

8

ernment of Jehovah. Is want of fortitude the heaven-provoking sin of man, and that so exclusively that all the sins forbidden in the decalogue, and all those enumerated in the 18th of Leviticus and the 1st of Romans need no attention and no reformation.

But why must this example be exhibited by Christ; why must a being who is perfectly innocent and holy suffer? Is fortitude so rare a virtue on earth, that none but he could possibly exhibit it? Could not one, who as a sinner deserved death, if he had afterwards become holy, especially if strengthened by God to endure the afflictions laid upon him;—could not such an one as Paul furnish an adequate example of fortitude to weak timid man, without that scene of horror, at sight of which,

"The fainting sun grew dim at noon?"

Let the Apostle speak for himself: "Are they ministers of Christ?—I speak as a fool—I am more: in labours more abundant, in stripes above measure, in prisons more frequent, in deaths oft. Of the Jews five times received I forty stripes save one. Thrice was I beaten with rods, once was I stoned, thrice I suffered shipwreck, a night and a day I have been in the deep; in journeyings often, in perils of waters, in perils of robbers, in perils by mine own countrymen, in perils by the heathen, in perils in the city, in perils in the wilderness, in perils in the sea, in perils among false brethren, in weariness and painfulness, in watching often, in hunger and thirst, in fastings often, in cold and nakedness." "Most gladly will I glory in my infirmities that the power of Christ may rest on me. Therefore I take pleasure in infirmities, in reproaches, in necessities, in persecutions, in distresses for Christ's sake; for when I am weak, then am I strong." Again; when Agabus foretold his sufferings if he went to Jerusalem, and his surrounding friends besought him with tears not to go, he replied, " What mean ye to weep and to break my heart; for I am ready, not to be bound only, but also to die at Jerusalem, for the name of the Lord Jesus." This, too, was not a childish empty boast, an overweening confidence in his own resolution:—he proved that he possessed it all, when put to the final trial. Are the sufferings then which mankind are called to endure, so much more severe than those of Paul; and was his resolution and that of all the other martyrs so defective as an example; that nothing would arm our flinching race with the needed nerve and energy, but the agony and crucifixion of the Son of God?

6. If the sufferings of Christ were merely his bodily sufferings, i. e. if they were not a manifestation of the anger of God for the sins of men, and thus a substitute for the curse of the law denounced against mankind; the examples of fortitude set by the Maccabees and Stephen, by Peter, Paul and Polycarp, by John Rogers and Latimer, were at least as perfect as that set by Christ. To satisfy you of this fact, I will recite an example. When Antiochus Epiphanes had conquered Syria, he carried the family of the Maccabees to Antioch; and, because they would not embrace idolatry, ordered them all to be tortured to death. Maccabeus, the eldest, was first stretched on the rack, and severely beaten; then fastened to a wheel and weights hung to his feet until his sinews cracked; then thrown into a fire till he was dreadfully burned; then drawn out, his tongue cut out and himself put into a frying-pan with a slow fire under it until he died. As long as he had life, he fervently called on God under these exquisite torments, and exhorted his brothers to a similar perseverance. His six brothers, and after them, his

mother Salamona, who had previously witnessed the martyrdom of her seven sons, were subjected to equally excruciating deaths.

When these and thousands of others came to the very time and place of their martyrdom, and saw the instruments of torture and death all prepared; the immediate prospect of their sufferings occasioned no overwhelming agony; no angel came down from heaven to comfort them; and neither of them cried out three times, as he prostrated himself to the earth, "If it be possible, let this cup pass from me." On the contrary, they went to the rack, the cross, and the furnace even, with alacrity, and until their last breath, rejoiced in the presence and the love of God. This, too, was the fact, when they had none of the peculiar supports by which he was sustained, and when they had no assurance of being raised from the dead on the third day.

According to a very different theory, it will be no difficult task, at the proper time, not only to explain the otherwise inexplicable scenes of Gethsemane and Calvary, but to show that the conduct of our Lord, while suffering for a condemned world, was a most illustrious example of patience and resignation,—an example, which we, according to our measure, and under our inconceivable inferior sufferings, may well be called on to imitate. But, on the given supposition, that all he endured was crucifixion, and that the great end of his death was to set an example of fortitude; I should be constrained to regard the actual result on his part, compared with that of other martyrs under far more severe and protracted agonies, as scarcely less than an absolute failure.

7. On this supposition why is the death of Christ an event of such inconceivable importance. He was not only "delivered up to die, by the determinate counsel and fore

knowledge of God," but his death has a pre-eminence given to it both in the Old and New Testament, which no no other event can claim. We have seen that it was the continual subject of prophesy. Was then the consolation given to our first parents to sustain them under their ruin merely this, that, after the lapse of four thousand years, the seed of the woman should bruise the head of the serpent, by setting an example of fortitude? Were impatience and timidity the curse under which the whole creation was so long to groan and travail together in pain; and was "the desire of all nations" at length to redeem them from this "curse of the law" by teaching them to endure bodily suffering. Was this the reason why the blood of Jesus "speaketh better things than the blood of Abel," that Abel, being killed outright, and not dying a lingering death, had no opportunity to show his fortitude. For this, did "Abraham desire to see his day;" and was this "what kings and prophets waited for, and sought but never found?" When Isaiah, at the distance of seven long centuries, saw from the mount of vision the spectacle on Calvary with so much distinctness, that in portraying the scene, he has not only thrown on the middle of the canvass the Man of Sorrows nailed to the cross between two malefactors, but on one side the very procession from the judgment-hall of Pilate to the top of the hill, and on the other the new sepulchre of Joseph hewn out of a rock in which he was buried;—could he so far mistake the grand design for which he suffered as to tell us that he was "smitten of God," that "the Lord laid on him the iniquity of us all," that "for the transgression of the people he was stricken," that "it pleased Jehovah to bruise him, and to put him to grief," that "he made his soul an offering for sin," and that it was the "travail of his soul" of which he died.

Can the Spirit of prophesy as he opened the curtain of futurity to the gazing prophet, have been so correct in presenting the scene itself, and yet so erroneous in stating the great end for which it was exhibited.

As the Spirit of Christ, which was in the prophets, revealed to them, with greater and yet greater clearness the sufferings of Christ and the glory which should follow, was an example of fortitude so grand a desideratum in the empire of God, that, before it was actually set, the angels, forgetting their wonted praises, could bend over in mute contemplation to look into that far distant manifestation of it which revolving centuries would at length unfold. Is suffering the chief business of heaven, of angels as well as saints, that they are interested in nothing but in learning how they may endure it. Was an example of fortitude so much the all in all in the view of "Him, who sitteth on the throne, that that strange council of heaven and of earth must be held on the holy mount, to prepare him who was to set it for the mighty achievement? Was it for this, that his face did shine as the sun, and his raiment was white as the light, and the voice came forth from the cloud of glory, "This is my beloved Son, in whom I am well pleased?" Is an exhibition of fortitude so absolutely *instar omnium*, in this broad Universe, that when made on Calvary, the choir of ten thousand times ten thousands, moved by one instinctive impulse, could turn their eyes away from the Uncreated Glory, and commence their new song of praise to him who made it, which is to continue forever and ever. Is this that display of matchless love, which kindles the raptures of eternity; and do the words of their anthem read, "Unto him that hath loved us—and set us an example of fortitude!—unto him be glory and dominion for ever and ever, Amen?"

8. On this supposition how shall we explain the incidents connected with the death of Christ.

Was the Sacramental Supper instituted to inspire us with fortitude; is it an exhibition of that virtue chiefly which we commemorate when we eat the bread and drink the wine in remembrance of Christ; and did Christ say to his disciples that same night in which he was betrayed, "This cup is the New Testament in my blood, which is shed—to set an example of fortitude." Was the mere death of the cross so immeasurably dreadful that, although it had been predicted for thousands of years that he should suffer it; although, if a super-angelic being, he came from heaven to suffer it; although, if a mere man, he had had the suffering in full view all his life; although he was prepared for it by the surprising interview on Mount Tabor; and although he went from Galilee to Jerusalem on purpose to die;—yet was it still so dreadful even in the anticipation, that although he was to die on purpose to set an example of fortitude, and he knew that all heaven was waiting in speechless expectation to see the long-hoped for achievement done—did he still, through the mere dread of bodily suffering, thrice cry out in low prostration, and with impassioned earnestness, "O my Father, if it be possible, let me not die, to exhibit an example of fortitude!"—and while his agony caused the sweat of blood to flow to the ground, did he need an angel from heaven to comfort him, because he must set such an example?

When he was nailed to the cross, did God forsake him because he was bringing to pass that very consummation which God himself so much desired, and which heaven and earth for four thousand years had heaved with throes unutterable to see accomplished. But after the whole creation had thus waited in mute anxiety for this divinely appointed manifestation; yet, when it was actually made on Calvary, was the scene so beyond conception dreadful, that the sun, unable to endure the sight, must wrap himself in funereal darkness, that the firm earth must quake, the solid rocks burst asunder, and even the slumberers under ground leap forth from their dark recesses. "O scene!"—the poet well might say—

"O scene, surpassing wonder!"

9. On this supposition what shall we make of the language of the Bible. Would they who adopt it, only make that language conform to their scheme, it must strike them as new and surprising. For instance, had Christ in fact said to Nicodemus, "as Moses lifted up the serpent in the wilderness, even so must the Son of man be lifted up to set an example of fortitude, that whosoever imitates that example might not perish, but might have everlasting life;" even he who was "a master in Israel," might have been excused for not knowing these things. And what meaning would there be in the language, "Herein is love: not that we loved God, but that he loved us and sent his Son to set us an example of fortitude?" Was timidity, or impatience under suffering, the great reason why men were the enemies of God, and fortitude the great means of our reconciliation, that Paul could write to the Romans,—"If, when we were enemies, we were reconciled to God by the example of fortitude set by his Son, much more, being reconciled, we shall be saved by his life." Is fortitude so far superior to faith, and hope, and love, that Paul could write to the Corinthians, "I am determined to know nothing among you save Jesus Christ, and the fortitude which he exhibited on the cross;"—and again—"We preach the fortitude of Christ crucified, unto the Jews a stumbling-

block, and unto the Greeks foolishness, but unto them who are saved, the power of God?" Had he written thus, and had he added, "God forbid that I should glory save in the fortitude of our Lord Jesus Christ;" it might have been said with emphasis that "in his epistles there were many things hard to be understood."

III. It is said that the Great End of Christ's death was *to perfect his obedience.*

This language has probably been borrowed from two passages in the Epistle to the Hebrews; in one of which it is said, that "it became him, for whom are all things, and by whom are all things, in bringing many sons unto glory, to make the Captain of their salvation perfect through sufferings;"* and in the other, that Christ, "being made perfect, became the author of eternal salvation to all them that believe."† Of this phraseology, different individuals may give very different interpretations.

1. It may be supposed to refer to the state, or condition, to which Christ was advanced subsequently to, and in part at least as a consequence of, his sufferings. In that case, it merely denotes that, as the reward of his sufferings, he was advanced to a state of perfect happiness and glory.‡ But if this be the true interpretation, neither of the passages refers to the great end accomplished by the death of Christ for the good of mankind; but both, to his own reward—to "the joy set before him for which he endured the cross."

2. It may denote that Christ could not become the

* Heb. ii. 10. † Heb. v. 9.

‡ See Wahl's Lex Gr Test. on Τελειοω. Wahl regards this as the true meaning; and if it be not, of which there may be a doubt, at least with regard to the passage from Heb. ii. 10, the true one is unquestionably the second which I have suggested.

Saviour of mankind, without suffering in their stead; and that he was rendered perfect as their Saviour, by actually enduring the sufferings necessary on his part as a substitute for their punishment. In this case, it is a direct assertion of the doctrine of the Atonement.

3. It may be supposed to denote, that the sufferings which Christ endured were necessary to render his personal obedience, and generally his holiness, perfect. But this is directly inconsistent with the supposition, that Christ was uniformly and always a perfectly holy being. Uniformly perfect holiness implies uniformly perfect obedience, and sufferings cannot be necessary to render it more perfect. As the angels need no sufferings to render their obedience and holiness perfect, so certainly Christ needed none. The testimony of God on this subject we have seen is absolutely decisive. Will it be said that his death was necessary to render his obedience perfect, under the dispensation to which he was actually subjected? But the question is, Why was the Son of God, when his obedience was already perfect, placed under such a dispensation? in other words, Why must a perfectly holy being suffer at all?

4. This phraseology has received a still different explanation. It is said that Christ's sufferings and death as an exhibition of obedience, were a powerful means of improving our virtue; and were so acceptable to God, that on account of them he has granted to mankind the forgiveness of sins that are past, and has also erected a glorious system of grace.*

Those who receive the doctrine of the Atonement, insist

* This is the scheme of Dr. Taylor of Norwich, the author of the Hebrew Concordance. If the reader is disposed to complain of the obscurity of the language, in which it is here stated, he is referred to the work itself, with the request that he will state it in language less obscure.

as truly as others, that the perfect obedience or holiness of Christ was indispensably necessary to render his death efficacious as an expiatory sacrifice; in other words that his sufferings would have been of no efficacy, if he had not been a perfectly holy being. But when it is said, that his sufferings were designed—not as a substitute for our punishment, but merely—as an exhibition of obedience; and as such were intended to be a powerful means of improving our virtue; we are compelled to suggest the following objections.

1. The sufferings of Christ on this scheme were absolutely unnecessary.

So far as positive duties were concerned, Christ's perfect obedience consisted in his perfect performance of all that were prescribed; and so far as sufferings were concerned, in his voluntary sinless submission to all that were inflicted. When it is said that "he became obedient unto death, even the death of the cross," it obviously denotes merely that he voluntarily submitted to death. His submission, therefore, so far as his sufferings were concerned constituted his whole obedience. But submission to sufferings is the same thing, as bearing them without complaint or murmuring. When, therefore, it is said that Christ submitted to sufferings to make an exhibition of obedience, it is the same thing as to say, that he submitted to sufferings to make an exhibition of submission; in other words—to show how well he could bear them.

We will then view his sufferings as ordained of God; as consented to, and endured by himself; and as affecting the character and condition of mankind. As ordained of God, they were appointed from eternity, and actually inflicted to see if he would bear them without murmuring.* God

* The first part of this theory, then, though differing in phraseology, appears when analyzed, to be identically the same with the preceding, which represents Christ to have died *to set an example of fortitude.*

demanded no atonement for sin, no satisfaction to his violated law: he wished nothing but obedience in order to forgive and bless mankind. Yet obedience to his law, or the perfect holiness of Christ, was not sufficient to become the meritorious cause of forgiveness and restoration to mankind. No obedience would satisfy, but obedience to agony and death; and that on the part of one, of whom God himself has testified, that "he knew no sin, neither was guile found in his lips." But if there can be wantonness in cruelty, it is found in subjecting a perfectly holy being to intense suffering, in order to see whether he will bear it. We had heard of the savage chieftain, who commanded several of his warriors in succession, to cut off each his right hand, in order to shew his obedience and devotedness to his cause; but probably none of us had suspected that it could find a parallel in the dispensations of God; and that too not towards men or angels, but towards his beloved Son, in whom he is ever well pleased.

As consented to by Christ, the step was one of extreme folly. It was a mere experiment on the firmness of his own nerves; as if a man should thrust his hand into the fire, to see how long he could hold it there. It was trying either how much suffering he could endure, or whether he could endure the prescribed sufferings without sin; and on either supposition was a mere wanton act of self-torment. Such an exhibition would find no parallel in the Indian expiring without a groan or a murmur, under all the varieties of savage torture; for he would escape if he could; nor any where else except in those maniacs in Germany, who not long since suffered their fellow maniacs to nail them to a cross, in order to prove their fortitude under suffering, and thus to perfect their obedience. And were any of us to act in the same manner, we should of course be regarded as equally bereft of our reason.

And what is the bearing of his sufferings on mankind. We are called upon to witness the strange spectacle of the Son of God, overwhelmed and at length destroyed by sufferings, which were prescribed by the Father, and consented to by himself,—not for his own punishment, or chastisement, or moral improvement; not as a manifestation of the displeasure of God against the sins of men; not to magnify the Law of God and make it honourable; but merely to show how patiently he could submit to agony and death. And this exhibition is to have a two-fold efficacy.

(1.) It is said to have been intended as a powerful means of moral improvement. But how? Was it, to prompt our confidence in God? To inspire us with this, we are elsewhere taught, that the innocent do not suffer; and that our sufferings here are far less than we deserve. But if God chose to inflict unmerited sufferings on his own Son, in order to see how he would bear them, he may also on us; and the bare possibility, that he may do this, is, in this murmuring world, sufficient to prompt the suspicion, when our afflictions are severe, that he has done it, and thus to destroy all our confidence in the equity of his dispensations. Was it to inspire us with fortitude under sufferings? As an example of submission to unmerited sufferings, we did not need it; because we have no such sufferings to endure. As an example of submission to sufferings generally, it is on the given supposition in various points of view a bad one. The consideration that God may inflict unmerited sufferings on us, as well as on his Son, merely to see how well we can bear them, is calculated to excite, not submission, but murmuring and rebellion. The example of Christ voluntarily subjecting himself to unmerited suffering, to show how well he could bear it, if it has any influence on us, will only prompt us to a similar exhibition—and that on the ground that our supererogatory sufferings are meritorious; and that, the more intense they are, the greater is the merit. This is exactly the Romish system of penance, and is at open war with the whole word of God. The example of Christ we have also seen was inappropriate, because he had great supports which are not vouchsafed to us; and, if he suffered nothing but the pains of crucifixion, was a far less perfect exhibition of fortitude, than that of many other martyrs. Was it to prompt us to obedience in general? It could do this, merely as it was an example of fortitude; for it exhibited no obedience but submission to suffering, which is only a definition of fortitude. We are then to go to Gethsemane and Calvary, and see the Son of God consenting himself, and subjected by the Father, to an overwhelming agony and an excruciating death, in order to show how well he could bear them; and, in the contemplation of the appalling spectacle, we are to grow wiser and better! How strange a seminary, to have been instituted by the Most High, for the moral improvement of mankind!

That the sufferings of Christ, so intense and overwhelming, viewed as a manifestation of the anger of God against our sins on the person of his Son, and as a manifestation on his part of a love passing knowledge, are powerfully efficacious in showing us the guilt and odiousness of sin, and in constraining us to love him who gave himself for us, is certain. But the theory, that he endured these dreadful sufferings in order to show how well he could bear them, and in that way to teach us fortitude or obedience, imputes such wantonness of cruelty to God, and such causeless self-torture to Christ, that, while its necessary tendency is, if believed, to shake our confidence in the

Divine wisdom and justice, it can neither inspire us with hatred for sin, nor with respect and love for the Saviour. The man who encounters imminent danger, or endures extreme suffering to save my life, is entitled to my lasting gratitude. But towards him, who comes before me and inflicts such sufferings on himself, merely to show how well he can bear pain, and in that way to teach me a lesson of fortitude or to promote my moral improvement, I know not what emotion I could feel except that of compassion. If Paul, when the disciples at Damascus had prepared the basket in which to let him down through a window by the wall, instead of consenting to escape, had announced his determination to deliver himself up to the governor under Aretas the king, in order to show them how well he could bear the pains of crucifixion, and thus promote their moral improvement, would they not have replied instinctively, and with good reason too, "Paul, thou art beside thyself; much learning doth make thee mad."

(2.) The other part of the moral efficacy of this exhibition on mankind, is through its efficacy on God himself. It is said, for some cause or other, to have been so acceptable to God, that on account of it he forgives the past sins of men, and establishes a glorious dispensation of grace. Whether the past sins here spoken of, denote the sins of the human race at large, committed before Christ made this exhibition, or the sins of every man, committed before he becomes a practical subject of its efficacy, is a matter of doubt. What also, on the first supposition, is the ground of forgiving the sins of mankind committed subsequently to this exhibition of obedience; or, on the second, those committed subsequently to the commencement of its practical efficacy on each individual, as well as those committed by the multitudes who lived before the exhibition was made, is equally uncertain. But, leaving this, we are told by the theory, that Christ's exhibition of perfect obedience to the law of righteousness, or his perfect holiness, was not sufficiently acceptable in the view of God, to procure the forgiveness of sins. He would not forgive them unless Christ also made an exhibition of obedience to sufferings and death, or showed how much he could bear without murmuring. But why so? According to the theory, no atonement was necessary, no manifestation of the anger of God against the sins of men in the sufferings of Christ. God was under no obligation to inflict the penalty of his violated law on the transgressor. He was just as able in the view of offended justice, and certainly in every other point of view, to forgive sin without, as with, the death of Christ. He was also just as merciful, or just as willing to forgive sin, in the one case as in the other. Why then was Christ's obedience to suffering and death, or his showing how well he could bear them, so much more acceptable to God, than his perfect obedience to the law of righteousness? Was it because Christ's exhibition of fortitude has peculiar efficacy as a means of moral improvement? We have already seen that, as presented in this theory, a fortitude under causeless sufferings, it has no such efficacy. Was it because God could not know how perfect Christ's obedience would prove, unless he actually submitted to the most excruciating sufferings? If this were true, what need was there of knowing it? But it is obviously untrue. He who is omnipresent, knew as perfectly before, as after, the death of Christ, how much suffering he could bear without sinning, and how well he would bear the sufferings which he actually endured. Was it because perfect obedience to the law of righteousness is in itself less acceptable to God than obedience to sufferings and death? To say this, is to say that God takes more pleasure in inflicting sufferings on perfectly holy beings, than in their perfect holiness. But perfect holiness is a perfect conformity to his own will—to what he himself supremely desires. God therefore has less pleasure in a perfect conformity to what he himself supremely desires, than in inflicting extreme sufferings and death on those who exhibit it; although they deserve nothing at his hands but the highest approbation and love.

In every point of view, therefore, in which we regard the death of Christ according to this theory, it was not only altogether unnecessary, and absolutely inefficacious in accomplishing the ends for which it is said to have taken place, but it also carries with it the most direct and palpable imputation on the wisdom and righteousness of God.

2. The Scriptures no where assign this reason. The declaration that Christ "became obedient unto death," as we have seen, denotes that he voluntarily submitted to death with resignation. In the two passages already quoted from the epistle to the Hebrews, there is not an intimation that, to make an exhibition of submission, or to show how well he could bear pain, was the end of Christ's sufferings and death; nor have I been able to find one in any other passage, throughout the sacred volume.

3. The deep interest which the death of Christ has excited, is on this scheme an inexplicable mystery. If it be true, angels and saints in heaven, and patriarchs, kings and prophets on earth, were occupied for many revolving ages, in looking forward to the arrival of the momentous period, when Jesus, by showing how well he could bear pain, should lay the foundation of the moral improvement of the human race, and perform a work so meritorious in the sight of God, that to reward it he would grant the forgive-

ness of sins that are past, and establish a glorious dispensation of grace on the earth. If it be true, God the Father, attended by Moses and Elijah, was manifested on Mount Tabor to Christ and the three disciples, to converse with him on his submitting to be crucified in order to show how well he could bear it. And this causeless infliction of suffering on the one part, and this causeless submission to it on the other, led the heavenly host to change their wonted melodies, and commence the everlasting song to him who, by showing how well he could endure the most excruciating sufferings, laid a broad and permanent foundation for the forgiveness and moral improvement of mankind. And this exhibition was so pleasing to God and so morally improving to men, that it effected the reconciliation of both, and led the spirits of the just, with a rapture before unknown, to say to him who made it, "Thou art worthy, for thou hast redeemed us to God by thy blood."

4. This theory wholly fails to account for the incidents connected with his death. According to it, his prayer in the garden must be thus interpreted : O my Father, if it be possible, suffer me to escape those excruciating miseries, which thou art about to bring upon me, in order that I may show how well I can bear them ! His agony on that occasion was owing either, merely to his lively anticipation of the ordinary sufferings of crucifixion, or to the anticipation of these, and of other sufferings which were extraordinary and peculiar to his individual case. If to the first ; that agony, on any principles consistent with his own fortitude, is wholly unexplained. If to the second ; no reason can be assigned for his extraordinary and peculiar sufferings except this—that, when the Son of God had voluntarily consented to suffer the ignominious and excruciating death of the cross, in order to show how well he could bear it,

the Father, not satisfied with that, heaped upon him far more intense and overwhelming agonies, in order to render the exhibition complete. Well, indeed, might the sun be darkened, and the earth tremble, and the rocks rend asunder, and the very dead come forth, at such a sight as this.

5. On this scheme, Christ has no exclusive right to the titles which he claims as peculiarly his own. If the sufferings of Christ were unusual, extraordinary and inflicted by God, we have seen that the theory represents God as inflicting them on his Son, in order to see how well he could bear them, and therefore cannot be true. If they were only the ordinary sufferings of crucifixion, the exhibition of obedience to sufferings, or of submission, made by many of the martyrs, even without the peculiar supports which he enjoyed, was at least as perfect as that made by Christ. Of course each one of these exhibitions, as made by men like ourselves, and as being far more appropriate to our circumstances, was a more powerful means of moral improvement, and therefore more acceptable to God, and a better foundation for the forgiveness of sins that are past, and for the establishment of a glorious dispensation of grace on the earth. But Christ's peculiar titles were given him in consequence of his sufferings and death. Every one of the martyrs, therefore, to whom I have referred, has even a better claim to these titles than Christ. Every one of them, therefore, on better grounds than he, can regard himself as the Lamb of God who taketh away the sin of the world, as the Saviour of sinners, and as the Redeemer of mankind. The apostle, too, was mistaken in supposing that there is no other name given under heaven among men whereby they may be saved, and the multitude of the redeemed, instead of turning to the one Lamb in the midst of

the throne, ought to associate with him thousands and tens of thousands who stand before it, and to say to the whole company of Saviours, " Ye are all worthy, for ye have redeemed us to God by your blood."

6. This theory, though devised and expressed with peculiar ingenuity and caution, in order that it may at least appear to correspond with the language of the Scriptures, is yet wholly inconsistent with many of the forms of phraseology in which the great end accomplished by the death of Christ is explained. The Scriptural writers represent all the sins of men, and not merely the sins that are past, as forgiven, in consequence of the death of Christ. They no where represent Christ's exhibition of submission to suffering, to show how much he could bear, as the great means of improving the moral character and condition of mankind, but every where ascribe this effect to the efficacy of Truth, accompanied by the influences of the Holy Spirit. They represent Christ as dying for the forgiveness of our sins, but we have seen that every possible reason for the exercise of forgiveness existed before his death, which according to this theory existed after his death. They represent Christ as our sin-offering, and as the passover sacrificed for us, but neither the goat of the sin offering nor the paschal lamb was sacrificed as an exhibition either of obedience or submission, or to show the Israelites how well either of the animals could endure bodily pain without complaint. They say that Christ made an atonement for our sins, but the Levitical atonement did not consist in the exhibition of fortitude made by the dying lamb for the moral improvement of mankind. They say that God laid on him the iniquities of us all, that he bare our sins in his own body on the tree, and that he was made a curse for us to redeem us from the curse (the penalty) of the law,

but neither of these phrases without gross violence can be explained to mean that he suffered crucifixion to show how well he could bear it.

IV. It is said that the Great End of the death of Christ was to furnish *a sign, a token,* that God is willing to pardon the penitent, and thus to persuade mankind to repent and turn to God.

A sign, a token, is a visible representation of a fact or a truth, and is intended either for information, for evidence, or for impression. The letters of the alphabet are signs informing us of the articulate sounds to be employed. The rain and the sunshine are signs proving the goodness of God. Baptism is an impressive sign of the truth that man needs cleansing from guilt and pollution.

According to this theory, God was in fact perfectly willing to pardon the penitent, independently of the death of Christ, and neither the threatenings of his law nor the welfare of his kingdom presented any difficulty in the way of an indiscriminate pardon, or laid him under any necessity of manifesting his anger against sin. Christ did not suffer and die to lay a foundation for pardon. His death was not a manifestation of the displeasure of God against sin, but was intended either to announce the willingness of God to pardon the penitent, or to furnish evidence of it, or to impress it on the mind. He did not procure pardon for us, he merely represented God's willingness to grant it.*

This theory can scarcely be stated without suggesting numerous objections to the mind of every attentive reader of the Scriptures.

* This theory is probably the favorite one, at the present moment, of those who reject the doctrine of the Atonement in this country, and yet do not avowedly renounce the inspiration of the Scriptures.

1. If it be true, the death of Christ was wholly unnecessary.

There was obviously no need of representing this truth at all. If there was, it was because the opposite principle, that God would certainly punish sin even in the penitent, was, previous to the death of Christ, most firmly riveted in the human mind. But why was it thus riveted? Not, certainly, because there was any willingness in the human mind to be punished, but because God had either explicitly in his word, or implicitly in the consciences of men, revealed his settled determination to punish sin. But if, previous to the death of Christ, he had revealed this determination, he had actually formed it. And if, in the death of Christ, he announced the contrary determination, it was because he had then changed his mind and actually formed the contrary determination. But, according to the theory, God was always infinitely willing to pardon the penitent, and no difficulty existed in the way of pardon before the death of Christ which does not now exist, i. e. his death removed no such difficulty, and furnished no new or additional reason for pardoning sin. If then there was any necessity of representing the willingness of God to pardon the penitent, either God originally formed and revealed his settled determination to punish sin when it was not necessary, and then, changing his mind without any reason, announced in the death of Christ his determination not to punish it, which is absurd, or, he originally formed and revealed his settled determination to punish sin because it was necessary to punish it, and then, changing his mind without any reason, and when none of the original necessity had been removed, he announced in the death of Christ his determination not to punish it, which is equally absurd. Of course, the death of Christ was a sign, a token, of God's changing his mind without any reason whatever, as well as of the fact, that he either originally revealed a settled determination to punish sin, even in the penitent, when no necessity of punishing it existed, and that, too, so clearly and impressively, that no other expedient which he could devise—no revelation, no voice from heaven, no miracle, no martyrdom of prophets or apostles, no incarnation and death even of an angel—nothing, in short, but the ignominious and excruciating death of his beloved Son could remove the impression, or that, when its punishment was originally necessary, and thus most impressively revealed, he subsequently announced a settled determination not to punish it, though none of that original necessity was removed. As we cannot admit these absurdities, we are compelled to conclude, that, on the very grounds on which this theory rests, there was no necessity of any sign or token to represent the willingness of God to pardon the penitent.

Again. This theory admits mankind to have been sinners, that is, transgressors of the law of God.* But, if a ruler is in fact willing to pardon those who have transgressed the laws, there cannot, in the nature of the case, be any difficulty in persuading them to believe it. The only alternative in his treatment of them is punishment or pardon. But they certainly do not wish to be punished, and as certainly they do wish to be pardoned or exempted from punishment. And the same motives which render them willing to be pardoned, would render them willing to believe, if the fact were really so, that the ruler was willing to pardon them. The human mind is always willing to believe what it wishes, even against evidence, but where evidence and inclination coincide, the case has never yet been known in which

* "For sin is the transgression of the law."—1 John 3. 4.

it was difficult to produce conviction. In some of these states it has not been necessary to announce the universal pardon of offences in order to inspire transgressors with the hope of obtaining it. The indiscreet multiplication of pardons on the part of the government, has been so efficacious in diffusing this hope, that the prisons have overflowed with the expectants of its clemency. In the Bible—the statute book by which God governs his kingdom in this world—there are numerous clauses which at least appear, and beyond all doubt have been very generally believed, to threaten transgressors with punishment, and that, too, neither very mild in degree nor very short in duration. Yet, with these minatory clauses staring them in the face, mankind have to a prodigious extent believed and been fully persuaded, that God would certainly pardon them, either whenever they should repent, or without any repentance at all. The history of the world ever has been, and now is, a practical comment upon this persuasion. If then these minatory clauses could have been expunged, or had not been inserted, the persuasion that God would pardon the penitent would have been universal. All that was necessary on the part of the Supreme Ruler, to secure the most implicit credence in this his gracious intention, was to announce it, and mankind would have gladly believed it without evidence.

But it may be said, "If the death of Christ was not necessary either to announce or to prove that God would pardon the penitent, still it was necessary for the purpose of impression. We are not creatures of mere abstraction but of sense and feeling. When we behold Christ dying to persuade us that God will pardon the penitent, this truth is exhibited to the eye and the heart, and is far more calculated to have a powerful efficacy on the man, than if it were addressed merely to the intellect." All this is true, provided there was any good reason for his dying. The question *Cui bono?* can never be put with stronger emphasis than to one who is about to sacrifice his own life. If my friend were to endure intense sufferings to save my life I should never forget his kindness. But if he were to come voluntarily and inflict them on himself, merely to announce a fact which he might have announced with his lips, or to prove that fact when I was too ready to admit it without proof, or to make an impression on my feelings, I should regard his conduct as the result either of weakness or lunacy. If Christ died to save me from the wrath of God, I can see why his dying love should constrain me to repentance and gratitude, but if he endured overwhelming agonies and an excruciating death, merely to excite sympathy or any other emotion of tenderness, or to convince me that God was willing to pardon the penitent, I see at once that he was under a delusion, and that he died for nothing, and though I may pity and regret his sufferings I cannot respect his good sense.

If mankind were not too ready to believe that God is willing to pardon the sinner on his repentance, yet the idea that the death of Christ was necessary to furnish evidence of this fact is most preposterous. If God *is* thus willing he could prove it without this amazing sacrifice. The capacity of God is at least equal to that of men, and he is able to make his feelings and purposes known to men with adequate evidence and emphasis without giving his Son to die either to announce, to prove, or to impress them. When he spake to the patriarchs, or delivered the oracle in the tabernacle or the temple, or sent messages by the prophets, he actually constrained those who heard or received them to perceive and to feel that the voice or the message came from God. In some way or other, also, aside from the death of his Son, he convinced the patriarchs, prophets and people of Israel, and that, too, as firmly and operatively as men are now convinced, that he was willing to pardon the repenting sinner. The difficulty with the impenitent Israelites was not, that on this point their evidence was not satisfactory, it was their readiness to believe that he would pardon them even if they did not repent. But if all good men before the death of Christ were both convinced, and adequately impressed with the truth that God would pardon the penitent, they were thus convinced and impressed by competent evidence and competent means of impression, and the same evidence and means of impression might have been furnished to all without his dying, and if their conviction and impressions were practical and sanctifying, the same evidence and means of impression might have had an equally powerful efficacy on all on whom they were brought to bear. The agony of Christ therefore was causeless, and his death a mere wanton waste of blood. It effected nothing which had not been actually for ages as well effected without it. His fervent supplication, therefore, "If it be possible, let this cup pass from me," —i. e. according to this theory, "If it be possible to persuade men that thou art willing to pardon the penitent, without my dying on the cross, let me not be crucified,"—was founded on a palpable mistake ; and instead of suffering himself to be betrayed by Judas he should have remained in Galilee and not gone down to the passover.

2. We call for evidence that the great end of Christ's death was to furnish a sign, a token, of God's willingness to pardon the penitent.

That the death of Christ was a sign of something is readily admitted ; for, as God always acts rationally or with design, there is no event of providence which does not express, if rightly understood, the real purpose of his mind. But the question is, was it the great end of Christ's death to furnish a sign, a token, of God's willingness to pardon the penitent?

Signs are either significant, or arbitrary. A significant sign, of itself, and without being announced as a sign, represents the thing signified, but an arbitrary sign, until it has been explicitly announced as representing the thing signified, does not represent it, and is not a sign of it. A violent blow intentionally inflicted on an individual is a significant sign, as it speaks for itself, and needs not to be announced as indicating the displeasure of him who inflicts it. The bow in the clouds is merely an arbitrary sign of God's covenant no more to deluge the earth, since it has no natural connection with the thing signified.

The death of Christ certainly is not a significant sign, or token, of God's willingness to pardon the penitent. Suffering is in itself an evil, and intense suffering a great evil. Suffering voluntarily inflicted by one being on another, if unexplained, is a natural and direct indication or sign of anger on the part of him who inflicts it towards the sufferer, and if the suffering be intense, of intense anger. Thus it is exhibited both by the Scriptures and by common sense. If a parent inflicts suffering on his child, the child of course looks upon it as an indication of displeasure; and unless it is clearly explained, will not view it even as a chastisement, but as a punishment. So naturally does the human mind regard it in this manner, that God, to prevent misapprehension, has thought it necessary to explain the sufferings of his children in the present life, and to inform us, that "whom the Lord loveth, he chasteneth, and scourgeth every son whom he receiveth." The overwhelming sufferings of Christ, therefore, if unexplained, are a significant sign of the intense anger of God against Christ himself, and can only be regarded in the light of punishment, inflicted on him as a manifestation of that anger. Unexplained, therefore, they cannot be regarded, either as a manifestation of God's anger against the sins of men, or as a sign of his willingness to pardon the penitent.

Was it then the great end of the death of Christ to furnish an arbitrary sign of God's willingness to pardon the penitent? If so, it is explicitly announced as such by God. But where are we to look for such an annunciation? Certainly not to the Scriptures. Among all the various forms of phraseology, in which the death of Christ is explained in the Scriptures, there is not one, in which it is said that the great end for which it occurred was to furnish *a sign, a token*, that God is willing to pardon the penitent. The cheering truth that God is willing and ready to pardon the penitent, and that every obstacle in the way of their pardon is removed, is indeed often urged from the fact that God laid on him the iniquities of us all; that he bare our sins, that he atoned for our sins, that he was a sacrifice for our sins, that he gave himself as a ransom to procure the forgiveness of our sins, that he has redeemed us from the curse of the law, (i. e. from punishment,) and that God has unequivocally accepted the sacrifice by raising him from the dead. But the idea that it was the great end of Christ's death to furnish a sign, a token, of God's willingness to pardon the penitent—to announce this willingness, or to prove it, or to impress it on the minds of men—is not asserted, nor even suggested, by any scriptural writer. This single fact will be enough to induce every one, who, on a subject of mere revelation, regulates his faith by what is actually revealed, to reject this theory altogether.

It will here be said that Christ is spoken of as a sacrifice for sin, and a sin-offering; that it is expressly asserted to be "impossible for the blood of bulls and of goats to take away sin;" that the animals offered in sacrifice were therefore merely signs and tokens of God's willingness to forgive the penitent; and that as Christ also was such a sacrifice, his death was merely a sign, a token, of the same truth.

To state this argument is so obviously to refute it that I fear you will regard an apology necessary for paying it any farther attention. The two first of the premises here stated we admit, but we ask for proof of the third, viz. "that the animals offered in sacrifice were merely signs or tokens of God's willingness to pardon the penitent." That they were signs of something we agree; but the mere fact, that their blood could not take away sin, certainly does not prove that they could have been signs of nothing else except of that willingness. If they could not take away sin, the death of Christ might, and according to the Apostle it did take it away; and of his death they might have been, and according to the Apostle they were, signs, or types.* But if they might have been, and in fact were, signs of Christ's bearing our sins, or taking them away, they answered one most important end; and we are not compelled, therefore, from any difficulty of discovering a sufficiently important end which they could have answered, to conclude that they must have been signs of God's willingness to pardon the penitent. Where then is the evidence of this fact? The Levitical law says no such thing. It speaks of these animals as, by their blood, purging, cleansing, bearing, taking away, and making atonement for the sins

* Heb. ix. 19—28.

of the offerer; of their being a ransom for his life; and of his sins as forgiven, in consequence of his offering the sacrifice. But, that the sacrifice of these animals was instituted to represent the willingness in question, there is not an intimation in the Pentateuch.

The offerer, in every case, by the very fact of presenting the animal at the door of the tabernacle, proved that he already most fully believed in, and was deeply impressed with, God's willingness to pardon the penitent. There was no need then of his sacrificing the animal; he might have preserved its life and taken it back again, as the end in view was already accomplished. If, then, these animals were sacrificed to announce, to prove, or to impress the truth that God was willing to pardon the penitent, they were always and of course sacrificed in vain; for the bare fact of his bringing the animal for a sacrifice, proved necessarily that the offerer already believed and was fully impressed with this truth. Certain it is, therefore, that these animals were not sacrificed as signs or tokens of God's willingness to pardon the penitent. If, then, the third of these premises is a mistake, the inference from them, that Christ died as a sign or a token of that willingness, is not supported.

Again. This theory is founded on the supposition, that the type is in all respects equal to the antitype; the sign to the thing signified; the shadow to the substance; the emblem to the reality. The argument is this: It was not possible for the blood of bulls and of goats to take away sin, but their blood was a type or shadow of the blood of Christ, therefore the blood of Christ did not take away sin. The force of this logic was doubtless realized by John the Baptist, when, as a harbinger of the Messiah, he made the public official annunciation of him to mankind, "Behold the Lamb of God which taketh away the sin of the world," as well as by Paul when he declared, "Christ was once offered to bear the sins of many," and by Christ himself when he declared at the sacramental table, "This is my blood, which is shed for the forgiveness of sins."

The position that the antitype, or the substance, has no efficacy or excellence which was not found in the type, or the shadow, will lead to singular results. Baptismal water is a type of the influences of the Holy Spirit; but baptism, the type, does not purify the heart; therefore, the influences of the Spirit, the antitype, have no purifying efficacy. David was a type of Christ. But David was not the Saviour of the world; therefore Christ was not the Saviour of the world. Elijah was a type of John the Baptist, but Elijah was not the harbinger of Christ; therefore John the Baptist was not his harbinger. Jerusalem and its temple were shadows of Heaven, and of the spiritual temple which God is erecting there; but Jerusalem and its temple were not destined for an immortal state of existence; the same therefore is true of heaven and of the temple of God on high.

It is singular that Paul, when reasoning in his Epistle to the Hebrews on this very subject, comes to the directly opposite conclusion. Having observed that the priests, the tabernacle and the utensils, the gifts and the sacrifices, employed in the ceremonial worship, were only types and shadows of the things in heaven,* he tells us, that as under both dispensations there was no forgiveness without shedding of blood, the high priest, under the first, went yearly into the holy place of the tabernacle, to offer a sin-offering for his own sins and the sins of the people; and Christ,

* Heb. viii. 1—5, and ix. 9—12, and 19—23.

under the new, not by the blood of bulls and of goats, but by his own blood, entered into heaven, to obtain eternal redemption for us; and actually obtained the redemption (i. e. the forgiveness) of the transgressions committed under the first dispensation;* that, as the law was merely the shadow and not the substance of the new dispensation, its continual sacrifices could not cleanse the conscience nor make the worshipper perfect, because it was impossible for the blood of bulls and of goats to take away sin; and therefore that Christ assumed a body, and, by offering that body once for all a sacrifice for sin, actually took away the sins of men, and then forever sat down at the right hand of God.† Thus the Apostle, instead of arguing from the inefficacy of the blood of bulls and of goats to take away sin, that the blood of Christ was equally inefficacious, derives directly the opposite conclusion, and insists that Christ offered himself a sacrifice for sin, that he might do that which the blood of bulls and of goats could not accomplish.

3. The deep interest manifested in the death of Christ by the heavenly world is, on this scheme, utterly inexplicable.

The conviction that God was willing to pardon the penitent, either was necessary, or it was not necessary, to the virtue and salvation of men. If it was not necessary, then Christ need not have died to produce it. If it was necessary, as the patriarchs and other virtuous men, who obtained salvation before the death of Christ, were so fully convinced of this truth, and so powerfully impressed with it, as to be rendered at least as virtuous, and as much entitled to salvation, without any knowledge of the death

* Heb. ix. 11—15. † Heb. x. 1—12.

of Christ, as we are with it; we therefore might also have been thus convinced and impressed, without that knowledge; and, on that supposition also, Christ need not have died to produce it. Why then are the angels represented as earnestly desirous for ages to look into the sufferings of Christ, and the glory that should follow? If the conviction that God was willing to pardon the penitent, was not necessary to the virtue or salvation of men, then they were occupied for ages in looking forward to see the Son of God die an agonizing death in order to furnish a sign, a token, of that which was in itself wholly unnecessary. If it was necessary; yet, as the patriarchs had it as fully as we, the angels were thus occupied for ages in looking forward to see Christ die, as a sign, a token of a truth, which had already been adequately represented to mankind, for every purpose connected with virtue and salvation. If this conviction was not necessary, then the God of heaven came down to earth, attended by Moses and Elijah, and met his beloved Son on Mount Tabor, accompanied by the three chief apostles, and while his face did shine as the sun, and the cloud of glory overshadowed them, they conversed together respecting his dying on the cross, to furnish a sign, a token of that which it was wholly useless to represent to mankind; and, if the conviction was necessary, they thus assembled, to converse together about his dying, to furnish a sign, a token of a truth, of which mankind had already all the means of evidence or impression necessary for their virtue and salvation. If this conviction was not necessary, then the whole choir of angels re-tuned their harps, and commenced a new and everlasting song, to commemorate the sign or token of a truth which it was wholly useless to represent; and, if it was necessary, they did this, when that truth had been for ages adequately represented.

4. The importance attached to the death of Christ, by the scriptural writers, is on this scheme excessive and hyperbolical. If the conviction of the truth in question was not necessary to the virtue or salvation of men, then Christ's dying to represent it, was not the great manifestation of the love of God, nor the sum and substance of the Gospel, nor the only thing in which an Apostle ought to have gloried. And if it was necessary; yet since we, as truly as the patriarchs, might have been adequately impressed with it, for every valuable purpose, without the death of Christ; their representation of its importance are, on this supposition, equally extravagant.

5. The titles appropriated to Christ in the Scriptures on this scheme belong equally to others. All the martyrs testified as fully as Christ did, the willingness of God to pardon the penitent; and many of them under sufferings far more severe than those of crucifixion. The death of every one of them therefore was, equally with his, an impressive representation of this truth, and each one of them is as truly as he, the Saviour, and the Redeemer; and instead of one only name there are tens of thousands of names given under heaven among men, whereby they must be saved.

6. The saints in heaven who died before the death of Christ are on this supposition totally mistaken. They became eminently virtuous men, and obtained salvation, without any knowledge of this sign, this token, of the willingness of God to pardon the penitent; and of course derived no personal benefit from his death. When, therefore, as a part of the church of the first-born they unite in the grateful ascription, "Thou hast redeemed us to God by thy blood," their gratitude is obviously unfounded; and they ought in good conscience to withdraw from the com-

pany of the redeemed, and give the glory of their salvation to the individual, if they can discover him, to whom it is due.

7. The willingness of Christ to suffer the death of the cross is equally unaccountable. If the conviction or the deep impression of the truth, that God is willing to pardon the penitent, was not necessary for the virtue or salvation of men, Christ either knew this fact, or he did not know it. If he knew it, his voluntarily dying as a sign, a token of this willingness, was a wanton throwing away of his own life, to accomplish an object known to be useless, and that, too, just after he had fervently prayed thrice, "If it be possible, let this cup pass from me;" and if he did not know it, he was left, after the impassioned supplications of Gethsemane, through a mere delusion on his part, to exhibit, before an astonished universe, during six hours of inconceivable agony, a sign, a token of a truth, which there was no need of representing, to promote either the virtue or salvation of mankind. If the conviction or the impression of this truth was necessary, yet Christ knew that unnumbered thousands, during four long millenniums, without any knowledge of his death, had been sufficiently acquainted and impressed with it, to become eminently virtuous and ultimately to ascend to heaven; and that if he did not die, other men, with similar means of knowing and of being impressed, might do the same. When, therefore, he earnestly wished, if it were possible, to avoid dying, he yet went voluntarily and deliberately from Galilee to Jerusalem, to make a most agonizing representation of a truth, which he knew had been sufficiently represented already for every purpose of virtue and salvation.

8. This theory gives no explanation of his early death. Whether the sign, the token, of the truth in question was

necessary for the purpose of annunciation, of evidence, or of impression, it might have been exhibited just as clearly and strikingly after a ministry of forty years as of four. How strange then as well as how unfortunate that he was crucified at so untimely a period!

9. Christ's explanation of his own death at the sacramental supper, "This is my blood, which is shed for the remission of sins," is totally inconsistent with this theory. The phrase, "blood shed for the forgiveness of sins," denotes blood shed to procure their forgiveness, and is most obviously a totally different thing from blood shed as a sign, a token of a previously existing willingness to forgive.

10. The violence and ignominy of his death were in this case wholly unnecessary. Mankind are not so hard to be persuaded of the truth, which of all others they are most willing to believe, that even the mission, the instruction, and the death of the Son of God, could not convince them of it, unless in addition to the ordinary pains of dying, he consented to endure the overwhelming agonies of Calvary.

11. The nature and degree of his sufferings, and his conduct with regard to them, it leaves equally unexplained. How deep the darkness which covers the scene in Gethsemane! If this long-wished for sign, this long expected token of the willingness of God to pardon the penitent, was so important as not only to be the object of anticipation and prophecy for successive ages on earth, but to occupy the minds of angels, to call down Jehovah from the upper skies, and to change forever the worship of heaven; and if Jesus had nothing before him but the pains of crucifixion; how unutterably strange and mysterious, that one so holy, so patient and resigned, so fearless of death, so enriched by the Spirit, so blest with the Father's love and safe in his protection, so conscious of the joy set before

him, and so secure of rising again on the third day, from the mere fear of crucifixion, a death which thousands have met without a groan, should thrice prostrate himself in an agony so intense and overwhelming, as to force from him first the thrice-repeated cry, "If it be possible, let me not be crucified, as a sign, a token of thy willingness to pardon the penitent!" and then the sweat of blood falling to the ground! Whence, too, on Calvary, that anguish of the mind, that "travail of the soul," in suffering which the pains of crucifixion were all forgotten? Did God inflict these sufferings upon him, and then forsake him, because at the expense of his life, he was exhibiting a sign, a token of the willingness of God to pardon the penitent? and was this the cause why the sun withheld its wonted beams, and the surrounding universe heaved as with its last convulsions?

12. It contradicts all the scriptural explanations of the death of Christ. Not an example can be adduced in which to die for another, or to die for our sins, denotes to die as a sign, a token of the willingness of God to forgive sin. The same is true of the phrases to die for the forgiveness of our sins, to become a sacrifice for sin, to make an atonement for sin, to die to reconcile us to God, and to bear our sins; every one of which has been proved to have an appropriate technical meaning, as used by the scriptural writers, that of dying to procure our exemption from punishment. When also it is said that we are justified by his blood; that we are saved from wrath by his death, that God does not impute our trespasses to us in consequence of his dying for us, that in suffering for us he gave himself an αντιλυτρον—a ransom in our stead; and above all that he hath redeemed us from the curse of the law—(the sufferings due for its violation) by being made a curse, (i. e.

enduring sufferings judicially inflicted) for us; and when we call to mind the several results of the preceding examination, we cannot fail, I think, to see that the theory in question is not only at open war with all the explanations of the death of Christ contained in the Scriptures, but inconsistent alike with all the phenomena attending that event, with the exalted character of Christ, and with the perfections of God.

V. It is said that the Great End of Christ's death was *to prove the Resurrection of the Body.*

If Christ died to prove the resurrection of the body, yet his death, apart from his resurrection, does not prove it. That he taught this doctrine is unquestionable: "Marvel not at this; for the hour is coming, in which all who are in their graves shall hear the voice of the Son of Man, and shall come forth; they that have done good to the resurrection of life, and they that have done evil to the resurrection of damnation." His dying as a martyr to the truth of this doctrine proves indeed that he was sincere in teaching it, but it does not prove that it is true,—for the very obvious reason that false systems of faith have often found their martyrs. When the Mohammedan dies fighting for his religion, is it true that there is a sensual paradise to which he will find admission because he avowedly believes it? or have we evidence that the polluted and sanguinary system of Boodh is true because the deluded Hindoo proves his sincerity by leaping into the Ganges, or throwing himself under the car of Juggernaut. Suppose then that Christ suffered death to prove the truth of this doctrine, still his death taken by itself proves nothing but his sincerity and his firmness. But though he thus evinced that he fully believed it, the question still arises, in this as in every other case, Was he he not mistaken? and the decision of this question will depend, not on the fact of his martyrdom, but on the evidence which he furnished of its truth.

That the resurrection of Christ proves the doctrine of a general resurrection is unquestionable; and it does so in the following manner. Before his death, Christ declared, before numerous witnesses, enemies as well as friends, that himself was to die and on the third day was to rise again. On this fact he staked his reputation as the Messiah the Son of God. He also, as we have seen, announced a general resurrection. Now the truth is, that Christ actually died upon the cross, was buried in the tomb of Joseph, and was raised from the dead on the third day. These facts we can prove by adequate evidence. But as God cannot lie, nor work a miracle to furnish evidence of a falsehood, we are sure, since Christ taught a general resurrection, that it will certainly take place.

So far is agreed on both sides. But when it is said that, to furnish evidence of a general resurrection, was the Great End of his death, we are compelled to doubt, and that for the following reasons:

1. The mere fact that his death and Resurrection do actually furnish this evidence, is no proof whatever that to furnish this evidence was the end for which he died, because, if he must die and rise again, and this, too, must be known to mankind, it was not in the nature of things possible that this evidence should not be thus furnished. Surely if the evidence is inherent in the event, so that the event cannot come to pass without furnishing the evidence, it does not therefore follow that to furnish the evidence was the great end for which the event took place. The fact, therefore, that the Apostles allege the resurrection of

Christ, as well as his other miracles, in proof of his divine mission and of the general resurrection, merely proves that they availed themselves of the arguments in their possession, but in no degree whatever shows the great end of Christ's suffering and death.

If there can be a doubt on this point, it will be removed by taking a part of the very case in hand. When Christ lay dead in the tomb of Joseph, there was some reason why he must rise from the dead. But if he rose, his resurrection would necessarily furnish this evidence. Will it then be maintained that the simple fact, that his rising from the dead would prove a general resurrection, is the great reason why the Son of God was not suffered to lie buried in the grave until the end of the world? If it would not have furnished this evidence, would he have been suffered "to see corruption," when Peter tells us "it was not possible that he should be holden of death?" Was to furnish this evidence—and not to organize his church, to commission his Apostles, and then to ascend to heaven that there he might overrule all things for the good of his church—the great end of his resurrection? If this does not follow, neither does it follow that it was the great end of his death.

2. The scriptural writers no where assert that Christ died to furnish this evidence. After his resurrection they appeal indeed to that event in proof of their own mission, and so they do to his other miracles with equal confidence. "Ye men of Israel," said Peter on the day of Pentecost, "hear these words; Jesus of Nazareth, a man approved of God among you by miracles, and wonders, and signs which God did by him in the midst of you, as ye yourselves also know."* It was evidence

* Acts ii. 22.

which grew out of the event, but is no where mentioned as its cause.

3. If Christ died to furnish evidence of the resurrection of the body, his death was wholly unnecessary. This will appear in various ways.

Patriarchs, and prophets, and other good men, who lived during the first four thousand years of time, either had clear evidence of a general resurrection, or they had not. If they had, they had it without any knowledge of the death of Christ, and so might the rest of the world as well as they, and in precisely the same manner. Of course, his death, on this supposition, was wholly unnecessary to prove the resurrection, for it was proved already. If they had not this evidence, still many of them, particularly Enoch, Noah, Abraham, Job, Moses, Joshua, Samuel, Elijah, Isaiah, Daniel, and the prophets, as well as Simeon, Anna, and John the Baptist, were as eminently wise and virtuous as any of those who have it; and in company with all the wise and good who lived before the death of Christ, as truly went to heaven as any who have lived since his death. Hence, those who are without this evidence can be as holy, and fully entitled to the divine favor, and as certain of a welcome in heaven, as those who possess it; and in that case, the evidence of the general resurrection is wholly unnecessary either for the virtue or salvation of mankind. Surely if, without the evidence of a resurrection furnished by the death of Christ, we could have possessed equal holiness, and been entitled to equal happiness, with Enoch and Melchizedek, with Abraham and Job, with Elijah and Daniel, his most important supplication, "O my Father, if it be possible, let this cup pass from me!" would not have been denied.

But if it was necessary that this evidence should be possessed by mankind, still it might have been furnished, and that in many ways, without the death of the son of God. The resurrection of the Body is one of the doctrines of the Bible and depends like every other doctrine on the general evidence that the Bible is the word of God. The question whether we have sufficient evidence of this particular doctrine depends therefore on the more general question whether we have sufficient evidence of the inspiration of the Scriptures ; for both must stand or fall together. For evidence of the divine inspiration of the Scriptures, we look to prophecies, to miracles, and to historical testimony, as well as to the writings themselves. Of the miracles which furnish this evidence, one, and a very important one, is the resurrection of Christ, but it no more fully proves it than the miracle of the five loaves, the raising of Lazarus, the gift of tongues, or the healing of the impotent man at the beautiful gate of the temple. Of the resurrection of Christ there were no eye-witnesses but the Roman guard, who have not left us their testimony ; and no one saw him after his resurrection except his personal friends. The eye-witnesses of these other miracles were very numerous, many of them the open enemies of Christianity, and the great body of them alive at the time of his death. The Apostles appeal to this fact with at least as strong confidence as to the resurrection of Christ: "Jesus of Nazareth, a man approved of God among you, by miracles, and signs and wonders, which God wrought by him in the midst of you, as ye yourselves know." The earthquake at the time of his resurrection, and the fact that his body was missing from the sepulchre, appear for the space of fifty days to have produced no effect at Jerusalem in persuading its inhabitants to believe in him as the Messiah. The gift of tongues, and the healing of the impotent man at the most public gate of the temple at the hour of prayer, wrought in the name of Christ before assembled thousands, were appealed to by his Apostles as evidence of his resurrection and of the truth of Christianity, "Ye killed the Prince of life," says Peter, "whom God hath raised from the dead; whereof we are witnesses; and his name, through faith in his name, hath made this man strong whom ye see and know; yea, the faith which is in him hath given him this perfect soundness in the presence of you all." After the evidence furnished by these two miracles, many thousands on the spot were converted to Christianity, but for fifty days the evidence furnished by Christ's resurrection did not convert even one. At the present time, also, we can prove these two miracles more directly, and at least as conclusively to the infidel, as we can the resurrection of Christ.

It may be said that the actual raising of Christ's body is the appropriate evidence of the doctrine of a general resurrection as it furnishes an example of the fact. I answer, the raising of the body of Lazarus, after he had been dead four days, proves as fully that a dead body can be raised as the raising of Christ. About his actual death there is less dispute; he had been longer dead, and the witnesses of the fact were far more numerous. It may be said that the case of Lazarus was a recalling to life, but not in the appropriate sense a resurrection—i. e. not a transformation of his corpse into a spiritual and glorified body. It is true; and from the fact that Christ's body when raised was flesh and bones, and that he ate with his disciples, it has been extensively doubted whether his body came forth from the tomb a spiritual and glorified body, or, whether, like the bodies of Enoch and Elijah, it was transfigured at the time of his ascension. We can maintain, therefore, that in point of fact evidence at least as conclusive of the truth of Christianity, and of the doctrine of a resurrection, has been furnished not only to the men of that age, but to those of every subsequent period.

But we are not compelled to maintain this position. The question is not, whether adequate evidence of a general resurrection is not furnished, but whether it could not be furnished without the death and resurrection of Christ; and on this point there can be no doubt. John the Baptist was as well known by the Jewish nation as Jesus. All Jerusalem and Judea had gone out to the banks of the Jordan to hear his instructions and to be baptized. He was beheaded by Herod on a most public occasion, and his dissevered head was brought in and exhibited before the whole of his court, in a charger. His death was known throughout all Judea, and Christ knew beforehand that he was to die. He might, therefore, most publicly have predicted John's death and resurrection, and staked his own character as the Messiah on the fulfilment of that prediction. Christ was certainly as able to raise up John as to raise up himself, and there would have been one most essential advantage. Those infidels, who regard the evangelists as well-meaning and honest, but deceived men, always insist that Christ was not dead but merely in a swoon when he was taken down from the cross and put into the sepulchre; and that instead of being raised to life, he merely came to, on the first day of the week. But the actual decapitation of John would have left no room for this allegation. If then Christ, on some most public occasion, had raised up John from the dead, and he had appeared again preaching repentance, baptizing, and announcing Jesus as "the Lamb of God, who taketh away the sin of the world," while the whole Jewish nation would have been witnesses of the astonishing miracle, Christ would have redeemed his pledge and proved the truth of Christianity, and in particular the doctrine of the resurrection, by evidence which no one could possibly gainsay.

Again. God could with perfect ease have raised up hundreds or thousands of his children in every generation, and that, too, after their bodies had seen corruption and begun to moulder into dust; and when they had re-existed long enough on earth to establish the fact and to furnish the necessary evidence, could have placed them on the same footing with Enoch and Elijah in heaven. To do this would have been certainly no more difficult than it will be to raise them at the last day. These men would have been a constant succession of living witnesses to the truth of this most cheering doctrine, as well as of the whole of Christianity. The proof would have been before our eyes and would have needed no help of argument, whereas, we are now driven to a long and laborious process of reasoning to establish the fact of Christ's resurrection, before we can prove by it the general resurrection or the truth of Christianity. Surely then it was possible in either of the ways pointed out, that the cup of suffering should pass from the Son of God. His sufferings and death were absolutely unnecessary, as evidence at least as conclusive of the doctrine of the resurrection might have been furnished, if he had not died.

4. On what principle, if this be true, can we explain the interest felt in the death of Christ, both in heaven and on earth? What means that anxious search for ages on the part of angels; that bending over, that they might look into the sufferings of Christ and the glory that should follow? When the resurrection of the body was revealed to them by God, was it so incredible that they waited in mute suspense for the development of evidence before they would

believe it? Why, too, those praises to the Lamb that was slain? Had he died to redeem the bodies of the dead from the grave, I can see why saints and angels should rejoice in this event. But he died, not to redeem, but merely to furnish evidence that God intended to raise them. Was this evidence wanting in heaven? Are they so faithless in the upper world that they cannot believe the word and promise of Jehovah, unless it is confirmed by the crucifixion of his Son, and yet, when their unbelief at length gave way, did they indeed break forth into one united song of praise because the sanguinary demonstation was furnished, and they could doubt no more? And do their minds so heave with rapture at the discovery of this evidence, that their new song of praise to the Lamb, who was slain to furnish it, must continue forever and ever?

How also shall we explain that unwonted meeting on the top of Tabor. When Enoch and Elijah had already ascended to heaven, each in a spiritual and glorified body, and there had been presented as the first fruits of the redeemer's victory over the grave; when the patriarch of Uz could rejoice because after worms had devoured his body, still in his flesh he should see God; when David, speaking in the person of Christ, could say, "Thou wilt not leave my soul in Hades, neither wilt thou suffer thine Holy One to see corruption;" and when the gracious promise had been given to Israel by Hosea, "I will ransom thee from the power of the grave; I will redeem thee from death: O death, I will be thy plague, O grave, I will be thy destruction;" was it, indeed, an achievement so hard for the Almighty to perform, so difficult for heaven as well as earth to believe, that He who spake from the overshadowing cloud must come down with Moses and Elijah to converse with Him who was to die upon the cross that he might furnish the long-wished for evidence?

Is this the reason why the sacred writers attached so much importance to the death of Christ? Does God commend his love toward us in that while we were yet sinners Christ furnished evidence of the resurrection? and could Paul glory in nothing but in the fact that that evidence was furnished? Why also these peculiar titles which no one else can claim? Do lambs reason and furnish evidence;—lambs that are slain, and by means of their blood; and, when they have done it, do we say that they have redeemed us; and does evidence of the resurrection "take away the sin of the world?" By discovering this evidence to us, does Christ save us from wrath, and hence gain the title of the Saviour of the world? Was the curse of the law that state of doubt and uncertainty from which he redeemed us by proving that God would raise the dead? And did he say to his weeping disciples around the sacramental board, "This is my blood of the new dispensation which is shed for many, to prove the resurrection of the body?"

5. On this supposition, why did he die so early in his ministry? His ministry, as we have seen, continued only three years and a half, and closed with his death; for after his resurrection, though he appeared in various instances to his disciples, yet he wrought no miracles, and communicated no instructions to the people at large and almost none even to his disciples—expressly reserving this office to the Comforter, whom he would send from the Father. But surely he whose motto it was, "I must be about my Father's business"—"I must work the work of him who sent me while it is day;" he who spent life in going about doing good, was not so soon wearied out by communicating

instructions fresh from heaven, and working miracles of mercy, that in three years he wished to leave off and die. Would not even one of us, imperfect as we are, if we could possess the same wisdom, and exert the same power, be willing to spend a far longer period in restoring the sick and the distracted, the deaf, the maimed and the blind, in raising the dead, and in imparting that truth which would prepare our fellow-men for heaven. How then could he say the night before his death, " Father, I have glorified thee on earth ; I have finished the work which thou gavest me to do ;" or on the Cross, " It is finished," when not a syllable of the New Testament was written, and but a small part of it communicated. Surely he might have died, if die he must to furnish evidence, at the age of seventy ; and if, too, he must be crucified for that purpose, he might have been crucified then. The death of a man of seventy, who is crucified, can be as certain, and it is at least as great a miracle to raise him to life, and therefore furnishes as strong evidence of that which he died to prove, as if he were only thirty-five.

6. On this supposition, what is the meaning of the scene in Gethsemane. The death of the cross was not a new and surprizing subject. It had been prophesied for four thousand years ; it had been the familiar subject of his contemplation through life, it was the very death which he came into the world to suffer, which he went from Galilee to Jerusalem on purpose to suffer, which he had just instituted the sacramental supper to commemorate, and concerning which he had just said, " I have a baptism wherewith to be baptized, and how am I straitened till it be accomplished." His conduct in the garden surely was not owing to weakness, or an effeminate fear of death. It was not owing to his mistake in apprehending the sufferings of

the ensuing day to be inconceivably more distressing than they actually proved. All he had to do was to be known to die, and then to come to life, in order to prove the truth of Christianity or the doctrine of the resurrection. Why then, when he was without sin, and had the Spirit without measure, and possessed an understanding so powerful, and a knowledge of the divine purposes so extensive, and such testimonials of the Father's love; when in him dwelt all the fulness of the Godhead bodily; when a little before on Mount Tabor he had met not only Moses and Elijah, but the Father of glory on the subject of this very death, and there had been transfigured and appeared in the glory of heaven; when all heaven was waiting in earnest expectation to see evidence either of the truth of Christianity, or of the doctrine of the Resurrection furnished to mankind by his death, and were all preparing to re-tune their harps for that "new song," which was forever to commemorate the achievement of furnishing this evidence; and when he knew that he should come to life in three days; why, I ask, in the name of sober reason, why this overwhelming horror and amazement; why this thrice repeated cry of anguish with the face upon the ground, "O my Father, if it be possible let this cup pass from me;" why that ineffable agony and sweat of blood, which forced an angel down from heaven to comfort and sustain the holy Sufferer? Ah! was it that he found mere bodily suffering so much that in these circumstances he could not go through with what he had undertaken; and with all these helps to sustain him did he, indeed, through the fear of mere death, cry out thrice, "O my Father! if it be possible, let me not be crucified, and then rise from the dead, to prove the doctrine of the Resurrection?" With all these helps and supports was he thus overwhelmed, when Peter and Paul, with scarcely one of them, and with no expectation of rising again on the third day, met the very same death with tranquillity and even with triumph?

7. Why, if this theory be true, was his death violent and ignominious? The argument is this: That the miracle of coming back to life after he was actually dead and known to be dead, proves the doctrine of the resurrection. But there are other modes of dying, and of being certainly known to be dead, besides crucifixion. Death is not so difficult an achievement in this dying world, that one must resort to a violent, ignominious and excruciating death, in order to die. And when one is really dead, the fact is so far from being a difficult one to prove, that it proves itself. The man who dies of a fever, in a few days is as certainly known to be dead, as if he had died upon the cross. The infamy, the violence, the tortures, do not add an iota to the certainty of the fact. It is also as great a miracle to be raised from the dead, when one is dead in one way, as in another. The raising of Lazarus, after he had been dead four days, was as direct an exertion of the power of God, as it would have been if he had been crucified. The violence and the torture of the death of Jesus were therefore needless, and the infamy was even worse; for his cross was to the Jews "a stumbling-block," and to the Greeks "foolishness;" and the former, we have seen, have ever reproached Christianity by denominating it, "The religion of him who was hanged." Yet all this infamy, and violence, and torture, so useless as to the purpose for which he died, so injurious to the extension of his religion, and so distressing to the Saviour himself, we are told by Peter, were only "what the hand and the counsel of God had determined before to be done."

Had Christ publicly predicted his own death as destined

certainly to occur on a given day and in a given place, and his resurrection on a given number of days or weeks afterwards; had he actually died when the given day arrived, and remained dead the specified time, and at the close of it had he returned to life, the attention of numberless witnesses would have been excited, and the fact of his being dead could have been as fully determined as it can now be; and by his appearing alive in the midst of his enemies for months or years afterwards, the evidence of his resurrection would have been far more clear and palpable than it is at present. The whole scene of shame and anguish through which he passed in the council-room of the Sanhedrim, in the palace of Herod, in the hall of Pilate, and on Calvary—the buffeting, the spitting in the face, the smiting on the cheek with the palms of the hands, the scourging, the crowning with thorns, the bearing of the cross, the piercing of his hands and his feet with the nails, the racking of his frame, and his public infamous death as a malefactor between two thieves, though appointed by God, and distinctly predicted by Isaiah, were only so much unnecessary torment; doing no good to mankind, not in the least increasing the evidence which he was aiming to furnish, and answering no purpose whatever except to inflict extreme and useless misery on One who was perfectly innocent and holy, and concerning whom God the Father twice said in an audible voice from heaven, "This is my beloved Son in whom I am well pleased." In the view of such a statement we inquire, in the language of Nicodemus, "How *can* these things be?"

8. How also, if this scheme be true, shall we explain the circumstances of his death. Was the unchangeable Jehovah, who a little while before had manifested on Mount Tabor such high approbation of his conduct, and of "the

death which he was to accomplish at Jerusalem," while it was only in prospect, so soon changed in his feelings, and displeased with him when that death was actually taking place? No mental sufferings on the cross could make his rising from the dead a greater miracle, or furnish stronger evidence of the resurrection of the body. Why then did "it please Jehovah to bruise him," "to put him to grief," and "to lay on him the iniquities of us all?" Why did he hide his face from him and compel him to exclaim "Why hast thou forsaken me?" when he was merely dying to prove the resurrection of the dead, and when he merited as well as needed his presence and his love more than at any other period of his existence? Is this the manner in which God treats his most faithful servants in the hour of their extremity? And should you ask Stephen, or Paul, or the great cloud of martyrs who are now on high, whether they were thus forsaken? would they answer, Yes? Had the sun, also, as he rolled around this world of carnage for four thousand years, been so little used to scenes of horror, that he must hide his face because he could not look down on one who was dying to prove the doctrine of the resurrection? Had the earth drunk in so little murdered blood, "from the days of righteous Abel to the days of Zechariah, the son of Barachiah," that she, too, must quake at such a spectacle? and the very captives of the tomb start from their iron sleep, and break their fetters and their prison?

9. On this supposition, why was Christ seen so rarely after his resurrection; and why, also, merely by his friends. If the fact, that he was to die in order to furnish evidence of the doctrine of the resurrection, had been divinely appointed, and long and often predicted, and eagerly expected and desired both in heaven and on earth, and had

occasioned the vision of glory on Tabor, and the scene of horror in Gethsemane, and the scene of universal convulsion, of darkness and of death on Calvary, surely it behoved him to render this evidence as irresistible and over whelming as it could be made. Yet, during the forty days of his residence on earth after his resurrection, he chiefly kept himself aloof even from his disciples, and was not seen by one of his enemies. The greater part of this period he was,—we know not where,—and only appeared, as we have already seen, ten times—five on the day of his resurrection, and five more during the thirty-nine following days of his continuance on earth. Of these ten instances, three were to solitary individuals—to Mary Magdalene, to Peter, and to James; two were to two individuals together—the first to Mary Magdalene and the other Mary, and the second to Cleopas and his companion, on the way to Emmaus; three were to the eleven; one was to more than five hundred at once; and one to the eleven Apostles certainly, and perhaps to others. But in no one of these instances were any of the enemies of Christianity, or any except his avowed followers present. But if to furnish evidence of the truth of Christianity, or of the doctrine of the resurrection, was the great object for which he died and rose again, why did he not, as he was personally known to almost all the population of Jerusalem, as well as to the Sanhedrim, why did he not go into the city, and exhibit himself publicly in the temple, and to all the inhabitants. He knew the pretence of the Jews, that his disciples had come by night and stolen his body away while the guard were asleep. How easy would it have been to put down this falsehood, by his appearing day after day before the whole multitude, and thus enabling his Apostles to turn to him and say, "Behold JESUS of Nazareth whom ye crucified, whom God hath raised from the dead!" What sensations would this have excited throughout Jerusalem; where would his enemies have hid themselves; and what would have become of the story that his disciples stole away his body. What would have been the excitement on the day of Pentecost, if, instead of Peter relating the story of his resurrection, he had come himself to the beautiful gate of the temple, and there had said to the countless thousands, as he said to Thomas, "Behold my hands and my feet: see, here are the prints of the nails." He foreknew, or, if he did not, the Father foreknew, that the fact of his resurrection would be questioned by infidels in every age, on this very ground, that he never was seen except by his personal friends. Why then, if furnishing evidence was the moving spring of this astonishing event, why did he not, when it was a thing so easy, furnish evidence of his resurrection, which would have banished every doubt, and hushed skepticism into perpetual silence. Never had any one the staff in his own hand so emphatically as Christ had after his resurrection; and if to furnish evidence of that resurrection, and thereby of the truth of Christianity, or the doctrine of a general resurrection, was the great point at which he was aiming, he was guilty of an extreme oversight, a palpable folly in his mode of using it, which I hope the advocates of this theory, even those who regard him as "a fallible, peccable man," will not impute to HIM, who, for some reason or other, was called, not only THE SON OF GOD, and THE SAVIOUR OF THE WORLD, but THE WORD, WHO WAS IN THE BEGINNING WITH GOD, AND WAS GOD.

10. We object to this theory, that it contravenes all the language of the Scriptures concerning the death of Christ. If the phrase, to die for us, might possibly have included within its largest meaning, to die in order to furnish us with

evidence of the resurrection of the body, yet an adduction of all the instances in which it occurs, proves that according to its settled uniform use by the scriptural writers, it has in fact no such meaning. But the phrase, dying for our sins, will admit of no such interpretation. Surely the great sin of man was not the want of evidence of the resurrection. Still less, if possible, can we force this meaning on the phrase, dying for the forgiveness of our sins. Did God refuse to forgive mankind because they had not been furnished with adequate evidence of the resurrection of the dead. What shall we say then of his dying as a sin-offering ? Was the lamb for a sin-offering daily sacrificed that he might come to life again, and thus furnish evidence that God could raise the dead ? What of his dying as an atonement for sin ? Were the demands of the law satisfied and the sins of mankind forgiven in consequence of the discovery of evidence ? Did God refuse to be reconciled to men, in consequence of their ignorance of this doctrine ? Does furnishing evidence mean the same thing as bearing our sins in his own body on the tree ? Was ignorance of the resurrection what the Apostle meant by the curse of the law, the penalty which it threatens to transgression ? and did he redeem us from the curse of the law by proving the resurrection of the body ? Until we are prepared to admit that the language of the Scriptures can mean any thing, and every thing, and nothing ; it is impossible for us to believe that to furnish evidence of a general resurrection was the great end of the Redeemer's death.

VI. It is said that the Great End of the death of Christ was to prove the truth of Christianity. Against this scheme I should allege the following objections :

1. It is highly derogatory to the character of God. It

supposes that the all-wise God, when he communicates a religion to mankind, cannot evince the truth or the divine origin of that religion, unless he gives his only begotten Son to die to prove its authenticity. Yet men, when they utter truth to each other, are not obliged to suffer martyrdom in order to evince that truth; and when they send messengers to each other, these messengers are not obliged to die in order to furnish evidence of their mission. Were this the case, God would have less power and less wisdom than man.

2. It contradicts known facts. God made revelations of his will to the patriarchs, and furnished them with evidence that the revelations came from himself, without commissioning some one to die, in order to prove their divine origin. He also communicated a new religion to the Israelites by Moses, and was able to evince its truth and its authenticity, without the crucifixion of his Son, or even that of Moses or Aaron. In the same way, therefore, as well as in many other ways, he might have proved the truth of Christianity, and the divine mission of his Son, without subjecting him to an ignominious and excruciating death. The resurrection of John the Baptist or of Stephen, or any other miracle equally great and surprising, if wrought in attestation of the truth of Christianity, would have been equally conclusive evidence of its truth, with the death and resurrection of Christ. Why, then, when the beloved Son of God, who was "holy, harmless, undefiled, and separate from sinners," cried out in his agony, "O my Father, if it be possible, let this cup pass from me!"—was not his most earnest prayer heard and answered? Was the import of that prayer, "If it be possible to prove the truth of the religion which I have taught, without my crucifixion, let me not be crucified?"

3. The death of Christ apart from his resurrection, does not prove the truth of Christianity, but merely his own integrity. Christ also never mentions his own death as evidence of the truth of his religion. He often appealed to the prophecies, to his own miracles, to the testimony of the Father, to his knowledge of the heart, and to the evidence inherent in his instructions, as conclusive proof that his religion is divine, but never announced the fact that he should suffer death to furnish additional evidence. The Apostles are equally silent on this head, and their uniform language, with regard to the object of his death proves that this idea never entered their minds. And with regard to his resurrection, conscious that the Jews had not seen him after it took place, they allege the many "miracles, signs, and wonders," which he had wrought before their eyes, the gift of tongues, and their own miracles which they were daily working, as evidence that he was risen, and that he was the Messiah.*

4. On this supposition, his death occurred at a most unfortunate period. No part of the New Testament then existed, or for a considerable number of years afterwards, and a large part had not been even orally communicated to the Apostles. Christianity, as a system of truths, did not exist, except in the imperfect and uncertain recollections of the Apostles. All the facts and truths which they had forgotten, as well as all which had not been communicated were lost by his death. The only hope that the former would be recovered, depended on the declaration of Christ, "When He, the Spirit of truth is come, he shall bring all things to your remembrance, whatsoever I have

* The reader is referred to the remarks on the preceding theory as equally applicable to this.

said unto you;" and the only hope that the latter would ever be known, depended on the similar declaration, "I have yet many things to say unto you, but ye cannot bear them now. Howbeit, when He, the Spirit of truth, is come, he will guide you into all the truth. He shall receive of mine, and shall show it unto you." If, then, Christ died to prove the truth of Christianity, why did he not defer it until Christianity existed, until his disciples were able to bear the communication of it from his lips—until it was all communicated and written down, and the New Testament completed under his own hand and seal. Had this been done, and had Jesus taken the volume thus finished, and declared, "I am now going to die, in order to prove the truth of this volume," the transaction would have had something in it definite and palpable. But what was the identical thing then existing, which his death proved to be true? Was it the collections of facts and sentiments which the Apostles recollected, or was it those which they had forgotten, and which the Holy Spirit was to bring to their remembrance, or was it the farther collection which they could not bear while Christ was living, and which the Holy Spirit was first to communicate?

5. This scheme will not satisfactorily account for the high importance imputed to the death of Christ both in heaven and on earth. When the angels knew that God could work any possible miracle, to evince the divine mission of his Son, and the truth of his religion, could they have been so anxious to look into the sufferings of Christ, if the great object of his death had been to furnish evidence which might have been as fully furnished if it had never taken place? Was the convocation on Tabor summoned merely to consult and decide on the best mode of furnish-

ing evidence? Was it because ten thousand times ten thousand and thousands of thousands of angels, and the four living ones, and the four and twenty elders regarded it as so difficult an achievement to furnish adequate evidence of the truth of Christianity, so far beyond the reach of any other miracle which Almighty God could work, that, when they saw it accomplished by the death of Christ, they broke out enraptured into that NEW SONG, which has often but erroneously been called the Song of Redeeming Love, but which should be called the Song of Demonstration, and did they say, "Worthy is the Lamb, who was slain to prove the truth of Christianity, to receive honour, and glory, and blessing?"

6. If this be true, what obligations did the ancient saints owe to the Saviour. They lived, and served God, and died, and ascended to heaven, without this evidence. If, then, we admit, that to redeem, means the same thing as, to furnish evidence of the truth of Christianity, still they were not redeemed, for they had arrived in heaven before the evidence was furnished. How then could they unite in the ascription, "Thou art worthy, for thou hast redeemed us to God by thy blood?" Again: If this was the salvation effected by Christ, as they were saved without the knowledge of the evidence which he furnished, Christ was in no sense of the word *their* Saviour; and if *they* were saved without Christ, so might we have been as well as they, and so might all mankind. There is therefore salvation in another than he; and there is some other name given under heaven among men, whereby they may be saved. The death of Christ, therefore, unless we blasphemously suppose it to have been the result of wanton and unparalleled cruelty, was founded on a mistake, and his whole mission was the result of a very doubtful necessity.

7. We cannot in this way explain any of the titles which are given him in consequence of his mediatorial work. Why did Christ merit the title of "The Lamb," "The Lamb slain," and "The Lamb of God." Is it the office of a lamb to demonstrate? Christ resembled a lamb, in that he was innocent, gentle, patient under sufferings, and in being slain as a sacrifice, but surely not in furnishing evidence. Neither is evidence the same thing with salvation, redemption or deliverance from wrath.

8. This theory furnishes a totally different explanation of this event from that officially assigned by Christ himself when he instituted the Eucharist: "This is my blood, which is shed for the remission of sins." Sins are positive transgressions of the law of God, and the forgiveness of them is the remission of their punishment. No torture of language, therefore, can make the forgiveness of sins the same with evidence of the truth of Christianity. The sins of men are not owing, solely nor chiefly, to want of evidence; nor has the evidence, which the death of Christ actually furnished, put a stop to sin. This theory cannot therefore be true, unless Christ himself was mistaken.

9. It gives no adequate explanation of his sufferings in the garden. Why must that agony exist at all? It did not augment the evidence of Christianity, and we hear of no similar event in the annals of martyrdom. Why, still more, must it rise to the hazard of life? If it was proper for him to go deliberately and die, merely to prove the truth of his religion, then his conduct was wholly approved by God; and he had no sufferings to endure but sufferings of the body. It was then the mere dread of bodily pain which led him thrice in deep prostration to pray that the cup might pass from him, which occasioned the sweat of blood, and made him need the presence of the sustaining

angel. And when he enjoyed the highest love of the Father, and had the Spirit without measure, and was to remain dead but three days, and then was to leave the grave in triumph; when he was to redeem and to save the world by furnishing evidence of the truth of his religion, and in forty days was to ascend to heaven and sit down on the right hand of God, it was simply the fear of dying which led him, unlike thousands of his followers, to shrink from that martyrdom which he came into the world to suffer.

10. The scene on Calvary, also, is a mystery equally inexplicable. As God approved of the purpose of his death, and he suffered, not in our stead, but to furnish evidence, no anger of God against our sins was manifested in his sufferings. God, therefore, did not lay on him the iniquities of us all, and it did not please Jehovah to bruise him and put him to grief. The darkness of the sun, too, at the time of the full moon, was doubtless owing to an ordinary eclipse; the earthquake was an accidental circumstance; and the evangelist was mistaken in supposing that many of the dead came forth from their sepulchres!

11. The whole conduct of Christ after his resurrection proves that this theory is erroneous;* and there is no one of the phrases employed by the Scriptural writers to account for his death by which it is not explicitly contradicted.†

As an appendage to this part of the subject, it is proper here to add, in the language of another, that "many," who reject the Atonement, "are dissatisfied with all these

* See the 9th head of the last general division.

† See the 10th head of the same. The argument in each case is applicable here, but to avoid repetition is omitted.

explanations, and think that the Scriptures ascribe the remission of sins to Christ's death, with an emphasis so peculiar, that they ought to consider that event as having a special influence in removing punishment, as a condition or method of pardon, without which repentance would not avail us, at least to that extent which is now promised in the Gospel."*

It will probably be thought, that this scheme of explaining the death of Christ, as it is embraced by many, should like the preceding ones, be subjected to a minute examination. To decline doing this is the result, not of choice, but of necessity. Were it fully bodied forth, so as to be tangible or even visible, it would be numbered as a seventh theory, and carefully investigated. But when it is said that without the death of Christ as a condition or method of pardon, repentance would not avail us in procuring it, at least to that extent which is now promised in the Gospel, we are at a loss how to interpret the language, and we look for additional information on the following points:

1. Is it intended that repentance by itself would procure us an inferior kind of pardon less advantageous than that now promised; or that it would avail us to a certain degree in procuring that now promised, but not altogether; or that it actually procures the pardon of a certain portion of our sins, but not of the remainder?

2. To what kind of pardon, on the first supposition; to what degree, on the second; and to how great a part of it, on the third; would repentance avail us, without the death of Christ?

3. On what grounds would repentance avail us, to that kind; that degree; or that portion?

* Rev. Dr. Channing's Sermon at the Ordination of Rev. Jared Sparks.

4. Why would not repentance also avail us either to the higher kind; or altogether; or to procure the remainder?

5. On what grounds does the death of Christ avail us in thus effecting what mere Repentance could not avail? Is it directly, as obedience, or suffering; or indirectly, as it leads us by its moral influence to a higher kind of repentance?

6. What is the specific difference between those two kinds, or degrees, or portions of our pardon?

7. On the third supposition, why cannot the death of Christ, alone and of itself, avail us in procuring also that part of our pardon, which repentance avails us to procure?

8. What passages of Scripture speak of such an inferior kind of pardon; or of the degree to which repentance avails us; or of the portion of our sins for which it is sufficient?

9. In what passages of Scripture is the death of Christ spoken of as procuring a higher kind of pardon; or as eking out our pardon, by availing us to an extent to which repentance could not avail us? Is it said by the Saviour, "This is my blood of the New Testament, which is shed to procure a better kind of pardon than that which repentance would procure;"—or by Paul, "Christ hath fully availed to redeem us from the curse of the law, when repentance could avail us only in part;" or by John, "The blood of Christ cleanseth—not from all sin, but—from those more heinous sins, which could not be washed away by the tears of repentance?

Until these points are distinctly stated, it is not possible to conjecture what the theory is, nor of course, by comparing with the word of God, to learn whether it is true or false. This is the only reason, why a more minute and marked attention is not paid to what, if fully conceived and fully stated, might have proved an additional explanation of this most wonderful event.

Thus have I endeavoured to examine the various theories devised to account for the death of Christ by those who insist that mankind need no expiatory sacrifice to save them from punishment. As they have successively passed in review before us, it has appeared, if I mistake not, that each one of them is utterly inconsistent not only with reason, but with the known phenomena attending the event, and with the plain explanations given of it in the Scriptures. On this point, however, as well as on every other connected with religion, it is at once your privilege and your duty, not, as in the days of types and shadows, to learn from those who minister at the altar, what you must believe and do, but to come in person to the tabernacle of the testimony, and hear for yourselves the voice of HIM who dwells therein. What that voice utters is distinct, and uniform, and level to the comprehension of those to whom it speaks. Listen to it, then, with attention and candor—with humility and contrition, and you will not err.

In completing the plan originally proposed, you may perhaps expect, as the opinions of those who receive the doctrine of the Atonement are on various points discordant, that their several systems should be separately stated and examined. These differences of opinion, however, are rather circumstantial than essential; and it is the design of these discourses, not to combat any one class of opinions, nor to defend any other, but simply to answer the question, *Why did Jesus the Messiah die upon the Cross?* All that now remains, therefore, is—to state what is regarded as the scriptural doctrine of Atonement, and then to compare it with the series of facts already recited, and with the plain declarations of the Word of God.

ATONEMENT is a word of extensive import, and needs to be explained.

Wherever one individual has a claim on another, the latter owes the first a corresponding duty. This duty may be either performed or not performed. If it is performed, the claim is discharged. If it is not performed, the failure either does not involve blame, or it does. If it does not involve blame, it is owing to some circumstance not originally contemplated, which, either for a time or permanently, renders it wrong for the one party to enforce the claim, and right for the other not to perform the duty. For such a failure, the party who originally owed the duty, need do nothing but show an excuse, viz. the circumstance which removes blame from the failure.*

If the failure does involve blame, an injury is done to him whose claim has not been satisfied. For this injury, a full and entire reparation is due; something which shall make full amends to the party injured, and leave him in as good a condition, as if the duty had been exactly performed.

There are injuries for which it is possible to make adequate reparation—such as the non-payment of a debt, or the non-rendition of a service when due; and others for which it is not possible to make such reparation—such as the transgression of a law. In cases of injury, the offended party has the same right to enforce reparation where it can be made, as he had before the injury to enforce the original claim. In cases where no adequate reparation can be made, if the offended party sustain

* This is the only proper use of the word *excuse;* for plainly that and that only is *an excuse* which *excuses* or *frees from blame.* A bad excuse, therefore, is no excuse.

towards the offender the relation of a ruler to a subject, and the injury done is the transgression of a law, he has a right to inflict such an amount of suffering, as will be a just and adequate expression of his anger for the injury done. Where reparation can be made, the offender also is as much bound to make it as he was to perform the original duty; and where it cannot be made, if the offended has a right to inflict suffering, the offender is equally bound to submit to that suffering.

The kinds of treatment, which the offended party may adopt towards the offender, are various. He may strictly enforce reparation, in a case where reparation is possible; or, where it is not, and the right to inflict suffering exists, may inflict suffering, until his displeasure for the injury is adequately expressed. Or he may, without either reparation or infliction of suffering, treat the offender as if he had done him no injury; and thus, without any ground or consideration, relinquish both the right to reparation, and the original claim. Or, in consequence of something done or suffered, in behalf of the offender, which, either conditionally or unconditionally, he consents to regard as an adequate reparation, or an adequate manifestation of displeasure, for the injury sustained; he may forgive the offender, and treat him as if he had not failed to perform the given duty. If the agreement to receive the thing done or suffered, as an adequate reparation, or an adequate manifestation of displeasure, for the injury, be unconditional, the offended party is bound to forgive the offender, and treat him as if he had not offended. If it be conditional, this obligation does not commence until the condition is complied with.

These remarks will serve to explain the general meaning of the word Atonement. AN ATONEMENT IS THE GROUND

OF FORGIVING AN INJURY. By an injury, is here intended, a blame-worthy failure of a duty. The atonement is in all cases something done or suffered, either by the offender, or a third party in his behalf. If it is something done, the offended consents to receive it as an adequate reparation, and if suffered, as an adequate expression of his displeasure, for the injury. The effect of it is, where it is unconditional, or the condition is fully complied with, to take from the offended party the right either to enforce reparation or to inflict suffering.

What the ground of forgiveness is, will usually depend on the nature of the injury. The non-payment of a debt, or the non-rendition of a service which is due, is an injury for which the subsequent reparation of the loss sustained either by the offender or a third party, is an atonement. The disobedience of a child is an injury to the parent. If the child humbles himself, and confesses his fault, the parent may consent to regard such humiliation and confession as an atonement. Strictly speaking, however, it is not an atonement, because there is neither reparation nor manifestation of displeasure, for the injury received; yet the parent treats the child as if it were.

Disobedience to a law is an injury to the lawgiver, as it is both a denial and a defiance of his authority. That authority is supported either by uniform obedience, or by punishment. Punishment is the infliction of suffering for disobedience. If wisely appointed, it is an adequate expression of the lawgiver's displeasure against transgression. By showing practically that the way of transgressors is hard, it is designed to support the authority of the law and secure obedience.

In cases of transgression, atonement takes the place of punishment. If the punishment merited be substantial suffering, atonement cannot be made by the offender himself. He cannot make it by future obedience, for that he is bound to render without any reference to past transgressions, merely to satisfy the future demands of the law. He cannot make it, by enduring a less degree of suffering than the threatened penalty, for that would not be an adequate expression of the lawgiver's displeasure; nor by enduring a greater degree, for when he has endured a degree of suffering equal to the penalty, the claims of the law are satisfied, and any farther infliction is unjust. In every such case, therefore, atonement, if made at all, must be made by a third person.

Where the transgression is *malum in se*, or *a moral evil*, and the punishment merited is substantial suffering, atonement cannot be made by a third person, except by the infliction of suffering. It cannot be made, either by the payment of money, or the rendition of service. If we admit that murder ought to be punished with death as an adequate expression of the displeasure of the lawgiver against this crime, and an adequate security against its perpetration, to receive the payment of any amount of money, or the rendition of any service, from a third person in behalf of the murderer, as an atonement for his murder, is to declare that the given sum or service is a reparation for the injury, and an adequate security against the perpetration of murder, which would be false. In every such case, therefore, if atonement is to be made at all, it must not only be made by a third person, but it must be made by the infliction of substantial suffering on the third person, as a substitute for the punishment of the transgressor.

To render the atonement adequate, the suffering thus inflicted on the third person need not, of course, be exactly the same in kind, or equal in degree, with that which would have been inflicted on the transgressor as a punishment. The kind of suffering may be different; for, if two kinds of suffering are equal in degree, they equally answer the end in view. The degree of suffering necessary to render the atonement adequate, will depend on the comparative importance of the third person and the transgressor, in the view of the subjects at large; and may be, in different cases, greater, equal, or less than that threatened in the penalty. All that is necessary to render the atonement adequate, is this,—that the suffering inflicted be seen to be as full an expression of the lawgiver's displeasure against the offence, or as decisive evidence of his determination to support his law, as would have been furnished by the actual punishment of the transgressor. When this is done, the whole design of punishment is fully answered; and, with perfect safety to the authority of the law, the transgressor may go unpunished. Such an atonement, however, in order to be just, must be voluntary on the part of the third person; and in order to be valid, must be consented to by the lawgiver.

If the suffering inflicted on the third person be the specific suffering, that is, the same both in kind and degree, with that which would have been inflicted on the transgressor, not only are the sufferings of the third person a substitute for the sufferings of the transgressor, but the third person himself is, in the strictest sense of the word, a substitute for the transgressor. In other words, while making atonement, he takes the identical place which the transgressor would have occupied while being punished. If the sufferings of the third person are different in kind or degree from those which would otherwise have been inflicted on the transgressor,—though the third person is not strictly speaking the substitute of the transgressor, as he does not while suffering take his precise place,—yet the sufferings of the third person are a substitute for the sufferings of the transgressor. In every case of atonement, therefore, the sufferings of the third person are a substitute for the transgressor's sufferings; and where the former are specifically the same in kind and degree as the latter, the third person himself is also, in the strictest sense, the substitute of the transgressor.

If the atonement be attended with no conditions, the transgressor's liability to punishment ceases as soon as it is made. If it be attended with any condition, that condition also must be complied with, before it can cease. Thus, if a third party receive on himself an adequate manifestation of the sovereign's displeasure for the desertion of an officer to the enemy, on the condition, that, if the deserter will within one year return to his allegiance, he shall be fully pardoned; if the deserter does not return to his allegiance, his liability to punishment, though suspended during the year, does not cease at all, and he is not entitled to forgiveness.

Adequate Atonement for a moral transgression, is therefore *such a degree of suffering, inflicted on a third person, with his consent, as shall be an adequate expression of the lawgiver's displeasure against the transgressor, and thus a substitute for his punishment, or the ground of his forgiveness.*

These remarks are explanatory of the Doctrine of ATONEMENT BY THE DEATH OF JESUS CHRIST. That doctrine supposes the following points:

That God is the rightful Sovereign of men, and as such entitled to their obedience:

That his government over them is a government of law, or a moral government; offering rewards to obedience, and threatening punishment to disobedience:

That mankind have universally disobeyed the Law of God, and are therefore liable to punishment:

That the authority of God's Law, and the safety of his empire, alike demand an adequate expression of the divine displeasure against the sins of mankind:

And that nothing, which men can do or suffer—no works of supererogation, no exhibition of contrition, no humiliation, no repentance, as well as no penance, or any other sufferings less than those threatened by the Law—can be a substitute for their punishment.

These points might, it is believed, be easily and most clearly established; but they are now mentioned by way of explanation, and not of discussion; as it is our present design, merely to compare the various theories devised to account for the death of Christ with the Scriptures themselves.

For man thus condemned, thus unable to deliver himself from punishment, the doctrine of Atonement supposes that the death of Christ was intended to be, and is in fact, a full and adequate method of deliverance, and that in the following manner. The sufferings and death of Christ were inflicted by God, and voluntarily endured by himself, as an adequate expression of God's displeasure against the sins of the world, on condition that pardon should be freely offered to all, and granted to those who actually repent and trust in Christ for salvation.

This doctrine, as we understand it, does not suppose that the sins of men were laid on Christ, in such a sense, as to effect a transfer of their sinfulness. Such a transfer not only would have rendered Christ the most guilty, odious being that ever can exist in the universe, but, as we have already seen, is a physical impossibility.

Neither does it suppose the sins of men to be so laid on

Christ, that strictly speaking he endured the precise punishment both in kind and degree, to which they were doomed. That punishment, as will be admitted by all who may be inclined to question this part of our explanation, was everlasting punishment in hell. Unless therefore the sufferings of Christ on the cross were identically the same thing as everlasting punishment in hell, the sufferings endured by Christ were not, strictly speaking, the precise punishment to which the human race were doomed. Of course, it does not suppose that Christ was strictly speaking, our substitute ; i. e. that he endured the identical punishment, both in kind and degree, to which mankind were doomed.

Neither does it suppose that the sins of men were so laid on Christ, that his sufferings were equal in degree, either to the everlasting sufferings of the whole human race, or to the everlasting sufferings of those who will actually be saved by his death.

Neither does it suppose that, strictly speaking, Christ paid a debt for us. We owed no debt, and of course none was paid. We were liable to suffering, and therefore suffering was endured.

But it does suppose, that the sins of men were so laid on Christ, that his sufferings were inconceivably intense and overwhelming; and that, being inflicted by God on a person of supreme exaltation and dignity, the object of God's supreme affection, " God manifest in the flesh," they were as full and as adequate a manifestation to the universe, of God's displeasure against the sins of the whole human race, as would have been made in their everlasting punishment. As such, it supposes them to be an offered substitute for the everlasting punishment of all mankind, and the actual substitute for the everlasting punishment of all who shall be saved ; so that if all mankind had been saved, no more suffering on the part of Christ would have been necessary; although none will be actually saved in consequence of it, except those who repent and believe.

The scriptural doctrine of Atonement, as we understand it, is therefore this—That the sufferings and death of Christ were inflicted by God, and voluntarily endured by himself, as an adequate manifestation of the Divine displeasure against the sins of the human race, on the condition that they should be offered to all men, as a sufficient ground for their forgiveness, or a substitute for their punishment, and that they should actually prove the substitute for the punishment of all who repent and believe.

This is the doctrine of Atonement as standing by itself and unconnected with any thing else. At the same time, all those who have held this doctrine have also held that, in the mission of the Holy Spirit as the agent, and in the truth of God as the means, of regeneration and sanctification, both of which were granted to men as the reward of the obedience and death of Christ, a broad and sure foundation was laid for the recovery of mankind to holiness and to God. In short, we believe that the death of Christ lays a sufficient foundation for saving the whole human family from the everlasting sin and misery of hell, and for raising them to the ever-increasing happiness and virtue of heaven; that none will fail of the salvation thus wrought out, but those who reject it; and that a multitude which no one can number out of every kindred, and nation, and people, and tongue, will actually escape that endless sin and misery, and partake of that ever-increasing holiness and joy.

Having thus learned what the doctrine of Atonement is, it remains to submit it to the same examination to which all the preceding theories have been subjected.

1. If this was the Great End of the death of Christ, it

was an event sufficiently momentous to justify the importance given to it in the Scriptures. No end, of which we can conceive as connected with this world, is equally important with the endlessly increasing happiness and virtue of mankind. The death of Christ might well, therefore, have been the result of the determinate counsel and foreknowledge of God. No subject could have been so interesting, as communicated to our first parents in Eden, or to Abraham, or Moses, or David, or Isaiah, or the succeeding prophets. That it was necessary as an atonement for sin, as an expression of God's displeasure against it, is most obvious from the fact, that no other way of forgiving sins has hitherto been devised, which does not declare the penalty of the law of God to have been absolutely unnecessary, and does not wholly subvert the authority of his government. If the angels contemplated the Father giving his Son to die, and the Son of God actually consenting to die, to effect this great salvation; and if they saw the countless multitude of the first born raised to immortal life in heaven; we can not wonder that this vast result of glory and of good, should have fixed their deeply interested attention for revolving ages; or that, when it was actually accomplished, they should have united in the new and universal song, "Worthy is the Lamb that was slain, to receive power, and riches, and wisdom, and might, and honor, and glory, and blessing." On this supposition, the death of Christ was indeed the great manifestation of the love of God to men; the highest possible evidence of his willingness to bless mankind; the sum and substance of the gospel; and the only thing in which an Apostle ought to have gloried.

2. This theory will explain the peculiar titles which are given to Christ in consequence of his death. In this his

great work, in dying as an atonement for the sins of the world, he stands perfectly alone. This is an honor, a distinction, a glory, of which no martyr nor apostle, no prophet nor patriarch, no angel nor archangel, can boast. Other foundation can no one lay ; and there is no other name given under heaven among men whereby we must be saved. We can see, therefore, why the Baptist, his forerunner, announced him to the human race as the Lamb of God, who taketh away the sin of the world ; and why he is styled by himself and his apostles, the Ransom, and the Deliverer, the Saviour of the world, and the Redeemer of mankind.

3. We can thus explain the deep personal interest felt in his death, by many who died before his coming. Their sins were forgiven, as truly as ours, in consequence of his atonement ; and their holiness, as truly as ours, was the purchase of his death. While they were on earth, therefore, they could behold in every bleeding victim, an affecting type of the Lamb, which God would provide for a burnt-offering, and, guided by the finger of prophecy, they could well look forward to the coming of his day, and rejoice in it, and be glad. On their arrival in heaven, they began fully to comprehend all that salvation means. There they witnessed the emotions felt in the hearts of angels, but which the tongues even of angels could not adequately express, on the first annunciation of a Saviour's birth ; when a multitude of the heavenly host, leaving the portals of the sky, and hovering over the plains of Bethlehem, shouted, in the hearing of the astonished shepherds, " Glory to God in the highest, on earth peace, and good-will to men !" And when, his work of agony and death all ended, the gates of heaven opened spontaneously to the ascending Conqueror, and the King of glory entered in ;

they might well be justified, as they cast their crowns before his feet, and began the sweetest of the songs of heaven, "Unto HIM who hath loved us, and washed us from our sins in his own blood, and made us kings and priests unto God, even his Father, unto HIM be glory and dominion, forever and ever, Amen!"

4. We can thus account for the fact, that the SON OF GOD was selected as the Saviour, and that he consented to suffer and to die. It was the purpose of Jehovah, to cause all his goodness to pass before the universe of intelligent beings, and by one decisive demonstration, to make them feel, as well as comprehend, the length and the breadth, the hight and the depth of the love that passeth knowledge. A world of sinners, all immortal, all condemned as the enemies of God, were to be rescued from endless darkness and death, and raised to the realms of light and life eternal. Some one must be found to take their place, and be made a curse for them; some one, the gift of whom should show the greatness of the Father's love; some one who was able to bear the sins of a lost world in his own body on the tree; some one of such high consideration and dignity, in the view of God and his intelligent kingdom, that, when he should drink the cup of wrath, heaven and earth should witness perhaps a deeper manifestation of the displeasure of Jehovah against the sins of men, than would have been made in their final condemnation; some one, too, whom his redeemed, as they beheld him on the throne of the majesty on high, could unite with the Father in their endless ascription of dominion, and blessing, and praise. Whom, then, in this broad universe, could we have selected for such an undertaking, but *Him*, who is the brightness of the Father's glory and the express image of his person, at whose name every knee shall bow, of things

in heaven and things on earth? And when he contemplated "the joy set before him," this achievement of never-ending glory, and of ever-growing happiness and virtue, who can wonder that he was willing to tread the wine-press alone?

5. In this way, we learn the reason of his early death. He came, as the Son of the Highest, to manifest the love of God to men in the purpose of salvation, to set an example of universal holiness, to prove his divine mission by his miracles, to die as a sacrifice for our sins, to rise from the dead as evidence of our justification,* and then to ascend on high, that in the possession of all power over heaven and earth, he might overrule all things for the good of his church. But he did not come to finish the canon of the Scriptures in person, nor to settle the constitution of the Christian church, nor by his visible presence to give efficacy to the gospel of salvation. This, as he expressly told his disciples, was the office of the Comforter, the Holy Ghost. In the immediate contemplation, therefore, of his own death, resurrection and ascension, he might say with truth, in his prayer at the close of the sacramental supper, "I have glorified thee on the earth, I have finished the work which thou gavest me to do;" and again he might also say,—"It is finished,"—as he bowed his head and gave up the ghost.

6. We can thus see why his death, rather than any other event of his life, not excepting even his incarnation, or his birth, should have been selected, as the object of public and perpetual commemoration by his church. If this theory be true, his death, taking into view its design, its

* That is, as evidence that his Atonement was accepted of God as a full atonement for our sins.

attendant circumstances, and its consequences, was not only the most surprising, but incomparably the most important event which God has yet made known to man; that which yields the richest tribute of glory to the King Eternal; that which best unfolds the treasures of Infinite love; that which procures for man, not merely all the blessings of the present life, but all the good which he can find in holiness and in God, through the ever-expanding life of heaven. His people, therefore, as they surround the sacramental table, can justify the institution; for they feel the force of his own language, "This is my body, which is broken for you."

7. We here find no difficulty in explaining why his death was public, violent, and ignominious. It was to be a manifestation of the divine justice, of the displeasure of God against the sins of men, and of the guilt and odiousness of sin, to be witnessed both by earth and heaven. All this was exhibited in the fullest manner by his most public death, accomplished, not by the direct agency of God, but by those, whom he came to save, nailing him to the cross, and imbruing their hands in his blood.

8. We can thus account for the fact that his sufferings were great and overwhelming—sufferings inflicted by God; sufferings not chiefly of the body but of the mind. The sins for which he was to atone were all the sins of the countless millions of mankind, all the determined enemies of God and of virtue, all destined to the wrath and curse of God, and to the torments of hell forever. As his sufferings were to be an expression of the divine displeasure, they must of course be inflicted by God. As Jehovah was to lay on him the iniquities of us all, and his death was to be at least as strong an expression of the divine displeasure against the sins of all mankind as their eternal con-

finement in the prison of his wrath, we see, not only why the Son of God must be selected as the victim, but why his sufferings must be, and must be seen to be, inconceivably intense and distressing. Such sufferings, a material body, especially one so weak and frail as the body of man, is not in its very nature qualified to endure. They must be principally the sufferings of the intelligent mind; the travail of the soul. And when he was stricken and smitten of God;* when Jehovah inflicted on his mind an adequate expression of his displeasure against all the sins of a condemned world, while we most easily believe that he made his soul an offering for sin, we do not wonder at that cry of agony, "My God, my God, why hast thou forsaken me!"

9. The scene in Gethsemane is, in this way, adequately explained.

The sufferings of Christ on the cross, which he here anticipated, we can readily believe, were at least from four different sources. One of these, and doubtless the least, was the pains of crucifixion, or the sufferings of the body. Another was his conflict with evil spirits. The apostle tells us that, having spoiled principalities and powers, at his death, he made a shew of them openly, triumphing over them with his cross. If so complete a triumph was gained, that, in his ascension, he led them captive, and made a show of them openly as his vanquished enemies, the conflict must have been for the time peculiarly distressing. Accordingly, when Judas, whom Satan had tempted to betray him, approached with the Roman band, he himself said of the season of his peculiar sufferings, "This is your hour, and the power of dark-

* Isaiah liii. 4.

ness." It was indeed the hour in which the powers of darkness were to make their most furions onset, the time when Satan was to bruise the heel of the Seed of the woman, the season of his expected and imagined triumph over the Son of God.

A third source of intense distress, was the infinite weight of responsibility resting upon him, during the season of his overwhelming agonies. This world had been created, as the Theatre of the Work of Redemption; and Man had been permitted to fall, that he might be redeemed. The fixed attention of heaven, earth and hell had been directed, for revolving ages, to the Great Atonement to be made by the promised Messiah. On the supposition, that he would well sustain the agonizing trial, all the dispensations of God to these three worlds had been adjusted. On that supposition, a countless multitude of penitent transgressors, with the curse of the law resting upon them, unless he should remove it, had, by anticipation, been justified, and admitted to heaven. On that supposition, a multitude of the heavenly host had ascribed glory to God in the highest, because there was peace on earth, and good-will to man. On the issue of that trial, was suspended the endless happiness or misery of a world. The great crisis of the universe was thus approaching. If he failed, not only were the hopes of men and angels blasted, but the glory of God was tarnished forever. Thus a weight, needing the strength of the Almighty to sustain it, would bear down upon him, while he was suspended on the cross.

His remaining sufferings were those directly and immediately inflicted by God. Not only was he to be forsaken of God, but Jehovah was to bruise him, and put him to grief;* and the sufferings actually inflicted on himself were to be, not only in the view of others, but to his own mind, as awful an expression of the Divine displeasure against sin, as would have been made to it, if he had witnessed the endless punishment of a revolted world.

In the garden his apprehension of all these sufferings was most lively and distinct. The overwhelming sorrows of Calvary were all present, and real, and endured by an anticipation so full and clear, that his sweat was as it were great drops of blood falling to the ground. Such an anticipation was necessary, that it might appear to the intelligent universe, not only how great his sufferings were, but that he was not mistaken nor surprised, and that while he was most conscious of their overwhelming weight, he voluntarily submitted to them all. Under the full consciousness of these accumulated sufferings, which no created nature could long endure, he cried out in prostrate agony, with his face upon the ground, "O my Father! if it be possible, let this cup pass from me!—nevertheless, not as I will, but as thou wilt:" in other words, "If it be possible, that the redemption of the world should be effected, without my drinking the cup of wrath, let me not drink it; nevertheless, not as I will, but as thou wilt." The very prayer, while it showed the intenseness of the sufferings, showed also the intenseness of his resignation.

10. We can thus easily account for the remarkable occurrences which preceded and followed his death. If it was an event, in which not only earth and heaven, but the great Sovereign of both, felt this deep personal interest, and if his sufferings were to be thus incomprehensibly great, Mount Tabor might well have witnessed that surprising

* Isaiah liii. 10.

scene, intended to prepare him for his decease, which he was to accomplish at Jerusalem; and, while he was transfigured before his astonished disciples, and his face did shine as the sun, and his raiment was white as the light, we do not wonder that they beheld there, not merely Moses and Elijah, but the overshadowing cloud of glory, from which they heard the Uncreated Voice, "This is my beloved Son, in whom I am well pleased." And when the wrath of the Almighty was poured out on his beloved Son, and he bare the sins of a lost world in his own body on the tree, great indeed would have been the wonder, if, when all heaven was veiled in sackcloth, the astonished sun had not withdrawn his light, or the earth had not quaked with fear, or the world of death had not heaved with new and strange commotions.

11. We thus learn why the Saviour was seen so little after his resurrection. His work on earth was finished and completed. The foundation was laid of that vast Temple, which the Divine Spirit, out of stones taken from this earthly quarry, and changed to living stones, was to build as the habitation of God on high. And, as he intended to furnish to mankind that amount of evidence of his religion, which would fully sustain their faith, rather than that which might be the basis of mathematical demonstration; he left the proof of his resurrection to the testimony and the miracles of his disciples, to the gospel which they preached, and to the influences of the Spirit who accompanied them; and, withdrawing from this lower world, he entered on his mediatorial reign in heaven.

Thus we see, that all the facts recorded in the Scriptures as connected with the death of Christ, are in perfect harmony with the supposition, that its great design was to make an atonement for the sins of the world. The theory also accounts for the *phenomena* attending the event. Let us now see whether it is also consistent with the *direct explanations* of that event given us by the scriptural writers.

Here we meet with a difficulty somewhat peculiar. It was necessary, in the preceding part of these discourses, to state the various *forms of phraseology* in which these explanations are given, and, by a critical investigation, to determine the exact meaning of each. What we there did leaves us here nothing to do, except to repeat what was there said; for the true meaning of these explanations is so identically the same with that of the theory which we are now considering, that all argument on the subject is out of the question.

You have already seen that the Son of God died for us; that he died for our sins; that he died for the forgiveness of our sins; that he died as a sin offering, or a sacrifice for our sins; that he died to make an atonement for our sins; that he died to reconcile us to God, or that God might not impute to us our iniquities; that in his death he bare our sins by enduring sufferings inflicted instead of our punishment; that he redeemed us from the punishment of the law; that he gave his life a ransom for us, to procure our pardon; that we are justified by his blood, and saved from wrath by his death; and that these several forms of phraseology have been proved to denote *that he suffered death, inflicted as the appointment of God to procure our forgiveness, or to save us from that manifestation of the divine displeasure, which would have been made in our punishment.* We need not add that, in barely stating these scriptural explanations, we have stated the identical doctrine of ATONEMENT BY THE DEATH OF JESUS CHRIST.

Thus, after a careful, and, so far as I know my own heart, an honest and fair examination of the Scriptures relative to this subject, I can come to no other result than this,—that, *To lay an adequate foundation for the forgiveness and salvation of a world, was the Great End for which Jesus the Messiah died upon the cross.* Of this, however, each of you will judge for himself. The Bible is in your own hands; and it is not a sealed book, to him who will read it. I ask none of you to believe any thing, merely because you hear it from this place. I urge every one of you to search the Scriptures most faithfully for himself, that you may know what the SPIRIT, who was in the prophets, the evangelists, and the apostles, has testified, concerning the sufferings of Christ, and the glory that shall follow. I do this fearlessly, because I know that this BOOK, like its AUTHOR, is light, and that in it there is no darkness at all,—"TO THE LAW AND TO THE TESTIMONY," is the Christian's motto: "if they speak not according to THIS WORD, it is because there is no light in them."

GOD'S CONSTANT TRIAL OF MAN.

JOB VII: 17. 18.

What is man, that thou shouldst try him every moment.

To try denotes, *to put to the test;* to place in such circumstances as will detect the character. The courage of a soldier is tried in the field of battle. The talents and industry of the student are put to the test by the daily recitation. The difficulties and temptations of public life try the firmness and integrity of men in power.

The text instructs us, that God so orders the daily events of life as to render them a constant trial of every individual. He places him in circumstances which will inevitably detect his character, and bring the hidden man of the heart out into open, naked view.

This truth, I know, is a painful one to many; it is frequently questioned and denied, and by those who admit it is too often forgotten. In considering it, I propose to show:

How the various events and circumstances of life try every man's character:

Why God so orders them, as to produce this result.

This trial is represented as carried on every moment. Of course we are to regard it as commencing when the mind begins to act, as continued from day to day, and as terminating at death.

Among these events and circumstances, I shall notice particularly,—

Afflictions. Men often speak of their afflictions as severe and distressing trials. By this language they intend a trial of their feelings, or of their fortitude. We ought, however, to regard them as a trial in a higher and more important sense, because they are one of the most efficacious means of determining the moral dispositions of our hearts. Afflictions do not come forth from the dust, nor spring from the ground, but they are in every instance immediately appointed and sent upon us by God. His hand takes away our property. Disease wastes our health at his command. Death comes as a message from him when he enters our dwelling. His design in sending affliction is to do us good. When it comes, his hand chastises us for our sins. He intends to make us feel the criminality of our sins, that we humble ourselves on account of them; that we break them off, and commence lives of holy obedience. When he deprives us of property, he intends that we shall resign our self-confidence and our inordinate love of riches, and transfer our affections to God and to heaven. When he visits us with sickness, he intends that we shall feel our frailty and dependence, and immediately prepare for death. When he takes away some one of our family, he aims at a similar result.

The afflictions which God sends have a very different effect on different men. As God sends them, he takes care to be present, and to watch their effect on each individual, from the time it is first felt, until it is forgotten. One man, when his property is taken away—whether by fire, or shipwreck, or the negligence or fraud of others, feels the hand of a present God chastising him, bows in submission to the stroke, confesses and laments his covetousness, and thus begins to lay up treasure in heaven. Another, under a similar loss, refuses to acknowledge God as sending it, murmurs at its severity, laments his ill luck, concludes to bear it because he cannot help it, and enters with new zeal on the acquisition of more. One man, when visited by sickness, becomes a real penitent and a humble follower of Christ. Another hardens himself against the voice of God; or, if he is alarmed by the near prospect of death, resolves to repent after his recovery and then forgets his resolution. In one dwelling, from which death has just torn away a wife or a husband, a parent or a child, you will find the survivors deeply mourning their loss, but not mourning for their sins,—unconscious that God has come near to them,—charging the event to the disease or the physician, and looking for consolation only to the present world. In another, you shall see them silent, submissive, sorrowing most of all on account of their sins, and finding sufficient consolation in the presence and the love of God. In every such case, God sends the judgment, reminds the individual that it came immediately from him, and then leaves him to act as he pleases. By the affliction, the character of the individual is so far determined and disclosed. He who is not subdued and brought to repentance, discovers the hardness and stubbornness of his heart, and practically says to God that, even when he feels his chastising hand and opens his eyes on death and judgment, he will not renounce sin nor return to his duty. God surveys the progress and result of the chastisement, and not only finds the design of it frustrated, but sees the individual on whom it was sent a more obstinate offender than before, more forgetful of God, and altogether less likely to attain salvation.

Blessings. The blessings we receive from God commence with our existence, are countless in their number and variety, and innumerable in degree. They are new every morning, fresh every evening, and repeated every moment. They are all not only gifts of his bounty, but are given in mercy—because they are bestowed on the evil and unthankful. They include the gift and preservation of life, all the enjoyment we have already received or now possess or hope for, the offer of Heaven, and the promise of happiness unmixed and eternal. They are intended to inspire thankfulness and praise, to lead us to supreme love, confidence, and obedience. This return, if we make it,—and it is the only return we can make,—will in itself be the greatest of all blessings.

While we are thus enjoying these blessings we are not always aware that every one of them is a trial. Their effect on different men is widely different. There are those, who daily remember from whence their blessings come, and daily ask, "What shall we render unto the Lord for all his benefits?" But how different is the conduct of others. While he feeds them and clothes them as children, they never acknowledge him as their Father. He watches over them every night, but they will not bless him in the morning. He guards them every day, but they will not spend it in his service, nor thank him in the evening. Should he preserve their property when exposed to peculiar danger, they have no perception of his goodness and never approach him to express their obligations. Thus every blessing they receive reveals their ingratitude; so that even at the close of life it will appear, that the goodness of God, instead of having inspired them with love, could not induce them to renounce transgression.

Temptations. Our path through this world is beset with temptations, and crowded with dangers. They arise from within and from without. They meet us before and behind; on the right and on the left. Every affection, every appetite, every object that we love, may be the means of tempting us to sin.

We are tempted to fraud and injustice in our transactions with others. This is the case in all the common concerns of life. When we buy, our avarice tempts us to represent the value of the article, or the market price as less, and when we sell, as more than they really are. In every such case, God looks on, witnesses our representations, and sees whether we love our neighbor as ourselves. In every contract we are tempted to overreach—if we can, and to impose on the confidence or simplicity of others. In every business and trade there are certain secrets familiarly known to those who pursue it, which constantly tempt them to impose on those with whom they deal. Are we poor; our poverty daily tempts us to cheat and steal. Have we property; that property gives us power to oppress the poor, and to defraud the simple. God places us in these circumstances on purpose to try us. He puts it in our power to gain by selfishness and dishonesty—he then leaves us to act as we please, and the result discovers our true characters.

We are tempted to acquire property by placing inducements to sin in the way of others, and by furnishing them with the means of sinning. All men who intend to live a life of sin, will pay a high price for the conveniences of sinning; and whatever our business may be, we find that the lusts and sins of those around us furnish the easiest and amplest means of support and emolument. When we engage in it, God submits this practical question for our decision,—Whether we will conduct it on the principles of the Bible, so as to do good and glorify him, or,—Whether we will become panders to the unholy appetites and passions of others. The temptation here thrown is often so strong that few are able to resist it. If we yield, we shall excite no observation, because we do only what others do. If we resist, we shall be thought unnecessarily precise and scrupulous. The result always discloses what is the state of the heart within.

We are tempted to impurity, in thought, word, and deed, and the opportunities of gratification are placed within our reach. We are tempted daily to sloth, to intemperance in eating and drinking, to the amusements and pleasures of fashionable life. Our hatred to others tempts us to slander them, our vanity leads us to exaggeration and embellishment, while in the case of those above us, our selfishness tempts us to flattery. Each of these temptations has its effect. It discovers the dispositions of our hearts.

Our opportunities of doing good. God informs us that we are his servants,—his stewards. Our business is *to do good*, and we have a vast field for doing good before us. As to the amount of good which every man is to do God has given us a plain rule—Do good, as you have opportunity, to all men. Whatever you do, do all to the glory of God. Every man's opportunities of doing good are peculiar to himself. God leaves us in these circumstances, and then says, "Occupy till I come." After this he exercises no control, no restraint over us. He merely looks on, and permits us to act as we please. We take our choice, and the result shows our characters. We are able to spend all of life in this great business; we are able wholly to neglect it, and to spend life in the pursuits of avarice, ambition, and sensuality. The conduct of men in this respect, also, is widely different. Some men are faithful stewards, and make doing good their sole employment. Others occasionally engage in it, not willingly, but by constraint. Others never once reflect that they were sent into the world for this purpose, and are always employed in serving their own selfishness, if not in gratifying their own lusts. In this particular, our daily business tries us. We shew this by our habitually carrying it on for God, or for ourselves. Our property tries us by the manner in which we employ it. We can hoard it, and thus live for the mere business of accumulation. We can expend it in the gratification of pride or the indulgence of pleasure. Or we can employ it in doing good. Our influence tries us. We can exert it to promote our own purposes or to secure the welfare of others. Our families try us. Our opportunities of doing them good are numberless. These commence in their infancy—they occur every day of their continuance through life. When a child is born, God says to us, "Take care of this young immortal and educate it for me. Its soul is worth all thy care, and all thy efforts. Be faithful and I will pay thee thy wages." Every day he tries us, whether we will do this duty or not. He inspires us with intense love for them. He opens heaven to our sight, and assures us that there is room there—not only for us but for them. He points us downward to a gulf of misery and tells us not to lead them thither. He thus informs us, that the question whether they shall spend their eternity in heaven or in hell, is intimately connected with our treatment of them in this momentary life; and with all these things before us he leaves us to decide for ourselves, whether we will faithfully seek their salvation in the ways of his appointment. At the same time he kindly warns us to begin early, as the work will be very difficult; and to do what we do with our might, because the time is short. He then looks on and watches what our conduct is from day to day. The result proves, in every case, whether, with all these motives before us, we are desirous of promoting the immortal welfare of our children. I need not say that in different families very different results are beheld. There are parents who daily remember that their children are probationers for eternity. By a holy example, earnest instructions and exhortations, by prayers and tears, they shew their faith in the Divine promises, and their determination to give a good account of their stewardship. The prayers of others are so faithless, their efforts so occasional and feeble, that they appear to be made merely to quiet their own fears, and with no view to a conscientious discharge of duty. Others still never do any thing in obedience to these commands, but leave the souls of their children as uncultivated as the heathen. We are tried by our domestics. We have powerful means of influencing them, by instruction, example, and prayer, to accompany us to heaven. While they live in our families is the time of trial, and God is present in our houses to witness the issue. We are tried by our fellow-men around us,—by the poor, and the ignorant, and the vicious,—whether we will exert ourselves to warn them of their danger, and to instruct and reclaim them; whether we will teach their children in the Sabbath school, and contribute to furnish them with Bibles, the preaching of the gospel, and all the various means of moral and religious improvement. We are tried by our neighbors and by strangers, whenever we have an opportunity to promote their eternal welfare, and to persuade them to seek that country to which we are invited to go. Every day furnishes us with such trials. Every day God directs us to use the opportunity as it offers, and he then waits to see what our conduct is. At the close of every day if we will but survey that conduct, we shall learn the result of the trial.

Our religious privileges. The Bible is given as a light to our feet and a lamp to our path. We have it in our own possession, and in our own language. It lies daily on the shelf, and tries us daily whether we will read it or not. If we read it, we are tried whether we will read it often and habitually, whether we will read it as the word of God, whether we will read it prayerfully and with self-application. Not a morning nor evening passes which does not bring us to this test; nor in which we do not thus disclose our characters, in which our Bibles do not testify for or against us.

The Sabbath is given unto us as such a privilege. All that is awful in the commands of Jehovah; all that is delightful in communion with him; all that is momentous in salvation, prompts us to keep it holy to the end of it, and to spend its sacred hours in his peculiar presence and worship. Every Sabbath thus is a trial of the state and temper of our hearts. As it approaches, God draws near to see how we prepare for its arrival,—whether we welcome it as one of the days of heaven, whether we consecrate it to him and spend it in his service and in the enjoyment of his communion, or whether we regard it with mere external decency; or openly and presumptuously profane it by amusements or business, by worldly thoughts, conversation, and conduct. We are taught, that the sanctuary is the house of God and the gate of heaven; that it is the place of his peculiar presence, where he meets his people to bless them, and where he is willing to meet and bless returning sinners. We are then tried every week, whether we will attend on its ministrations or absent ourselves; whether we will go with reverence and humility to meet God, to worship him, to listen to his truth, and to seek pardon and salvation, or whether we will go to gratify curiosity, or taste, a critical or captious spirit.

Every evangelical sermon is a direct and painful trial of our characters. In every such sermon the way to heaven is clearly pointed out. Our danger and our guilt are set before us. The invitations of the gospel, and the sufficiency and willingness of Christ to save us, are unfolded. The danger of delay and the necessity of now accepting the great salvation are disclosed, and all possible motives are brought to bear on our consciences and our hearts. When we hear every such sermon, life and death, heaven and hell, are set before us. God submits to us the plain identical question,—"Will you repent and accept salvation, or not? and he then leaves us to decide for ourselves. We do decide; we choose one or the other, and that in every case. Every minister when he has preached such a sermon, can close the book and say to the people, "Life and death, heaven and hell, are this day set before you and presented for your choice. You may have eternal life if you will; but to have it, you must choose it. But if you do not choose it, you will choose death." Every such sermon, whether we will or no, has an important effect on our welfare. It brings us to a stand, and compels us to take God for our portion or to reject him. This is true of this sermon if it be really of this character. If it declares to you faithfully the whole counsel of God, it will be to every one who hears it a savor of life unto life, or a savor of death unto death.

Revivals of Religion. At such a season God is near, and every day and hour reminds us of his presence. He does not merely come to the sinners around us, but he comes to us *in person.* He brings us directly before him, so that our minds see him. We know and feel that he is come on an errand of infinite love. We stand before his throne of grace, from day to day and from hour to hour. We behold him seated thereon, and see the omnipresent Spirit face to face. All that is awful in power, in holiness, in justice, is blended with all that is lovely in goodness and mercy. When he speaks, he does not—as at other times—address sinners in general; he speaks immediately to us. There, while we stand before his throne, and beheld the very features and expression of infinite love, he calls us by name and puts the question directly :—"Guilty, ruined, as you are, will you now turn from your transgressions, and come back, and acknowledge me as your Father and your God? Will you now come and apply to your soul that blood of Atonement which was shed for the remission of your sins? Relent, and I will have mercy on you. Return, and you shall be a son, a king, a priest unto God." With these proposals many sinners comply. Believing that he who gave his Son to die for them is willing to forgive and bless them, they go to him as their Father, and take their place among his children. Many others, though they thus see God and hear him speak to them, linger and hesitate from week to week, and from month to month, until God retires and leaves them to themselves. Such a season is, at times, the most fiery trial through which the soul is ever made to pass. The sinner acts knowingly, wilfully, deliberately. While he sees heaven above open to welcome him and hell from beneath moved for him to meet him at his coming, while his eye is fixed on God and his ear is listening to his voice, he says to Jehovah,—"I will not have thee for my portion. I will not renounce my sins. I will hold on my way to death."

We are also briefly to consider, why God thus orders the events and circumstances of life so as to be a constant trial of our characters.

He does this, I would say particularly, to prepare men for the judgment of the great day. On that day he must demand an exact account from every human being of the affections of the heart and of the external conduct, that he may reward us according to our works. He must, of course, place men in circumstances which will infallibly try them and shew of what their hearts are constituted.

If a single angel, or a single man, should be found in that day who had not been placed in such circumstances, the judgment could not proceed, for the necessary preparations would not have been made.

He does this, I would add, to make known our characters to others. God intends that all his creatures shall know, that he is just when he judges, and clear when he condemns. If he should admit a single angel or a single man to heaven, who could not justify himself on his trial, according to the known public condition of justification, either under a dispensation of law or a dispensation of grace, he would be accused of partiality and a violation of his promises. If he should condemn any one who could thus justify himself, the whole universe would be witnesses of the injustice. The Divine character must not be suspected. Heaven and earth must be satisfied that, in every case when he sends sinful creatures to the abodes of woe, they deserve to be forever banished thither, and that they are thus rewarded only according to their works.

He does this, also, to make us know our own characters. God intends that the conscience of every impenitent man shall pronounce his own sentence, and be perfectly satisfied that it is right. He intends that the sinner's mouth shall be stopped, that the world of misery shall never hear a solitary complaint or murmur against the rectitude of his administration, and that it shall be the heaviest part of the sinner's punishment to know forever that he deserves it. God makes every day, and hour, and moment, therefore, every thing which the man possesses or covets, every individual whom he knows, and every action, word, and thought of his life, the means of trying him and of shewing to himself as well as to others, the true character of his heart. Thus it is that the sinner, whether he will or no, in every case, let him do or not do, choose or refuse, speak or be silent, is always acting out his character and exhibiting himself. The record is drawn not only on the book of God's remembrance, but on the tablet of his own memory. Many of these lines now seem, indeed, to be almost obliterated, and many of the transactions forgotten; yet the time is approaching when every line and word will appear as fresh as when it was first written, and all the transactions of life will come back in their original depravity—to glorify the justice of God, and to seal his own lips in endless silence and despair.

An application of this subject should be readily made by every one. I need not say, then, how solemn our condition in this world! We cannot act, nor speak, nor feel, nor think,—we can neither move nor exist, but we are furnishing the materials out of which we are to be judged. We are always revealing the secrets of our hearts, and thus furnishing evidence either for or against ourselves. Like a skilful limner, each one of us is ever occupied in painting his own likeness, the picture of his soul. Every moment, as he adds a new touch of the pencil, the features become bolder, the expression is stronger, and the resemblance more exact. At length the portrait is finished, and it is then hung up, to be gazed at by God, by the universe of intelligent creatures, and by the painter himself. Unlike all the other works of man, the canvass will never decay, the coloring will grow more distinct and vivid through eternity.

No less evident is it, that each of us personally has been thus placed on his trial, and has been thus disclosing his character. Let me then ask you, my hearer, what has been the result of this trial hitherto? The hand of God has chastised you with afflictions. Has he seen you bowing in submission, or refusing to regard his chastisements, and discovering a temper which afflictions cannot subdue? He has tried you by great and constant blessings. Have you not discovered a heart which blessings could not melt, affections which kindness could not win? You have been daily exposed to temptations. Cannot the eye of memory trace on the picture you have been drawing, the lines of fraud and oppression, of intemperance and sensuality, of falsehood and calumny, of hatred and revenge? Every day has afforded you numberless opportunities of doing good. Have you been exhibiting the character of the unprofitable servant? Your religious privileges have been always great. What must they affirm of the character of your hearts? How have you appeared when tried by the Bible; by each returning Sabbath; by the house of God; by the invitations of mercy? Have you hitherto shown that you love sin too well, to be drawn from it by the joys of immortality, or to be frightened from it by the groans of despair?

A great preparation, as we see, has already been thus made for the day of judgment. That day cannot come on until all things are ready for its arrival; and God has taken care so to order the events of his providence, that the preparations for the judgment shall advance just as rapidly as the wheels of time roll on. Not a human being has gone into the world of spirits, whose character has not been completely developed, and the account of his conduct has been taken and sealed up against the arrival of that day. That account will be lodged in the archives of heaven until the judgment shall be set and the books be opened.

As our use of our religious privileges is thus disclosing our characters, it is evidently a very solemn thing to hear the faithful preaching of the gospel. When God sends you the gospel, my hearers, he is in earnest, and he does not send it in vain. You do not trifle when you send messages to each other, and God does not trifle when he sends the message of salvation to you. Jesus Christ did not ascend the cross for a trifling purpose, and the Holy Ghost was not sent to strive with you for nothing. "The word that goeth out of my mouth," says God, "shall not return unto me void; but it shall accomplish that which I please, and shall prosper in the thing whereunto I send it." The word which you hear is quick and powerful, and sharper than any two-edged sword. Defend yourselves as you please against it, it will inevitably penetrate your hearts, and try and disclose your characters. You may come to the house of God from habit or thoughtlessness, or for mere amusement, and hear this message as if it were not a message to yourselves, and would have no influence on your future welfare. If so, the time will at length arrive, when you will feel the evil effects of such stupidity and presumption. Christ informs you that his word shall not be lost upon you. "He that rejecteth me, and receiveth not my words, hath one that judgeth him: The word that I have spoken, the same shall judge him at the last day." When you come to the sanctuary, and Christ with his salvation is offered to you, you either embrace the offer, or you practically say to Christ,—"I reject thee as a Saviour, and refuse the salvation which was purchased by thy blood." This very thing you are each of you now doing; and when you and I meet at the judgment, and there give an account of this Sabbath and this sermon, the Judge of the quick and the dead will then shew to you that, while I am now speaking, every one of you is either receiving or rejecting Christ. In this hour of trial and decision, when you are choosing between heaven and hell, may God grant you his Spirit, that you may come out humble penitents and sincere believers.

If a Revival of Religion is so fiery a trial, ought you not, my unconverted hearers, to think solemnly of your own condition? You live in the midst of such* a work of grace. You know that God is present, on an errand of infinite mercy. Not a day, nor an hour passes by you, when you do not stand before him and see him on his throne of grace, and hear his voice offering to you glory, honor, and immortality. He employs peculiar means to bring you to repentance. You that are young, have line upon line, precept upon precept. You that are parents, and others that have attained adult years, have had new and unusual efforts made for your salvation. For months you have been standing on the very brink of the unseen world, and the curtain has been drawn, and while the

* A Revival was in progress when this discourse was originally delivered.

glories of heaven from above have burst upon your sight, you have seen the smoke of the pit which is ascending forever and ever. With all these objects in view, Jehovah has come forth from his hiding place, not to punish and destroy, but to purify and save. Here, on his throne, he has been surrounded, not by that glory which no eye can see and live, but with those softer and lovelier beams of mercy which shine from the face of Jesus Christ. Here he has been for many weeks and months, waiting on you to be gracious. And yet you have until now trifled with all this greatness and goodness, and with a madness at which demons stand confounded, have practically said to him,—"I will not have thee to reign over me. I will not hear thy voice. I will not accept pardon at thy hands. Thy love does not melt me,—thy thunders do not awe me." Poor, delirious hearer, need you wonder, should you hear him swear in his wrath that you shall never enter into his rest?

THERE IS NO DIFFERENCE.

ROMANS III: 22.

For there is no difference.

THE first three chapters of this epistle are the longest discussion of the moral character of man, to be found in the Scriptures. The Apostle, to shew the excellency of the gospel, takes a full survey, first of the Gentiles, and then of the Jews, and declares both to be in a ruined condition, alike guilty in the sight of God, and alike incapable of being justified by works of law. Having established this fundamental position, he declares that men, though condemned by law, are not without hope, because God in the gospel had provided a righteousness for sinful man through faith in Christ, which he would accept of all who believe in him; and that in their need of this righteousness, there was no difference between one man and another, because all were alike sinners and alike under condemnation. "But the righteousness of God, which is by faith in Jesus Christ, is manifested unto all and upon all them that believe; for there is no difference; for all have sinned, and come short of the glory of God." This, then, is the result of Paul's investigation of this most interesting subject. After surveying the whole world,—Jews and Gentiles,—after declaring that they are all under sin; that the whole world is guilty before God, and that no flesh can be justified in his sight, he concludes by putting all men on one common level, and declares that there is no difference between them. This account of the character and condition of man I know is a very different one from that which we should be inclined to give, if left to ourselves; and it directly tends, if believed, to humble our pride, and, if disbelieved, to provoke our resentment. Instead of bringing mankind together into one common group of deformity, we make numerous distinctions, and at every step elevate ourselves while we depress others. We first separate savages from civilized men, and Mohammedans and Heathens, from Christians. We next expel murderers and robbers, thieves and adulterers, and all other infamous persons, from the class in which we include ourselves. We then exclude atheists, infidels, and sceptics. We then withdraw from those who disregard the nicer shades of morality and are guilty of offences which the law of the land will not reach. Finally, perhaps, we remove from the ignorant and the clownish, and retreat within the pale of refinement and intelligence. Here we regard ourselves and those with whom we associate, as the truly respectable and virtuous, and conclude that there is a wide and fundamental difference between ourselves and the various classes from whom we have withdrawn.

It may, then, be well to pause a moment and inquire, why Paul's conclusions and our own are so directly contradictory. The reason is this. Paul had been led by the Holy Spirit to adopt very different rules for measuring characters from our own. We refer our conduct to the law of the land, or the laws of fashionable life, or to professional or national customs; Paul referred it to the holy, perfect, and comprehensive law of God. We compare ourselves with those of our own class, or with those beneath us; Paul compared us with saints and angels in heaven. We forget the duties which men owe to God, and think only of those which they owe to each other; in estimating their character, Paul fixed his eye chiefly on the former. Even in our estimate of the latter class of duties, we look only at the external conduct; Paul looked only at the motives from which that conduct flowed, and regarded it as virtuous only when it respected the glory of God. We view men merely as inhabitants of this world; Paul viewed them as on their way to the judgment, and as candidates for a higher and a nobler state of existence. He brought them,—not to the standard by which we measure one another here,—but to the standard by which an infinitely pure and holy God will measure us to determine whether we shall be admitted to his presence and allowed to associate with saints and angels. Taking this broad and comprehensive view of the subject, he tells us that there is *no difference* between Jew and Gentile, or between one man and another, but that all stand on one common level.

It is my design to explain the meaning of the passage, and then to establish the principle which it affirms.

What then is the *meaning* of the Apostle when he says, that there is no difference between one man and another? I shall endeavor to answer this question, first, negatively, and then, positively.

There is no allusion here to the external circumstances of men. Paul knew, as well as ourselves, that there is a very wide difference between men as to birth, family connexions, the advantages of early education, manners, rank, property, power, and influence.

Neither is there any reference to the corporeal or mental endowments of man. Paul was aware that, while one man has a perfect body, and a healthy, vigorous constitution, another is lame, or blind, or deaf and dumb, and another is the prey of hereditary disease and destined to an untimely grave. Neither was he ignorant that, while one man has a powerful and well-balanced mind, possessing the various faculties in their just proportion, another is destitute of taste, or memory, or judgment, or the power of reasoning or invention, while another is an idiot, and another the victim of hereditary delirium.

Neither does the Apostle intend that men are alike in their tempers, or in their instincts, which, when called into exercise, we sometimes call the native virtues of the human character. Owing partly to native constitutional temperament, partly to education, and partly to the influence of prosperous or adverse circumstances, one man is cheerful, while another is habitually gloomy; one is sweet tempered, and another is morose; one is frank and affable, another is reserved and distant; one is unsuspecting, another is jealous; one is mild, gentle, amiable, while another is rough and violent; one is not easily provoked, another is irritable; one is humble, timid, contented, while another is bold, ambitious, and aspiring; one is tender-hearted, another is unfeeling; one is meek and patient, another is unforgiving and revengeful. He knew also that most men possess natural and conjugal affection, while some are without it; that some men are capable of friendship, while others can neither cherish it themselves, nor prompt it in those with whom they associate; that some seek to promote the public welfare, while others regard nothing but their own. This difference between these classes of men is very great. Those who belong to the first class, in each instance, will be pleasant and agreeable friends, neighbors, and connections, while those belonging to the second, will be uncomfortable in all the relations of life. If individuals of these different classes are converted, it will require a far greater measure of grace in one of the latter than in one of the former, to exhibit the beauty and loveliness of religion. Nay, some of those latter, who give decisive evidence of piety, owing to their peculiarly unhappy native tempers, are far less amiable and pleasing associates than some of the former, who furnish no such evidence. Of all these diversities of Christians the Apostle was fully aware when he said that there is no difference between one man and another, yet he overlooked them all when he threw mankind into one promiscuous group, and employed none but the dark colors of sin and guilt to sketch the moral likeness of the race. Is it asked, why he overlooks those diversities? I answer: He knew that these heavens and this earth were soon to be burnt up; that then all mankind would be inhabitants of the world of spirits; and that that world is made up of heaven and hell, with no intermediate region. He looked at these native virtues, and saw that they might, and that they all do, often, exist without any spirit of obedience to the law of God, without any love to him or regard to his glory; that these very diversities are found in the different animals; that they grow either out of instinct, or selfishness; that they are perfectly consistent with impenitence and rejection of Christ; that an infidel or an atheist may possess them all; that they are often found in men of openly debauched and profligate lives; that they may all exist in their highest perfection, and yet not qualify their possessor for the presence of God or the enjoyments of heaven.

Neither does Paul here intend to deny that there is a wide difference in men as to their native or acquired propensities to particular sins. One man is peculiarly propense to the indulgence of anger, another to fraud, another to falsehood, another to debauchery, another to intemperance.

Neither means he to assert that all men are alike in their morals, or that all are equally wicked, or that all men are as bad as they can be. A youth who has ventured but a little distance in the course of sin is far less corrupt than an old transgressor ; and the difference in the depravity of persons of the same age is often very great. Some men lead a life of crime and enormity, others are occasionally vicious, and others are externally and really decent and reputable in their morals. If also we could examine the hearts of decent and moral men, we should find some of them far less deformed and polluted than others.

As little does he refer here to difference in degrees of guilt, or to any difference which the grace of God has affected in the human character. He is speaking of men in their natural, unrenewed state.

Neither, finally, does he regard any difference effected in man by the means of grace, where actual grace is not imparted. Under the privileges of the gospel, one man is punctilious in his observance of all the external duties of religion, while another treats them all with absolute indifference.

What, then, is the Apostle's meaning, when he says that there is no difference between one man and another ? A reference to the context will enable us to answer this inquiry. In the 9th verse he looks simply at the characters of men, and asks, "Are we Jews better than the Gentiles? No, in no wise, for we have before proved, both Jews and Gentiles, that they are all under sin." In the 19th and 20th verses he brings the whole race of Adam before the final bar on their trial as under law, and finds that every mouth is stopped; that all the world are compelled to plead guilty; that no flesh, not an individual, is justified or acquitted, but that all are condemned. And, in the following three verses, he declares that all men stand in equal need of that righteousness which is by faith in Jesus Christ, which God has agreed to accept instead of the perfect righteousness of the law. It is then, when he views men as candidates for salvation, when he sees them, not only incapable of being justified, but actually condemned, and needing justification through Christ, that he places them all on the same level, and denies that there is any difference between one man and another.

I shall next proceed to establish the principle of this passage.

This, in itself, is far from being an enviable undertaking. To reflect that we stand on the same level, in any sense, with criminals, and profligates, and others of the worst of mankind, is a most distressing consideration. Yet if God places us on the same level in the decisions of the final day, in the question of acquittal or condemnation, it is desirable we should know it; and it will require no very remarkable degree of humility, to believe that his estimate of us is right.

I would observe then particularly, that when God describes the native character of man, and pronounces mankind to be fallen, without holiness, and deplorably wicked, *he no where intimates* that there is any difference between one man and another. We are told in the context, that all have sinned and come short of the glory of God, and that Jews and Gentiles are all under sin. In the 14th Psalm, which is there quoted, we are told that Jehovah looked down from heaven, not merely on the Gentiles or the Jews, but on the children of men, to see if there were any of them that sought after God. We are then immediately told of the result of this universal survey. In this result, God does not classify men by nations, or as civilized and barbarous, or according to their professions or circumstances. We hear nothing of good and bad men. He groups them all together. " There is none righteous ; no, not one. There is none that understandeth ; there is none that seeketh after God. They are all gone out of the way ; they are together become unprofitable ; there is none that doeth good,—no, not one." When he says in Jeremiah, " The heart is deceitful above all things, and desperately wicked," he does not say this of the heart of a thief, or of a robber, of an adulterer, or a murderer ; nor does he say it of the heart of a savage, or of a Gentile, or a Jew. He says it without qualification ; and when he immediately adds, " I, Jehovah, search the heart, to reward every man according to his works," he lets us know that he is speaking of all men who will be summoned before the final bar ; in other words, of the whole race of Adam. When God pronounces mankind sinners, desperately wicked, and without holiness, his language, as we thus see, is in the fullest possible degree universal ; he puts no difference between one man and another.

2. There is no difference as to *the condemnation* in which all men are involved. This necessarily follows from the fact that they are all sinners and without holiness ; for " he that offendeth in one point, is guilty of all ;" and " cursed is every one that continueth not in all things writ-

ten in the book of the law, to do them." But the fact is itself asserted in many forms. Thus in the context it is said, that all the world is become guilty, i. e. liable to punishment, before God. We are also told that, previous to faith in Christ, all men are under condemnation. "He that believeth not, is condemned already," and "the wrath of God abideth on him."

In the *tidings of the gospel* all men are put on one level. "Fear not," says the angel to the shepherds, "for behold! I bring you glad tidings of great joy, which shall be," not to the Jews merely, nor the Gentiles merely, nor to sinners merely, but "to all people." In the same manner the multitude of the heavenly host shouted, "Glory to God in the highest," because there was "peace *on earth* and good will to *men*,"—i. e. to all mankind. In the same manner Christ was the Saviour, not of the Jews only, but also of the Gentiles. He is the Saviour of all men, but especially of them that believe. In the gospel, all mankind receive one common *message*. The gospel is to be preached to all men. "Go ye," said Christ, as he was ascending to heaven, "and preach the gospel to all nations." The gospel is to be preached to every creature. The message of reconciliation is to be sent to all men without distinction. "God," says Paul, "hath given to us the ministry of reconciliation; viz. that God is in Christ reconciling the world unto himself, not imputing their trespasses to them, and hath committed unto us the word of reconciliation." He then tells us what this word is, and by whose authority it is delivered. "Now then, we are embassadors for Christ, as though God did beseech you by us, we pray you in Christ's stead, 'Be ye reconciled to God.'" This was the message from God, sent not to the heathen only, but to the whole world; and proclaimed, not merely to outlaws and profligates, but to every creature. But a call to reconciliation implies enmity. By this call of the gospel, then, all mankind are placed on one footing, and charged with enmity to God, and the command to be reconciled, is addressed to every creature without distinction.

Pardon is, in the same manner, offered to all men indiscriminately; but pardon, I need not say, is the remission of deserved punishment.

All men, I would add, are declared to be alike as to their need of *regeneration*. Christ was not speaking of the Jews, nor of the heathen, nor of the abandoned and profligate simply, when he said, "Except a man be born again, he cannot see the kingdom of God." His proposition is as absolutely universal as language can make it. The declaration, Except a man have eyes, he cannot see, is equivalent to the declaration, No man can see without eyes. Of course Christ's words, Except a man be born again, &c., is precisely equivalent to the words—No man who is not born again, can see the kingdom of God. Here, then, there is no difference. Every man living, whatever his native temper or character, must experience the change of regeneration, if he is to be admitted into the kingdom of God. "If any man be in Christ, he is a new creature." "Every one that loveth, is born of God." "Every one that believeth, or worketh righteousness, is born of God."

The agency of the Holy Spirit is just as necessary to produce this change in one as in another. No degree of sweetness of temper; no cultivation of the native virtues, or of the social affections; no external decency of character; no observance of the duties of religion, will exempt any man from this necessity. Except a man be born of the Spirit, he cannot enter the kingdom of God. This excludes every man without distinction, who is not born of the Spirit. "As many as believed" on the name of Christ, says John, "were born, not of blood, nor of the will of the flesh, nor of the will of man, but of God."

All mankind stand on one common level as to *justification*. All men, without exception, are declared incapable of justification on the ground of obedience. "By the deeds of the law no flesh shall be justified." We are "saved, not of works, lest any man should boast." To convince the Jews that this was true of every man, the Apostle tells them, that even Abraham could not be justified by works. "If Abraham were justified by works, he hath whereof to glory." In the same manner it is said, that all who are justified, are justified by faith alone. Therefore we conclude, that a man is justified by faith, without the deeds of the law." "The righteousness of God, by faith of Jesus Christ, is manifested upon all them that believe." We are justified freely by his grace, through the redemption that is in Christ Jesus."

Neither, we may add, is any difference made between one man and another in the *requirements of the gospel.* Mark tells us, that Jesus came into Judea, preaching the gospel of the kingdom, and saying, "Repent ye, and believe the gospel." These commands are of universal application. "Except ye repent, ye shall all likewise perish." "God now commandeth all men every where to repent." "He that believeth, shall be saved; and he that believeth not, shall be damned." The most moral and virtuous men must therefore repent and believe, as truly as the most abandoned, if they are to obtain salvation; and will as certainly fail of it, if they do not.

In the article of *death*, all men are placed on one level. Death is the wages of sin; and death has passed on all men, because all have sinned. Not a child of Adam is here exempt. Whatever distinctions we may be disposed to make between ourselves and others as to disposition, or temper, or decency of life, death disregards them all, and says to us, " You have earned your wages, return to your dust." This has been his solemn language to every one. Of all the unnumbered millions of men who have lived in past generations, there is not a solitary survivor. Multitudes of them, in every age, have boasted of their native virtues, and thanked God they were not as other men ; but death has laughed at those discriminations, and taught them in a most affecting and awful manner that they were " children of wrath," being children of disobedience, " even as others." Of all who are now living or shall live hereafter, not one will fail to receive this distressing conviction that there is no difference. Death, the common leveller of all terrestrial distinctions, sent by God as the common executioner of the human race, will treat the man of respectability and virtue with as little ceremony as the outlaw and the profligate. There is no difference, either, as to the circumstances of death. The amiable, virtuous man, dies as early as the villian. His death is attended with equal suffering and equal humiliation. Go to the chamber of sickness, where the man thus most distinguished is expiring, and then repair to the dying bed of the most abandoned of mankind, and you will see that all these distinctions are vanished and forgotten. You will see them both writhing and tossing with pain ; their flesh is alike wasted ; the face of one is as pale and ghastly as that of the other ; the voice of each is dumb ; a common palsy benumbs their limbs ; the same cold sweat settles on their foreheads ; the pulse of life in both is still ; the lamp of life is for each put out in never ending darkness. See them in their coffins, and one is as quiet, as powerless, as loathsome as the other, and needs as much to be removed from the sight of all the living. Follow them to their burial. They lie side by side under the same clod of the valley. The grave of one is as deep, dark, silent, as that of the other. One of them as truly as the other may "say to corruption, thou art my father, and to the worm, thou art my mother and my sister." They will mould with equal rapidity into one common dust, and in a few years, every trace of both will be blotted out from under heaven.

The *judgment day* also tells us, that there is no difference. I have already remarked that Paul is here speaking of men in their natural, unrenewed state, and that he has no reference to the distinction made between them by the grace of God. That difference, I admit, is very great, and it will be seen and felt to be infinitely great, on the final trial. But when the Judge shall separate mankind, he will divide them into two classes only, the righteous and the wicked; and the righteous will consist of those, and of those only, who are clothed in the robes of Christ's righteousness and not in their own. Those on the right hand will all have been renewed by the grace of God; will confess that they deserve condemnation, even as others; and that it is grace alone which has made them to differ; and will place all their hope in the blood of Christ. Those on the left hand will stand in one promiscuous crowd, and will be grouped together as the common enemies of God and the kingdom of holiness. The earthly distinctions of birth, education, manners, rank, talents, and fortune, as well as of respectability and decency of life, will be all forgotten. The man who was here cheerful, sweet-tempered, affable in his manners, liberal, amiable, and compassionate in his disposition, if he died in impenitence and unbelief, will then see himself placed side by side with another, who was habitually gloomy, morose, jealous, covetous,—who was violent, ambitious, unfeeling, and revengeful. He who prided himself in the purity of his morals, will perceive that the Judge has not separated him from the vile and the profligate. However respectable in the view of his fellow-men; however numerous or great in degree his virtues; however distant he thought and kept himself from the abandoned in this world, when he then looks on his companions on the right and the left, before and behind him, will behold among them, liars, thieves, and robbers, adulterers, and murderers, and see himself regarded by the Judge as possessing a common character of guilt and debasement, and involved with them in a common ruin. When the trial is finished, the same sentence of reprobation, "Depart, ye cursed, into everlasting fire, prepared for the devil and his angels," will be pronounced on them both. They will go away in one indiscriminate crowd to receive the same dreadful allotment. They will be all shut up in the same prison; will be companions with one another, and with devils and damned spirits, will drink from the same vials of unmingled wrath, and will be shrouded in the same blackness of darkness forever.

What, then, in conclusion, are the practical reflections which we should universally make. As one of these, I may say, we perceive the reason why the doctrines of grace have been so unpopular and offensive. When Christ preached to Nicodemus the universal necessity of regeneration to Jew and Gentile, the latter exclaimed with astonishment, "How can these things be?" Paul tells us that the cross of Christ was "to the Jews a stumbling-block and to the Greeks foolishness." The reason was, that

Christ died for all. He was a propitiation for the sins of the whole world. No man could come to the Father but by him. All were reduced by his cross to one common level of sin and ruin. Had he taught us, that those only whom we regard as vile and profligate, need to be cleansed by his blood, and must be born again,—but that we, who regard ourselves as amiable and moral, as cherishing kind and good feelings towards others, and as deserving and receiving from them the meed of respectability and worth, need not be born again,—the offence of the cross would have wholly ceased, and all its enemies, Jews, Mohammedans, heathens, atheists, and infidels, both speculative and practical, would have been numbered among its friends. I do not say this from mere conjecture, but found the declaration on facts. The bitterest enemies of the cross of Christ are those who deny the doctrines of regeneration and atonement; who say that they themselves need no change of heart, and who expect to be justified without the cleansing efficacy of the Redeemer's blood.

As clearly are we instructed as to the true value of the native virtues of the human heart.

These unquestionably render us agreeable and amiable in all the relations of the present life. But this life is but a moment; and yet the character here formed endures through eternity. Death introduces us to the world of *spirits;* to heaven or to hell. The one, a world of unmingled holiness and joy,—the other, of unmingled sin and misery,—are the only regions which we shall then inhabit.

What will be then thought of these virtues, my hearer, which you now so highly value? Whether you possess any or all of them, and in whatever degree, they now make no difference between you and others in the view of God. He pronounces you to be as truly fallen, without holiness, and desperately wicked; to be as really condemned already; that the tidings of the gospel are as joyful tidings to you; and that the command, "Be ye reconciled to God," is as truly addressed to you, as he affirms these of robbers and adulterers. He asserts also, that you as truly require the blood of Christ to wash away your guilt, and the influences of the Spirit to remove your pollution; that you are utterly incapable of being justified by any works of righteousness which you have done; that the commands of the gospel, "*Repent and believe*," are as fully addressed to you, as binding on you, and as indispensably necessary to be obeyed; that death as certainly awaits you, in as distressing and awful circumstances; that your body will be as low in the grave and moulder into as humble common dust; that, if unrenewed by the grace of God, you will stand in the judgment on the same left hand, will hear the same sentence of damnation, be shut up in the same prison, and linger out the same eternity of hopeless misery, as those whom you now regard as the vilest of mankind. I appeal to your own conscience, if in each case, I have not proved from the express declaration of the word of God, every one of these positions. If so, they are true. Of what avail then are those virtues in which you boast yourselves, and on which you fondly rely? They are nothing but a mask, which you draw over the face of your soul; which prevents you from appearing to yourself and to others as you appear to the eye of God. But, believe me, death will strip off this mask, and shew you in your real character to *your own eyes;* and, when you drop the body, and go naked and without disguise into the world of spirits, where all things are seen in their true colors, you will appear to yourself and to every being in the universe just as you now appear to the eye of God. There the dreadful glory of God shines with unclouded brightness, and in its intolerable light, wicked beings will see all the features of guilt and impurity which make up their own moral picture. Cast away then all dependence on your own virtues; trust alone to the righteousness of Christ.

MAKE YOU A NEW HEART.

EZEKIEL XVIII: 31.

Make you a new heart.

THIS is a command of God, addressed to impenitent men. That it binds the conscience like every other divine command, and was given to be obeyed, must be admitted. It is a command, however, to which little or no attention is ordinarily paid by those to whom it is addressed. Many seem not to know, that such a command is to be found in the Bible. Others, if they know this, are unmoved. Others, still, deny that they need a new heart. And others, when the command, "Make you a new heart," is brought home to them, reply, that they *cannot* do this.

To individuals of the first three classes I shall not now address myself. If there are any such persons present, I will barely remind them, that, when God utters this command, "Make you a new heart," he subjoins, "For why will ye die?" I need not explain what this death is. Yet this is the awful motive which God himself has suggested, to prompt them to an immediate compliance.

To persons of the fourth class, to those who allege that they *cannot* make themselves a new heart, our attention will now be directed. The number of these is very great. Rarely indeed, do I urge this duty on any individual, but he replies,—"I ought to be a Christian, and I wish sincerely that I was one. But we cannot convert ourselves. We must wait God's time. If we do as well as we can, God will do the rest."

Unhappily for the church, this is no new language. When the heretic, Pelagius, in the fifth century, denied that the Holy Spirit changes the heart, and contended that men actually change their own hearts, Augustin and his friends, to destroy this error root and branch, insisted that men not only want *inclination*, but *capacity*, to change their own hearts and turn to God. If they were *willing* to do this, they would be still *unable*.

This unhappy mistake has been handed down from that hour to the present. The reformers were too much occupied to detect it. We find it, therefore, incorporated in all the creeds and confessions of the Protestant churches. In the writings of some eminent divines, we do indeed read that the sinner's impenitence is charged upon his choice, but at other times they represent him as destitute of capacity to repent. Even Baxter, the most consistent of them all, is at times inconsistent with himself.

The truth is, that the subject of moral agency has not been thoroughly investigated by the divines of Europe. No one of them has given the world a treatise on this subject, in any high degree important or valuable. Andrew Fuller, the only exception to this remark, acknowledges the source whence his own views were derived. It was the divines of our own country who first vindicated the moral government of God; who taught mankind that God does not require bricks without having first given them straw; and that nothing hinders men from doing their duty but the want of inclination.

This truth was first promulgated in our own churches about seventy years ago. It was at first vigorously opposed, but it is now universally received by the ministers of New England. Within a few years it has made rapid progress in the regions lying south and west; and it has already found numerous and powerful friends and defenders on the other side of the Atlantic. The time is not distant, when, on this subject, "the eyes of them that see shall not be dim;" when no preacher shall tell the impenitent sinner that God has commanded him to do what he has not the capacity to perform.

Though this truth is so extensively received by ministers and Christians, yet it has made but little progress among those who are not Christians. Even now, when we urge the sinner to repent, he almost of course tells us that he *cannot*. The reason is obvious. He was taught so when a child, and he loves the delusion. He knows that God commands him to repent, if he would not perish. But to do this, he is neither ready nor willing. When you press this command home upon his conscience, and this danger upon his fears, if he cannot find some lurking-place, he will be compelled to submit. What his shelter is, he cares not, if he can only live undisturbed. At first he says, perhaps, with Pelagius, "Men are free agents; they do convert themselves. I can safely postpone repentance for the present, and turn to God by and by." Should you take the sword of the Spirit, which is the word of God, and drive him from this refuge, he flies to another. He then concludes with the Arminian: "Religion is a gradual thing. I do not believe in these sudden conversions. The seed must be sown, and by and by there will be a crop.

I must use the means of grace, and God will do the rest." If you force him from this retreat also, he resorts to the doctrine of efficacious grace. "No man can convert himself. We must wait God's time. Our own efforts will not avail. All that we do before regeneration, is sin. When God is pleased to convert us, he will convert us." Here his conscience is lulled, and his fears are laid asleep. God indeed commands him to repent, but he cannot, and therefore it is not his duty to attempt it.

From this "refuge of lies" the sinner must be driven, or he will perish. No man feels guilty for sinning, if he thinks he could not help it; and no man will attempt to repent, if he knows that he cannot. Pour the arrows of truth upon him like hail; under this shelter, not one of them can reach him. The only resource is to drive him from his lurking-place, and then to prostrate it in the dust.

Many of you, my hearers, I doubt not, have found a shelter under this miserable delusion. When urged to repent, you say that you cannot; and you have said this so often and believed it so long, that you deem it a doctrine of the Bible. He who attempts to refute it, seems to be driving you from a refuge which the Bible has furnished you for continuing in impenitency. Alas! if it were indeed true, you would be in a fearful condition. *You cannot repent;* and yet, if you *do not*, you must perish.

In discussing the subject which is thus suggested, I shall consider:

The meaning of the command, that the sinner make himself a new heart.

The meaning of his excuse, that he *cannot* do this.

To what extent his excuse is valid.

The real difficulty of his rendering obedience.

1. The meaning of the command. In the language of the Bible, " a new heart" is a heart which repents of sin; which believes in Jesus Christ; which loves God and obeys him. For a sinner to make himself a new heart, is the same thing as to begin to repent and believe, to love and obey. The text, then, is an express command of God to impenitent sinners, to begin the exercise of repentance, faith, and love.

2. The meaning of the excuse, that he cannot make himself a new heart. This excuse is capable of two interpretations. By the words *cannot*, *unable*, *impossible*, we sometimes denote the want of natural capacity;—for example, the want of knowledge, of understanding, or of bodily strength; and sometimes, the want of *inclination*. When a man wants natural capacity to do some particular thing, we call that which prevents him a *natural* or *physical* inability; when he wants inclination merely, we call it a *moral* inability.

The Scriptures use these words in both these meanings. They say, that with God " all things are possible," and yet they say, " It is impossible for God to lie." These two passages would contradict each other, did not the first refer to a physical, and the latter to a moral impossibility. In the same manner we say, that the Devil cannot love. In this we do not allege natural incapacity as an excuse for his malice; we only mean, that his infernal disposition prevents him from the exercise of love.

We apply this language to all the common concerns of life. An honest man cannot steal, because he is incapable of such villany. If a thief cannot steal, it is because nothing is within his reach. The poor widow could not give, because she had previously cast her two mites into the treasury. The miser cannot give, because he will not.

The sick man cannot work, because his strength is gone; the sluggard, because he is too indolent. In all languages we find words corresponding with *cannot*, *unable*, *impossible*, used to denote merely *the want of inclination*. There is a real propriety in using language in this manner, and for two reasons. One is, that our disinclination to do a thing is strong enough to render it just as certain that it will not be done, as the want of capacity would render it. Thus, it is as certain that the ever-blessed God will not lie, as if he had not capacity to lie. It is as certain that a holy angel will not sin, and that an infernal spirit will not repent, as if a natural impossibility prevented them. The other reason is, that, while a want of inclination to do a given thing lasts, it is impossible that it should be done. Thus, so long as I do not choose to raise my arm to my head, it is as impossible to raise it as if the arm were dead; and if I never should choose to raise it, I should never be able.

When, therefore, the sinner says, "I cannot make myself a new heart," or in other words, "I cannot begin to repent, and believe, and love," his language is liable to two very different constructions. It may either mean, "I am not willing to repent, to trust in Christ, to love God and obey him," or it may mean, "I have not the necessary faculties to enable me to repent, and believe, and love."

3. To what extent is the sinner's excuse valid? If by this language he intends that God has not given him the faculties necessary to enable him to repent, and this be true, the excuse is a good one. In this affirmation, common sense and the Bible perfectly harmonize. The idiot acts like a fool, yet no one blames him. The lunatic may utter profaneness or blasphemy,—may destroy his own life or the life of his neighbor, yet for these acts no one holds him responsible. An impenitent sinner may become deli-

rious, and if he dies in this state, he will perish, yet the preacher who should visit such a man and then tell him that it was his duty to repent, would be deemed a lunatic himself.

The Scriptures confirm this decision of common sense. They make our capacity the measure of our obligations. In the parable of the talents, of him who received ten, other ten were required, so also of him who received five, and so of him who received one; "of every man," says our Lord, "according to his several ability." Had there been a servant who received nothing, of him nothing would have been required. We know that this is true in the case of the idiot. To him nothing is given, and of him nothing is required. On the same principle, "To him that knoweth to do good and doeth it not, to him it is sin." His knowing, or not knowing, decides the question of guilt or innocence. On the same principle, "where there is no law, there is no transgression." Where is there no law? The answer is: When the law is absolutely unknown. On the same principle, our Lord says to the Pharisees, "If ye were blind," i. e. if ye had no knowledge of your duty, "ye should have no sin." In the final day, as we learn, a wide difference will be made among those who are to be the subjects of punishment, and this will be precisely measured by their difference of knowledge and capacity. "He who *knew* his Lord's will, and did it not," like the impenitent sinner under the gospel, "shall be beaten with many stripes." He who *knew not* "his Lord's will," or, who *knew it imperfectly*, "and did it not," like the impenitent heathen, though even his knowledge renders him without excuse, "shall be beaten with few stripes." And he who *knew it not at all*, and did it not, like the idiot, shall not be beaten at all. Though this is the general rule of God's government, and the obvious rule of justice, it may be imagined that an exception is made in the doctrine of original sin. But God takes effectual care in the Bible to guard against this mistake. He tells us that the son shall not bear the iniquity of the father; that the righteousness of the righteous shall be upon him, and the wickedness of the wicked upon him; that the soul that sinneth, it shall die; and that every man shall bear his own iniquity. In other words, no man shall bear the punishment of Adam's transgression, but merely of his own.

If, then, my hearer, you have no capacity to obey the command in the text, you are as excusable for not obeying it, as an idiot, or a lunatic, or a beast of the field. The command is not addressed to you. Christ does indeed say to his ministers, "Go, preach my gospel to every creature." An idiot is a creature, and so is a beast of the field. Yet the minister of Christ is not to carry the gospel to them, nor to command them to repent. And why not? Because they have not the requisite capacity. If, then, you have not the requisite capacity to repent, the gospel, for the same reason, is not sent to you, and repentance is not your duty. If there be such a person present, I unhesitatingly say to his *friends*, (he will not *understand* me himself,) you need not let your unhappy relative come to this sacred place. He has no more to do with the Sabbath, or the sanctuary, or the Bible, than an idiot or a lunatic. If he has been always thus destitute of capacity, you need not entertain any apprehensions as to his destiny. To whom nothing is given, of the same will nothing be required. If heretofore he had capacity and lost it, there is no remedy, for, unless God restores it, nothing can be done.

But your excuse, "I cannot make myself a new heart,"

may mean, "I have no inclination to repent, nor to believe, nor to love God." If you mean this, the excuse will not avail you. What is its real import? That you love sin too well to renounce it, or to trust in Him who offers to save you from it, or to love God and obey him. Your excuse, then, lies in *the fact* that you love sin, or in *the degree* to which you love it.

I appeal to your own conscience, whether either of these excuses can be pronounced valid. Will the *fact* that you love sin and are unwilling to renounce it, avail you? Can any being commit sin who does not love it? Can he go on in sin unless he is unwilling to renounce it? Will not this plea, then, excuse all the sin that has ever been committed? Is not this love to sin, *itself sin?* Do you not, then, plead your sin as an excuse for your sin? And do you think that your Omniscient Judge is weak enough to be thus blinded?

But you will say, "I am a descendant of apostate Adam. I was conceived in sin, and shapen in iniquity. When I sin, I only indulge the propensities of my nature. God gave me these propensities, and I cannot resist them." If you mean that, in consequence of the fall of Adam, you have lost the faculty of willing and choosing, I deny it, and appeal to the Bible and to your own consciousness for evidence that you are mistaken. There is not an hour of your life in which you do not choose or refuse. I also reply that, if you can prove that you have lost this faculty, you are not a moral agent—you are not an accountable being, and have never sinned. If you mean that, in consequence of the fall of Adam, you and all his posterity do sin, and love to sin, and choose to sin, I admit it. But how, I ask, does any being incur guilt? By *choosing* to sin. If, then, you choose to sin, God will not ask the question, How you came to choose it? Acting as a parent, you never think of asking, how your child came to choose to disobey you? Sitting as a judge, you do not ask, how the murderer came to choose to destroy his neighbor's life, or the thief to take his neighbor's property. All you ask in either case is, was the act a voluntary, wilful act? To justify punishment, all that is necessary is, to find an accountable being who has chosen to break a law which he was bound to obey. This is exactly your case.

Or will the *degree* to which you love sin, avail you? Let me then ask, Is your little child, who has just begun to disobey you, guilty and deserving of punishment; and is an older child who has been long and obstinately rebellious, innocent? Will you pursue and punish the young and faltering offender because he has violated the law of the state when he was afraid to do it, and will you let the old and hardened offender escape because he loved the villany so well that he could not help it? Do you excuse Satan because he is so full of all subtlety and all malice that he cannot help perpetrating every crime within his reach? What an excuse will this be in the eye of Omniscience! On the judgment day, those unhappy beings who will be sentenced to the lowest hell, may all allege this intense love of sin as their apology; and this very apology,—their intense love of sin,—will be the cause of their singularly dreadful sentence. Are you, then, secretly relying on such an excuse as this? Go to your closet. Meet the God whom you are refusing to obey, face to face, and there settle this controversy. There, while you remember that he is looking at you and surveying your heart, look up and say to him, "I love sin so well that I cannot forsake it." Honestly make the experiment. If it is a good excuse, it will stand in the judgment, and if you can urge it then, you can urge it now. Do not think of trusting to any excuse in that hour of awful decision, at which your voice would falter were you to utter it now. Try it, then, when you leave this house. Your soul is worth the experiment.

4. What is the real difficulty of the sinner's obeying this command? This question is entirely practical. No person ever becomes in earnest concerning his salvation, who is not compelled to answer it.

This difficulty, I would then observe, *is not on the side of God.* There is no defect in the atonement of Christ. This is full and complete; as full for Judas as it is for Peter; so that God can be just, and yet justify every one who believeth in Jesus.

Neither are you prevented, my hearer, by the want of knowledge, for you have all the knowledge that the Bible contains.

God will not take any pleasure in your death. "As I live, saith the Lord God, I have no pleasure in the death of the wicked." You will not allege that God is unwilling that you should repent. Why has he revealed his word, and given his Son, and sent his Spirit, if he is not willing?

You will not assert that Christ is not willing. He who hung on the Cross, need furnish you no evidence that he is willing to save sinners.

You are not prevented by the want of invitations. "Come unto me," says Christ from his throne of glory, "all ye that labour and are heavy laden, and I will give you rest."

The greatness of your sins does not prevent you. "Though your sins be as scarlet, they shall be white as snow; though they be red like crimson, they shall be as wool."

On the side of God, then, nothing exists, to prevent the

sinner from obeying the command of the text, but everything to prompt him to render obedience.

This difficulty, I also remark, consists not *in the Sinner's need of any additional faculties.* You cannot name the faculty that is wanting. I make the appeal directly to your conscience. What is that faculty of the mind, which, were you to possess it, you could repent? This question has been put a thousand times, and no man, Christian or sinner, has ever yet given the answer.

What faculty, I would ask again, has the mind of a Christian, which your mind possesses not? Know you not many real Christians, of inferior talents and knowledge to your own? Here your pride of understanding will give me an affirmative answer.

I will, then, enumerate your faculties. You have an understanding, to know God and his right to your obedience. You have a conscience, to feel the weight of obligation. You have intense desires for happiness, and an intense aversion to misery. You have motives strong enough in heaven and hell, if motives can be strong enough to prompt you to repentance. Finally, you have a heart that can sorrow, and trust, and love.

I then inquire, what other faculties possesses the Christian, or what others do you need, to render you capable of becoming a Christian? Perhaps, however, you will reply: "I need a *relish* for spiritual objects. Did I possess this, I should become a Christian." I admit, that if you possessed a relish for spiritual objects, that you would already *be* a Christian, but not that you would *become* a Christian. But you deceive yourself by this figurative word, relish. Our relish for the various kinds of food depends on the bodily appetite, and is not a mere matter of *choice.* But it is not thus with the relishes of the mind. What do I mean when affirming that I relish bread? That I love bread. What do I mean when affirming that I relish the character of God? That I love God. When, therefore, you tell me, that you have no relish for the character of God, and that, therefore, you cannot love him,—but strip the declaration of the figurative dress in which you have disguised it, and we have the naked fact, that you *do* not love the character of God, and therefore you *cannot* love him. On your own ground, the want of *love* is the only difficulty, and not the want of *capacity*.

But this plea, that the sinner has not capacity, is to accuse God of injustice and folly. In his law, God commands every man to love him. In the gospel, God commands every man to repent and believe. You say, that you have not capacity to obey these commands. What then should we think of God, if he had said to the stones of the streets, "Thou shalt love the Lord thy God with all thy heart?" If he had said to the beasts of the field, "Repent ye;" if he had said to the fowls of heaven, "Believe on the Lord Jesus Christ." Why would this have been folly? Merely because stones and beasts and birds have no capacity to obey. If they had this capacity, they would be proper subjects of moral government. If, then, sinners have no capacity, the folly of giving you these commands is equally great. Still more palpably would these commands be marked with injustice. God not only commands; he affixes a most awful sanction. What should we say of the parent who had required his child to do what he could not do, and had then threatened a severe punishment if the child should not obey? What say you of Nebuchadnezzar, who ordered his wise men to be cut in pieces because they could not discover a dream which he had forgotten? Yet when the judgment of the great day is over, God will send away great multitudes into everlasting punishment because they did not love him, and other multitudes because they did not repent of sin and believe in Christ. What kind of a government, then, does Jehovah exercise over his creatures? He first commands what they cannot perform, and then punishes them through eternal ages because they do not obey. Surely this is despotism without a parallel. And is Jehovah such a tyrant as this? Will you go and meet him and tell him this; and intend you, when he summons you to your trial, to rise up before the assembled universe and excuse your disobedience, by substantiating this charge against his character?

You may allege, that man originally had the needed capacity, but has lost it. This does not remove the difficulty, even in the case of Adam. A man is guilty, and ought to be punished, for putting out his own eyes. Yet when they are once put out, and you have punished him for that offence, you would not then also punish him because he could not see. But, if Adam was guilty for not obeying, after he had lost his original capacity, his children were not guilty. They never forfeited their capacity, for they never had it. If they had lost their reason by the fall of Adam, would this command be binding on them? Why not? It would have been just as true then, as now, that man originally had capacity, and that he afterwards lost it. And if loss of capacity would not have exempted from obedience then, neither does it exempt now.

The slothful servant brought the same charge against his Lord: "Lord, I knew thee, that thou art a hard man; reaping where thou hast not sown, and gathering where thou hast not strawed." This was his excuse for doing nothing. But the charge was false. When his Lord commanded his fellow-servants to bind him hand and foot and to cast him into outer darkness, he appealed to the very talent which the servant had brought wrapped in a napkin, to prove its falsehood and to justify his own sentence. Yet the impenitent sinner not only wraps his own talents in a napkin, but wastes his lord's money; and then, to excuse his sloth and perverseness, brings this very charge against the righteousness of God. Look well, then, my friend, to the ground on which you stand. You are intending to go to the bar of God, and there to justify yourself for a life of disobedience against Him. Believe me, God understands himself. He knows what he is doing, when he commands you to repent. He will not commit his character, in the face of heaven and earth. He tells you, that he will be seen and felt to be just, when he judges. "Hath he spoken, and shall he not make it good?" Will you, then, rise up in the judgment and say to him, "I knew thee, that thou wert a hard master, reaping where thou hadst not sown, and gathering where thou hadst not strewed." Take care lest he reply, "Out of thine own mouth will I judge thee, thou wicked and slothful servant."

The very language of the law also proves that want of capacity does not prevent obedience. Its language is, "Thou shalt love the Lord thy God with all thy strength; i. e. *as much as thou canst. Can* you *not* love God, as much as you *can* love him? No matter, then, what your capacity is; you can obey this law. If you *cannot* love God *at all*, you obey it in not loving him at all.

According to this scheme, I may add, there is no mercy shown in God's government. If men can not obey the law, to punish them for disobedience is despotism. Of course, there can be no mercy in pardoning them, for mercy is deliverance from deserved punishment.

What an exhibition, then, is made of the justice, the

wisdom, and the grace of God! His justice commands them to do what they cannot, under the penalty of eternal death. And then, rather than that one jot or tittle of this unjust law fail, he gives his Son to die on the cross, to deliver them from a most unjust punishment. He then offers them salvation on the conditions of faith and repentance,—conditions with which they have not capacity to comply, and yet threatens them with a far sorer punishment if they do not comply. Did Jesus then ascend the cross, and did the multitude of the heavenly host come down, shouting, "Glory to God in the highest,"—to mock a ruined world with such an offer as this?

Facts also prove that the sinner wants not capacity to obey this command. "Not many wise men after the flesh, not many mighty,—are called; but God hath chosen the weak things of the world to confound the mighty, and the foolish things of the world to confound the wise." "I thank thee, O Father! Lord of heaven and earth, that thou hast hid these things from the wise and prudent, and revealed them unto babes." The same has been true in every age. In the day when God shall separate the righteous from the wicked, it will appear, that many little children had capacity enough to repent and believe, while men of wisdom and experience had not. Then, multitudes of the feeblest intellect will be found to have been wise unto salvation, where men of brilliant talents and powerful understanding have been confounded. Then, the poor degraded Hottentot, scarce elevated above the beasts that perish, will be found to have loved the Lord his God, while the scholar and the gentleman of Europe and America, educated in the dwelling of refinement, and perhaps of piety, *could not* love.

The reason for the necessity of the Holy Spirit's renewing agency also proves, that there is no defect in the sinner's capacity. Were there any such defect, the first thing for the Spirit to do would be to remove it. But when this Omniscient Agent comes to the sinner's mind and examines it within and without, his eye is able to discover no such defect as this. Every power and faculty of the soul is in full exercise. He finds sufficient understanding, and knowledge, and memory, and imagination. He finds a will which chooses and refuses, and affections which can love and hate, can hope and fear, can rejoice and be sorry. He finds a conscience which is able, if the sinner has not seared it with a hot iron, to distinguish between right and wrong, and to feel the weight of obligation. All is right, but the will and the affections. Nothing hinders the sinner but an unwilling heart, and all that the Spirit does is to render it willing.

This difficulty, I would then remark, is merely the want of inclination. It follows, irresistibly, from what has been already proved. We have seen that, on the side of God, every difficulty in the sinner's way is removed. God also commands him to repent. He offers him heaven, if he obeys; and tells him that hell is his portion, if he disobeys. The sinner, we have seen, is also *able* to repent; still he refuses, and does not repent. But if he is not prevented from without, and has also the requisite capacity, what can prevent him but the want of inclination?

The Scriptures allege this as the reason. They do this, in their commands. They say to the sinner, "Choose you this day whom you will serve." They say, "Whosoever will, let him take of the water of life."

They do so, in assigning the reasons of his punishment. He is punished because he hated knowledge, and did not choose the fear of the Lord. They, who are excluded from the marriage supper, are those who are bidden and would not come.

They do this, in express declarations. "Ye will not come to me, that ye might have life." "Ye hate the light, and will not come to the light, lest your deeds should be reproved."

What takes place in the sinner's conversion shews this. This may be well illustrated by a familiar case. You learn that your child is beating his brother, and send a servant commanding him to stop. The servant delivers the message, and the child knows that it comes from yourself. But, because you are at a distance, and he does not see you, he refuses obedience and still persists. You yourself then come in sight, and raise your hand, or speak to him; he then stops in a moment. God sees the sinner transgressing his law every day and hour, and holding on his course to perdition. He sends his servant, with a message to the sinner, commanding him to stop. "Stop, sinner, says the servant of God, or you will perish." The sinner knows that the message comes from God. But God is out of sight, and the danger at a distance, and the gratification at hand; and he will not stop. By and by the Spirit of God comes to the sinner, and looks at him, and speaks to him with his still small voice; and the sinner, looking up, sees and knows that it is God himself who commands him to stop. Now, indeed, he stops, and is willing to repent, but he loved sin so well that, like the child, he would not do it when the message of God was brought to him by a servant. My hearer, you here see your precise case. I come as the servant of God, and bring you his message. You know that it is his command, but you will not obey. Your excuse is, that God does not come to you in person, and bring you the message himself. The child was just as able to stop when the servant spoke to him, as when he saw his father approaching. You are just as able to repent, when the servant of God commands you, in his name to repent, and as fully know it to be your immediate duty, as you would be if God himself were to approach and make you feel that he thus commanded you. Remember that God himself is present when his servant delivers you this message. He observes and records the manner in which you treat his command; and he does it to bring it out on your trial as the ground and measure of your last sentence.

This Discussion would be incomplete, without several Reflections. We understand what the sinner's excuse means. When the embassador of God brings to him the command to repent and believe, the sinner's lips say, "I *cannot*," but his heart says, "I will not." This, my friend, is precisely the answer which God himself hears uttered by your heart every time that his known command is brought to your mind. Remember, that you utter this language when you know that God is in sight, and when, if you would but open your eyes, you would see his eye fixed upon you and marking your decision. This is the very language which he will *now* hear you utter, if you now refuse to obey him. And do you wonder that he, who knows his Lord's will and did it not, shall be beaten with many stripes? Does the declaration of Christ surprise you, that "it shall be more tolerable for Sodom and Gomorrah, in the day of judgment, than for you?"

The meaning of the awakened sinner's excuse, when he says, "My *heart* is so wicked, that I *cannot* repent," is thus also understood. My hearer, what is your *heart?* It is *yourself*. Do not, then, lay the blame on your heart, and thus shift it from yourself. Tell the simple, naked truth: "I am so wicked, that I will not love God, nor forsake my sins, nor trust in my Saviour."

Equally evident is the nature of the sinner's dependence on the Holy Spirit for regeneration. It is a *moral* dependence, merely. The sinner is so wicked that he will never turn to God, unless the Holy Ghost turns him. If he would but choose salvation himself, he would have it. Because he will not choose it himself, the Spirit of God comes to him and renders him willing.

Let me urge you, then, my unforgiven hearer, to lay aside every excuse, and listen to the known and plain commands of God. Needs it much faith to believe, that the commands of God are reasonable and right? Calls it for much sacrifice of pride, to admit that you cannot offer a good excuse for disobeying God? If God commands, and you refuse to obey, either you or God, must be in the wrong; and which, think you, in the day of judgment, will make out his case? Until you abandon every evasion, and every attempt at evasion, and come to this conclusion, "I can have no excuse for disobeying God," you will never repent.

When, then, does God command you to repent? Now. To-day. This hour. Did you not seek to hide yourself behind some "refuge of lies," you would be compelled this very moment to repent of your sins, or directly to brave the wrath of the Almighty.

Come, then, and let your heart say what your conscience has already said,—"God commands me to repent now: I have no excuse for disobeying him; I will not seek to find one. I will arise, and go to my Father, and will say unto him, "Father, I have sinned against heaven, and before thee." Believe me, that, while you are yet a great way off, he will have compassion on you. While he welcomes you to his family as a returning child, he will say to those who surround his throne, "Rejoice with me, my children, this day; for this my son was dead, and is alive again; he was lost and is found."

REGENERATION, A SOVEREIGN WORK.

JOHN III: 8.

THE WIND BLOWETH WHERE IT LISTETH, AND THOU HEAREST THE SOUND THEREOF, BUT CANST NOT TELL WHENCE IT COMETH, NOR WHITHER IT GOETH: SO IS EVERY ONE THAT IS BORN OF THE SPIRIT.

OUR Lord declares in the context, that a man must be born of the Spirit, to enter into the kingdom of God. For this he assigns two reasons. The first is, that he who has not been born of the Spirit, but has merely experienced the first or natural birth, is not fit for the kingdom. "That which is born of the flesh, is flesh." The second is, that he who is born of the Spirit, is fit for it. "That which is born of the Spirit, is spirit. In the text he points out the manner in which the Spirit operates, in effecting this change. "The wind bloweth where it listeth, and thou hearest the sound thereof, but canst not tell whence it cometh and whither it goeth, so is every one that is born of the Spirit." In this comparison we should observe, in what respects the blowing of the wind and the influence of the Spirit in regeneration are said to resemble each other. Both are free, on their part; both are uncontrollable, on ours; and both are secret. "The wind bloweth where it listeth." No man can regulate the wind, and determine in what direction it shall blow. So far from this, he cannot tell whence it cometh, nor from what place it takes its rise, nor from what cause it proceeds. No man can determine what effects it will produce. So far from this, he does not even know whither it goeth. In the same manner the Spirit of God works as he pleases. No one can regulate his operations. No one can foretell at what time, in what place, and in what persons, they will commence, nor to what extent they will be carried on.

We are thus taught, that the Holy Spirit is entirely free and sovereign in the work of regeneration. In illustrating this principle, I shall endeavor to establish these two propositions:

That God acts as free, and sovereign, in the work of regeneration; and

That his acting thus, is in itself right.

That God is thus free and sovereign, will be evident from the following considerations:

Particularly, in the choice of the *Persons* on whom he is to bestow his grace, God acts according to his own pleasure. This truth is confirmed, both by the Scriptures, and by our own observation. When our Lord began his public ministry he selected his disciples. In doing this, Mark tells us, that he "called unto him whom he would." The twelve whom he ordained, were fishermen and publicans. This choice contravenes all the principles on which we should have acted. Had we been left to choose those who were to be the apostles and pillars of the church, we should have selected men of learning and talents. But if they must be ignorant men and men in humble life, why not carpenters, or husbandmen, as well as fishermen and publicans? Certainly there is nothing in the occupation of a fisherman, which qualifies him to preach the gospel. But if they must be fishermen and publicans, why must they be these rather than others? Matthew tells us, that "Jesus, walking by the sea of Galilee, saw two brethren, Simon and Andrew. And he said unto them, 'Follow me.' And going on from thence, he saw two other fishermen, James, the son of Zebedee, and John, his brother, mending their nets; and he called them." Were there no other fishermen on the sea of Galilee, or in Judea, but these? When Jesus was passing by that sea and saw those others; why did he not call them? Others were as good as they. They were as well informed and possessed of as much understanding. Why, then, were these singled out? The fact that Jesus called these fishermen, was the reason why they followed him. It was the reason why they went to heaven, and why they will sit with him in the final judgment, and why they will be admitted to distinguished honor in the church on high. What a difference will there be between their situation through eternity, and that of the other fishermen on the sea of Galilee! Yet this difference will all be owing to the single fact that Jesus *called them*, while he passed the others by.

The same truth was impressively exemplified at the crucifixion of Christ. If we had been present on that occasion, and had been called upon to select the individual, whose sins Christ would then forgive, and whose soul he would sanctify, perhaps the last man whom we should have named, would have been one of the malefactors. They were robbers, hardened in guilt, and justly condemned to that ignominious death. After they had been nailed to the cross, also, they joined with the multitude in reviling Jesus. What men were ever more unlikely to repent. Yet one of them, just as life was about to expire, repented and believed in Jesus. If mercy was to be shewn in this manner, why was it not shewn to both the malefactors? Or, if it was to be shewn to but one of them, why to this one, rather than to the other? So far as appears, there was no difference between them as to their guilt. Why, then, this vast difference in their allotments; one of them in Paradise, the other, as we have the best reason to believe, in the world of misery?

Had we been present with Saul of Tarsus and the band of soldiers who accompanied him on his way to Damascus, and had we known that one of the company was to be made a subject of divine grace, should we have selected as that individual the furious, persecuting bigot, who had just before consented to the death of Stephen and made havoc of the church; who was still breathing out threatenings and slaughter against the disciples, and was even now on a journey to Damascus to seize them and bring them bound to Jerusalem; or one of the ignorant soldiers who had never even heard of the name of Jesus?

In these instances, and in others like them, in the New Testament, how can we account for the fact, that such a difference was actually made between those who were converted to God and those who were not? Will it be said that the disciples were called because Christ, being omniscient, saw that those individuals were the proper persons for the work he designed them, rather than the other fishermen; that this was eminently true in the case of Paul; and that something of this nature must be also supposed in the case of the penitent thief; and that therefore he called these persons, rather than the others? I admit it. And this is unquestionably true in every other case. This is also the very principle for which we contend. When we say that God is free and sovereign in this work, we do not say that he acts without a good reason in any case; but that in every instance of regeneration, for reasons which are always the best, but which he has not thought proper to disclose to us, he acts freely and according to his own pleasure; and that his own choice determines him with regard to every person, whether to convert him or not.

This account of the subject, given in the Scriptures, is confirmed by daily observation. As we look around upon our fellow-men we see numbers every where who give satisfactory evidence that they are the subjects of regeneration. We see also a still greater number who give no such evidence. The first class differ from the second, only because God made them to differ. If we examine these two classes we cannot discover any rule by which God is governed in the work of regeneration. Sometimes God bestows his grace on men who are ignorant and of very humble capacity, who seem to stand on the lowest verge of intellect, while he passes by other men of learning and wisdom. Often he confers it on the poor and the unknown, while he denies it to the rich and the honorable. We are often apt to wonder that certain individuals around us,—men of talents and wealth,—are not renewed. If some one or other rich man were to become a Christian, we often say,—what an amount of wealth would flow into the treasury of the Lord. If such a man of splendid and powerful talents were to become a Christian, how much good might he not do to the church of Christ. God does not see fit, however, to put their wealth or their talents in requisition. He passes them by, and calls into his kingdom the beggar and the outcast. Sometimes he selects persons of rough native tempers, who, if they become Christians, will exhibit very little of the Christian character, and yet does not renew others around them who are distinguished for native sweetness of temper, and who might exhibit the graces of piety in all their beauty and loveliness. Sometimes we see the children of wicked parents, made the subjects of renewing and sanctifying grace; and the children of pious parents, left to final impenitence. Abijah, the child of Jeroboam—the son of Nebat, who made Israel to sin, had some good thing found in him towards the Lord God of Israel, while the children of Eli and Samuel had not. Occasionally we see those who have been gross sinners, nay, those who have been openly and scandalously profligate, brought to repentance, while those who are far less hardened, perish in their sins. This, I admit, is not common. Yet in every age of the church, God has manifested his sovereignty in the work of conversion by examples of this nature. The conversion of old sinners is also not frequent. Yet we sometimes see sinners of this description become penitent, when those who are young seek salvation a long time and yet do not obtain it.

God appears to act according to his own pleasure, also, as to the *Time* of bestowing his grace. The Scriptures mention several instances, in which children were sanctified from their birth. It is the common belief of ministers, that such instances occasionally exist at present. When such a case occurs, what reason can we give for the selection? Why was this child thus sanctified at the very dawn of life, when his brothers and sisters and the children of the neighboring families were not? The only answer to this question is, "Even so, Father, for so it seemed good in thy sight." Still more frequent are the instances, in which persons are converted to God in early childhood.

God thus takes some in the morning of life into his service; he permits others to go on in sin through youth and manhood, and in old age, when they are unable to serve him, he calls them into his kingdom. We find a remarkable difference in those who are earnestly seeking salvation, as to the length of time which elapses before they find it. When the power of the Holy Ghost is felt upon the heart; when the attention is arrested to the interests of eternity; when the conscience is enlivened; when a deep sense of guilt is felt and the danger of the wrath of God is strongly realized; we see some almost immediately become the subjects of repentance towards God and faith in the Lord Jesus Christ. Others continue, not only for months, but for years, convinced that they are sinners, and that without a personal interest in the mediation of Christ, they must perish, and still they make no progress in the way to heaven. To give up seeking salvation, they dare not; yet when they attempt to pass through the straight gate and enter on the narrow way, they grope for the wall at noonday as the blind. Remarkable instances of this nature occur in every revival of religion. On such occasions we sometimes see those who have been openly profligate, becoming in a few days the subjects of regeneration, and proving the reality of the change wrought in them by a life of holiness; while others, who are amiable in their manners and correct in their deportment, continue a long time convinced of their sin and danger before they are renewed.

God is equally free and sovereign in the *Manner and Circumstances* of bestowing his mercy. If we knew that during the existing year, one hundred of the persons now present would become the subjects of renewing grace, we could not conjecture the time, the place, the occasion, nor the circumstances, in which God would bestow it on any one of them. If we possessed the spirit of prophecy and could know every sermon and every prayer which they would hear, every chapter and religious book which they would read, and every religious conversation to which they might listen,—every means of grace, in short, at which they would be present; we could not probably select, in a single instance, *that one*, which the Holy Spirit would make effectual. Two men shall be sitting on the same seat at church, listening to the same sermon; one a youth, the other, a man of gray hairs. The truth of God shall be faithfully preached. The youth will, perhaps, resist it; while the gray-haired sinner will perceive for the first time that it is quick and powerful, and sharper than any two-edged sword, and by means of an agency of which he is not conscious, will yield to its influence. It is in consequence of this fact, that means, apparently the most powerful, are often ineffectual; while those which seem the least likely to produce the effect in question, are followed with a blessing. All of us have heard the story of the Virginia planter, now a faithful and zealous preacher of the gospel, who severely whipped his pious slave for praying with the other negroes, and who soon after became a Christian in consequence of hearing the same slave's praying earnestly for his forgiveness. I myself once knew a lofty-minded young man of fine talents, enter a place of worship, to divert himself with the style and delivery of the preacher, a man of seventy-five years of age, eminent for piety, but of moderate talents, and unusually awkward in his manner. He left the place, however, not merely ashamed of the spirit with which he entered it, but convinced that he was a sinner, and anxious to learn the way of salvation.

In the immediate effects produced by this divine agency

in different cases, we see similar proofs of sovereign power in the Agent. Some are drawn to the Saviour by the cords of love; others are driven from perdition by the fears of wrath. Some find their attention arrested, while listening to a representation of the love of God; others, of the sufferings of Christ; others, of the agency of the Holy Spirit; others still, of the dreadful punishment which awaits the finally impenitent. In some of these instances the heart may be melted, and yields at once. In others, it is overwhelmed with terror, under a sense of its own sin and desert of the anger of God. In some, also, the evidence of a genuine conversion is so strong as to leave no room for doubt. In others, it is so feeble, that years may pass away before the subject of it ventures to profess the religion of Christ.

In selecting the *Places* where, at a given time, the work of regeneration shall be carried on, God also acts according to his own pleasure. I need not tell my audience that there are places where, for a long period, no marks of God's renewing agency are visible. The gospel is faithfully and powerfully preached, and yet, to most who hear it, it appears to become a savor of death unto death. At the same time, in some neighboring town, no one is left to doubt whether God is present. All who dwell there feel and acknowledge his presence. Many of them rejoice that his power and glory have been manifested. Others are so conscious of the fact that they also believe and tremble. The inhabitants of the latter place in great numbers give themselves up to God. Those of the former go to their graves in impenitence. What, let me ask, has occasioned this difference? Why is all the surrounding region enveloped in clouds and gloom; and why over this little favored spot have the clouds dispersed, so that those who dwell there can look through, and see the face of heaven, and behold the light of the Sun of righteousness? Still more sovereign is the exercise of God's grace at this moment, in the distinction which he often makes between Christian and heathen lands. This town in which we live is a remarkable example of this nature. It was settled by as pious a race of emigrants as this world ever saw. For one hundred and thirty years, pure and undefiled religion revived and flourished among the inhabitants. But for the last seventy, no one who dwells here has beheld an extensive revival of religion. During that period two generations have gone to the grave; the rich man and the ancient, the proud man and the honorable, as well as the poor and the outcast; and how few of them, is there any reason to hope, were the subjects of repentance towards God and faith in our Lord Jesus Christ? And what is the fact at this moment? The gospel is preached in its purity to Tartars, to Hindoos, to Hottentots, and they hear it and obey it; while here in the land of the Pilgrims, how many thousands seem to be more beyond the dominion of that gospel which Jesus published and which Paul preached, than were they in the centre of New Holland! Two children are born the same year. One of them is born in the mansion of refinement and piety, is given up to God in baptism, and early taught the way to heaven. The other is born in a Hottentot cabin, and knows of no god but an an image of wood. God, however, sends him a missionary, who preaches to him salvation by the blood of Christ. His heart is opened to receive the truth, and he is baptized into the name of Jesus. The other continues impenitent, and his parents perhaps go to their graves without any evidence that their prayers have been heard. Take a still stronger instance. A faithful minister of Christ, in this commonwealth, preaches to a congregation for thirty years, and is all that time left to mourn, because he labors in vain and spends his strength for naught. Another stations himself in a Hottentot village, and before he is able to master their language, he sees that his sermons in broken Hottentot have been accompanied with a blessing, and that half of those who hear him are inquiring the way to heaven.

We see, then, that in the choice of the persons on whom to bestow his grace,—in the time, in the manner and circumstances, and in the places in which he bestows it, God acts as if he were free and sovereign.

Our second proposition is, that God's acting thus is in itself right.

That it is right in God to regenerate those, whom he actually regenerates, every one will admit. The only question, therefore, is,—Whether God is under any obligation to convert those who are not converted. We say that he is free from any obligation of this nature.

Particularly, God is under no obligation from his *Justice.* Regeneration is the communication of holiness to a mind which is entirely destitute of it. What is holiness ? It is love, or benevolence ; love to God with all the heart, and to our neighbor as ourselves. What is sin ? It is disobedience to the law which requires this love. Why does not a sinner obey this law, and thus become the subject of this love ? It is not from the want of excellence in God, or of knowledge of that excellence on the part of the sinner. It is not from the want of a conscience to feel the force of his obligation to obey the law, nor from the want of motives to induce obedience, nor from the want of a capacity to love and hate. It is, simply, from the want of choice. Whenever the Omniscient Spirit examines man's heart to see what is the difficulty, he discovers none but this, that he *will not* obey. Not a sin has he ever committed, but it was *voluntary*,—the result of choice. And all that is now wanting to the sinner's regeneration is, his being willing, even for a single moment, to obey that great command,—Thou shalt love God supremely and thy neighbor as thyself. The Holy Spirit undertook the office of the Sanctifier, not because there was any physical defect in the sinner's mind, but merely because he has an *unwilling heart*. What claim then, has any sinner on the justice of God to convert him, and how would he urge his claims when called upon to state them? Were the beasts of the field commanded to love God, they might truly say that they have not capacity to discern his moral excellence, nor consciences to feel the force of obligation; and they might, therefore, justly demand a new creation before they could incur guilt. But all that the sinner can allege is, that he loves sin so well that he is not willing to obey God; and he therefore insists that God shall make him willing. How must such a claim as this sound in the ear of God's justice!

If the sinner can justly claim regeneration, then he has a right to eternal life. In other words, God had no right to punish him, nor to refuse to admit him to heaven. But if it was unjust to punish the transgressors, then Christ's death was unnecessary to save him from punishment. And if the sinner had a right to heaven, then Christ's righteousness was unnecessary to purchase heaven. Of course the mediation and death of Christ were unnecessary, and salvation is not a matter of grace but of justice.

Eternal life is the greatest gift which God can give. It is to give Himself to the sinner as his portion. It is to allow him to dwell in his own immediate presence forever. If the sinner had perfectly obeyed the law, he could not have asserted a title to such a portion as this. If he had received it, it must have been merely as a free gift; and to a free gift, in the very nature of the case, we cannot lay claim. But the sinner, instead of perfect obedience, has always disobeyed, and can claim therefore nothing but punishment.

But he may say, I have been long endeavoring to obtain salvation, and it would be now unjust to cast me off. Let me then ask him, in reply,—Had you any right to salvation before you began to seek it? This question, we have seen, he must answer in the negative. We ask, then, again,—Does any thing you have hitherto done, merit salvation? The Bible is here explicit. It tells us, that the best efforts of the most eminent Christian do not in the least merit salvation. If, then, the sinner's efforts had been the result of holiness, they could not on the ground of justice have merited any thing. What shall then be said of the efforts which he has actually made? He has read his Bible, and attended public worship, and attempted to pray, and contributed to the poor and to religious charities, and led a sober, moral life, and he has often felt a strong apprehension that he should finally perish. If he has done all this, and have not love, Paul tells him, that he is nothing. Has he not done them all, because he believed and trembled, and because he hoped that the gift of God could be purchased with such a price as this? Has he in this way advanced a step towards holiness? Is he not a greater sinner now than when he began? Can he then have acquired any claims on the justice of God? Instead of this, has he not offended God anew, by refusing to obey the great law of the gospel dispensation, "Repent and believe." Originally, then, he had no claims on the ground of justice, and he has subsequently acquired none.

God will be, therefore, perfectly just, should he not convert him.

The sinner may also say, that his parents were unusually pious : that they gave him up to God, and prayed earnestly and often for his salvation. But his parents did not merit any thing for themselves ; still less, therefore, do their prayers or their efforts merit salvation for him.

Neither has such a person any claim on the *Holiness* of God. A holy being does indeed love holiness wherever he finds it. But there is nothing even in the best services of any impenitent person which such a being can love. He cannot name an exercise of his heart, or an action of his life, in which God can discover holiness.

As little is his claim on the *Mercy* of God. To speak of claims on the divine mercy, is a solecism. The very term, mercy, implies that we have no claims whatever. It is, in the nature of the case, impossible to exercise mercy towards any one who is not justly condemned.

God is under no obligations from his own *Veracity*, to convert him. God has made no promise to any impenitent man whatever. Sinners are not the children of the promise, nor the heirs of promise. The promises were made to Abraham and his seed, but sinners are not the seed of Abraham. Promises are made only to those who have faith to trust in them. God has laid many commands on sinners, requiring them to repent, and believe, and obey, and threatening them with his sore displeasure, if they do not. He has also promised them eternal life if they do. But there is not, in either Testament, a single promise on the part of God that he will regenerate any sinner. God has no where laid himself under bonds to any one who is destitute of holiness. The sinner might spend one hundred, or one thousand years, in just such efforts to obtain salvation ; and, if he should fail of it at last, the veracity of God would be still inviolable. Nay, these very efforts would have only served, for the time, as his excuse for not repenting of his sins and believing in Christ.

Neither has God laid himself under any such obligations *by any thing which he has done.* The sinner may allege, that he has been long seeking salvation, and that others who began long after him, have found it. If the sinner has sought it, still he has not merited it ; and, if others have received it, God replies to him, " May I not lawfully do what I will with mine own ?" He may allege that those who are far more guilty than himself, have been pardoned. True ; God had a right to manifest the riches of his grace in forgiving them, but this did not bind him to forgive others. The sinner cannot then complain, unless he had a right to forgiveness himself. He may allege that the number of those who will be saved, will be very great. It will. Yet the salvation of each is a matter of mere grace on the part of God. Any one of them might have perished, and so might all of them, and yet God would have been perfectly excellent. If God is pleased in his mercy to save them, he manifests the riches of his grace, but he does not lay himself under any obligation to save others.

The subject, as all perceive, is directly practical. As one of its lessons, we may observe, that a moral life will not secure for any man his regeneration. It is a most difficult thing to persuade men of this truth. Many a hearer surveys his life, and it differs so little from the lives of many Christians, that he must believe that God regards it with some degree of approbation. The young ruler's conclusion was the same. He had kept the whole law from his youth up. Had he been present at the crucifixion and seen the thief on the cross, he could not have believed it possible that mercy should have been extended to him rather than to himself. Yet the thief on the cross repented, and is now in Paradise. But the young man whom Jesus loved, went away from him, and never returned. If the grace of God is freely given, it is not given as the reward of morality. Should the most moral man now living, mention his morality in his prayer for the gift of God's saving grace, how would God regard it? Would he not remember before opening his lips, that it is not by works of righteousness which we have done, but according to his mercy he saves us; and would not this truth compel him to be silent? We must be justified, either by faith, or by works. To him that worketh, i. e. doeth all his duty, " the reward is reckoned of debt. But to him that worketh not, but believeth on him that justifieth the ungodly, his faith is counted for righteousness." If the sinner expects to obtain salvation in any degree by his morality, he rejects the gospel. The salvation of the gospel is merely of grace. If the moral and immoral man both continue impenitent, both will perish. If either of them is saved, it will be wholly owing to unmerited grace. If, then, the moral man does not renounce his dependence on his morality, and trust in nothing but the righteousness of Christ, he will certainly come short of eternal life.

As little can regeneration be purchased by our prayers, or other religious observances. The impenitent man often flatters himself that there is something meritorious in his use of the means of grace. He thinks of the difference between himself and others. He reads his Bible, and venerates the Sabbath, and goes to the sanctuary, and prays,—it may be in his family and in his closet,—and they do none of those things. So did the Pharisees and Scribes, and thanked God they were not as other men. They intended to purchase heaven by these services, and so does the hearer in question; forgetting, that "they that are in the flesh cannot please God."

But the hearer may say, If these services have no merit, and do not avail any thing to procure my salvation, then I will give up my Bible, and the Sabbath, and prayer. I answer; This is a controversy which you must settle, not with me, but with God. He requires of you repentance, and faith, and love. What is your language to him? If you will let me offer prayers, and read my Bible, and go to the sanctuary, without faith and love and repentance, I will do so. If not, I will give them up. But, in either case, I will not repent, nor believe, nor love. The sinner needs ask now but his own conscience, how this controversy will be settled?

It is no objection to any one's coming to Christ, that he has been a very great sinner. If God is entirely free and sovereign in communicating his grace,—if morality cannot purchase salvation,—then a great sinner has just as much a right to repent and believe as one who has committed fewer sins. "Pardon my iniquity," said David, "for it is great." The greatness of his sins was the very reason why he asked for pardon, and why he urged his plea. Is there then present any one who has grown old in sin, or sinned against great light and strong conviction, or who has committed great and enormous sins—so great, that he fears that God cannot forgive them? Let me tell him, this day, that God is free and sovereign in granting his mercy. This day he offers you pardon, on the simple condition that you will accept of it. Go to him, then, in all your sin. Go now; and though your sins are as scarlet and as crimson, they shall become whiter than snow.

What, then, is the immediate duty of every impenitent hearer? It is, to repent of his sins, and to believe in Jesus Christ. Why should not every such person comply with this demand? Have you not trusted long enough to your prayers, and your punctual performance of the external duties of religion? Have they advanced you a step towards heaven? Is not enough of life wasted already? Is not the day of life to many far spent, and are not the shadows of the evening approaching? Why, then, continue any longer in this wretched course, when, if you do not repent, you must perish; if you do not believe, you must be damned?

THE CHURCH.

1 TIM. III: 15.

THE CHURCH OF THE LIVING GOD, THE PILLAR AND GROUND OF THE TRUTH.

THE great design of Christ's mission was to redeem sinful man from the curse of the law, and from the bondage of sin. To secure its accomplishment, he has directed those who are thus redeemed to form themselves into a voluntary association, as his visible followers, and to become a peculiar people, distinguished from the rest of mankind by holiness of life. This association is known by various names in the Scriptures, but its proper designation as an organized body is, The Church, and, The Church of Christ.

This association was established immediately after the Fall, when God revealed to our first parents the covenant of grace. It was established also as a permanent institution, to exist so long as the work of redemption should continue to be carried on; it has been always peculiarly dear to its founder, and has received from him numberless marks of his constant protection and attachment. It existed and flourished under the patriarchal form, in the family of Seth, during the ages before the flood, and in the family of

Shem, until the recovery of Israel from Egypt. It became national in its constitution, at the giving of the law on Mount Sinai, and was ultimately extended to the whole family of man immediately after the crucifixion of Christ. While it has thus assumed three forms in different ages of the world, yet it has been always one and the same Association, founded on the same covenant, existing for the same purposes, and composed of men possessing visibly the same character.

It is my intention to consider:

The Nature of the Church; and

The Design of its institution.

In considering its Nature, I would observe:

It is a *voluntary association.* In its present form, all men are freely invited to join it; and none who wish to do this may be lawfully excluded, if they possess the requisite qualifications for admission. None, however, may be compelled to join it, for those who are its members, become so by their own voluntary act. They may not, indeed, subsequently leave it, for at their entrance they voluntarily covenant, that they will continue its members through life, seeking its prosperity and submitting to its discipline. All its members have a right to its privileges, and none can be deprived of them unless they disobey the laws by which the community is governed.

The more advantageously to answer the design of the association, it is divided into *numerous smaller associations*, each of which is called a church, having its own members and government, but constituting a part of the Church universal.

Though its members are subject to the laws and rulers of the countries to which they belong, yet the association is *subject to no legislator but Christ*, and to no laws but such as he has established. The civil magistrate, as such, has no connexion with it, nor any right to regulate its concerns. "My kingdom," said the Redeemer, "is not of this world." If the magistrate in any degree undertakes to control it, he thrusts himself into the place of Christ, and usurps his authority.

The members of this community are *all on an equality.* The king and the beggar, the sage and the peasant, if connected with it, stand on one common level. The rich and the poor here meet together; the Lord is maker of them all. Christ has indeed committed the care and oversight of the church to two classes of officers, pastors and deacons. They are to regulate its external concerns, and to watch over its welfare. But its internal regulations,—the admission and exclusion of its members, are left to the church itself. One class of the officers is elected by the church, and every member is eligible. The other class maintain their own succession; yet every member possessing the requisite qualifications, is, on his request, admitted to their number. Thus, according to the charter which it has received from Christ, it is, in the management of its own concerns, a pure democracy,—subject to no regulations but those which itself has made, and those which Christ has given it.

Its members *profess to be the friends of Christ.* This profession he has required to be public. It is made when each individual is united to the body itself, to point him out to the members and the world, as an avowed disciple and follower. In this profession they avow their faith in Christ and in the truths which he taught; dedicate themselves and all that they have to his service; covenant to obey him; and are baptised into his name. At stated seasons also they meet together, to celebrate his death, and to dedicate their children to him in baptism.

In its present state it consists of *numerous divisions*, each of which has no connexion with the rest. These differ widely in their government, their belief, their purity, their discipline, and in their forms of worship, and of administering the ordinances. All of them also are exceedingly imperfect. Some churches do not require the prescribed qualifications for the admission of members, nor in the officers of the church. These soon grow corrupt in doctrine, and discipline, and life, and ultimately cease to constitute a part of the Christian community. Other churches, however careful, are liable to deception, and admit members who are not really qualified for admission. The consequence is, that no local church of any considerable numbers can, probably, be found, which has not some members of this character. Christ himself, however, taught his disciples that this would be the fact. This prediction led them to expect that the tares would always be found mingled with the wheat.

Such is a brief account of the nature of this Association, the Church of Christ, as it now exists, and substantially, as it has existed since its first institution.

We are also to consider the Design of the Church's institution.

This was, particularly, to furnish mankind with *standing evidence of the truth of the Christian Religion.* That such a body as the Church exists, is certain. That it has existed in its present form from a short time following the crucifixion of Christ, is also certain from historical evidence. It has in its possession a book, called the New Testament. The gospel of Matthew,—a part of that book,—was written, as we may learn from such evidence, eight years, and that of Mark but twelve years, after Christ's death. These contain a full account of his birth, life, miracles, and instructions; of his institution of the Church; of his death and resurrection; of his commission to the apostles and their successors to convert all nations to his religion; and of his ascension. These accounts were in the possession of the eleven apostles, who were eye-witnesses of every transaction; of his other disciples, who had witnessed most of them; and of his enemies who had seen many of them, and were able to contradict them all if they were not true. Yet no contradiction of them is left on record. The eleven apostles did not contradict them. Instead of this, they everywhere preached Jesus of Nazareth, and converted thousands and hundreds of thousands to the faith of Christ. The other followers of Christ did the same. The enemies of Christ opposed the diffusion of his religion by persecution and violence, but never dared to contradict the truth of the gospels. Thus the facts of the perpetuation of the Church, and of its constant possession of the New Testament, furnish us the highest evidence which the nature of the case will admit of the truth of the gospel history, and far higher evidence than we can procure in any other case, of the truth of any fact transmitted from antiquity. It is thus owing to the Church of Christ, that its members and mankind at large are furnished with evidence which will not admit of a doubt, that all the events recorded in the life of Christ are literally true, and that the Christian religion is, of course, divine.

The Church was also designed, to *transmit the truth of God in its purity.* Within a very short time after the death of Christ, numerous churches were formed in Western Asia and Eastern Europe; and not long after, in the south of Europe and the north of Africa. The consequence was, that copies of the Scriptures were early and widely diffused. Every church at least, and many private Christians also, had a copy. Thus widely circulated, they could not be destroyed by the most vigorous efforts of persecution. Equally vain was every attempt materially to corrupt them. The Church was soon divided into sects, and each sect possessed numerous copies of the Scriptures. No sect, in attempting to establish its own sentiments, could misquote the Scriptures, or attempt to circulate incorrect copies, without detection. The same has been true in every age. Copies of the Scriptures have been always thus multiplied. The Church has been always divided, and each division has watched the conduct of every other to see that no attempt was made to corrupt the purity of the written text. We have thus far higher evidence that the text of the Bible is genuine, than with regard to any other book. Thus the Church has been "the pillar of the truth."

Controversy has always existed also with the world, about the genuineness of Christianity; and among the different divisions of the Church, respecting the true meaning of the Scriptures. Against an unbelieving world, the whole Church has united to defend the divine origin of Christianity. The external defence of natural and revealed religion in opposition to Atheists and Deists, has thus been so effectually secured that it cannot be attacked. In settling the real meaning of the Scriptures, these divisions of the Church which have been most distinguished for holiness and for love to Christ, have always united in supporting the real truth of God. This controversy has been long continued, and much of it is now brought to a close. Wherever it is still maintained, if ably conducted, truth always gains, and error loses. When finally brought to a close, the real meaning of the Scriptures will be so firmly established, and the true nature of Christianity so universally understood, that no material error will afterwards find adherents. In this sense the Church will deserve the title—"The Light of the world."

The Church was no less designed, to *preserve the religion of Christ* through every age. The great means of preserving the religion of Christ in the world have been the Sabbath, the preaching of the gospel, the circulation of the Scriptures, and the religious education of children. In heathen and Mohammedan lands there is no Sabbath, and of course no knowledge of God or salvation. But the reason why they have no Sabbath is, that they have no church of Christ. The moment the Church is established, there that moment the Sabbath begins to dawn with healing in its beams. In lands which are called Christian, we perceive that religion always flourishes in proportion to the strict observance of the Sabbath. In those places in which no respect is paid to the Sabbath, there we see is no religion; but wherever the Sabbath is faithfully devoted to God, there religion flourishes. But wherever there is no church, there is found no Sabbath; and wherever a real church of Christ exists, there the Sabbath is kept holy. Its members observe it in its purity, and they preserve it from profanation by others.

The same things are true of the religious education of children. The Church of Christ, at any given period, is made up almost exclusively of those who have been religiously educated in childhood. In Christian lands, very few, comparatively, of those who have not been religiously educated, have become truly pious. But wherever religious education flourishes, there religion flourishes. But religious education owes its existence to the Church of Christ. In those places where there is no church, there is also no religious education. Were the Church to discontinue the religious education of its children for a single generation only, the parents would go to the grave, and none would rise up to take their places. In this short period the Church would become nearly, or quite, extinct. It is the children of the Church in this generation who will chiefly constitute the Church in the next. It is because so many of them, when children, are trained up, imperfectly indeed, yet really, in the way they should go, that, when they are old, they do not depart from it. The Church takes care of its children. Its sons become as plants, grown up in their youth. Its daughters are as corner-stones, polished after the similitude of a palace.

This is no less true of the preaching of the gospel. In lands where the gospel is not preached, religion does not exist. In lands where religion once existed and flourished, but has since disappeared, religion began to decline when the gospel ceased to be preached in its purity; and when such had been the case for a length of time, religion wholly disappeared. But the preaching of the gospel is entirely owing to the Church. Preachers of the gospel are trained up in the Church. The Church alone investigate the qualifications of preachers. Wherever a Church, to a good degree pure, exists, there the gospel is preached in its purity. Wherever a corrupted church is found, there a different gospel is preached from that of Christ. And wherever the church has become extinct, there the preaching of the gospel ceases.

Thus we are indebted to the Church of Christ for the observance of the Sabbath, for the religious education of children, for the preaching of the gospel; in a word, for the preservation of religion. In this respect, the Church is, eminently, "the salt of the earth."

This design has also been, to *diffuse* the religion of Christ. If the Church of Christ had not been established, Christians, could we suppose them to exist, would not know each other as such. They would never meet as Christians, and, of course, they could not confide in each other. But if there were to be no mutual confidence, nor even knowledge, even could we suppose them possessed of the disposition to do good, their efforts must be only feeble and unsuccessful. The work to be done is immense, the difficulties to be encountered are apparently inseparable. Each individual would accordingly feel, that his own efforts and contributions would avail nothing. He would see none to rouse him, to encourage him, nor to assist him; and should he make exertions, would have no opportunity to learn their fruits. In such circumstances, I need not say, no efforts could be made.

How different from all this is the actual state of things? Christians, because they are embodied into a church, meet together. They know each other as Christians; as one body, having one common interest, and that—the best of all interests. They see that Christ has ever had a church in the world, that it grows and flourishes, and their hearts are encouraged. The work to be be done is great; but they know that there are many laborers. The sums to be contributed for the conversion of the world are great; but the funds on which the contributions are to be levied are inexhaustible. The difficulties to be overcome are great; but there are vast energies of body and mind employed in overcoming them. Thus their efforts are concentrated, while their hearts are united. And while wonderful effects are seen to be produced by this oneness of exertion, the labor to each is comparatively light. In this way, the establishment of the Church as a union of Christians, who have one body and one soul, is the moving spring in the conversion of this world.

The entire history of the church confirms these conclusions. Wherever the apostles went, they planted churches. Those churches educated and supported evangelists, and circulated the Scriptures. In every subsequent age, wherever the Christian religion has been planted in a heathen land, God has made use of the instrumentality of the church in planting and watering. At this day, we see the same great process going on before our eyes. It is the Church, which sets in motion the wheels by which this mighty work is carried on. It is the Church, which first forms the plan for distributing Bibles and tracts. It is the Church, which educates evangelists and supports missions. I cheerfully admit that multitudes not belonging to the Church, do much towards this object. Still the great amount of labor and funds is yielded by the Church; and it is owing to her example and solicitations that any thing is done by others. Thus the Church of Christ is the great instrument, and the source of all the other instruments, employed by the Holy Spirit in the recovery of mankind. Without the Church, the work would not have been begun; and were the efforts of the Church to cease, the work would be finally relinquished.

The Church is no less designed, to *unite mankind ultimately into one family.* As mankind are all descended from the same parents, they should have constituted one great family and treated each other as brethren. Had mankind been a race of virtuous beings, such would have been the reality. The Fall not only left us without love to God, but without love to our neighbor. Instead of loving happiness, as such, man's supreme object is to promote his own. Instead of feeling a common interest which binds them together, mankind are actuated, each by a private, separate interest. Selfishness is the native universal character. It begets distrust, and is thus the repelling principle of our nature. Instead of drawing men together, it drives them asunder. It may, indeed, induce individuals to associate for a time, because their selfish purposes coincide and can be best promoted by co-operation; but it does not unite them, nor give them a common interest. All men are conscious that this is the true character of man. They know that they are selfish themselves; that their own interest is at all times the ruling motive. And they have no doubt that other men are like themselves. We prove by our daily conduct that this is our own estimate of the human character. No man exercises confidence in a stranger. Why? Because he knows that the stranger is *a man*, and therefore a selfish, depraved being. If we lived in a world of virtuous beings, we should exercise confidence, because we should know that they would love our happiness, and seek to promote it as truly as their own. The history of man has been, accordingly, a history of selfishness. To a vast extent, this history has been made up of war and desolation on the part of nations; of bloodshed and rapacity on the part of rulers; of fraud and theft, robbery and murder, between man and man. And when these more violent effects of selfishness among individuals have not appeared, there have still been clashing interests, contentions, alienation, and hatred.

This vast multitude of disunited beings Christ proposes to bring together into one family, and unite them as brethren. This effect he is now accomplishing by the instrumentality of his Church. That it may be accomplished, a new character must be communicated to mankind. Where the Church exists, the means employed are the preaching of its ministers, the religious education of children, and the prayers of Christians. Where these means are faithfully employed, this new character is actually and extensively communicated. The Holy Spirit creates the heart anew after the image of Christ. Wherever this takes place, mankind begin to lose their native selfishness, to love their neighbor as themselves, and to seek his happiness as their own.

In this manner, so far as the Church of Christ extends, mankind have already, partially at least, become one family. It is already established in Europe, Asia, Africa, and America, in New Holland, and the isles of the sea. It embraces in its limits the king and the beggar, the master and the slave, the sage and the peasant, the child and the man of gray hairs, the Brahmin and the Soodra, the white man and the tawney, the red man and the negro. But the Church knows no distinction of birth or endowments, of age or condition. With her, the cast and complexion are nothing. Those who enter her pale, come on one footing,—that of ruined sinners, needing pardon, and hoping for it only through the blood of Christ. The Church receives them because they possess the character of Christ,—the love of doing good. They come to unite themselves by one common covenant, to the same Father, Redeemer, and Sanctifier; and to acknowledge as their brethren all the members of the common family.

But the Church is constantly receiving accessions to its numbers. These accessions are large, and are rapidly increasing. Christ has also promised her that they shall increase, until all people, nations and languages are included among her children. It is thus that the scattered

22

family of man will be ultimately reunited, and, in the language of Christ, will become "one flock in the one fold, under the one Shepherd."

This Design has also been, to advance *its members in holiness, and thus to prepare them for heaven.* The grace of God, when imparted to the soul in regeneration, is as a grain of mustard seed, or a little leaven. The soul is in a very slight degree sanctified, and needs a very great change wrought in it before it can be prepared for a world of holiness. Some undoubtedly are removed to that world, within a very short period after they are born of the Spirit. But this is not usually the fact. God has need of the services of his children in this world; and he keeps them here in a state of discipline, that they may be purified themselves, and may be the means in his hands of saving others. It is chiefly owing to their union in the church, that this object is accomplished. To the Church there always remains the keeping of the Sabbath. That sacred season returns every week, a type of that everlasting rest which remains for the people of God. It brings with it salvation. It calls off the mind from this world and all things temporal, and fixes its contemplations and affections on heaven.

In the Church, the Word of God is preached. This word is explained to the understanding, enforced on the conscience, and impressed on the heart. It contains spiritual life, and is the great means of sanctification. It contains all that the Christian needs to believe and to do, to prepare him for heaven. His duties of the heart and life are set before him, heaven is brought near to invite him, and the love of Christ to constrain him.

The members of the Church meet with one another for prayer. They watch over each other's failings, they provoke one another to love and good works, especially to labor for the salvation of others, and to educate their children for heaven. The very object for which they are united, is, in this sense, to promote each other's spiritual prosperity, and to walk hand in hand in the straight and narrow path that leads to heaven.

In the sacrament of the Lord's supper, this great purpose is eminently promoted. Here they remember the agony of the garden, and the still deeper agonies of the cross. When they see the emblems of his broken body and shed blood, Christ tells them, "This is my body, which was broken for you: This cup is the new Testament in my blood, which was shed for many, for the remission of sins." While the heart here flows out in penitential sorrow, the Christian trusts with new faith in the efficacy of the Great Sacrifice, and covenants with new strength to put away sin and lead a life of holy obedience. Thus every grace is enlivened, heaven is brought near, the praises of the Church on earth and of the Church in heaven are mingled. Thus, also, the soul is prepared for a richer feast, for a nobler worship, for communion with a more pure and glorious church, and for the enjoyment of the immediate and blissful presence of the Lamb, when it shall see as it is seen, and know as it is known.

As a practical lesson, it may be observed, that when we compare the Church of Christ with other associations of men, the design of its formation is seen to be absolutely peculiar. Other associations are formed for the accomplishment of objects which belong solely to this world. Men are united in civil communities, to secure life, liberty, and property. Smaller associations are formed for the promotion of commerce, agriculture, and manufactures; for the advancement of the arts; for the promotion of science and learning; and for the reformation of morals. All these are desirable objects, and are happily promoted by the united wisdom and energy of those who are thus associated. Yet these associations regard man merely as an inhabitant of this world, and in no degree as accountable and immortal. They multiply the enjoyments of life, and some of them expand and invigorate the mind. Yet even those formed for the improvement of morals, aim simply to make man a more decent inhabitant of this world, but in no wise to fit him for a better.

The object of the Church of Christ is, to make men better. It regards man as fallen, and aims to raise him to a higher level than that from which he fell. It regards him as accountable, and seeks to prepare him to render his final account with joy. It regards him as immortal, and aims to secure to him glory, honor, and peace, in that world where his eternity will pass away.

The bond which unites this Society, we may add, is no less peculiar. It is not fear. Fear may bring men together in communities and nations, but it will never unite them. It is not selfishness. This may induce a few to associate for a time, for worldly purposes, but can never be either universal or permanent. It is not conjugal or natural affection. That may bind together the family, but beyond their little circle its influence is lost. But we need a principle,—a bond, which shall bring all the descendants of Adam together into one family, and unite them as the children of one common father. Such a bond none of the wise men of this world ever formed or imagined. But Christ taught his disciples what this principle is, and in the Church we see its influence exemplified. This principle, this bond, is *brotherly love*. "A new commandment I give unto you, that ye love one another." This principle, this bond, is not mere benevolence. It is also the love of virtue, or the love of good men because they are virtuous. The Church is an association of good men; of men who are associated for the purpose of promoting all the happiness which is in their power. In this they resemble Christ. Living together, they see this character in each other; and because they love the character of Christ himself, they are constrained to love it as visible in his disciples. Though many members, they are one body, having one Head, and animated by one Spirit. Often, indeed, this bond has not preserved the church from confusion and discord. But this has been owing to the unchristian conduct of its members, and not to any imperfection in the nature of the bond. As the Church grows better, this perfect bond is beginning to exert its proper influence; and the time, we trust, is not distant, when the whole human race will become one family, by becoming children of the same Heavenly Father, and be bound together by brotherly love.

The Church, we may be then assured, is safe. He who made this world for the sake of the Church; He who has directed his whole system of providence to promote her welfare,—will not forget her. He, who took care of her during the waters of the deluge, and in Egypt, at the Red Sea and in the wilderness, in the land of Canaan, and in the captivity;—He who defended her during bloody persecutions, and watched over her during the long night of Popish superstition,—will not forsake her at the dawn of a better day. He who loved her and gave himself for her, has assured her, "Behold, I have loved thee with an everlasting love. I have graven thee on the palms of my hands. Thy walls are ever before me. He who toucheth thee, toucheth the apple of mine eye."

WHY MANY CHRISTIANS MISTAKE THEIR OWN CHARACTERS.

2 Cor. xiii: 5.

Know ye not your own selves?

The original word in the context rendered *prove*, denotes that kind of trial by fire, to which the artist subjects a piece of metal, to determine whether it is base metal or pure gold. If inspiration deemed such care and fidelity to be necessary in making the investigation which is here enjoined, in order to prevent self-deception, instances of such deception must be frequent; for rarely indeed do we find those who are thus careful and faithful in trying their own characters.

It must be obvious, that there are but two mistakes with regard to this subject, which we can commit. One is, for Christians to believe that they are not Christians. The other is, for those who are not Christians to believe that they are such. As such mistakes are always violations of the duty of knowing ourselves; as they are of course attended with unhappy consequences, and may easily be fatal; I propose at this time to lay before you some of the reasons why one of those mistakes is often made;—in other words, why true Christians frequently mistake their religious character.

In every such investigation, the question to be decided is one and the same. It is this: Am I a Christian? The true answer to this question is always the declaration of a fact. In order that the reality of a fact may be proved, two things are necessary. First, sufficient evidence of the fact must exist. Secondly, the real evidence of its existence must be collected and laid before the mind. As a general answer therefore to the question, Why does a real Christian sometimes conclude himself to be an impenitent sinner, it is owing either to the fact that, in consequence of his very low attainments in piety, scarcely any evidence exists of his piety; or to the fact that, although sufficient evidence of his piety really exists, yet he neglects by faithful self-examination to collect that evidence and present it to his own mind.

This general answer, though we see it to be logically true, and though it comprehends every answer which can be given to the question before us, yet is at once felt by the mind to be less minute and particular than a case so important and interesting demands. While, therefore, we are compelled to descend to a more minute statement of the reasons why persons fall into this mistake, we wish it to be remembered that no reasons can be assigned which are not comprised in these two: the want of evidence, or a failure to discover whether there be evidence or not.

The Inquiry, then, which I propose to answer, is this:

Why do men often believe that they are not Christians, when they really are?

One cause of this mistake is, *the very depressed state of their religious affections.* Such affections really exist in the mind of every Christian, and constitute all that within him which gives him a right to the name. In many Christians, however, they are exceedingly imperfect. Often they do not exist at all. Often when they really exist and are in exercise, they are so low in degree as to leave their existence doubtful. Often also they are so blended with natural feelings, or with sinful affections, as to render it impossible for the mind to distinguish between them. Two examples will illustrate this difficulty. A Christian parent wishes the salvation of his child. Does he wish it merely because natural affection instinctively prompts him to desire its welfare? Or does he wish it, also, because he wishes the glory of the Godhead to be manifested in its salvation? A minister wishes and prays for a revival of religion among his people. Does he do thus merely, though perhaps unconsciously, to extend his own reputation and influence, and secure the attachment of his people; or because he really loves and prays for the salvation of their souls? I need not inform those who know anything of their own hearts, how apt our best affections are to be thus tainted with selfishness; how prone the hearts even of Christians are, when they profess to act for God, really to act for themselves. Even Paul could say, "The good that I would, that I do not; but the evil that I would not, that I do. I find then a law that, when I would do good, evil is present with me. O wretched man that I am, who shall deliver me from the body of this death!" If Paul could say this of himself, in whose heart the flame of holiness burned with a clear and steady light, what language ought those Christians to use, whose piety is like the smoking flax—not yet kindled into a flame? Such a person looks back on the period since he began to deem himself a Christian. The retrospect affords him little ground for consolation. He can find intervals of time, often of considerable length, in which his affections and conduct differed, if at all, yet imperceptibly, from that of an impenitent sinner. If he had any evangelical affections, they were all but frozen. If he had any spiritual life, it was almost dormant. At such times also he sees that there was another law in his members warring against the law of his mind, and bringing him into captivity to the law of sin. He will indeed see other intervals of a brighter aspect. Yet the light thrown over them will be so uncertain, that he will not know whether it is the light of self-righteousness, which shines from a fire of his own kindling; or whether there is blended with it the faint light of holiness shining dimly, yet really kindled by the Spirit of God. In such a life, little evidence of piety exists; and of course, in the survey of it, little evidence can be discovered. When the mind looks at the darker intervals, it indulges gloomy apprehensions that it is still impenitent. And even those which are less dark, are surrounded by so dim and dubious a twilight, that it scarcely dares to hope.

A second cause of this mistake is, *the commission of gross sins.* This was the case with David. All the manifestations which he had enjoyed of the divine favor were forgotten, when he contemplated the enormous sins which he had committed in his conduct towards Uriah. Even the divine declaration, that he was the man after God's own heart, ceased to yield him any satisfactory evidence of his piety when he remembered his dreadful guilt. Even this could not prevent him from saying, "I cry in the day time, but thou hearest not; and in the night season, and am not silent. I am poured out like water, and all my bones are out of joint; my heart is like wax, it is melted in the midst of my bowels. Wash me thoroughly from mine iniquity, and cleanse me from my sin. For I acknowledge my transgressions, and my sin is ever before me. Against thee, thee only have I sinned, and done this evil in thy sight. Behold, I was shapen in iniquity, and in sin did my mother conceive me." The same was probably true of Peter, after his denial of Christ. Even our Lord's assurance that he was possessed of faith, and his promise that that faith should not fail, were probably forgotten when he went out of the judgment-hall—to weep over his ingratitude and guilt.

There are Christians who are, at times, so far left to themselves, that they commit sins of a character peculiarly aggravated. They may not indeed be sins alike gross and monstrous with those of David and Peter. They may be sins which, if they were known, would not be thought sins by most men. A Christian can commit sins which, in the nature of the case, an impenitent sinner cannot commit. None but a Christian can be placed in those circumstances which must exist, to permit their being committed. They may be sins committed in consequence of temptations, of which the mind is conscious at the time, when the guilt of the conduct is brought directly into view, when conscience and the Holy Spirit strive powerfully with the mind to prevent the commission, and when God has recently favored the mind with peculiar manifestations of his favor. Conduct which, under other circumstances, might perhaps have passed almost unnoticed, will at such a time appear to be attended with peculiar aggravations. The Christian who has thus back-slidden, or who has fallen into more public and scandalous but perhaps not more heinous sins, will not, like Peter and David, have received direct personal assurances from God that he was his child. Neither will he, like them, be able to look back on such clear evidences of his own piety. Under such circumstances, when he contemplates his temptation, his fall, and the guilt which he has incurred, it is not surprising that he should relinquish the hope which he had before fondly cherished, and conclude that, if he had been a Christian, he could not have discovered so much degeneracy and ingratitude. At such a time, the thick cloud of guilt which envelops his mind will hide from his view the glory of God in the face of Jesus Christ; and all around and within will be gloom and uncertainty.

Still another cause is, *the ignorance of divine truth*, of which many Christians are the subjects. All persons familiarly conversant with those who are under convictions of sin, know, that ignorance of the truth of God and of the way of salvation is the cause of much of the anguish of mind which is then endured. The reason is obvious. They perceive their guilt and danger, and they have no adequate views of the way of escape. The same is true of such Christians as have no distinct conceptions of what is meant by repentance, faith, and holiness, and no adequate views of what are real evidences of personal piety. The truth of God, as it is revealed in the Bible, is the great means of sanctification. "Sanctify them by thy truth: thy Word is truth." But into a mind thus ignorant, truth can scarcely find admittance. If admitted, it can scarcely act, and cannot manifest its proper efficacy. This may be illustrated by a parallel case. A mathematician explains to an ignorant man the geometrical truth, that the three angles of a triangle are equal to two right angles. Suppose him for the moment thoroughly to understand it: of what use will it be to him? Yet the mathematician, by the help of this truth, will first build a ship, and then circumnavigate the globe. In the same manner, communicate what truths you please to an ignorant Christian, if he comprehends them at the moment, he does not know how to apply them; and for this reason, they scarcely become in any degree the means of his advancement in holiness. Knowing imperfectly what a Christian ought to be, he continues a very imperfect Christian. Conduct which an enlightened conscience would at once condemn, he does not suspect. Principles which such a mind would reject as false, he embraces. Not knowing what are the evidences of piety, he does not labor to possess them. It is not surprising that such persons should walk in darkness, and grope for the wall at noon-day as the blind. Perhaps few things are more frequently discovered in Christians, in those possessed of sound understanding and who have long been Christians, which ought to give pain, than this unhappy ignorance of the Truth of God; of that Holy Word which was given us as a light to our feet and a lamp to our paths while walking towards heaven. To such persons Paul addresses a most necessary reproof: "For when for the time ye ought to be teachers, ye have need that one teach you again which be the first principles of the Oracles of God, and are become such as have need of milk, and not of strong meat."

Another still is, *the unfairness which many discover in judging of the evidences of their own piety.* This remark is now and then applicable to individuals who have professed Christianity; but it chiefly applies to a class of persons often found in our congregations who are real Christians, and yet are without the pale of the visible Church. These persons were usually educated under pious parents, and do not recollect when they first began to be conscious of guilt and afraid of perdition. They had been always instructed as to the way of salvation and the terms on which it was offered. At some distinct period they became more deeply interested in religious subjects, felt a more lively consciousness of guilt, and became the subjects of faith, repentance, and holiness. They were not conscious, however, of peculiarly distressing apprehensions of the wrath of God, nor of their own danger of final perdition. Yet they found themselves impelled to their closets, they knew not why; and, almost without being conscious of the fact, discovered new beauty and excellence in all spiritual objects. God thus distinguished them by his forgiving love, and thus reasonably expected and required of them at such a time lively gratitude, as well as perfect fairness and sincerity in their treatment of Himself. Instead of the conduct which gratitude and sincerity dictated, they concealed their feelings in their own bosoms. Often, while in the company of Christians—especially of their parents or their minister, they ardently wished that they could be willing to unfold the state of their hearts; and when they left them, resolved, that they would do this at the next favorable opportunity. Shame, however, or a distrust of Christ, or an unfair estimate of the evidence of their own piety, or a determination to be more holy before they should profess the gospel, held them back, and the secret remained in their own breasts. In this very conduct they were punished. As they did not publicly profess to be Christians, they could not properly act as Christians; just as a man who has not been licensed to practice law or to preach, cannot with propriety appear at the bar or in the desk. Neither could they feel that confidence which they needed, to enable them to withdraw from the influence of this evil world,—from its principles, its follies, its temptations, and its sinful indulgencies. They were chiefly cut off also from intercourse with Christians, and their love was rarely prompted towards them. Not believing themselves also to be converted, they felt no covenanted obligations, they were guilty of sin with less reluctance, and often for long periods—chiefly or wholly—neglected the duty of prayer. Occasionally they have brighter and better seasons, and the strong affections of their souls are prompted towards God and spiritual objects. Yet these seasons do not differ so materially from the time in which they became Christians, as to induce them to act; and their progress in holiness, through a lapse of months and years, in consequence of these disadvantages, is so slow and so irregular, that they do not discover it. They remain in an apparently amphibious state. Neither themselves nor others can determine to which kingdom they belong; whether the life which they live in the flesh, is natural or spiritual life. The tender mercy of the Holy Spirit indeed sustains them, and keeps them from finally falling away. Yet all this time they have no evidence which seems to justify them in professing Christ's name before men. This is the proper and deserved punishment to which God subjects them, for the conduct of which they were guilty when they became his children. How long persons continue in this state, does not appear. That they do not go to their graves in it, is not certain. That they would always remain in it until death, were it not for some peculiar occurrence in God's spiritual providence towards them or others around them, we cannot doubt. If however the time arrives, when Christ has any work for them to do as his open and professed followers, he comes to them while they are wandering in a labyrinth in which there is no way, takes them by the hand, and leads them forth to light and certainty.

The causes which have been already mentioned, are all included in the general one: *a want of sufficient evidence.*

Those which I am about to mention, will be included in the other general one: *a failure to discover the evidence which really exists.*

One of these is, *the immense importance* of the case to be decided. This is no less than whether we are the children of God, and entitled to heaven; or whether we are still the children of wrath. The decision of any question of vital importance even to our temporal welfare, will excite a deep interest in the mind; and prevent that calm and quiet exercise of the intellectual faculties which seems to be necessary, if we are to arrive at certainty. Still more is this true of a question which is felt to involve our final welfare. When approaching its decision, the mind feels the peculiar danger of self-deception. To form too favorable a decision; to believe itself renewed, when it is not; it knows may easily be fatal. But to conclude itself impenitent, when it is really sanctified, though it may deprive us of present comfort and retard our progress in holiness, yet will not lull us into a fatal security, but will rather prompt us to increased watchfulness, and make us more anxious to seek eternal life. Thus mere policy seems to determine the mind of such a Christian to a false conclusion, and instead of finding his safety in his piety he finds it in his unbelief. Although he does exercise some degree of confidence in Christ, for without it he could not be a Christian; yet the principle on which he mainly acts, is that of distrust. He cannot consent to go even to such a Saviour, and commit himself unreservedly to him, trusting in his faithfulness to keep him from falling. He does not believe that Christ will thus keep him, unless he first makes himself a better Christian, if he is one at all, and in this way recommends himself to his notice. He intends, therefore, to gain all the advantage he can from this course of doubt and unbelief; and then, when he has made sufficient progress in holiness, to look to Christ alone for security. What a delusion! To believe that he can be safe without depending on Christ, when his faith is feeble and faint, and yet intend to depend upon him when it has grown stronger. As confidence is the principle of moral attraction, uniting those who indulge it, so distrust is the principle of moral repulsion, necessarily separating all by whom it is exercised. Were such a Christian to treat his friend as he treats his Saviour, their friendship would terminate finally and forever. But his Saviour is long-suffering, and slow to anger, and plenteous in mercy. While, however, he acts from these selfish, disingenuous motives, he ought to expect that frank and delightful communion with his Saviour which confidence alone can justify.

Another may be found in *the character, and circumstances, of those who make it.* Some men are constitutionally gloomy. They look, as we familiarly say, on the dark side of every thing around them, and are at least as prone to do this in spiritual as in temporal things. Were such a man and another who is habitually cheerful to become Christians at the same time, to possess equal degrees of piety, and to be equally faithful in self-examination, the amount of evidence which would induce the latter to hope, might lead the former almost to despair. The same individual also will, at different times and under different circumstances, assign a different weight to the same evidence. The state of the bodily health often has an influence on the views and judgment, of which we are not aware. I knew an individual, a preacher of the Gospel, a man of an unusually calm and collected mind, and believed by all who knew him, to be a man of very uncommon piety, in consequence of that loss of tone and energy to which all sedentary men are liable, reduced to absolute despair, not only as to his actual possession of holiness, but as to the hope of ever obtaining it for the future. This state of mind continued for several years, until a change of country and climate restored his health, and with it his cheerfulness. After this he did not hesitate to believe, that all his gloomy apprehensions and conclusions were without foundation. The best spiritual guide to a man in such circumstances is a discreet and skilful physician. The hopeless derangement of our worldly circumstances is occasionally attended by results equally unhappy. Few men can contemplate the utter ruin of their property, without seeing every object around them covered with gloom.

The backsliding and fall of those who have been supposed to be Christians, often occasions the same mistake. Sometimes real Christians thus backslide and fall. They commit presumptuous and scandalous sins, and dreadfully dishonor the Church of Christ. Others who were believed to be Christians, fall away, and are never brought to repentance. And Christians who think humbly of their own attainments, and are disposed to think others better than themselves, when they behold such conduct in others,—in those perhaps in whose piety they had strong confidence,—are prone to doubt not only their own piety, but that of almost all other professors. They see that the persons in question were deceived in believing themselves Christians; well, therefore, may they distrust themselves. Did we realize how much Christians are prone to confide in men, and how little in God, this fact would not appear surprising.

Christians often mistake their religious character, in consequence of *comparing themselves with others.* In such comparisons they usually overlook the great mass of Christians, and single out a few individuals who are eminent for piety. They read the life, or the diary, of some person of distinguished excellence. They see how holy and unblamable he was; how frequent and delightful his communion with God; how ardent his love; how firm his faith; how deep his humility; how thorough his repentance; how bright his hopes; how strong his consolations. Were they to read such accounts to quicken their own progress towards heaven, the perusal would be very profitable. But to derive from them a criterion of personal piety, is to come to the strange conclusion, that there are no Christians but those who are eminent Christians.

This mistake is often heightened by the indiscreet conversation of those who have professed to be Christians. There are those in the visible Church, who appear to find their chief enjoyment in communicating their own religious feelings to others. For this they are always prepared; and in doing it they are always fluent and fervent. They often mention their own deep sense of sin and contrition of spirit, without mistrusting, perhaps, that they wish to be distinguished for their humility. Their zeal is so animated and ardent, that it would continually lead them into mischief, were it not restrained by the prudence of others. Their religious comforts and joys are usually transports, if not actual visions of Christ and of the glories of heaven. The persons who thus converse, are sometimes unquestionably pious. Yet most of what they deem the brightest evidences of piety is but the effects of a heated imagination. Humbler Christians of more sedateness and good sense, listen to these representations, and are misled by them. Deeply sensible of their own imperfections, they are ready, of course, to esteem others better than themselves. When they examine the state of their own minds they find no resemblance to these glowing descriptions. Their sense of unworthiness is perhaps great, but so little compared with what it ought to be, that they can only mourn that it is no greater. Their religious comfort is usually a faint and trembling hope; and rarely rises so high, as to deserve the name of joy. The result of the comparison is, that they conclude those who thus converse to be the peculiar favorites of heaven, and themselves to be so unlike them, that it is scarcely possible that they can be true disciples.

This mistake is also occasioned by our *assuming false tests of the Christian character*. From my own observation I am convinced that no error is more common among Christians in this country, than to look for their chief evidences of a man's piety in the manner and circumstances of his conversion. We know this to be the case with some other denominations. I wish that I could say, it is not of our own. On this scheme, if a man is a child of God, he must know the time when he became such, if not also the very place, and the posture of the body. At the time in question, he must have passed through a series of views and affections, following each other in a certain prescribed order. He must state the event, or the conversation, or the sermon, which first arrested his attention; the distress, which succeeded, accompanied by increased hostility to spiritual objects, and the comfort which followed. If these events follow each other in the proper order, and in quick succession, the piety of the individual is not questioned. Not a few real Christians, especially among those who were born under the roof of piety, and were there taught in infancy the truth of God, the comprehensive nature of his law and the justice of its penalty, whose consciences were thus enlightened from the beginning, and who have always known the fulness of God's mercy in Christ, when they look back on their past lives, are unable to come to any certain conclusion as to the period when they became Christians. They can remember various periods when they felt a peculiarly deep sense of guilt, and an unusual tenderness of conscience; and they almost dared to hope in each of them, that they were the children of God. Yet no one season, perhaps, was so distinguished above others, that they could single it out as certainly the period when the event took place. Much less can they point out the week, the day, and the hour, and still less the place or the posture. Nor can they mention the text of Scripture, the sermon, or the event of providence, which the Holy Spirit employed to fasten their attention on spiritual objects. These facts distress them, and lead them to fear that they want the clearest and best evidences of their own regeneration, if they are not wholly without evidence. Would they in their self-examination confine themselves to the only important question, Am I a Christian? and see whether they possess those evidences of the Christian character which the Scriptures mention, they would reach a different result.

The near resemblance of these affections which are evangelical, to corresponding affections which are not, involves many real Christians in the same mistake. Every evangelical affection and grace has its counterfeit. Thus an impenitent person may exercise a species of love to God, to Christ, to his fellow-men, and to Christians; a species of hatred to sin, of repentance, of faith, hope, joy, humility, and zeal; a species of relish for the word and ordinances of God; he may also evince a species of obedience in his life, which himself and others may mistake for evangelical. Some true disciples, knowing this fact, instead of allowing it to have its proper and intended effect—that of quickening them in their progress towards heaven and making them more faithful in self-examination, are prompted by it only to despondency and relaxation of effort.

Christians also often mistake their religious character, from *the mercenary views with which they perform the duty of self-examination.* They enter on this duty, not to ascertain the real fact; not to humble themselves under their sins; not to enliven their consciences, warm their affections and invigorate their obedience; but simply to obtain comfort and peace from the discovery of evidence that they are Christians. No conduct is more absolutely selfish. None can be more foolish. They thus frustrate the very object which they have in view. Instead of spending life in searching daily after evidence of their piety, they should spend it in bringing forth the fruits of piety. Were God to inform such persons by a voice from heaven, that they were his children, it would ruin them forever. They can hardly endure the little evidence which they already have. The only person who can safely endure the strong, clear evidence of piety, is he who is eminent for his piety. Thus to look after religious enjoyment in the knowledge of our safety, instead of seeking it in the affections and duties of the Christian life, is in itself merely sinful. It is demanding that we should know that we are Christians, when we will not discover the character of Christians. The man who does not bring forth the fruits meet for repentance, faith, and love, and yet attempts to find evidence that he possesses these graces, has a task to perform which no one will envy him. "Show me thy faith," says James, "without thy works," i. e. if thou canst; "and I will show thee my faith, by my works."

Suffer me to remark, in closing, what evidence does this

investigation furnish us, "that the heart is deceitful above all things?" How are we impelled to ask, Who can know it? We expect to find this declaration true of every impenitent heart, both as to temporal and spiritual subjects. But here we see those, who are not only bought with blood, but renewed in the divine image, discovering in their most secret retirements, when most conscious of the presence of God, and when transacting the most solemn business between God and their own souls, this very obliquity, and deceiving themselves by their own inventions. Before Him, who requireth truth in the inward parts, how does the heart of a Christian look? O what need have we, Brethren, if we are Christians, that our Great High Priest in the Heavens should ever live to make intercession for us!

EVERLASTING LIFE, ALREADY BEGUN IN THE BELIEVER.

JOHN III: 36.

HE THAT BELIEVETH ON THE SON, HATH EVERLASTING LIFE.

ETERNAL LIFE is the life of the inhabitants of heaven, and is usually supposed to begin when the Christian enters the heavenly world. The Baptist here shows us that this opinion is a mistake, and instructs us to regard every man as in possession of eternal life from the moment when he believes. He does not say, He that believeth on the Son *is entitled to*, or *shall have*, eternal life; but he, that believeth on the Son, *hath*, i. e. he has now, he *already possesses*, eternal life—the same life with that enjoyed in heaven.

When I say, *the same life* with that enjoyed in heaven, you will not suppose that I intend the same in all its attendant circumstances. You will not imagine, for example, that I suppose heaven to be the same place with earth; or the state of existence of a separate spirit to be the same with that of a spirit, dwelling in a frail, dying body; or the objects visible to the two, in the two different worlds, to be identically the same. Eternal life, however, does not consist in merely being in heaven, or in viewing its external glories: for if an impenitent sinner were now in heaven and saw all of God, of Christ, of angels, and of just men made perfect, which the bodily eye can see, he would not possess eternal life; and if an angel were to come down to this world and remain here on the service of God until the general resurrection, he would be still as truly in possession of eternal life as he is at present. Neither will you suppose me to intend the same life, in degree and perfection. The eternal life of the Christian who has just entered heaven, is exceedingly inferior in degree to that enjoyed by Gabriel or Paul; still in its nature and properties, it is one and the same.

With these explanations, I shall endeavor to show you in what respects the believer is already in possession of eternal life. In doing this, however, I shall not draw my illustrations from the character and condition of a young Christian, who has just begun to live; nor from those of a Christian who is so diseased with worldliness, that the symptoms of life are scarcely perceptible. To render the exhibition of this truth clear and striking, you must turn your eyes on one whose heart is warm, whose pulse is vigorous, whose limbs are active, and who is gaining the stature and strength of a full grown man. Eternal life is begun in such a Christian, because:

The same principle of life is already communicated to his soul. Life, as an entity, has various natures, it exists in various degrees, and may be possessed in any inferior degree without being possessed in a degree which is superior. For example, a plant has vegetable life and yet does not possess consciousness, feeling, or motion; a beast has animal life, yet does not possess reason, imagination, or conscience ; a man may have rational life in full perfection, and yet not possess the least relish for spiritual good ; and an angel does possess spiritual life in full perfection, and yet can not possess that inherent, divine life, which is peculiar to the Uncreated Spirit. If the testimony of God can furnish evidence of the fact, the souls of men by nature, as to the possession of any degree of spiritual life, are dead. They are without motion, or have no spiritual activity ; they are without feeling, or have no spiritual affections or desires ; they are without consciousness, or have no perception of the excellence of spiritual objects. Instead of any signs of life, a moral decay has commenced, which will render it necessary to remove them from the sight of all the living and to bury them in an eternal grave. In this sense of life, they do not exist, nor constitute a part of the spiritual creation of God, any more than a mineral belongs to the vegetable creation, or a vegetable to the animal creation, or an animal to the intelligent creation.

Yet, of those who have been thus dead, multitudes are now dwelling on high, who are flourishing in all the youth, and health, and activity of heaven. The question then arises, when did this surprising change take place ; when did this new and eternal life begin ? We are not left to conjecture how, when, or by whom, it was accomplished. We know negatively, that it is not effected by death, for death is simply a destruction of the animal life, followed by a separation of the soul from the body ; and it is therefore a mere physical, and not a moral, change. As such, it has no tendency to cause eternal life to commence, and vast multitudes experience death, who will never possess eternal life. Neither does it commence after death, either in the sinner or the Christian : for as he who is unjust or wicked at death will be unjust still, and he who is filthy will be filthy still; so he only who is righteous previous to his death will be righteous still, and he who is holy will be holy still. That the Christian at death is divested of all imperfection and sin, is certain; yet this will be only carrying on the work of sanctification more rapidly, and not the communication of a principle of life which did not previously exist. We know also affirmatively, that the Son of God is the bestower of it, for he giveth life to whom he will; that the Spirit of God is the agent who communicates it, for it is the Spirit that quickeneth; and that it commences at regeneration, for John tells us, "This is eternal life, to know thee, the only true God, and Jesus Christ whom thou hath sent."

The life thus communicated is *new*, as absolutely new, as if feeling and motion were imparted to a vegetable; or reason and conscience to an animal. It is called spiritual life, because the subject of it then commences a spiritual existence, and begins to belong to the spiritual creation; and perhaps, also, because it is found in its highest perfection in the pure spirits of heaven. It is not only new, but it is the same in its nature with the eternal life of heaven. We here do no violence to language; for, when the seed in the ground begins to germinate, we say that the germ has the same vegetable life which afterwards exists in the full grown plant; and that when the embryo is quickened, it possesses the same animal life which exists in the man. He who possesses it, becomes a living, spiritual being. Before its implantation, though surrounded by spiritual objects, he exhibited no symptoms of life, no circulation within, no consciousness of the objects without. But afterwards, the heart propels the warm current of feeling through the soul, the eye discerns the moral beauty and excellence of God, the ear hears his voice, the tongue speaks his praise, and the hands engage in his service. This spiritual life thus begun, does not expire with the body. It is a flame kindled from the fires of heaven, which never can go out. It is a seed from the garden of Jehovah, planted here, and nurtured with infinite care; that it may be at length transferred to its native soil, there to wear a verdure ever vernal, and yet be ever loaded with the fruits of Paradise. Like the soul in which it is found, it fears not the waste of nature nor the ravages of death, and is alike undecaying and immortal. As beheld in the saint in heaven, it is but a continuation of the same spiritual existence on which the Christian enters here. In both worlds, as we shall soon have occasion to remark, he is surrounded by the same spiritual beings, and discovers towards them similar emotions. There he feels indeed a stronger love to God, a livelier gratitude towards him, a fuller confidence in his goodness, a more tender affection to the Saviour, a more entire complacency in holiness, a more intimate union to his brethren, and a more absolute good will to the universe of being; yet all these various exhibitions of holiness, though new, purer, and more constant, really exist, and are called into exercise in the present world.

That the same living principle animates the breast of the believer in both worlds, is obvious also from the fact, that it is nourished by the same aliment. "I," says the Saviour, "am the living bread which came down from heaven; and the bread that I will give is my flesh, which I will give for the life of the world." Here the believer sees that this sacrifice of Christ is the only reason why he is not subjected to eternal death; and the moment will never arrive in heaven, when he will not know that, were it not for the same sacrifice, he could never have been admitted to that world of life. Here it is the sight of

God, the discovery of his manifold perfections, especially as they are unfolded in the beauty of redeeming love, which wakes up gratitude, confidence, and joy, and which calls forth adoration and praise ; and it is only a nearer sight of God, a brighter discovery of the same perfections which he will enjoy in heaven. Here, while he receives and cordially obeys the truth of God, his soul is refreshed and purified ; but this stream of living water which has broken out here in the desert, comes from that Uncreated Fountain to which the heavenly Shepherd conducts his flock.

He possesses and uses *the same spiritual Faculties*, which he will employ in heaven. It is not merely true of the spiritual being, the renewed man, who has been thus formed by the Great Quickener of the intelligent universe, that he is alive ; that by approaching him, as you approach a sick man, you can barely hear him breathe, and feel his heart palpitate and his pulse beat ; but he exhibits the more positive and obvious symptoms of life. As living, healthy, active men, have faculties, which they continually employ ; so he has spiritual faculties which are called into constant exercise.

He has a spiritual *Consciousness*. When any virtue, any grace, of the spirit, for example, Christian love, is presented to his mind as the subject of contemplation, he not only perceives its nature intellectually, i. e. either by a metaphysical investigation of the principles from which it proceeds, or a consideration of the fruits which it produces ; but he also perceives its nature experimentally. He himself exercises this grace ; he knows what it is to love God ; he can turn the eye of his understanding inwards, and his own consciousness tells him the nature of Christian love. So when the holiness of God is the subject of meditation, it may be of use to him to investigate intellectually the nature of holiness, and to consider its effects; but as holiness in all beings is one and the same in its nature, he has a shorter, a clearer, a livelier way of understanding that nature, and that is, from the consciousness of his own mind.

He has a spiritual eye, or discernment. "The natural man receiveth not the things of the Spirit of God, for they are foolishness unto him; neither can he know them, for they are spiritually discerned; but he who is spiritual, discerneth all things." His view of spiritual objects is not merely a sight of their physical and intellectual properties. This the natural man has, and often far more clearly than the spiritual. It is also a sight of their beauty,—their excellence.

He has a spiritual ear. Once the whole contents of the book of life might have been poured into the ear of his understanding, and yet his heart would not have heard a syllable. Now the ear of his heart is open to catch the sounds of divine truth. Once, if you explained to him his duties, it was preaching to the winds. Now he listens, that he may hear what is the will of God. Once the notes which angels sung, fell powerless on his ear. Now the harp of Orpheus is not so sweet and ravishing, as the melody of redeeming and sanctifying love.

He has spiritual feelings. Once, when motives were addressed to him, connected with his personal interests, his fears or his hopes, or those which should have prompted gratitude, love or confidence, not a sensation was excited. But now, when his soul comes in contact with the excellence and beauty of the Divine mind, with the glory of God shining in the face of Jesus Christ, or with the communion of saints, or the blessedness of the heavenly world; the life-blood of the soul flows warm and rapidly from its fountain through every artery, and every vein throbs with new and unusual pulsations.

He is surrounded by the *same spiritual Objects*. That an object may be present to an individual, it is not enough that he merely knows its existence. I know that London exists, yet it is not therefore present to me. Nor is it enough, that it affect his senses or his mind. I can see the sun or a distant mountain, and the spectacle produces an appropriate effect, yet neither object is thus made present. Nor is it enough, that the object be near. I may be present in the same room with one who is deaf or blind, and he may still not perceive me. In that case he is present to me, but I am not present to him. In addition to all this, the mind must be in such a sense conscious of the nearness of the object, as to be led to think of it, and feel and act towards it, as present. When objects are in fact present, we become conscious of this by evidence of the fact conveyed to our minds. And here I may observe that it makes no difference what the evidence is, provided it is real, and is perceived. Thus the mind of a deaf and dumb man may become conscious of my presence by seeing me, or still more by perceiving those articulate motions which my fingers utter; and a blind man, by hearing my voice or feeling my hand. As most spiritual objects are not discernible in the present life by either of the five bodily senses, God has furnished the mind of the Christian with an additional sense, by which he becomes conscious of their immediate presence. This sense is, faith. In the Bible, God tells him that these objects exist, and that they are present to him. By means of faith, the evidence of their presence is thus presented to his mind, and he is led to think of them, and to feel and act towards them accordingly. "Faith," says the Apostle, "is the substance of things hoped for, the evidence of things not seen." He does not indeed realize the presence of these objects in the same manner as they do in Heaven, neither does he realize it as vividly, and joyfully, and operatively; yet when the vision of his faith is clear, and strong, and comprehensive, he does realize it as truly, as actually, as he will when he escapes from his prison and sees as he is seen.

He sustains *the same Relations* now, which he will sustain in heaven. The relations which we sustain, depend on our birth. By his first birth the believer becomes a child of Adam, a member of the human family, and a relative of all his posterity; as well as a nearer and more intimate connection of that individual family from which he is immediately descended. It is on this oneness of descent and blood that all the relations of the present life are founded. By his second birth he becomes a member of that family which Paul denominates, " the whole family in heaven and earth." His connection with that great family does not, however, commence in the heavenly world; for, if so, it would be described simply as the family in heaven, and not as the family—a part of which is in heaven, and a part on earth. He, as truly as those who are in heaven, is born from above, claims a heavenly origin. This birth does not take place in heaven, but on earth. " If any man be in Christ," i. e. a Christian, " he is already a new creature." " Every one that believeth, is born of God; every one that loveth, is born of God." Neither does this sonship of the Christian commence hereafter, but here. " Beloved," says John, " we are now the sons of God; and it doth not yet appear what we shall be." " The Spirit itself," says Paul, " beareth witness with our spirit that we are the children of God." He is as truly a child of the Lord Almighty, and has the same right when he approaches the throne to call him, "Father!" "For ye are all," says Paul, "the children of God by faith in Christ Jesus." "And because ye are sons, God hath sent forth the Spirit of his Son into your hearts, crying, 'Abba, Father." This relationship, on one side paternal, on the other filial, is as real, as permanent, and, if it be not the Christian's fault, as readily acknowledged by God, as it will be in heaven. He is as truly a friend and brother of Jesus Christ. He is as fully entitled to call the Holy Spirit, his Sanctifier and his Comforter, and to receive from him as constant supplies of purity and peace, of holiness and joy. He is as nearly related to the angels. The church of the redeemed as truly know him to be one of their number, remember the day when his name was announced as one of the new-born children of God, and are ready to welcome him to the house of their Father.

He possesses now all *the Rights*, which he will possess in heaven. He is already justified. Faith in the righteousness of Christ is the simple and single condition of his justification; and with that condition he complied, when he first became a Christian. As faith entitles him to all the benefits of Christ's obedience, so his title is made out,—not when his final trial is over; not when he enters heaven; not after a long life of holiness; but when he first believes. If, like the thief on the cross, he dies instantly after conversion, he is as truly a partaker of Christ's righteousness, as he would be, were he to outlive Methusaleh, or as he will be in the great day of decision. He does not need the trial of that day, nor any previous trial, nor an actual admission to heaven, in order that he may be justified. The fact that he believes in Christ as his Saviour, is known to God, to Christ, and to all the flock above, for the good

Shepherd has said to them, "Rejoice with me, my friends, for I have found the sheep which I had lost."

His right to his future inheritance is thus a vested right. His title is not only made out, but written down in the records of the upper world. "The Spirit itself," says Paul, "beareth witness with our Spirit, that we are the children of God ; and if children, then heirs, heirs of God, and joint heirs with Jesus Christ." Surely, the inheritance of Jesus Christ is vested ; and if the believer is a joint heir with Christ, then his inheritance is vested also, and the one can be no more defeated than the other. Like an heir during his minority, while under teachers and governors, he has not indeed come into full possession of that inheritance. Like him, however, he receives many an earnest of his title, in that pleasant provision made for all his wants from the stores of his father's bounty; but, unlike him, he cannot, in consequence of fraud or violence, or death, come short of his inheritance at the last.

He moves and acts in the *same Theatre.* Action, which is nothing else than voluntary motion, is of course the result of Choice or Volition : and volition is the result of two things; the Character of the mind willing, and the Objects in the view of that mind which furnish it with motives. The question, Whether the objects presented at any time to the view of the mind, will have the force of motives, prompting that volition which results in action, depends wholly on the character of that mind. The same set of objects may be presented to the view of two different minds, with directly opposite results: on one their influence will be powerless, exciting no desire, calling forth no effort; on the other they will exert their whole power, and call forth all the energy of the soul.

The Theatre, in which an intelligent being moves and

acts, depends upon the scenes and the objects actually before him, in the view of which, his mind habitually puts forth his energy. The book of nature and the book of revelation spread out two scenes, and two classes of objects, wholly distinct and unlike each other; the things which are seen and temporal, and the things which are unseen and eternal. The latter class of objects are made known and presented to the mind of a worldling under the gospel, as truly as to the mind of a Christian; and may, if he pleases, act with their full and appropriate influence on his soul. But unhappily his treasure is on earth, and his heart is there also. The consequence is, that earthly things are the only things which are habitually present to his mind. These alone, prompt desire, and call forth and occupy the whole energy of his being. This world is the theatre, in which he lives, moves, acts. His eye sees nothing beyond it. Its vision is bedimmed by his lusts; and it is always turned downward on the earth. Conscience does indeed at times inflict a pang, and a dread hereafter will for a moment cover the scenes around him with gloom. But he shuts his eyes, till the gloom is dispelled, and then opens them anew, only to fasten them more intently on the things beneath. Would he first clear his vision, and then turn his eyes upward, eternity with all its awful realities—nay, heaven with its immortal glories, would burst upon his sight, and wake up a feeling, an energy, which its own everlasting day would only strengthen and ennoble. But the unhappy man loves nothing, and therefore sees nothing; he feels nothing, and therefore acts for nothing, but what is of the earth, earthy. At first, the gratifications of pleasure, afterwards those of power, or wealth, or fame, alone move his heart and constitute his whole inventory of real good. In this narrow theatre he acts his wretched part, until the drama closes and the curtain falls.

Not so with him, that believeth. Faith has cleared his mental vision; and as the objects which he supremely loves are the things above, his eye is lifted from earth and directed towards heaven. This life, instead of including his whole being, and all the objects for which he lives, is merely the first scene on which he is called to act in the drama of existence. From this world he looks outward, and sees it to be a speck, an atom, in the creation of God. From it he also looks upward, and sees that brighter world where Jehovah dwells himself, and where his glory shines from the face of Jesus Christ with no intervening cloud; where the hosts of angels, as ministering spirits, wait his bidding, ready to minister to the heirs of salvation; and where an innumerable multitude of the just made perfect already surround the throne. As he looks around him, he sees his fellow-actors vanishing from the stage of life, and entering by thousands and millions into the world of spirits. As he casts his eye beneath, he beholds a broad and crooked path conducting downwards to the world of woe, and most of his fellow-actors, as they leave the stage, take the path to that melancholy world, and sink into its deep and dark recesses. The sight awakens all the feelings of his own soul, and, with a compassion resembling that which is felt above, he becomes a worker together with God and all holy beings in rescuing them from everlasting woe. Thus heaven, earth, and hell, are the Theatre in which he now lives, and moves, and acts his part; and when he puts off these vestments of clay and is arrayed in the glory of the hosts on high, he will still appear in the same Theatre, acting a nobler part—a higher character—in the same great Drama,—the Work of Redemption,—the first scene of which was the Temptation and Fall of Man, and the last scene of which will be the ascending of Christ after the Judgment of the Great Day, with all the hosts of Angels and the whole Church of the Redeemed, into that New Heaven, that masterpeice of wisdom and glory, in which Jehovah himself will love to dwell forever, and which will be a full reward for the agony of Calvary, and for the toils and the sufferings of seven thousand years.

He partakes of *the same Enjoyments.* This is a consequence from what has been already said. If he has the same principle of life, possesses the same spiritual faculties, is surrounded by the same spiritual objects, has the same rights, and is engaged in the same business, with those in heaven, it can scarcely fail to be the fact that his pleasures are the same; and that they are the same we have the most abundant evidence. This part of our subject is at once so refreshing and so fertile, that it might most pleasantly and advantageously occupy a separate discourse. I can here allude to but a few particulars.

One great delight of the heavenly world is found in the knowledge of God. "This is eternal life, to know thee, the only true God." In the endless variety of his works, both material and immaterial, the believer discovers here as truly as he will hereafter, abundant evidence of Jehovah's wisdom, power, and goodness; while the course of providence unfolds to him in conjunction with these perfections the divine immutability, justice, and mercy. In the Word of God all these perfections are drawn out in living characters; and this supplies the place of that immediate revelation of God which is made in heaven: so that here he sees God as in a mirror, instead of seeing him face to face. He lives, too, in a world where the brightest manifestation of God ever beheld in the universe, was first made,—a manifestation in the view of angels so far surpassing every other, that, when the Word was made flesh and dwelt among us, they not only left the upper world to see this great sight, but they also tuned their harps anew and sung, "Glory to God in the highest; peace on earth; and good-will to man."

Another source of heavenly bliss is loving God with all the heart. The Christian on earth loves God also supremely, and can at times literally exclaim, "Whom have I in heaven but thee, and there is none on the earth whom I desire beside thee!" In heaven the manifestations of the love of God communicates a joy, too great even for the souls of angels to contain; the Christian here also finds that love when richly shed abroad in his heart, a sober certainty of heavenly bliss. In heaven he will be admitted to a near and intimate communion with God; and there is not a moment of his life on earth in which he is not at liberty to be alone with God as his Father, in which God is not willing to welcome him into his presence as a child tenderly beloved, in which he may not have communion with God in all that he is, and has, and does, and in which God is not willing to commune with him in all his wants and sorrows and emotions.

To Jesus also he may come unspeakably near, as God manifest in the flesh. With Him, his disciple can commune concerning all that he did and all that he suffered, while on earth; and all that he is doing and will do for the salvation of his church.

To the Holy Spirit, the dispensor of the grace of heaven, he can come with wants as pressing and desires as strong as his nature will sustain; with the supporting assurance that he, who thus hungers and thirsts after holiness, shall be filled, and if he were in heaven he could receive no more.

Here, too, as well as there, he can join in social worship with the children of God. When that consecrated season comes round which is a type of the everlasting rest of heaven, God invites his children to meet him in his earthly temple; and when there assembled, he reveals himself to them in all the riches of his goodness and his grace. There, as the believer sees Him who is invisible, he can say with conscious certainty, "Behold God in very deed is in this place. This is none other than the house of God, and this is the gate of heaven." There, while he dwells in the secret place of the Most High and abides under the shadow of the Almighty with an assurance resembling that of heaven, he says of Jehovah, "He is my refuge, and my fortress; in him will I trust."

It is for the believer and the unbeliever, on this occasion, each to make a faithful application of this sacred theme to his own breast.

FELLOWSHIP WITH THE FATHER AND THE SON.

1 John i: 3, 4.

AND TRULY OUR FELLOWSHIP IS WITH THE FATHER, AND WITH HIS SON JESUS CHRIST. AND THESE THINGS WRITE WE UNTO YOU, THAT YOUR JOY MAY BE FULL.

Two leading thoughts are here suggested by the Apostle: Real Christians have fellowship with the Father, and with his Son Jesus Christ; The knowledge of this fact should be the cause of peculiar joy. We are then naturally led to contemplate,

The Nature;
The Reality;
The Extent; and
The Desirableness; of this Fellowship.

The *Nature* of this Fellowship first demands our attention.

Fellowship and Communion are words of the same import, and are employed indiscriminately as translations of the same word from the Greek. That word, as well as the verb which we render, *to partake*, are both derived from an adjective, signifying, *common;* and *to have or enjoy in common*, is the original idea of the phrases, *to partake*, and *to have communion*—or *fellowship*. Fellowship, then, is that relation subsisting between two or more individuals, in consequence of which they *have things in common*. Such a relation, we are told, subsists between real Christians on the one part, and the Father and his Son Jesus Christ on the other.

To understand the Nature of this Fellowship, we must consider the state of the mind which it implies; and the things in which it exists.

It implies *mutual Knowledge*. On the part of the Christian, it implies a knowledge of the true character of God. He must know him as the eternal, self-existent, and Omnipresent Spirit; infinitely great; knowing all things past, present, and to come; infinitely and unchangeably wise, holy, just and good, merciful and true; as the Creator, Proprietor, Benefactor, and Sovereign of all things. I have said he must know his *true* character. If his conceptions of God are false; if, for example, he supposes him to have a bodily shape, or to be mutable, or not to be the enemy of sin, or a God who will acquit the guilty, his communion is with a false God, and not with Jehovah.

The Christian must know the End, or Purpose, for which God made and governs all things: the manifestation of his own glory in the supreme and eternal happiness of virtuous beings. He must know the general laws of his empire, and the great principles of his government: that he governs all beings and events according to a plan formed in eternity; that he takes care that, while his creatures follow their own wills, they accomplish his purposes; that he rewards the obedient, and punishes the disobedient, forever.

He must know the works of God: his Works of Creation, both in the heavens and on the earth ; and his works of Providence, both in this world and the world of spirits, towards men and angels, in time and in eternity—that he may discover the wisdom and power, the goodness and mercy, the justice and truth, manifested in them all.

He must know the Word of God: the Truth which it unfolds respecting the character of Man; the Duties, which it enjoins ; the Character, which it requires ; and the Motives, which it presents.

He must understand the Work of Redemption : the true character of the Redeemer ; the design of his mission and death to atone for sin, and to procure the mission of the Spirit ; the conditions on which Salvation is offered, Faith and Repentance ; the agency of the Holy Spirit in converting and sanctifying the heart ; the Privileges to which the believer is entitled, here and hereafter ; the Promises respecting the future glory of the Church, both on earth and in heaven ; and the endless separation of the righteous and the wicked at the General Judgment.

On the part of God and of Christ this fellowship implies an exact knowledge of the Christian's character, his conduct, circumstances, wants, sufferings.

This fellowship also implies *mutual Love.* Mere knowledge may exist in any degree, without producing communion. The devils know all the things just mentioned ; yet their knowledge only renders them more hostile to God, to his designs and his kingdom. The communion we here contemplate, is sincere and cordial ; and cannot exist without love.

On the part of the Christian this Love to the Father and his Son Jesus Christ must be supreme ; so that his love to all other things even to his nearest connections, is comparatively hatred. It includes supreme benevolence towards God, or joy in his happiness; complacency in his character; gratitude for his goodness; submission to his will; joy in his government; and friendship to his designs.

On the part of God and of Christ it implies a desire for the happiness of the Christian, and complacency in his character—so far as it is holy, compassion for his wants and sufferings, and the forgiveness of his sins.

It implies *Union.* We may both know and love the character and designs of another, and there may be still no communion with him. We may know that a monarch is engaged in diffusing useful knowledge among his subjects, in promoting their religious interests, and in generally seeking their happiness; we may love him for this conduct; yet we cannot have communion with him, unless some connexion subsists between him and ourselves which creates a common interest. By nature no such connection subsists between God and man. We are aliens from his family, and feel no common interest with him or his children. If we are to feel this interest, we must assume and sustain a new relation to God. He must adopt us into his family, and we must become his children. This relation gives us a title to be interested in all that concerns God, and at the same time assures us that he is interested in all that concerns ourselves.

It implies *Co-operation.* Intelligent beings are active; and their purposes, their designs, are the objects nearest to their hearts. If two such beings are to have communion with each other in any important degree, they must have common designs, and must co-operate in the measures adopted to fulfil them. If a wife does not co-operate with her husband in promoting the temporal welfare or the salvation of their children, she has no communion with him in these important objects. The same is true of God. He has infinitely important and glorious designs which he is ever carrying on in the presence of his creatures. In his great condescension he permits and invites them to co-operate with him in their accomplishment, and he instructs them as to which are necessary. If the Christian under these circumstances does not co-operate with God ; communion between them cannot exist.

It also implies *Intercourse.* I intend by this word, that relative situation of two intelligent beings in which their minds meet ; in which they become mutually conscious of each other's thoughts, feelings, designs, and measures. If a husband were banished to a distant country with one half of his children, while the wife remained at home with the remainder ; during this separation their mutual love might exist, their relation as husband and wife would continue ; and they might diligently and successfully co-operate in securing the salvation of their common family, by a faithful discharge of the duties devolving on each. Still, if they could neither see each other, nor write to each other, nor in any way hear from each other, they could have no communion in this common good.

The same is true of God and the Christian. They must enjoy mutual intercourse. Their minds must meet on those subjects, on which they commune. Each must be conscious of the views, feelings, purposes, and measures, of the other with regard to these objects ; each must know that the other has this consciousness ; and for this purpose they must be conscious of being together, and must actually confer with each other.

If all these things exist ; if God and the Christian feel this mutual love ; if they are united in the relation of Father and child ; if they co-operate with each other ; and if they maintain a holy and delightful intercourse ; I see not that anything can be wanting to a full and perfect communion between them.

We are next to notice the *Reality* of this communion. This I shall argue, both from the Scriptures, and from the Nature of the case.

The Scriptures abundantly assert this, and in a direct form. The Text is an example. "Truly our fellowship is with the Father, and with his Son Jesus Christ." So Paul thus writes to the Corinthians,—"God is faithful, by whom ye were called to the fellowship of his Son Jesus Christ,"—and to the Hebrews, "We are made partakers of Christ, if we hold the beginning of our confidence steadfast unto the end." God promised this communion under the Old Dispensation. "I will meet you saith the Lord; and I will commune with you in every place where I record my name." Christ promised it to his disciples, immediately before his death. "If a man love me, he will keep my words; and my Father will love him, and we will come to him, and make our abode with him." "The world shall not see me, but ye shall see me." Henceforth I call you not servants, for the servant knoweth not what his master doeth, but I call you friends; for all things that I have heard of my Father, I have made known unto you." In his Intercessory Prayer, Christ prayed that all his followers might enjoy this communion; "That they all may be one, as thou Father art in me, and I in thee, that they also may be one in us. I in them, and thou in me, that they may be made perfect in one." Christ also promised after his ascension, that he would thus commune with his people. When he appeared to John in the Apocalyptic Vision, he said to him in the message sent to the Church in Laodicea, "Behold! I stand at the door and knock: if any man hear my voice, and will open the door, I will come in to him, and sup with him, and he with me." The common blessing pronounced on all Christians by the direction of God is, "The grace of our Lord Jesus Christ, and the love of God, and the communion of the Holy Spirit, be with you all. Amen." In accordance with this truth, good men in all ages have regarded communion with God as the greatest of all blessings. Thus Moses said to God, in the tabernacle of the congregation: "If thy presence go not with me, take us not hence." Thus David expresses his own feelings on this subject: "Whom have I in heaven but thee, and there is none on the earth whom I desire beside thee? As the hart panteth after the water-brooks, so panteth my soul after thee, O God! My soul thirsteth for God, for the living God; when shall I come and appear before God? O God, thou art my God; early will I seek thee. My soul thirsteth for thee, my flesh longeth for thee, in a dry and thirsty land where no water is, to see thy power and glory as I have seen thee in the sanctuary. Because thy loving-kindness is better than life, my lips shall praise thee."

This is also declared, in all the representations given of the connection between Christ and his disciples. He is the vine, and they are the branches. But the vine and its branches partake of a common sap and a common life. He is the head, and they are the members. But the head and the members of the natural body have a common blood, a common life, and a common consciousness. He and they are friends. But friends feel a common interest, and partake in common blessings and enjoyments. He and they are brethren, and therefore joint-heirs. They are the Bride, the Lamb's wife. But the possessions, the enjoyments, the interests of husband and wife, are in common.

This truth is also evident from the nature of the case. The Bible makes the Christian acquainted with the perfections, designs, government, works, and word of God, as well as with the character and the work of Christ, the mission of the Spirit, the nature, terms, and means of salvation. God also perfectly knows the character and circumstances of the Christian. The Christian loves the character of God, and approves of his measures; and God loves the Christian, so far as his character is holy. A most intimate union subsists between him and Christ as the Saviour, as well as between him and God. He has been adopted. God has become his Father, and he is God's child. "Beloved, now are we the sons of God; and it doth not yet appear what we shall be." As a son he feels a common interest with his father in all that is his. And God as his Father, and Christ as his Saviour, take a lively interest in his welfare. The Christian, so far as he is able, co-operates with God in his designs and measures. "We are laborers together with God," says Paul. God also co-operates with the Christian, in his designs and measures, so far as they are right, and so far as success will prove a blessing. A constant intercourse also exists between him and God. God is always present with him. He surrounds the Christian day and night, and is acquainted with all his ways. Not a day passes, in which he comes not frequently into the presence of God. What the mind of God is, what are his affections, and designs, and measures, he knows from the Bible. God also knows, by inspection, what are the feelings, wants, desires, and purposes of the Christian. In prayer and contemplation, his mind meets the mind of God on these subjects. They confer together as a man converses with his friend. At the same time, the Christian is conscious, at such seasons, that God thus knows his views, feelings and purposes; and God is also conscious that, through the Bible, the Christian is acquainted with his. Thus the Omnipresent Spirit is present to the soul of a Christian, and holds a communion with him which is far more intimate, confidential, and delightful, than the latter can hold with any created being.

What, then, is the *Extent* of this communion?

By its extent, I intend the number and variety of those things which God and the Christian possess and enjoy in common. It should be noticed that I am here speaking of the Christian, who has not only shaken off his original worldly character, but who has also advanced towards the stature of a man in Christ Jesus. These things, I apprehend, are far more numerous than many who appear to be Christians seem to imagine. They may be arranged under two classes: those things which belong to God; and those which, in a subordinate sense, belong to the Christian. In the first, the Christian communes with God; in the second, God communes with him. The second class, I need not say, is small, and, though interesting to the Christian himself, is comparatively of little moment. The first is boundless in the number of its objects, and infinite in its importance.

The Christian enjoys a holy and elevated communion with God, while he contemplates the divine perfections and glory. The perfections of God render him what he is, and constitute all his own happiness and glory. God dwells on his own perfections with supreme complacency and delight. The Christian, conscious of his own relations to Jehovah, while he casts his eye upward, sees God's various perfections, like the rays of the sun, all blended in one effulgence of glory; and, while he rejoices in the beauty of the all-perfect Mind, he is able to say, "This God is my God, my Father, my portion, forever and ever."

At other times his mind, with a prismatic power, separates these blended perfections, and surveys each in its own appropriate beauty.

Sometimes the goodness of God passes before him and melts his soul into fervent gratitude and admiration. While the cords of love draw him near to his great Benefactor, till there is no distance to separate them, he is ready to exclaim, "Oh that men would praise the Lord for his goodness, and for his wonderful works to the children of men!" It was at such a season that Jacob said, "O God of my father Abraham, and God of my father Isaac! I am not worthy of the least of all the mercies, and of all the truth which thou hast showed unto thy servant; for with my staff I passed over this Jordan, and now I am become two bands." It was after such a contemplation that David was led to cry out, as he sat in the house of the Lord, "Who am I, O Lord God, and what is mine house, that thou hast brought me hitherto."

Sometimes, as he ascends in heavenly contemplation, he has clear and bright discoveries of the purity and holiness of God. Of this Isaiah had a wonderful representation in his vision in the temple, when he saw the Seraphim covering their faces with their wings, and heard one say to another, "Holy, holy, holy, is the Lord of hosts; the whole earth is full of his glory." The sight produced the deepest self-abasement, and the prophet cried out, "Woe is me! for I am undone, for I am a man of unclean lips, for mine eyes have seen the King, Jehovah of hosts." Job had similar communion with God in his holiness, when he said, "I have heard of thee by the hearing of the ear, but now mine eye seeth thee. Wherefore I abhor myself, and repent in dust and ashes."

Sometimes he ponders with delight the truth and faithfulness of God, as manifested towards himself, and especially as manifested towards the Church, and her children in all generations. While this view produces unshaken confidence, he gives to God the glory: "Thou art a God that keepest covenant and mercy. Thy truth is as the great mountains, stedfast and immovable. Behold God is my salvation; I will trust and will not be afraid."

Sometimes God reveals himself in his infinite greatness; and while the Christian is ready to sink, he cries out with Abraham, "How shall I, who am but dust and ashes, take upon me to speak unto God." Should he contemplate the vastness of creation and the countless worlds of which it is composed, he says with Isaiah, "Behold! all these are as the drop of the bucket, and as the small dust of the balance!"

The Christian instructed by the Bible, communes, as we have said, with God, in his designs and purposes. Once, when he looked back to the beginning of the creation, when there was nothing but God, and remembered that then God formed his plan for the creation and government of all things; that then every globe and every atom, with all their various motions, as well as every intelligent being, with all his thoughts, desires, words, and actions, through Eternity were present to the divine mind; and that all subsequent events were merely the execution of this original plan; his heart rose up in rebellion against God. Now he looks upward and views the very same eternal purposes of God with joy and adoration, and he asks, "Shall I not rejoice that infinite goodness chose, and infinite wisdom devised, and infinite power will forever execute that plan which will manifest the glory of Jehovah in the supreme and eternal happiness of virtuous beings?

The Christian has communion with God, in his government. He looks upward, and sees Jehovah on the throne and all things beneath his feet, and every thing is just as it should be. Wicked beings in hell and on earth are hostile to this government, and wish to overturn it. But his language is, "Jehovah reigneth, let the universe rejoice; let the multitude" of worlds "be glad thereof." He rejoices that Jehovah is Almighty, and with a filial confidence can draw near to the throne and exult in the sunshine of that power which can crush the universe to dust. Even when he looks down on the world of misery and sees the punishment of the enemies of God, he can say with the hosts of saints and angels, "Alleluia, for the Lord God omnipotent reigneth."

He has communion with God, in the works of Creation. Sometimes when he meditates on the immensity of creation, especially when he surveys the clear starry firmament, and then ascends to its author, he exclaims with David, "When I consider the heavens, the work of thy fingers, the moon and the stars which thou hast ordained,—Lord, what is man!" At the same time, with filial love and confidence in the highest exercise, he can say, "My Father made, upholds and governs them all, and they will constitute that immense and eternal kingdom in which he will expend all the stores of his goodness and all the riches of his grace." When too he recalls his eye to the objects around him, and surveys "the bounteous store of charms which nature to her votary yields;" when he contemplates the perpetual succession of sublimity and beauty, of novelty and variety visible in the mountain and the valley, the woodland and the plain, the land and the sea, the changes of the seasons and of day and night, the majesty of the storm with the terrors of the volcano and the earthquake; he sees in each of these the manifestations of the same power and wisdom. And when he contemplates the unnumbered millions of the beasts of the field and the forest, of the birds of the air, of fishes in the sea, of reptiles and insects; he says with holy adoration, "All these wait upon *thee*. Thou givest them their meat in due season." Thus every object which he sees leads him to commune with its Author.

He has communion with God, in the works of Providence. When clouds and darkness are round about him, he rejoices that justice and judgment are the habitation of Jehovah's throne. His eye sees a God employed in all the good and ill that chequer life. In seasons of prosperity he says, "Thou makest me to lie down in green pastures; thou leadest me beside the still waters." In seasons of affliction he asks, "Shall I receive good at the hand of the Lord, and shall I not receive evil also?" It is then sweet to reflect that "whom the Lord loveth, he chasteneth, and scourgeth every son whom he receiveth." With Job, when the affliction is extreme, he can thank God for sending it. The Lord gave, and the Lord hath taken away, blessed be the name of the Lord." If his means of support for himself and family are diminished, he can say with confidence, "The Lord is my Shepherd; I shall not want." When dangers thereaten him, he knows that God sent them, and that God controls them, and his language is, "The Lord do unto me as seemeth him good."

He communes with God, in his Word. He never opens the Bible, but he hears the voice of God speaking to himself. It is God who communicates every truth it contains; and however mysterious or humbling, he believes in it and welcomes it as the truth of God. It is God who dictates every precept; and as he reads he resolves to obey. He not only accedes to, but rejoices in every threatening, as a sanction of a holy and righteous law. Every encouragement draws him nearer to God. Every promise he lays hold of in its fulness, whether it assures him of a glorious reward for his own faithfulness, or tells him of the future triumphs of the Church.

But in the Bible, it is his peculiar delight to commune with Christ. He approaches him as a Saviour mighty to save, and says with Thomas, "My Lord and my God." He communes with him in all that love which he manifested, as the angel Jehovah, to Patriarchs, and Kings, and Prophets, before the day of his coming. Knowing that he came to seek and to save that which was lost, he comes to him as a sinner justly condemned, who can find no one but Christ to save him from perdition. He surveys his character, and it is all glorious within and without. He receives his instructions as able to make him wise unto salvation. He dwells on his holy and perfect life, and resolves to walk in his steps. He contemplates his sufferings; and while he owns that no other sacrifice could atone for his sins, the love of Christ constrains him to devote himself a free-will offering to that Saviour who died for him. Every contemplation of his death leads him to more thorough hatred and renunciation of sin, to stronger and more prevailing faith, to a life of purer obedience; and the sincere language of his heart is, "God forbid that I should glory, save in the Cross of our Lord Jesus Christ, by whom the world is crucified unto me, and I unto the world." He communes with Christ as an ascended and glorified Saviour. Looking upwards, he beholds him on the throne, possessing all power in heaven and earth, holding the keys of death and of hell, and giving eternal life to whom he will.

Remembering that He who died to save the Church is

overruling all things for its good, he feels that the Church is safe, and that all his own efforts for its extension and prosperity will be crowned with success and acknowledged in the final day. He attempts nothing therefore in his own strength, but everything in the strength of Christ; and looks for no blessing in his efforts for the conversion of his children or of others around him, or for the recovery of a world lying in wickedness, unless he secures the co-operation of the Holy Spirit.

God also communes with the Christian, in all those things which are immediately interesting to himself. The Christian has daily wants; and he goes to his heavenly Father and tells him of them all, and then comes away with the gracious assurance that he shall not want any good thing. He has many sins, great and aggravated, but he is not afraid to spread them out before the eye of Infinite Purity, because he is sprinkled with the blood of sprinkling; and he comes away with a sweet assurance that his sins are covered and his transgressions forgiven. He has the business of life to transact; and he daily commits it to God, and finds that God directs his steps. He has daily duties to perform; and while he continually seeks the divine guidance, a voice within him says, "This is the way, walk thou therein." He looks to God to provide for his family; and He who feeds the young ravens when they cry, tells him that he will not leave his children to hunger or thirst. Dangers always surround him; but he finds that he who dwelleth in the secret place of the Most High, abides secure under the shadow of the Almighty. The souls of his children call forth his earnest cries and his faithful efforts; and he takes hold of the comprehensive promise, "I will be a God to thee and to thy seed after thee." He needs the daily presence and blessing of God in his house; and he finds the words of Christ sweetly verified, "If any man love me he will keep my words, and my Father will love him, and we will come to him and take up our abode with him!" He knows that death is before him; but he can often say with David, "Though I walk through the valley of the shadow of death, I will fear no evil; for thy rod and thy staff they comfort me." And when the hour of death has actually come, and he is summoned away into the unseen world, he perceives his Saviour present, and is able to say to him without a doubt, "Lord Jesus, receive my spirit."

Thus in all things, whether relating to himself and his own personal and relative interests, or to God—to his perfections, government and works, or to Christ—to his mission and kingdom, the Christian may say, in the language of the text, "Truly our fellowship is with the Father, and with the Son Jesus Christ."

We are also to notice the *Desirableness* of this Fellowship.

After what has been already said, it needs scarcely be observed, that it increases the Christian's resemblance to God. The character is continually affected by surrounding objects. Men are ever exerting powerful influence on each other. No two individuals can associate familiarly without assimilating in character. The expressive proverb of common sense, that 'a man is known by the company he keeps,' and the declaration of inspiration, "He that walketh with wise men shall be wise, but the companion of fools shall be destroyed," teach us how prevailing is this mutual influence. Especially is this true, where one of the individuals is greatly superior to the other in energy of character. No one can be the intimate friend of a man of uncommon depravity without becoming thoroughly corrupted; and no one can associate with a man of distinguished piety and virtue, without becoming like him in the purity and excellence of his character.

How great then, how transforming must be the influence exerted by God! The energy of his character is infinite. In daily communion with him we come into his immediate presence, and while we dwell with reverence and delight on his uncreated beauty and glory, we surrender ourselves to his influence, and are gradually formed into the same character. "But we all," says the Apostle, "with open face beholding, as in a glass, the glory of the Lord, are changed into the same image, from glory to glory, as by the Spirit of the Lord. This is the true secret of the Christian's growth in grace. His soul, like the dawning light, shineth more and more unto the perfect day; and when admitted to the unclouded presence of God and of Christ, in heaven, this resemblance will be complete. "Then," says John, "we shall be like him, for we shall see him as he is."

Must it not afford an equal security against temptation and sin? Joseph, in the hour of peculiar trial, found his safety in fleeing immediately to the Divine protection: "How shall I do this great wickedness and sin against God?" In this refuge, David tells us, was his daily safety: "I set the Lord always before me; because he is at my right hand, I shall not be moved." Every Christian also, who, like David, leads a life of daily communion with God, can testify as he did, "He that dwelleth in the secret place of the Most High shall abide under the shadow of the Almighty. I will say of the Lord, 'He is my Refuge and my Fortress; in him will I trust." The Christian never so distinctly discovers the odiousness of guilt and sin, as when he contrasts it with the purity of God. His habitual consciousness of the Divine presence and his habitual contemplation of the Divine perfections restrain the disposition to sin, and render his victory easy and certain. When Satan comes near to seduce him and lead him captive, he has a refuge in the Divine presence whither the adversary of his soul dare not follow him. When the world spreads its snares around him, if God is with him, and his hand supports him, he finds that his feet are not taken. If his own lusts rebel, the presence of God brings them into immediate captivity. "This I say then," exclaims the Apostle, "walk in the Spirit, and ye shall not fulfil the lusts of the flesh."

Nor is this fellowship less supporting in every species of trial. If dangers surround the Christian who thus walks with God, he can firmly say, "The Lord is my Portion: I will not fear what man can do unto me. Surely he shall deliver me from the snare of the fowler and from the noisome pestilence. He shall cover me with his feathers, and under his wings will I trust. His truth shall be my shield and my buckler." If the events of Providence are dark and mysterious, he can remember that justice and judgment are the habitation of God's throne. If his property is taken away, he has a treasure in God of which nothing can deprive him. If his friends prove false or are removed by death, Jesus is a friend who cannot die, and who will never prove faithless. If the valley of death is before him, its glooms are dispelled, its terrors gone, for Jesus himself is there.

It yields, we may add, a corresponding enjoyment. What can be a source of higher joy than a firm assurance that our peace is made with God, that sin, the sting of death, has been taken away, and that heaven is our eternal inheritance? But communion with God will give us this assurance. There is, however, if possible, a higher joy than this, which it will also impart. Our personal blessings must indeed be secure, if we are to possess any high enjoyment. Yet that state of the mind is not the happiest, in which it often reflects on the question whether its blessings are secure. That question, probably, never occupies the attention of the inhabitants of heaven. There is in God himself an infinite fulness of good. If the mind is rightly attempered to enjoy him, if it has a suitable relish for his spiritual beauty and glory so that all other things appear as worthless, God can manifest himself to that mind in such a manner and to such a degree, as to satisfy every desire. The discoveries of Himself may be easily rendered so clear and bright, as to draw forth every affection of the soul until it is lost in the depths of Infinite love. This enjoyment is absolutely pure. It has no earthly nor animal mixture, for it springs up in a rational and purified mind, while loving with all the heart Him who is Infinitely lovely. It is solid and substantial, for it rests on the love of God. It is satisfying, for he who drinks of this Uncreated fountain perceives all other enjoyments to be broken cisterns that can hold no water. It is elevated, for it is derived from Him who is higher than the heavens. It is unfading and without end, for He who bestows it is infinite and eternal. This enjoyment, the earnest, the commencement of life eternal in the soul, springs from fellowship with God; and the degree in which it is possessed will depend on the nearness, the purity, and the constancy of this communion.

Such a fellowship, it is apparent, is also the highest honor to which a rational being can aspire. We deem it the peculiar honor and privilege of angels, that they always behold the face of God. Yet this is the very honor to which the humblest Christian is admitted, whose fellowship is with the Father, and with his Son Jesus Christ. Every day he is admitted to the immediate presence of God. He sees him as the world sees him not—as his Father, Redeemer, and Sanctifier, as his Mediator, Comforter, Guide, and Portion. He not only sees him, but is permitted to come near to him, and to converse with him face to face. When he calls him his Father, God owns him as a child. When he looks to him as his Saviour, Christ acknowledges him as one ransomed by his blood. When he addresses him as his Sanctifier, he finds that the Spirit of holiness dwells in him as in a living temple, making him a partaker of the divine nature and preparing him for the more immediate presence and enjoyment of God in heaven. What honor, let me ask, can be compared with this? To be admitted even once into the presence of a powerful monarch, is accounted a high distinction. To be thus admitted daily is the peculiar privilege of nobles and princes. But the Christian, partaking of this fellowship is admitted into the immediate presence of the Monarch of the Universe, not once, nor occasionally, but daily and hourly, whenever he is willing to approach him. He may converse with God in the most unreserved and confidential manner, may communicate all his feelings, make known all his wants, confer with him respecting the prosperity and glory of his kingdom, and be employed by him in the same work in which angels are engaged—the work of recovering immortal minds from ruin, and raising them to glory, honor, immortality. This is the honor that cometh from God only.

This subject, so sacred, so searching in its tests, is its own application both to the Christian and to the impenitent hearer.

HEAVEN.

HEBREWS XII: 22.

THE HEAVENLY JERUSALEM.

JERUSALEM was the peculiar residence of God below; the place where he manifested his presence, his goodness and his grace, as he did no where else on earth. Heaven is the peculiar residence of God above; the place in which his presence is felt, his goodness displayed, and where his glory shines forth as it does no where else in the universe. This is the reason why the one is made a type of the other, and why the latter is styled by the Apostle in the text, "the Heavenly Jerusalem."

This passage may fitly invite us to a contemplation of Heaven, as it is described to us in the Scriptures. This is a subject which the Scriptural writers continually introduce. Their own feelings instinctively led them to the contemplation, and they appear to wish to describe it, as that residence above which we are all urged to secure, and which the children of God will forever occupy. But a few of the more prominent particulars of this description can be included in a single discourse.

Heaven is described as a *Place.* I know that it has been much disputed whether Heaven is a *State*, or a *Place;* whether it is the *happiness* enjoyed by separate spirits, or the *region* in which it is enjoyed. This dispute seems to have arisen from misapprehension. When it is said that Heaven is a place, it is not intended that it is a globular or a material world like the earth or the sun, to which its inhabitants are confined by the attraction of gravitation. Neither will those who regard Heaven as a state affirm, that its inhabitants never enjoy each others' society, and that they float in eternal solitude on the ocean of Immensity, but in the enjoyment of God.

If those who deem Heaven to be a place had described it as *that portion of the universe, where saints and angels are gathered together, where they see and converse with each other, and where they behold the glorified body of Christ*, probably the dispute would not have arisen.

It is usually said that *place* or *locality* is not predicable of separate spirits, and that a spirit cannot be said to be *in place* at all, except with respect to its operations on matter. This, however, is obviously said rashly, and without evidence. A created spirit is not omnipresent. If, then, separate spirits exist and are not everywhere, they are somewhere.

Both common sense and the Scriptures show us that this conclusion is sound. The soul of a living man is in his body, in a sense in which it is not in the body of another man. When the body moves, the soul moves with it from one place to another. At death it ceases to be present with the body, and goes away. The separate spirit of Moses was as truly present on the Mount of Transfiguration as the body of Peter, and as truly left the Mount after the interview with Christ. In the same manner, the souls of the righteous are spoken of in the Scriptures as going to heaven after death ; and the angels are represented as descending from heaven and as ascending in return. They also teach us that the souls of the wicked are not mingled with those of the righteous, but are separated from them and gathered into another place. At the present time, the bodies of Christ, of Enoch and Elijah are in heaven ; and those of the righteous, after the Resurrection, will all ascend to Heaven. It is not, therefore, merely in accommodation to our weak and imperfect conceptions that heaven is uniformly spoken of in the Scriptures as a place. Though we conceive of no solid, material world on which its inhabitants move, and to which they are confined, yet, when we know that angels and saints are there assembled, and dwell together with Christ, and behold his glory, it is with metaphysical exactness that we represent heaven as a *place*, and not merely as a *state* of existence.

Heaven is a place of *great Extent.*

Our views of the extent of heaven are often exceedingly inadequate. This may be partly ascribed to the manner in which heaven is described in the Scriptures. There it is often represented under the image of a *House*, to show the endearing relation which God sustains to its inhabitants. If we view heaven as a house, they constitute a family of which God is the Father and they are the children. As children, they live in his presence, partake of his bounty, and constantly enjoy his paternal love. Instead of receiving this delightful instruction from the language, we too often make use of the image of a house to narrow our views of the extent of heaven.

Heaven is represented as a *Temple*, and its inhabitants as priests offering incense around the altar. Yet, so gross and earthly are our conceptions that, instead of learning from this delightful image that heaven is the residence of pure and spotless minds, and the place where the spiritual beauty of Jehovah shines forth, we give to Heaven itself a material subsistence, the shape of a church or a temple far above us, indeed, and in dimensions somewhat larger than the temple of Solomon.

Heaven is often described as a *City*, with walls, and gates, and streets, and buildings. As the capital of a great empire, in which the monarch and his court reside, is the seat of power, the centre of intelligence, and contains the richest displays of art and magnificence ; so, when heaven is represented to us as the city of the living God, the residence of angels and saints, who are the nobles and princes of his empire, we are taught that it is the seat of his government, the place where the magnificence of creative wisdom is displayed, the spot where all the intelligence respecting his vast empire is collected. Yet we too often interpret the language literally, and our minds dwell on the image of a large city until our views of its extent become diminutive and low.

The Scriptures, did we properly observe their language, would correct mistakes of this nature. They not only speak of heaven as a house, a temple, a city, but also employ images to describe it which imply a far greater extent. They speak of it as a *Country*, and a *Kingdom;* the country to which the righteous have gone, the kingdom which they will inhabit forever. They also represent it as a *World*. "They," says our Lord, "who shall be accounted worthy to obtain that world, are equal to the angels, and are the children of God."

When the Scriptures represent it as the residence of separate spirits, they authorize us to form views of its extent as almost unlimited. Material worlds were formed for the residence of sluggish, material bodies, and need not therefore be large. But separate spirits, we know, move with a rapidity incomparably greater than that of light, and approaching that of thought itself. If, then, the extent of Heaven corresponds to the nature and faculties of its inhabitants, and is large enough for them to expatiate freely, our minds can set no limits to its extent. Solomon, in his prayer at the dedication of the Temple, conveys to us this idea, in the most impressive manner. Alluding to the immensity of God, he says, "Will God indeed dwell on the Earth! Behold the heaven and heaven of heavens cannot contain thee!" If he had not supposed the extent of heaven to be immeasurably great, compared with that of the earth, his language would have been without force or meaning.

Heaven is a *very populous world.*

The native inhabitants of heaven are exceedingly numerous. Wherever the angels are mentioned, the language employed indicates that their numbers are very great. They are described as a host or army: "Who doeth according to his will in the army of heaven, and among the inhabitants of this lower world." They are mentioned as numerous hosts or armies. John tells us that he saw the armies of heaven following after Christ. And Job, by asking the question, "Is there any number of his armies," teaches us that even the number of the armies of heaven cannot be reckoned.

Whenever the sacred writers refer us to the number of the angels, they either use the greatest numbers ever employed in the language of the Scriptures, or they inform us that the number is too great to be computed. Thus Daniel tells us that, when the Ancient of days sat upon his throne, "thousand thousands ministered unto him, and ten thousand times ten thousand stood before him." In the same manner, John asserts that the number of the angels whom he saw about the throne was "ten thousand times ten thousand, and thousands of thousands." The first of these numbers taken literally, denotes one hundred millions; and, when used in connection with the second, is a Hebrew idiom expressive of a number which is great beyond all possible computation. It is also mentioned as a characteristic of Jehovah, that he numbers the armies of heaven and calls them all by their names, as if this were a task which no one else were able to accomplish. And in the context Paul teaches us that we are to understand by these and similar representations that the Holy angels are literally without number. "But ye are come to an innumerable company of angels."

The number of saints in heaven is also very great. John, when describing heaven as it existed when he was upon earth, speaks of the spirits of the just as a vast multitude which no one can number. To these we must add the many millions who since that period have ascended to heaven, if we would learn the whole number already assembled there. If we look forward to the arrival of the Latter Day, we learn that the number of those who are every year to enter heaven will be continually and rapidly increasing. During the long reign of Christ on earth, this world will be nothing but a nursery for heaven. One generation will pass away, and another will come in rapid succession, and each will furnish its hundreds and probably its thousands of millions to the upper world. If then the redeemed in heaven, in the time of John, were a multitude which no one could enumerate, how vast beyond conception will be their number on the morning of the Final Day!

Heaven is a world *peculiarly connected with that in which we dwell.*

As the city of the Great King, the metropolis of his empire, Heaven is connected with every world throughout his vast dominions. The metropolis of an extensive empire is the centre, the heart, from which life, activity and influence circulate to the remotest provinces, and to which they unceasingly return. The various worlds and systems of worlds in the universe are the provinces of the empire of God. As distinct governments, they are entrusted to the nobles and princes of his court; who are accordingly spoken of as Thrones and Dominions, Principalities and Powers, in heavenly places. As these celestial beings visited our first parents in paradise, so we cannot doubt that they visit all the various worlds entrusted to their care; and these maintain uninterrupted intercourse between the metropolis and every part of the empire.

The connection between this world and heaven is far more intimate than that which subsisted before the Fall of Adam; in various respects it is more intimate than that which can subsist between heaven and any other world. It is not placed, like other worlds, merely under the operation of the general laws of the empire. By the work of redemption it has been singled out from the rest of the universe, and placed under a dispensation of grace. The great design of this dispensation is to recover the inhabitants of this world from ruin, and to gather them together in heaven. This consummation is the reward of the righteousness of Christ; and is a far more glorious exaltation than that which the perfect obedience of the first Adam could have secured for his posterity. This work of the New Creation began immediately after the Fall, and has continued to the present moment. Whenever one sinner is converted, the intelligence not only reaches heaven, but occasions more joy in the angels of God than the perseverance of ninety and nine just persons who need no repentance. The angels, however, are not mere passive spectators of this work. As ministering spirits, they are sent forth to minister unto them who are the heirs of salvation, to protect them from their enemies, and to conduct them safely to heaven. The way from this world to heaven has thus become a high-way in which the angels of God are continually ascending and descending.

The King of heaven has, also, in a peculiar manner been present in this world. As the Angel Jehovah, he appeared to the patriarchs, on Mount Sinai, in the Holy of Holies, and to the prophets of Israel and Judah. In the fulness of time he became flesh, and dwelt among us, and we beheld his glory. In this world and in this alone, has God assumed a local habitation—the body of the Man Christ Jesus; and no nature, but the nature of man, has ever been received into a personal union with the nature of God. No race of creatures but our own can look up to heaven, and there beholding him who sitteth on the throne, even the Lamb that was slain, can say, "This glorious Person, in whom all the fulness of the Godhead dwells and whom all the angels worship, was made in all respects, sin excepted, like unto us his brethren, and is Emmanuel, God with us." In three instances, God the Father has been also manifested on earth: once at the baptism of Christ, again on the Mount of Transfiguration in the voice and the cloud of glory, and again by a voice from heaven a few days before the death of Christ. In one also the Holy Spirit has appeared among us in a bodily shape, like a dove. Since the ascension of Christ, the Spirit has constantly dwelt on earth, as the Sanctifier, by his divine influence renewing the souls of men and preparing them for heaven. Those whom he renews are born from above, and are made the heirs of heaven. While here, they are mere pilgrims, on a journey to heaven. There a place is prepared for them by Christ; and thither, when they die, they instantly ascend.

Thus heaven and earth have become intimately connected. Jesus of Nazareth is head over all things in heaven and earth. A vast multitude of the human family have already been there admitted. Many more are now on their way. Soon peoples, nations, and languages, will enter on this journey. At the final consummation, all that part of the human family which God intended to recover from a state of ruin, will be collected in heaven; and heaven and earth will be "no more twain, but one."

Heaven is a world of *knowledge*.

There will be no error in heaven; for none of the causes of error will there be found. Prejudice will not there close the eyes against the discernment of truth. Pride will not there lead it to investigate those things which it cannot comprehend. The love of sin will not bias and warp its decisions, in favor of falsehood. No liar will be found there, to deceive with regard to facts; no sophist, to mislead with regard to principles. The love of truth is there the only character, and its influence is controlling over every heart. The knowledge of heaven is not, like much of ours, mere doubt or conjecture. It is attended by certainty. God, the Sun of the Intelligent Universe, shines on every object of contemplation within the reach of saints or angels; and the eye of the mind looks on, and sees it as it is. This certainty of knowledge is much insisted on in the Scriptures. John, describing the vision of Christ at his coming, thus affirms: "We shall be like him, for we shall see him as he is." "Now," says Paul, "we know in part: but when that which is perfect is come," i. e. when we arrive at our perfect state, then this partial knowledge will be done away. With his present knowledge he compares himself to a child; but then he will be a man, and put away childish things. "Now," he says, "we see through a glass darkly; but then face to face. Now I know in part; but then shall I know even as also I am known."

The inlets of knowledge will be wonderfully changed. Here the soul is confined to a narrow house of clay, and has no medium of communication with the surrounding universe except through the senses; three of which convey perceptions to the animal nature merely, and only two to the intelligent nature. Had it not been for these five dark windows through which a little light from without is let in, the soul would have been wrapt in perpetual night. From this dungeon the disembodied spirit of the believer goes forth to the regions of light and day. Like a prisoner set free he expatiates freely and gladly, and is lost in astonishment at the beauty, grandeur, glory, which every where surround him.

The desire of knowledge, which is here feeble and possessed but by few, is one of the most distinct characteristics of the inhabitants of heaven. Here, a few hours' mental labor exhausts our powers, and the mind is compelled to relax its efforts. There, it will be incapable of weariness or decay, and possess the activity and energy of a separate spirit. Here, the faculties are feeble; the discrimination is imperfect, the memory treacherous, the imagination grovelling, and the reasoning powers are sluggish and erring. Who can conceive of the change wrought in the embodied mind, when its faculties shall qualify it to converse with angels, and to appear with dignity in heaven!

How strong will be its memory, when impressions once made will never be effaced. How lofty its imagination, when it can ascend with safety to the consecrated heaven, where the ever-blessed Three dwell in holy and blessed communion forever. How intuitive its reason, and how strange its discoveries, when conclusions now learned only by the most difficult demonstrations, shall be seen to be true at a glance and by bare inspection, and shall be taken for granted at the outset of its researches. What attainments will be made in knowledge by a mind of such faculties in that world of truth and certainty, through the progress of everlasting ages?

The kinds of knowledge which the Christian will acquire in heaven, deserve our notice. He will acquire a knowledge of *Events*. The angels were present on the morning of the Creation. Then "the morning stars sang together, and all the sons of God shouted for joy," when they saw, at the command of Jehovah, suns and planets starting into existence. They were acquainted with the original state of heaven; they beheld the fall of Lucifer and his angels, the happiness of Eden, and the fall of our first parents. They have been constant and attentive observers of the providence of God, not only in earth and heaven, but in every other world through his vast dominions. Especially have they watched the work of Redemption. They remember how this plan of mercy was first intimated, how it was gradually unfolded in heaven and on earth; and the whole history of every part of it is fresh in their memory.

Heaven, as the metropolis of the Divine empire, is also the centre of intelligence. No event which occurs in the Universe is too small or trifling to be immediately known in heaven. In this world not a beggar can die who is the child of God, but angels are present to conduct him home.

Not a sinner can be converted, but new songs of joy are heard through the multitude of the heavenly host. The Scriptures inform us, how constantly the angels are going forth from heaven as the messengers of God to do his pleasure. As they return they doubtless also communicate the events which they have beheld on their journey. These events unfold the goodness and glory of the Supreme Governor, the wisdom of his counsels, the variety of his dispensations, and the increasing happiness and virtue of his empire.

He will acquire a knowledge of *Other Worlds.* That he will gain this by communication, we have just seen. That he will also gain it by personal inspection, the Scriptures place beyond a doubt. The spirits of Moses and Samuel, and the glorified body of Elijah, have visited this world, and are equally able to visit every other part of the Divine empire.

He will gain a knowledge of *truths*, or principles. This will, probably, be true of the principles of natural science. These, as established, were to be known, that God might be glorified. Yet many truths relating to the organization of minerals, the structure and growth of vegetables and animals, particularly the nature and laws of vegetable and animal life, and the ordinances of heaven, never can be known by our present limited faculties. But truths relating to mind, or the laws by which intelligent and moral beings are governed, will there especially interest the attention. Of these how little do we now know? On a few plain subjects God has shed a clear and satisfying light. But clouds and darkness rest on all that lies beyond. When, for example, we attempt to contemplate the introduction of Moral evil into the Universe, or the Decrees of God, or the freedom of Man, or the transmission of a fallen nature to the posterity of Adam, or the election of those who are saved, or the self existence and eternity of God, or the doctrine of the Trinity, or the manner in which the Holy Spirit renews and sanctifies the soul, how feeble does the grasp of our minds appear, how much is there that seems to need a further explanation ; how ready are we to wish, that Paul or some other of the Apostles were present, that we might state our difficulties and have them solved ? Of all these truths, those which are immediately connected with the work of Redemption will be dwelt upon with peculiar interest, because they especially display the glory of God to principalities and powers in heavenly places.

He will acquire a knowledge of *intelligent beings.* With those who are in heaven, the saints and angels, he will be present ; and will see as he is seen, and know as he is known. In the vast population of the Universe also, in the endless variety of their characters and circumstances and of God's dispensation towards them, he will discover manifestations of the Divine perfections ever varying and ever new.

Above all things he will gain a knowledge of *God.* In heaven the perfections of Jehovah shine forth with as strong an effulgence as the eyes of angels can endure. In contemplating and adoring the All-perfect Mind, they have been employed since that Mind spoke them into being. What progress have they not made ? What knowledge can they not communicate ? Where is there such a school of theology as this ? 'If an angel from heaven,' says Baxter, 'would come down to earth, to tell us all of God that we would know and might lawfully ask ; who would not turn his back on libraries and universities and learned men, to go and discourse with such a Teacher ? What travel should I think too far, what expense too great, for one hour's talk with such a messenger ?' This knowledge, I add, will grow forever. They will never, indeed, arrive at that Uncreated Heaven, whither creatures cannot go, and where the Sacred Three dwell alone; but they will mount up towards it, and draw continually nearer and nearer, through eternity.

Heaven is a world of *Happiness.*

Nothing will there exist either within or without the mind, to excite uneasiness, or to create pain or sorrow. The power of sin over the spirit will be forever destroyed. Not one impure or unholy thought, or affection, or purpose, will ever enter within its chambers. Not one restless, unhallowed, ungratified desire, nor a feeling of remorse, will ever disturb its repose. Its subjection to the will of God, will be perfect and unchanging. The government of the universe will be seen to be in the right hands; and all things throughout the mighty empire will appear to be exactly right, and to be laboring together to display the perfections of Jehovah and the immortal happiness of his virtuous creatures. The will once so turbulent and restless, will be lost in the will of God, and will thus be always perfectly satisfied because the will of God will be always perfectly done. The uneasiness of faith will subside in vision. The aspirings of hope will be quieted by enjoyment.

There will "be no night there," for immortal natures do not need the refreshings of repose. Their vigor only grows by exercise. Their faculties, instead of decaying, only strengthen and heighten under the labors of eternity. Not one deformed or disgusting object will be seen. Nothing that defileth or that worketh abomination, will ever be admitted. No scenes of distress or sorrow, no example of the frailties or sins of good men, will be there beheld. The bodies of the saints will be all glorious without; the minds of saints and angels will be all glorious within; while the glorified body of Jesus, invested with an uncreated splendor becoming the visible Representative of the Omnipotent spirit, will be the light, the sun, of the heavenly world. And if any other objects are there presented to the sight they are only shadowed forth by the streets of gold, and the walls of living gems, and the gates of pearl in the Apocalyptic vision.

In heaven the social affections of the mind will be forever refreshed and satisfied. Our Lord tells us that many shall come from the east, and from the west, from the north and from the south, and shall sit down with Abraham, Isaac and Jacob, and all the prophets in the kingdom of God. There all holy men of past ages are now assembled. There are Enoch — who walked with God, and Elijah — the chief of the prophets, who were singled out from the sons of men and translated that they should not see death. There is Abraham, who conversed with God, face to face. There is Moses, who led the church through the wilderness and then entered the heavenly Canaan. There the sweet Psalmist of Israel, who taught the Church on earth to sing the praises of God and the Lamb; and is now, perhaps, the chief musician of the heavenly choir. There is Isaiah, rejoicing in the seed of the virgin and the victories of the Church. There is the disciple whom Jesus loved, and his companions; and there is the apostle of the Gentiles, in company with Stephen, though he consented to his death. There are the martyrs of the Church, the faithful evangelists and ministers, and missionaries of the Cross. There, too, are the Reformers, and all those other distinguished men who have contended for the faith; and there are all the humble followers of Jesus, whom God has gathered out of every kindred and people and tongue. There, also, the Christian will find his pious ancestors, whose prayers secured him the divine blessing; with his pious parents who gave him up to

God in infancy, and by prayer, instruction, and holy example, led him in the pathway to heaven. There, too, he will see that faithful minister, or that devoted Christian, whom the Holy Ghost employed to bring him to repentance.

Mingled with the Church of the Redeemed, he will see an innumerable company of angels, pure and holy spirits, the princes of the Universe, originally made to inhabit the holy place and to stand in the presence of God. Among them are Gabriel — the harbinger of the Messiah from heaven, and the multitude of the heavenly host who sung the song of Bethlehem. All of them are ministering spirits, and among them he will discover the angel to whom the ministering to his own salvation was especially entrusted by God.

In heaven he will dwell in the immediate presence of Christ, that he may behold his glory. He is the light of heaven; and in Him, as in a central point, the rays of uncreated light are all collected, and from his face the effulgence shines forth to enlighten, warm, and bless the happy inhabitants. This effulgence will transform saints and angels into the same image, from one degree of likeness to another, in a never ending progress. He is the medium of communication between the Omnipresent Jehovah and the holy inhabitants of heaven. He is the temple in which Jehovah dwells, the only visible manifestation of the Godhead through the Universe. In him infinite perfections centre, and from him they shine forth with a softer radiance. On his face holy intelligences will forever look, and behold the glory of God. In knowing Christ, they will know God. He calls them his friends and brethren, and will admit them into the same near and familiar intercourse to which the twelve were admitted on earth. Their communion with him will be most intimate, resembling that between him and the Father. It is the intercourse of love, of a love that passes knowledge, of a love to which even angels will in some respects be strangers; for they can never shed the tears of contrition and repentance, they can never say, "Thou art worthy, for thou hast redeemed us to God by thy blood." There, He will feed his flock like a shepherd, and lead them in green pastures, and conduct them to living fountains of water. There He will reign over them, only to bless them; and they shall reign with him forever, and be partakers in his glory and blessedness. He himself will teach them the knowledge of God, and make them new and unceasing manifestations of his love. As the ages of Eternity roll on, He will employ the stores of his own exhaustless bounty to bless them; He will enlarge their faculties by fresh communications of truth; He will sanctify them wholly, and reveal new glories of the All-perfect Mind in a progress becoming only more rapid and blissful forever.

MUTUAL RECOGNITION IN HEAVEN.

2 Corinthians i: 14.

AS YE ALSO HAVE ACKNOWLEDGED US IN PART, THAT WE ARE YOUR REJOICING, EVEN AS YE ALSO ARE OURS, IN THE DAY OF THE LORD JESUS.

It has been often asked, Whether in the future world, we shall remember the events and associations of the present; Whether we shall hereafter know those, with whom we have been connected here by friendship or by blood. Were this the inquiry of mere curiosity, I should not attempt to answer it. But it presents a subject of contemplation, on which the voice of Revelation is far from being silent. It is prompted, also, by feelings, which I would cherish myself, and which I respect in others. It may, at the same time, furnish strong consolation and powerful motives to christian faithfulness. I shall proceed accordingly, to present the subject, as it is exhibited both by Reason and the Scriptures.

While thus proposing to derive aid from Reason, I am well aware that unassisted Reason can here shed no light; that on this subject nothing is easier than to pursue the rovings of fancy, and that our only safety lies in following the Word of God. It has been my earnest wish that this Word might guide me far from the regions of conjecture, into the plain path of truth and certainty. At the same time, as every truth in that Word flows from Him who is pure Reason itself, we are not only assured that every such truth accords with reason, but are constrained to believe that on all subjects within the grasp of the human mind, this accordance can be seen and proved; and that it is, of course, the duty of a preacher of that Word to show in every case that Reason and Revelation perfectly harmonize.

At the first stage of this inquiry it is fair to ask him, who takes the Negative, Whence do you derive your opinion? From the Scriptures no passage has been adduced hitherto, and none, I venture to say, can be adduced, which either directly or indirectly asserts it, or which declares any other principle from which it may be fairly inferred.

Do you conclude from *the nature of the case*, that the soul loses all or any of its powers, and particularly its memory, at death? Would not the proof of such a loss involve also the proof, that the soul is material and mortal.

Do you learn this principle from *the death-bed?* Do the vivid recollections of the past, and the clear and strong anticipations of the future, which we often witness, both in the saint and in the sinner, at the moment of death, convince you that mind which, even amid the agonies of dissolving nature, is all life, all energy, is destined when those agonies are past to become inactive and lifeless?

Is your opinion the dictate, even, of *Natural Religion?* In what mythology, which regards the soul as immortal, do you fail to find the events and associations of the present life intimately connected with the happiness of the future? In the fabled descent of Orpheus, we see Eurydice recog nizing her husband, cherishing for him her wonted affection. and consenting to return with him to their former home. Do not Pythagoras and the early Brahmins insist that, in each successive transmigration of the soul, the events of the preceding states of existence were remembered; and did he not distinctly declare that he had been Æthalides, the son of Mercury, then the hero Euphorbus at the seige of Troy, then Hermotimus the prophet of Clazomenœ, and afterwards a fisherman, before he became the son of Mucsanchus? Do you not hear Ulysses and Æneas in their visits to Hades, conversing familiarly with their departed friends, as well as with the heroes and sages of earlier times? Did not the prospect of an admission to their exalted society furnish great consolation to Socrates and Cato, in the near prospect of death? Ask the Mohammedan, what awaits him beyond the river of death; and he will point you to a paradise of active but licentious joy. Inquire of the Hindoo widow, what prompts her to fire the pile on which she is reposing by the corpse of her husband; and she will answer, 'The hope of a happier union, in a world, where death and separation are unknown.' Inquire, too, of the dying Indian, why his buffalo-robe and his tomahawk, his bow and his quiver, must be buried with him in the grave; and he will tell you, that he is going to the land where his fathers are gone, and that in that milder region he shall need them when engaged in hunting, or in war.

As then neither revelation, nor the nature of the case, nor any system of mythology, popular or philosophical, lends any direct support to this opinion, I conclude that it is the result of mere feeling; and the objections usually alleged against the opposite opinion, confirm this conclusion. These we shall consider hereafter. With these preliminary remarks I shall now procceed to the direct discusssion of the subject.

1. The souls of men do not lose their personal identity, when separated from the body. It was a favorite opinion of the heathen philosophers, and has been avowed by some who call themselves christians, that the soul is a spark, or an emanation from the essence of the Deity ; and that when the intervening obstructions presented by the body are removed, it immediately returns, and is absorbed in its original Fountain. When meeting with such notions in poetry, we regard them as mere creations of fancy, and are amused or delighted ; but when we are called on in sober prose to believe in them as revealed truths, or as matters of fact, we instinctively hesitate, and ask for evidence to support our faith. In this case all the evidence is contrary.

We are not *God*, nor *a part of God;* either when in the body, or when out of it. God does not consist of parts, nor is he susceptible of division or addition. Angels, though separate spirits, have as absolute a personal identity as men. They are perfectly distinct from God, and are not a part of him. He charges them with folly, and they are not clean in his sight. Can this be said of himself? But if this be true of those pure spirits who never sinned, how much more emphatically is it true of ourselves, even when separated from the body. The angels, also, are perfectly distinct from each other. All the representations of Scripture teach us that they are not blended, or united into one common mass of being, like two portions of air or water when brought together ; but are separate, individual existences, possessing each his distinct consciousness and exhibiting his own personal characteristics. As such they have their respective offices, as thrones and dominions, principalities and powers ; and their respective duties, as messengers and ministering spirits. As such, God, their maker, numbereth them and calleth them all by their names ; and as such, they know each other's stations, histories and characters.

To conclude, because we know each other by our faces, voices and persons, our attitudes and movements, that separate spirits, not having these helps, cannot therefore distinguish one another, is wholly unphilosophical. Two individuals, natives of distant countries and personally strangers, if mutually and intimately informed of each other's histories, characters, views, and habits of thinking, may, by conversation merely, mutually discover each other. A lost child, after time has changed every trace of that image which was imprinted on his parent's memories, may, by the recollections of childhood, identify his birth-place and parentage. The angels, we have seen, do in fact thus distinguish each other ; nor are we left to the mere argument from analogy with regard to departed spirits. Several of them since their decease have actually revisited this earth. The spirit of Samuel came from the unseen world, to announce to Saul his tremendous doom. The spirit of Moses was present with Christ and his three disciples, on the mount of Transfiguration ; and was not only seen there by them, but conversed with Christ in their hearing and in language which they understood, respecting his decease which he should accomplish at Jerusalem. These departed spirits had as really a separate individual existence and a distinct personal consciousness, as they had in the present life. They were not only known as such by God, but actually made themselves known to men on earth. Saul knew as certainly that the spirit of Samuel announced his awful doom at Endor, as he knew that the living Samuel reproved him after the battle with Amalek. The three disciples had as clear evidence that it was Moses, the lawgiver of Israel, who came to the Mount in company with Elijah, as they could have had, if he had reanimated his former body.

Separate spirits, therefore, possess as distinct a personal identity as embodied spirits; and if they can establish this fact to spirits inhabiting material bodies and thus impeded in all their perceptions by these dull organs of sense, much more can they do so to one another.

2. Separate spirits have a conscious, active existence, between death and the resurrection. On this, as on every other subject, the language of the Scriptures is uniform. Moses and Samuel, we have seen, were living, conscious spirits after their death. Christ said to the penitent thief, "To-day shalt thou be with me in paradise." It is usually objected, that "one day is with the Lord as a thousand years." True: but it is not so with man; and as Christ knew that the thief would understand him to promise that, before the close of the day then passing, he was to be with Christ in Paradise, we must admit, unless we regard him as insincere or mistaken, that the separate spirit of the penitent thief was before the close of that day actually with Christ in Paradise.

In the parable of the rich man and Lazarus, Christ informs us, that Abraham and Lazarus were living, conscious beings in a state of happiness, and that the rich man was in a state of misery, while the five brethren of the latter were still alive on earth.

In his conversation with the Sadducees, Christ teaches this truth in the direct form. The Sadducees denied a future state, as well as the existence of angels and spirits. To confound Christ on this subject, they put the senseless case of the woman who had had seven husbands. To show them their mistake, Christ appealed to their own Scriptures:

—"But as touching the *resurrection of the dead*"* — as our version renders it, ("But as touching *the future existence of the dead*" — as it ought to be rendered) "have ye not read that which was spoken unto you by God, I am the God of Abraham, and the God of Isaac, and the God of Jacob? — God is not the God of *the dead*, but of *the living*." Some, supposing that Christ advances this passage as a proof of the resurrection of the body, have charged him with inconclusive reasoning; and had he done so, I do not see how the charge could be obviated. What is the argument, according to our version? God said to Moses long after the three patriarchs were dead, "I am the God of Abraham, and the God of Isaac, and the God of Jacob." — But God is not the God of *the dead*, but of *the living*. Therefore — What? Therefore, there will be a resurrection of the body. How does that follow? And what possible connection is there between the premises and the conclusion? Obviously there is none. The word 'Ανάστασις, here erroneously rendered *Resurrection*, comes from a verb, signifying *to stand up again;* and denotes either *the future existence, the standing up again*, of the soul in another state of being — or *the future existence, the standing up again*, of the body at the Resurrection. Here, the connexion shows us it means the former; and when so rendered, the argument of Christ is irresistible. As God is not the God of *the dead*, but of *the living;* and as God was the God of Abraham, of Isaac and of Jacob, in the time of Moses, after the death of the three patriarchs, therefore Abraham, Isaac and Jacob, after their deaths were living, conscious beings; and therefore, still more generally, departed spirits are living, conscious beings in a separate state of existence.

* Matthew xxii. 29—33. Mark xii. 24—27. Luke xx. 34—38.

3. The separate spirits of the righteous are in heaven. Many who would have disdained the name of Papists, and have ridiculed the doctrine of a Purgatory, have yet believed that there is a region of happiness in the world of spirits, distinct from heaven, where the righteous live until the resurrection. For this opinion, however, I can find no scriptural warrant. Christ said to the dying thief, " This day shalt thou be with me in Paradise." Those who hold this opinion, imagine that the soul of Christ between his death and resurrection did not go to heaven, but to this region of the world of spirits which they call *Paradise*, in distinction from heaven ; and that thus the promise to the dying penitent was made good. What the word, *Paradise*, means, it is not difficult to determine, for it is used only in two other places. Paul tells us, " I knew a man in Christ, above fourteen years ago, who was caught up *into the third heaven :* I knew such an one caught up *into Paradise*, where he heard unspeakable words, which it is not lawful for man to utter." Paradise, then, is the third heaven. But the third heaven with the Jews is, always, *the heaven of heavens :* the *atmosphere* being the first, and the *starry heaven* the second. Christ says, in Revelations ii, 7, " To him that overcometh, will I give to eat of the tree of life, which is in the midst of the Paradise of God ;" and in the 22d chap. John says, " And he showed me a pure river of water of life, clear as crystal, proceeding out of the throne of God and of the Lamb. In the midst of the street of it and on either side of the river was the tree of life." It will be admitted that the holy city where the throne of God and the Lamb, in the midst of which was the river of life upon its banks, was heaven. Christ, therefore, by the paradise of God in the midst of which was the tree of life, intended *heaven*. Christ's declaration to the thief was, accordingly, an ex-

press promise that, before the expiration of the day, he should be with him in heaven.

That Christ himself went to heaven at his ascension, that he is now there, and not in some other region of the world of spirits, will probably be admitted by those who remember the declaration of Mark, "So then, after the Lord had spoken unto them he was received up into heaven, and sat on the right hand of God:" — that of the angels, "This same Jesus, which is taken up from you into heaven, shall so come in like manner as ye have seen him go into heaven:" — and those of Paul, "We have a Great High Priest, who has passed into the heavens, Jesus, the Son of God," and "Christ is not entered into the holy places made with hands, but into heaven itself, now to appear in the presence of God for us." But if this be so, the point in question is easily decided. Christ promised all those who believed in him, that they should be with him after he left the world: "In my Father's house are many mansions: I go to prepare a place for you. And if I go, I will come again and receive you unto myself, that where I am, there ye may be also." This was the place where his glory was displayed to them. "Father! I will that those whom thou hast given me, be with me where I am, that they may behold my glory!" From the declarations of Paul, also, we learn that when the righteous are absent from the body they are present with the Lord; and that when they die, they are with Christ. As then He is in heaven, they are there also.

4. The faculties of the soul are not diminished by its separation from the body. The nature of the case evinces this. The state of existence to which the separate spirit is introduced, is incomparably more noble and exalted than the present state, and requires faculties proportionally more noble and exalted. But the wisdom of God is every where

displayed in fitting the things which he makes for the purposes for which he makes them. This is true in minerals, and vegetables, and in all the various tribes of insects and reptiles, of fishes, birds and beasts. Especially is it exhibited, in preparing the various orders of intelligent creatures for the various spheres in which they are to move. We see this in infancy and childhood, in youth and manhood. We see it also still more strongly marked, in men and angels. Had human beings been so constituted as to possess the full size and strength of manhood at their birth and gradually to diminish in the vigor of their faculties and the size of their bodies through childhood, youth and manhood, until in both they became like new born infants; or had men, while destined to inhabit these sluggish bodies and to be confined to the surface of this material world, been endowed with the power and the speed of angels; and had angels, though intended as the messengers of God, the couriers of the starry universe, been created as feeble in their powers and as sluggish in their movements as men;—neither we, nor they, could have regarded these arrangements as proofs of creative wisdom. Since then saints, at their death, are raised to that heaven where angels dwell, to move in their exalted society, and to share in their elevated pursuits, we are hence fully assured that their intellectual faculties, instead of being impaired at the period of their translation, will be only expanded and ennobled.

This obvious conclusion of reason is fully confirmed by the Scriptures. Paul, treating on this very subject, tells us, 1 Cor. xiii., that "now we know in part; but when that which is perfect is come," (i. e. when we arrive at our perfect state in heaven,) then this partial knowledge shall be done away. To show the difference between the intellectual faculties and the knowledge of the Christian, in this world, and in heaven, he compares the one to those of a lisping infant, and the other to those of a full-grown man. "When I was a child (in the Greek, a lisping infant*) I spake, I reasoned, I thought, like such an infant; but when I became a man, I put away childish things." "Now," he adds, "we see through a glass darkly, but then face to face. Now, I know in part; but then shall I know, even as also I am known."

Our Lord places this subject, if possible, in a still stronger light. "They," says he, "who are thought worthy to inherit that world, are equal to the angels, and are the children of God." As the angels are perfectly holy and happy, saints cannot equal them in their degree of holiness or of happiness, unless their intellectual capacity is equal. But, if the intellectual faculties, generally, will be thus enlarged and invigorated, why should we suppose that the *memory*, without which permanent progress in any kind of knowledge is impossible, instead of gaining a proportional degree of strength and expansion, will only be enfeebled? Why must the mind of the saint thus limp in its intellectual progress; one of its powers being crippled, and thus disproportioned to the rest? No; if he is equal to the angels in perception and taste, in fancy, and reason, and judgment, he cannot, he will not, be inferior to them in the power of memory. The events and associations of the present life, instead of fading and vanishing from the tablet of memory, will seem to have been traced upon it anew; for they will be graven there as with "the pen of iron, and the point of a diamond."

5. The deep interest felt by the inhabitants of heaven

* Νήπιος.

in the affairs of this world, forbids the supposition that the events of the present life will be ever forgotten. We clearly gather from the Scriptures, that, heaven perhaps excepted, there is no world in the universe, on which God keeps his eye fixed, with such deep interest, as on this. "He created all things by Jesus Christ to the intent that now unto the principalities and powers in heavenly places might be known by the Church the manifold wisdom of God." This world then is the theatre, in which the glory of God is especially to shine forth to the hosts of heaven, and on which the greatest of all his works is to be performed. One great end, for which the angels were made, was to minister to Christ as the Saviour, and to the heirs of salvation. The Son of God left the throne on high, took on him the nature of Man, and lived and died in this world. As Mediator, he is the immediate Ruler of heaven and earth, that he may conduct many sons unto glory. The work of salvation is the great object of attention in heaven. It is so to Christ. Not a sinner is converted, however humble, weak or polluted, but the good Shepherd says to his friends, "Rejoice with me, for I have found my sheep that was lost." It is so to the angels. "Likewise I say unto you, There is joy in the presence of the angels of God over one sinner that repenteth." It is so to the saints in heaven. "There is more joy in heaven over one sinner that repenteth, than over ninety and nine just persons who need no repentance." Christ is deeply interested in them. "He is head over all things unto the Church." He knows them all. "My sheep hear my voice; and I know them; and they follow me; and they shall never perish; neither shall any one pluck them out of my hand." Saints and angels know them, because they have rejoiced over their conversion. The angels are deeply interested in them, because, as ministering spirits, they have ministered to their salvation. The saints feel an equal interest. "Wherefore," says Paul, "being compassed about by so great a cloud of witnesses, let us run with patience the race that is set before us." The witnesses here referred to are all those, who died in faith, from the beginning of the world. Like the crowd of spectators, who witnessed the races at the Olympic games, he represents this triumphant assembly as looking down, and surveying the race which the Christian is running on earth.

This deep interest, felt by heaven in the church on earth, is felt in every age of the church, and in degrees proportioned to its numbers and prosperity. But do Christ, and angels, and saints feel this intense interest in every Christian, while he is here; and yet lose it all, and immediately forget him, when he dies and goes where they are? Do all heaven exult in the conversion of a sinner; and yet not know him, when he comes arrayed in spiritual beauty, to meet a cordial welcome in his Father's house? Do the assembly of the blessed look down upon him from the battlements of heaven, as he runs the Christian race; and yet forget him, the moment he has gained the victory, and comes to receive his crown?

This knowledge of the character and conduct of Christians on earth, possessed in heaven, is exceedingly minute and exact. Christ of course knows them perfectly. The means of knowledge which the angels possess are very abundant. If they are sent forth to minister to the heirs of salvation, to watch over their welfare, to succor them in temptations, and to guide them to heaven, they must watch their conduct, must see the effect of the temptations which they meet, and must know many of their sins; and with such experience, discernment and opportunities as they enjoy, must thoroughly understand their characters. If also the fact, that the saints in heaven are witnesses of the race run by the Christian on earth, is urged as a powerful reason why he should exert himself to gain the prize; their opportunities of understanding his character, and of knowing his sins, are far greater than is generally supposed.

But do they *gain* this knowledge, merely to *lose* it? Are the memories of saints and angels thus treacherous after death? Or have they both the power of remembering what they please, and from an accommodating good nature do they agree to forget the sins of Christians on earth?

Many of the sins of good men have been very heinous, and are on record in the Scriptures. God has taken care that some of the sins of Noah, of Abraham, Isaac and Jacob, of Moses and Aaron, of Sampson and Eli, that of David in the case of Uriah, those of Solomon, Hezekiah and Manasseh, the denial of Christ by Peter, the persecutions and murders of Saul of Tarsus, should be recorded by the pen of inspiration, and read by the whole body of the Church. Cannot the angels, too, read the Bible, and, if need be, refresh their memories; and do not the saints in heaven know what is in the Bible? Did God then wish these and similar events not to be known or remembered, when he thus published them to the innumerable millions of the past; and when he took effectual care to place them on the imperishable leaves of that volume, which is to be the daily manual of the church throughout Millennial ages?

6. A distinct knowledge of the events and associations of the present life will be indispensable to a state of retribution. Reason and Revelation lend their united attesta-

tion to this truth. Events and actions are important, not usually in themselves, but in their consequences. Adam's eating the forbidden fruit was in itself an event of no more consequence than my eating an apple ; but in the train of consequences which it drew after it, it was important, if we except the death of Christ, (which, indeed, was one of those consequences,) beyond all the other events united which have occurred in this world from its creation to the present moment. In this view, the conduct of every man, and the events which occur to him in this world, are of infinitely more importance to him than those of the world to come. This is his time of trial; and of the scenes in which he mingles, of the associations which he thus forms, and of the transactions in which he engages, he will feel the direct consequences throughout the progress of duration. In every day and hour of eternity, the dispensations of God to him will remind him of his conduct in the present life. He will be rewarded according to his works. If a lost sinner, "he will eat of the fruit of his own ways, and be filled with his own devices." If a redeemed penitent, the measure and kind of his reward will bring his whole life on earth continually into view—the measure of holiness which he gained, and the sins which were forgiven.

The account given us of the Day of Judgment, permits us not to doubt here. That day is "the day of the Revelation of the righteous judgment of God." It is the day, which is to disclose all the events and associations of time, and to prepare Heaven, Earth and Hell, for the retributions of a coming eternity. God will then bring every work into judgment, with every secret thing, whether it be good or whether it be evil." Every thought, affection, motive and purpose, every word and action of life, with all their various circumstances, will be therefore revealed. As God will on that day cause the intelligent universe to see, that all his dispensations in time, and all his judgments in eternity, are righteous; it follows that all the relations which we sustain in life, all our various sublunary associations and connections, must be then distinctly remembered and reviewed. But if *these* are remembered, so, necessarily, will the individuals be remembered, to whom we sustained these relations. The remembrance of the one necessarily implies that of the other. When parents give an account of their conduct towards their children, husbands and wives an account of theirs towards one another, children towards their parents, magistrates and ministers towards their people, and their people towards them, partners, friends, associates, neighbors and companions in iniquity towards one another; it is obviously impossible that they should do this, and not remember the several individuals, with whom they have been thus connected, over whom they have thus exerted a powerful influence, and whom they have thus helped to fix forever either in heaven or in hell. But it is precisely as important that the justice of God towards his creatures should be seen and felt in every coming day of Eternity, as at the Day of Judgment.

Lost sinners, while they endure the punishment of eternity, must know the conduct and the events of the present life, in their own case, if they are to understand the justice, and see the appropriateness, of the punishment which they suffer; and they must possess a similar knowledge in the case of others, if they are to see the propriety of *their* punishment. But if they will remember their sins, and the events of which they were spectators here, they must and will of course also remember the persons, with whom they were here associated. All their sins, except those of the heart, all their visible conduct of omission and of commission, their life of worldliness and impenitence, and their rejection of the offers of grace, have been exhibited in the view of thousands; and have had a most pernicious influence, not only on their own children and posterity, but on their friends and neighbors and their posterity, through succeeding generations. In many of these sins also, they have had associates and partners in iniquity. They cannot look back upon these events in the abstract. Each act of sin is indissolubly connected with the time, the place, the circumstances and persons; and the recollection of the sin, in every case, must and will involve the recollection of the manner of its commission, and of the persons who were partners in it, or who were corrupted or injured by it.

In the same manner, the righteous will remember, not only their own conversion to God, and their own exercises of love, and acts of obedience, but those of others also; that they may understand the appropriateness of the reward bestowed on each. But the remembrance of these, in every case, will necessarily involve a distinct and perfect recollection of all the persons, with whom they have been associated in the present life, and the influence for good or for evil which they have actually exerted.

This remembrance is absolutely essential to their character and circumstances, as redeemed sinners in heaven. If humility and gratitude are to be in full exercise there, they must look back on the rock whence they were hewn, and on the hole of the pit whence they were digged; they must remember the number, greatness and aggravations, of their sins, and be conscious of their deep depravity, if they are adequately to glorify the mercy of the Father, or the love of Christ, or the grace of the Spirit, in their salvation.

They must remember and know the individuals, to whom, under God, they are indebted for eternal life:—their pious parents, who faithfully governed and instructed them, and set them a holy example, and prayed and wrestled for them with many tears; the faithful minister, who was perhaps the means of their conversion; the pious members of the church, who walked with them in the way to heaven; and the angel, to whom as a ministering spirit they were entrusted, in their progress through a wilderness of temptations and dangers:—if they are adequately to feel and express the gratitude, which they owe them for their earnest and successful efforts in guiding them to eternal life. These events are the most important, which will occur to them in all the progress of their being; because they were the foundation, on which were built their everlasting life, and holiness and joy. Not a day, not an hour, will occur in the long year of eternity, which will not, by the power of association, bring up to distinct view the events, the persons and the connections, of the present life. Will Abraham forget leaving his country at the call of God, or the sacrifice of Isaac? Will Moses forget that he was the leader of the Church through the wilderness, or his sin at the waters of Meribah which excluded him from the earthly Canaan; or Joshua, that, instead of Moses, he led them into the promised land? Can Enoch and Elijah be ever unconscious that they were translated, that they should not see death? Does David forget that he wrote those Psalms, which convey the praises of the church to heaven; or that he wrote the 51st Psalm, after Nathan had reproved him for his dreadful guilt in the affair of Uriah? Has Isaiah forgotten his distant visions of that latter day glory, which is now brightening on his view in the heavenly world? Does the blessed Virgin forget that she was the mother of the Saviour of the world; or that Gabriel came, as a harbinger, to announce his birth? Do the Eleven forget that they were the bosom friends of Jesus on earth; or Paul, that his labors and his writings have been the means of salvation to millions which cannot be numbered?

On this portion of the subject the Scriptures are also explicit. John informs us, that he saw "under the altar the souls of them that were slain for the testimony of Jesus. And they cried with a loud voice, 'How long, O Lord, holy and true, dost thou not judge and avenge our blood on them that dwell on the earth;' and it was said unto them that they should wait for a little season until their fellow-servants and their brethren, that should be killed as they were, should be fulfilled." Here, the saints in heaven were remembering the events and the associations of the present life, as well as carefully observing the providence of God towards those who followed them. In Rev. i. 10, also, John informs us that he heard the whole assembly of the first born join in the ascription, "Unto him that loved us, and washed us from our sins in his own blood;" and on a subsequent occasion, they exclaimed, "Thou art worthy; for thou hast redeemed us to God by thy blood, out of every kindred, and people, and nation, and tongue." Their sins on earth, therefore, had not faded from their memories; nor the countries, and nations, and families, to which they belonged.

7. This truth is taught, directly and explicitly, in the Scriptures. In proof of this, I allege the text, As ye have acknowledged us in part that we are your rejoicing even as ye also are ours in the day of the Lord Jesus;" and the parallel passage, 1 Thess. ii. 19, 20, "What is our hope, our joy, our crown of rejoicing. Are not even ye in the

presence of the Lord Jesus at his coming. Doubtless we are your rejoicing even as ye also are ours." Paul had begotten these Christians in Christ Jesus through the Gospel. He here declares that in the day of judgment they will not only be raised up together, and will know each other in this most endearing relation, but will be a mutual joy and rejoicing to each other in Eternity. He will rejoice in them as his spiritual children, and they in him as their spiritual father.

He tells the Hebrew Christians, "Obey them that have the rule over you, for they watch for your souls as they that must give account, that they may do it with joy and not with grief." This is a plain declaration, that in the day of judgment, ministers will know their hearers,—those who have not become Christians, as well as those who have.

Christ informs us, Matth. viii. 11, "Many shall come from the east and the west, from the north and the south, and shall sit down with Abraham and Isaac and Jacob in the kingdom of God;" and in the corresponding passage in Luke, Luke xiii. 28, "There shall be weeping and gnashing of teeth, when ye shall see Abraham, and Isaac, and Jacob, and all the prophets, in the kingdom of God, and you yourselves thrust out; and there are last which shall be first, and there are first which shall be last." The assertion that they shall see these patriarchs and prophets in the kingdom of God, implies that they shall know them,—otherwise, it can be no motive to labour for the attainment of heaven; and the fact that intense suffering will be then endured by many from the great reverse then experienced in their relative condition, evinces that not only individuals, but their former circumstances in this world, will be distinctly known and remembered.

Paul consoles the Thessalonian Christians who were mourning their deceased friends, with the reflection that they will see them again in the day of the Lord Jesus; and that they and their beloved friends will be ever with the Lord, or live together forever in his presence. This plainly implies that, in the future world, they would know their departed friends and rejoice with them; and it is, indeed, an effectual ground of support and consolation.

Many other passages, did the time permit, might be adduced in support of this position. I hasten to notice three Objections, which are usually brought against the principle of this Discourse.

It is said, that the recollection of our own sins will diminish the happiness of heaven. Contrition and Penitence, I reply, are not painful but delightful emotions. The Christian on earth is never more satisfied with the state of his own heart, than when the tears of godly sorrow are flowing from his eyes. The saints will be forever conscious that they have been welcomed into heaven, only as redeemed sinners; and when they bless the Lamb because he has washed them from their sins in his own blood, I may safely appeal to any Christian—Will this be ever a painful ascription of blessing and praise?

It is said also, that the recollection of the sins of others will diminish our esteem and affection for them. Our estimate of those who dwell in heaven, I reply again, will be regulated according to truth, taking in their whole existence. We may estimate the past character of an individual, as very different from his present character; and the one does not interfere with the other. We may wholly condemn his past conduct in given instances; and yet wholly approve his present character. The sin of David in the matter of Uriah was almost unparalleled in its enormity;

yet his present character deserves and commands perfect esteem and love. Stephen will not love Paul the less as a holy being, although the apostle once consented to his own death. Had this not been the case, an imperishable record would not have been made of the failings and sins of some of the most distinguished saints in heaven.

It is also said that it will lessen the happiness of heaven, to remember such of our friends as have been denied admission to its bliss. This objection may imply not merely, that our personal friends have failed of salvation ; but that they have failed of salvation, in consequence of our unfaithfulness. In this sense, I answer, it is well founded. The happiness of every individual in heaven will be "*according to his works.*" Those who have been eminently faithful in the discharge of every duty here, will have a very high capacity both for holiness and happiness there ; those who have exhibited inferior faithfulness will have an inferior capacity ; and those who are saved, yet "so as by fire," will find the measure of their own capacity wonderfully less. The first class will "shine forth as the sun in the kingdom of their Father ;" the second will "shine as the stars forever and ever ;" and the third will only shine "as the brightness of the firmament." It is true, that every saint in heaven who has manifested great unfaithfulness in seeking the salvation of his own relations, or in the performance of any other duty, will be an everlasting *loser* by such unfaithfulness. In every age and in every moment of eternity, his capacity—both for holiness and happiness—will be greatly inferior to what it would have been, had he been in the full sense a faithful servant. Each will possess his own appropriate measure of holiness and happiness ; yet the various measures, though differing thus widely, will be all absolutely full. This fact, however, is no objection to the principle for which we contend. It is only a necessary consequence of the great rule of righteousness, that the saints shall be rewarded according to their works.

This objection may refer, however, to the simple fact, that our impenitent friends have failed of salvation. As thus understood, I answer, that the predominant and only feeling of heaven is, "Whom have I in heaven but thee, and there is none on the earth whom I desire beside thee. Let God be glorified, and I am happy forever!" Moral character, holiness, is there the only foundation of love. Its inhabitants love those whom God loves and hate that which he hates. None will be banished from heaven to the world of despair but the irreconcilable enemies of God, the unbelieving, and polluted, and abominable,—those who have proved themselves to be the fit companions of the devil and his angels—those whom no means and no motives, no warnings, no terrors, and no manifestations of love, could recover from the character of hopeless sin and obduracy. Viewing them as possessed of this character, the mind of the saint will say, "The will of the Lord be done!" Isaac will say this in the case of Esau, Eli in that of Hophni, and Phineas and David in that of Absalom. Why they were not "gathered," will be known; and it will be seen and felt to be right. To have "gathered" them, possessing their present character, it will be distinctly seen, would have tarnished the glory of Jehovah and interrupted the peace and joy of the heavenly world.

Extended as has been this exhibition of the subject, I must be indulged for a moment in several Reflections.

Need I say, then, that we have here presented a delightful theme of contemplation to the dying Christian? He is going away from a world of sin and sorrow, but he is not going to a land of strangers. At his second birth he was born from above, the land to which he is going is his native country, there is his Father's house. There his best friends and kindred dwell. There are his pious ancestors, whose prayers called down blessings on his head. There are his pious parents, who became, perhaps, the means of his immediate conversion. There are many of the wise and good, who have been his fellow-travellers in the upward path. There is the angel, who ministered to him as an heir of salvation; and there is that vast assembly of saints who felt new joy over his repentance, who watched all his progress to the shores of death, and who are ready to welcome him as a brother among many brethren. Who would not go to such a world? With such a prospect before him, who would not say:

> "Fill'd with delight, my raptured soul
> Can here no longer stay."

We have here also, abundant consolation in the death of pious relatives and friends. Their works on earth are ended, and do follow them. In God's time, in the best time, they have been removed to the heavenly Jerusalem, to an innumerable company of angels, and to the assembly of the first born; and to Jesus the mediator of the new covenant; and to God the Judge of all. Who would wish them back? They are gone from us, but they have not forgotten us. If we are the children of God, they are gone as our forerunners; they are among the great cloud of witnesses, who watch our progress, and are already preparing to welcome our arrival. They still remember their labors of love towards us, and are expecting soon to unite with us in their nobler worship and enjoyments.

I need not add, How solemn is our condition in this

world. When we say that the present is a state of trial, and the future a state of retribution, we have told but one half of the story. God intends that every intelligent being in the world of spirits, whether he is welcomed to the great palace or is shut up in the eternal prison, shall know that his allotment is strictly just, that he is rewarded exactly according to his works. In every passing hour of eternity, as we look around us and within us, we shall be conscious, why our allotment is what it is; and shall distinctly know, that the harvest which we are reaping is the legitimate produce of the seed which we have sown. The deeds, which we now do, are not done in vain, are not destined to be forgotten. Each moment are they distinctly written down by two very different writers, in two very different books;—by God, in the book of his remembrance; and by the man himself, however unconscious he may be of the fact, in the book of his own memory. The record, written by the man himself, is as true, as full, as perfect, as that written by God:—nay, to be still more exact, it is written down *in the very same words*. It is a record wonderfully comprehensive, comprising every work and every secret thing. In writing it, we are all of us most diligently employed. Wherever we may be, and however engaged, whether busy or idle, by day or by night, at home or abroad, in a crowd or in solitude, each one of us is always occupied in writing out a full and perfect history of himself—an auto-biography of his own soul, in which there is not one omission or one mistake. At death, the work is finished; and when the soul—the living man—forsakes the body, leaving all things else behind him, he carries this imperishable volume in his hand to the judgment-seat of Christ. There, as the Judge, from the book that is open before him, reads off the story of his life, the man perceives that the two records exactly correspond ; and when he departs, to enter on his destiny of bliss or woe, he carries with him this little volume as his inseparable companion, to tell him every moment of eternity why he has received his allotment in heaven or in hell.

ADDRESS ON THE GREEK REVOLUTION.

THE shores of the Archipelago, during the last three years, have presented a most interesting spectacle to the contemplation of the civilized world. A nation once pre-eminent in moral greatness, but for centuries subjected to a tyranny more oppressive than this world ever saw, in the commencement of 1821, revolted from the Turkish government, and on the 30th of March declared to mankind that they were free and independent. The pledge then given, they have since labored to redeem, in the face of Europe and the world. Solemnly appealing to God for the justice of their cause, while they have made known to Christian nations their wrongs on the one hand, and their comparative weakness on the other, they have invited them, by all that is illustrious in their past history, by all that man holds dear, or regards as sacred, to aid them in this decisive struggle for liberty and for life.

When this call first echoed from the shores of the Peloponnesus, we might well have expected to see the nations of Christendom hurrying, with a noble emulation, to deliver the suffering Greeks, and to drive back their oppressors beyond the shores of the Caspian. As Christians, as men, we may well wish that this expectation had been realized. But the events of the past three years are now recorded by the pen of history; and the descendants of the present generation will blush for the cold, unfeeling selfishness of their sires, when they learn, that the surrounding nations, with a strength sufficient in a single week to have levelled the throne of the Sultan in the dust, could stand coolly by, and, during three years of toil and agony, could see their brethren, alone and single handed, maintain the dreadful conflict.

The Committee, to whose care the national contributions for the Greeks are entrusted, have publicly requested the clergy of our country to address their congregations in behalf of this injured people. Who can doubt the propriety of this request? Were the case of the Greeks *our own;* were *our* country thus oppressed, invaded and desolated by a cruel and blood-thirsty enemy; would it not be demanded of every minister of Christ, that he should raise his voice in behalf of his suffering countrymen? And is the great rule of Christian benevolence—"Thou shalt love thy neighbor as thyself"—to have no influence *here?* Is it mere political declamation to plead the cause of suffering millions, to tell you of their wrongs, and to ask you as individuals to feel for them, and to help them. Shall the clergy of Switzerland and Germany urge the claims of the Greeks on the sympathies of their countrymen; and shall the clergy of America be silent?

On the present occasion, without assuming the garb of the politician, or usurping the chair of the legislator, we may take that view of the Revolution in Greece, which, as freemen and as Christians, we ought to take; we may examine its immediate bearing on the cause of Liberty and the welfare of Religion; and thus may learn what feelings we ought to cherish, what conduct we ought to pursue.

In endeavoring to exhibit such a view of this Revolution, the following arrangement of topics will be pursued :—

It has broken out in an interesting country :
That country is inhabited by an interesting people :
Many things indicate their ultimate success :
The struggle is an eventful one :
What is our own duty ?

THIS REVOLUTION HAS BROKEN OUT IN AN INTERESTING COUNTRY.

Greece, including the whole of Epirus and Macedonia, has a length of 500 miles by an average breadth of 150 ; exclusive of its numerous islands, and its ancient colonies on the eastern coast of the Archipelago. Lying between the 36th and 43d degrees of latitude,* almost surrounded by the sea, and every where intersected by ranges of mountains, it enjoys a climate unrivalled for its pleasantness and salubrity, favorable to the culture of the best productions of the soil, and to the most vigorous growth of the body and the mind of man. The clearness of its sky, and the delightful temperature of its seasons have ever been the admiration of the traveller ; while the uncommon longevity of its inhabitants has shown their auspicious influence on human life.

It is a land of hills, and vallies, and brooks of water ; exhibiting, in its native scenery, all the varieties both of beauty and of grandeur. Its soil is distinguished for its fertility ; and its productions for their variety and excellence. While its vallies yield the finest fruits of tropical climates, all the choice harvests of the temperate zone

* D'Anville.

wave in the richest luxuriance on its plains and its highlands.

Few countries in the world have the same advantages for security and defence. On the northern frontier, ranges of lofty mountains separate it from Thrace and Dalmatia. The eastern, southern, and western are guarded by the best of all bulwarks—the ocean. The numerous ridges of mountains, intersecting the interior, with their steep fastnesses and abrupt defiles, form a succession of impregnable ramparts. These, terminating in bluffs and high grounds on the shore, are the sites of numerous fortifications, which line the extensive sea-coast.

Greece has no rival on the Mediterranean in her advantages for navigation and commerce. Her many islands render her the mistress of the Archipelago and the Levant. Her continental territories, embosomed in the sea, and every where penetrated by gulfs and bays, are a mere collection of larger and smaller peninsulas. These numerous and deep indentations supply the want of navigable rivers, and bring the waters of the ocean within a moderate distance from every village, and from every dwelling.

The seas which encircle Greece, while they give her an easy access to the productions of the surrounding countries, furnish her a near and unfailing market for her own. On the north-east, the extensive and rapidly increasing commerce of the Black Sea comes, through the Hellespont, to her door. Her ancient colonies, the rich countries of Asia Minor, are an integral part of her territory. With Syria and Egypt she is in immediate contact. Through the Red Sea she opens on Arabia and Persia, on India and China. The Barbary States and Italy are merely her frontiers; and more remote are the markets of western Europe and America.

The whole country is *classic* ground. As the birth-place of freedom, as the early and favorite habitation of genius, of eloquence and of fancy, as the theatre where the arts attained their highest perfection, Greece is a consecrated soil; endeared above every other to the artist, the scholar, and the patriot. Her vallies and mountains, her plains and rivers, her towns and villages have all been celebrated in story, and immortalized in song. The relics of her past glory are still majestic amid the solitude of time. The traveller, gazing at her broken columns and her falling temples, while he dwells with admiration on the beauty and grandeur of their perfect state, and remembers that the united world has toiled more than two thousand years in vain to furnish rivals to Phidias and Praxiteles; gives up the hope of finding them, until Greece is once more the dwelling-place of freedom, and the nursery of the arts.

In the present state of the continent of Europe, with the doctrine of legitimacy and the divine right of kings supported by three millions of bayonets, Greece is the only spot of ground where freedom, during the present generation, can find rest for the sole of her foot.

Greece borders on Turkey, hitherto the bulwark of the Mohammedan religion. It approximates, also, to the Barbary States, to Egypt and Arabia, and is not remote from Persia: the only considerable countries where that religion now prevails.

The religious associations of Greece render her peculiarly interesting to the Christian. Taken in her most extensive limits, she was the seat of the seven churches of Asia, of the churches of Galatia, Pontus, Cappadocia, and Bithynia, of Colosse and Thessalonica, of Philippi and Corinth. She is the seat of the primitive Greek church, and is immediately connected with the other great branch of that church in Russia. She is also in the near neigborhood of the churches of Armenia and Syria, and of the Coptic church in Egypt; and is not remote from the church of Abyssinia, and the still existing but newly discovered church of Chaldea.* At the same time, four-fifths of all the JEWS, hitherto known, surround the seas, whose waters are commanded by the Archipelago. A few miles from these waters, also, lies JERUSALEM, the common mother of Jews and Christians, and destined ere long to unite them both into one church, and, by their combined efforts, to gather in "the fulness of the Gentiles."

Thus Greece is a country eminently interesting in itself, in its productions, in its commercial advantages, in the relics of its former glory, and in its political and religious associations.

THIS LAND IS INHABITED BY AN INTERESTING PEOPLE.

They are interesting from their Descent. So extensive and powerful has been the influence exerted by Greece, so exclusively have the efforts of her genius and taste been selected by other nations as their models, so numerous are the trophies every where raised to her superiority; that he, who would escape from them, must go out of the precincts of the civilized world. The sculptor cannot take up his chisel, nor the architect his square; the painter cannot hold his palette nor the musician strike his lyre; but he remembers who founded that school of the arts, in which he was instructed. The mathematician still submits himself to Euclid as his master and his guide. The rhetorician boasts that he is the pupil of Aristotle and Longinus.

* See Appendix to XIX. Report of British and Foreign Bible Society, pp. 101—103.

The orator keeps the image of Demosthenes always before his eye. The highest aim of the statesman is to emulate the wisdom of Solon and Lycurgus. The poet ever wanders in thought among the groves of Parnassus, and drinks of the Castalian fount—if haply thereby he may catch the inspiration of Homer and of Pindar. The warrior, fighting for his country, hopes that an ever-verdant wreath of glory may encircle his brow, entwined from the laurel of Leonidas. The patriot as he looks around him, and reflects with conscious dignity that he is *free*, remembers with heart-felt gratitude, that Freedom first uttered her voice in the councils of Athens and Sparta.—Go where we may ; see what we may ; retrace what period we may since the downfall of Greece ; we cannot forget the influence which she has thus exerted in humanizing the manners, in kindling the genius, in refining the taste, or in elevating the pursuits of man ; nor shut our eyes on the voluntary and universal homage thus paid to her greatness and her glory.

In tracing the descent of the modern Greeks, we cannot fail to remember that the great body of the church of Christ, in the days of the Apostles, were Grecians. Among these, were Luke and Timothy, and many of the friends and companions of Paul. Stephen and Polycarp, and many of the early martyrs, as well as most of the distinguished fathers of the church, were Greeks. Greece, including Asia Minor, was the first Christian country. In the language of Greece, the New Testament was written. It was at Constantinople, then the very heart of the Grecian world, that Constantine the Great established Christianity as the religion of the Roman empire. The Greeks were then, and for centuries afterwards, the proprietors of the vast territories of Europe and Asia, now subjected to the Grand Seignor. *They* fought the battles of the Church against the Saracens, against Mohammed, against the Caliphs and the Turks. Nor was it until the year 1453, that their empire was destroyed, in the capture of Constantinople by Mohammed the great.

They are interesting from their Sufferings. Since the period of that capture, or for the space of nearly 400 years, they have been abandoned, by the common consent of Europe, a prey to Turkish domination; and subjected to a slavery, which, in all the odious features of brutality and cruelty, of rapacity and pollution, lacks a parallel in the annals of this world. Since that time, wherever they have lived, whatever character they have sustained, they have been compelled to feel, from day to day, that every Turk whom they met was a master, and every Greek a slave. The Sultan, and under him the Pasha, and under him the Bey, and under him the Aga, was *avowedly* the proprietor of all their estates, and the disposer of their lives. Their wives, their daughters, were never secure from violence. Life always hung in doubt before them. Property could be safe, only as it was concealed.

> "The fruits of toil were *labell'd on the door;*
> The pride of wealth, the gleanings of the poor."

To the Greek, no house has been a sanctuary; no temple a refuge. Wherever he has cast his eyes, he has seen the crescent frowning on the churches of the living God, the Bible supplanted by the Koran, and the ministers of Jesus driven out to make room for the imams of Mohammed.

They are interesting from their attachment to their Religion. Notwithstanding the oppression under which they have groaned; notwithstanding the threats and the bribes held out by the proselyting spirit of the Mohammedans; they have, as a people, adhered to their open profession of the Christian faith; and regularly maintained their clergy and the worship of God. It may be said that their Christianity is deformed by many corruptions, and concealed under a mass of useless ceremonies. I admit the fact. Yet, look at the Christianity of western Europe—of England as truly as the rest—in 1453, the æra of the capture of Constantinople; or look at the Christianity of southern Europe at this moment; and you will see it altogether more corrupted, and more absolutely concealed under the enormous mass of ceremonies which envelop it. Since the period of their captivity, they have neither felt the motives, nor possessed the means, of reforming their religion.

They are interesting for their commercial enterprise. The commerce of the Greeks is an anomaly in the history of nations. Elsewhere, commerce has flourished either when left to itself, or when encouraged by the fostering hand of government. In Greece, it has flourished in spite of opposition and rapacity. Those who engage in it are pillaged by the Turkish governors, are defrauded with impunity by the Turkish merchants, and exposed by their very success to the loss of liberty, property and life. Yet thus pillaged, thus defrauded, they have extended it, with unbending resolution and increasing activity, until it covers all the shores and harbors of the Mediterranean. According to a statistical table published in 1813, we find them, eight years previous to the revolution, possessed of 615 merchant vessels, armed with 5,878 cannon, and manned by 17,526 seamen. Since its commencement, the number of vessels has rapidly increased, for the small island of Hydra alone now possesses upwards of 600. The beauty and swiftness of their vessels evince their skill in naval architecture; while their seamen are celebrated through the Mediterranean for the dexterity with which they manage their ships.* It is owing to these causes, that, for a series of years, they have been the common carriers of the surrounding world, and have engrossed in their own hands almost all its local commerce. To mention a single example of their enterprise—In the late convulsions of Europe, many of the Hydriote merchants acquired large fortunes, by carrying corn from Odessa, on the Black Sea, for the supply of the armies in Spain; and many of them now trade as far as the West Indies. In addition to this,† the Greeks have carried several important branches of manufactures to a perfection unknown in Western Europe.

They are interesting from their love of Literature. Schools, which are accessible to all classes, are extensively established throughout the country; and the great body of the people, as we learn from our own missionaries as well as other travellers, can read and write. Where there are no schools, the mothers instruct their children. The college at Haivali, founded in 1803, had 200 students, and a competent number of professors, supported by the liberality of the citizens. That at Scio, founded ten years earlier, and supported by the merchants, had, immediately before its destruction, from 700 to 800 students,‡ 20 professors, chiefly educated in Europe, an athenæum, and a library of 10,000 volumes.§ The course of instruction in literature and the sciences was rapidly approximating to the European standard of perfection. Beside these, public schools of a respectable character were found at Yanina,

* North American Review, and Blaquiere's Report to the Greek Committee of London.

† Jowett's Christian Researches. ‡ Missionary Herald, April, 1821, p. 103.

§ North American Review.

at Athos, at Athens and at Patmos. More than 500 of the finest young men of Greece regularly received a still higher education at the universities of western Europe.* Several printing-presses have been established, several newspapers circulated; and information is regularly communicated in them of the latest discoveries in science and the arts, and of the benevolent efforts which characterize the present age. Many of the classics of ancient Greece they have republished; many of the best writers of England, France and Italy, they have translated into the modern Greek. This has been done chiefly at the expense of wealthy individuals, from national pride, from patriotism, and the love of letters. Allow me to add here, what, in a single word, will give you an adequate impression of this subject; and what, as an inhabitant of this peninsula, I can add with honest exultation; that while reading the account given by Jowett of the munificent patronage extended by the Greek merchants to learning and the arts; I easily forgot that the traveller was at Scio, and thought for a moment that he was in the metropolis of New England. Let it be remembered that this ardor was felt, that these efforts were made, when the rod of the oppressor was unbroken; and when none but a faint and distant hope was cherished by Greece, of the restoration of her freedom. Even the bustle and exhaustion of war could not restrain this ardor. The seat of government had not been established in Tripolizza for three weeks, when a Turkish mosque was converted into a Lancasterian school, and seventy children were immediately enrolled. Two other such schools, one at Missolunghi, the other at Gastouni, were established, by Mavrocordato, almost in sight of the infidel army.†

* There were 500 Greek youths in the German universities, at the commencement of the war.

† Blaquiere's Report.

They are interesting from their love of Liberty. I well know that they have worn the most galling yoke for four centuries. Yet they have not worn it tamely and patiently; but because without arms, without foreign assistance, with far inferior numbers, with their country all garrisoned by janizaries, and with the enormous pressure of Turkish power upon them, it was *physically impossible* for them to shake it off. Yet this is not the first revolution, which they have attempted. For the last fifty years, no seeming opportunity has offered of liberating their country but they have at once embraced it.

Faintly, very faintly do we realize how intense was the courage, how devoted the patriotism, which impelled them to the present revolt. The numerous and strong fortresses on the coast, in the interior, and in the islands were occupied by the Turks. To keep all things quiet, and to sound the alarm on the approach of danger, Turkish soldiers were quartered on every town and village. In addition to these, the Turks had a large and disciplined army; the Greeks had none. The Turks had a powerful navy; the Greeks had none. The Turks had arms; the Greeks, without a license could not possess fire-arms, and were almost without a bayonet. The Turks had a regular government; the Greeks were a scattered, unorganized population. The Turks had money and all other resources in abundance; the Greeks had no public treasures, and none of the *materiel* of war. The Turks had their resources at command, and could strike in a moment. The Greeks did not even know that, as a people, they should act in concert; and, if they *did* this, it must be after months of uncertainty and delay. The Turks were an enemy—not, like the British in our revolution, 3000 miles off—they were at hand, even at the door. By a powerful fleet they could land an army on any part of the coast, and shelter it under the cannon of their own fortifications. They were an enemy, too, ferocious, brutal and sanguinary beyond a parallel; accustomed to pay no regard to age or sex, to "dignity of rank or sacredness of function." When they entered on the war, the Greeks perfectly understood this character of the Turks. They well knew that they put in jeaopardy not only their own property and lives, but the safety of their dwellings, the lives of their children and their aged parents, and the purity of their wives and their daughters. They had no promise of foreign aid; and the issue of former insurrections had taught them, in letters of blood, that no faith was to be put in any encouragements or promises of the neighboring powers, when it was their interest to forget them. They knew that the conflict was terrible beyond example; and that they must maintain it alone, with no prospect of help but from God. Brought to this awful crisis, with all that the heart of man can love at hazard, they moved in one embodied host into the field of death, declaring to Turkey and the gazing world, "WE WILL BE FREE; OR WE WILL PERISH."

I need not tell you, how far they have maintained this declaration. Fighting alone, at this dreadful disadvantage, amid murders and desolations which have made the world turn pale, they have marched forward undismayed, in one firm unbroken phalanx, to victory and freedom.

MANY THINGS INDICATE THEIR ULTIMATE SUCCESS.

To feel the full force of this remark, we must contrast their condition now, with what it was when they "put on the harness." Then the country was covered with Turkish troops; now not a soldier is found in the Morea. Then all the fortresses were in the hands of the enemy; now by the last intelligence all those in the Morea, most of those southward of Epirus and Macedonia, and many in the islands have been captured. Then they had no military force but a mere mob of brave men, who had left their fields and their shops to fight for their country. Now they have an experienced army of 50,000 men. Then they were without muskets; and two-thirds of them actually went to the field with no weapons but sticks;* now they are well armed and well equipped. Then they had no park of artillery; now they have a full and well disciplined corps, commanded by Europeans, and perfectly equipped for the reduction of any of the fortresses yet in possession of the enemy. Then their officers had never seen a battle; now they have often led their men to danger and to victory. Then the Turks were sure of conquest; now they expect to be beaten, and the Greeks calculate to beat them of course. Then the Turks had a powerful navy; now many of the finest ships are destroyed, while the Greeks have raised up a formidible fleet which commands the Archipelago. Then the Greeks had no credit; now, at a moderate premium, they raise the sum of £800,000 sterling in London, and are offered twice that sum if they will take it. Then their hopes of success were shivering in the wind. Now they have fought through three campaigns; and in the two last have met almost the whole force of the empire; and still they are conquerors.

The late destruction of the Turkish fleet by the providence of God, in the sea of Marmora, has raised the courage of the Greeks, as much as it has depressed that of the enemy. Should the Porte persevere in its obstinate re-

* Blaquiere's Report.

fusal to adjust its differences with Russia; should Persia persist in declining to ratify the treaty of Bagdad; a powerful force will be necessary on the Danube, and another on the Euphrates. To provide for and to direct these two armies, and that destined against Greece, in the approaching campaign; to equip a new fleet; to prevent in the mean time the ravages of the Greek squadron; to keep the Hellespont open; and to raise the drooping spirit of the people; will require the collected wisdom of the Divan, and the whole resources of the government. In addition to this, the official request of the consuls at Smyrna—those of England and France, of the Netherlands and Austria made in December last to the senate of Ipsara, that the Greek fleet might not enter the gulf of Smyrna, nor make any attack on the shipping or the fortifications, lest their consular establishments should be jeoparded; is a frank acknowledgment, that the Greeks had then the entire command of the Archipelago.

We ought not here to forget that they have established a free constitution of government; wise in its provisions; securing to the citizen every civil and political right; modeled in its bolder features after our own; and clearly evincing that the constituent members of their General Congress are men of superior and enlightened minds—men, to whom their public affairs, at this eventful crisis are most judiciously entrusted. Neither ought we to forget that, throughout the whole war, the officers and men, both of the army and navy, have evinced a patriotism and a valor, not surpassed at Thermopylæ or Marathon.

No man can look at these facts, without perceiving that both the actual and comparative condition of the Greeks is far better than it was, and their prospect of success incomparably brighter. *What is to be*, however, we do not know; neither is it our province *to prophecy*. Of three things we may be sure:—Without putting forth all her strength, Turkey will not surrender Greece.—During the present summer the great contest will doubtless be decided. —And its decision under God, will depend on the single question, *Whether Greece can command the resources of war*. If wisdom in her statesmen, if conduct in her chiefs, if fearless valour in her warriors, if pure disinterested patriotism in all her citizens can achieve her independence—Greece will be free.

THE STRUGGLE IS AN EVENTFUL ONE.

The issue of this struggle is big with consequences, not only to the combatants themselves, but to the surrounding countries, to the Oriental churches, to the Jews, to the Mohammedan religion, to Europe, and the world.

If the Greeks fail in this contest—which may He, who rules this lower world, forbid!—their sun will go down in darkness and in blood. If they are not utterly extinguished as a nation; yet will their "final hope be flat despair." They will see before them a night of slavery, to last through centurial ages, and giving the promise of no returning day. All the miseries, which fiendlike rage, revenge and pollution can inflict—miseries, of which the fires and blood of Scio were but a type, will be heaped upon them. In that catastrophe the Turk has felt the pulse of Europe, and learned how much its cabinets will bear. By one decisive act of terror, forever to put down the spirit of revolt, thousands on thousands of the choicest sons of Greece will be given up to indiscriminate massacre. Her wives and her daughters will glut the slave-market, until no more purchasers can be found. Her colleges and schools, her libraries and her press will be burnt up. Every vestige of genius, taste, and magnificence, now standing, will be swept away. Her warriors and statesmen, her clergy and her scholars, will be devoted to utter extinction. Colonies of Greeks will be driven away into Asiatic captivity; and their places supplied by hordes of Mussulmen. Nothing will be left undone to set a terrible example of the consequences of revolt, before the eyes of the other nations subjected to the Turkish yoke.

If they fail, the power and courage of the Ottoman Porte will be proportionally increased. Hence the chains, long fastened on Armenia and Chaldea, on Syria and Arabia, will only be riveted anew. The Mohammedan religion will gain new strength; and the churches of the East will cease to hope for the termination of their long and abject servitude. The period of the Jews' dispersion will only be prolonged; for Jerusalem will still "be trodden down of the Gentiles," with no apparent prospect that "the times of the Gentiles will be fulfilled."

If they fail, Freedom, driven from her last retreat, will take her final flight from the continent of Europe, and leave its subjugated millions in darkness and in chains.

That this is the very result desired and aimed at by the parties to the Holy Alliance, is plain, is palpable, from the nature of the case, and from their own conduct.

There are but two kinds of government;—one founded on the principle, that all power is originally vested in the people; the other on the opposite principle, that all power is originally vested in the monarch, and that he exercises it by a divine right over his subjects. These two principles are directly hostile to each other, and lead to opposite system of administration. While the people are shrouded in ignorance and accustomed to the yoke, they easily coincide with the monarch, and willingly confess that they were born to be slaves. But there is a certain point in the progress of knowledge—the knowledge of their own rights and their own strength—when, in point of fact, they incline to the other opinion; and conclude that themselves are the only fountain of power; that government ought to be administered, not for the aggrandizement of the ruler, but for the good of the citizen; and that the most effectual method of securing this object is to establish their own form of government. When any nation has reached this point of knowledge, a despotic government never has existed, never can exist over it, without the constant and powerful pressure of military force; and there is no source from which nations acquire this knowledge so rapidly as from example.

This is plain, simple reasoning, founded on plain, obvious facts, and has not escaped the attention of the cabinets of Europe. Arbitrary as they are, their only safety lies in preventing their subjects from reaching this point of knowledge, and from witnessing any near examples of successful resistance to the divine right of kings. That this is the principle on which they act, that they have combined to avert this much dreaded crisis, and that these are the means by which they intend to avert it, is plainly asserted in their own official declarations. If we wanted any corroboration of these, we might find it in Naples and Piedmont, in Portugal and Spain; and, if at length, we shall not find it in the "Sea-girt Isle" and on these western shores, it will be because the Lion and the Eagle have combined to guard the passage.

This train of thought furnishes the true reason why—when, to succor the Greeks, their own subjects have al most risen in insurrection, and the swords of their warriors have "leaped instinctively from their scabbards;"—they have yet stood by and viewed the murder of the Patriarch, and the massacre, rapine and pollution of Scio and Cyprus, with a cold and calculating indifference. It has not been owing to the difficulty or expensiveness of the undertaking. It has not been owing to the conflicting interests or the jealousies of the Four great powers. Had the Czar, as he drew his sword in defence of Greece, solemnly protested in the face of heaven and earth,—that his only purpose was to deliver his suffering brethren from extermination, that he would never sheath it until he had driven their oppressors from Europe, that he himself would not touch an acre of their territory, but would guarantee the whole of it, together with the Bosphorus and the Hellespont, to the Greeks, as a free, sovereign and independent nation ;—all the jealousies of rival powers would have been hushed ; and the whole continent of Europe, but for this single principle, would have bidden him God speed.

If, however, in this struggle, the Greeks shall prevail ; a very different train of consequences will ensue. Instead of this long midnight of slavery, deeper and blacker than the midnight of the grave, they will open their eyes on a bright and brilliant morning, to be followed by a long and glorious day. The shackles of slavery will be broken—to be riveted no more. Claiming their ancient limits to the northern frontiers of Macedonia and Epirus, they will occupy a territory, including their numerous islands, of 75,000 square miles—a territory, as we have seen, strongly fortified by nature and by art—a territory eminently healthful, productive and delightful, and every where accessible to the approaches of commerce. They will start into existence as an independent nation with—our own number—three millions of people. They will have been taught lessons of practical wisdom in the school of adversity. The efforts made in the cause of freedom will have roused the whole intellect of the nation, and called forth talents worthy to deliberate in the councils of Greece. If their commerce, when manacled by Turkish despotism, and fleeced by Turkish rapacity, could yet cover and almost command the Mediterranean; whither will it not go, what will it not accomplish, when, moving free as air, it is fostered by a wise and parental government? If their manufacturers, when ground in the dust, could yet acquire a skill, which brought western Europe bending at her feet; to what an extent of enterprise, to what a height of perfection, will they not advance, when roused to emulation by the market of the world? If when robbed, and spoiled, and trampled on as a nation of slaves, they could yet patronize letters, and educate their choicest young men abroad, and found universities, and establish the press, and translate and publish the best authors of ancient and modern Europe; what patronage to learning and science will they not yield, what seminaries will they not endow, what progress in letters will they not make, what illustrious authors and artists will they not rear, when all their wealth is their own; and when all the motives which can actuate freemen, arising from the remembrance of their former greatness, or from personal distinction or national glory crowd upon their minds? If centuries of persecution did not warp them from their religion, when the Bible was possessed merely by their clergy, and science shed upon them only a dim and uncertain light, and they were dissociated from the christian world; how will their conceptions of Christianity be cleared, and their attachment to it strengthened, when they are welcomed into the family of christian nations, and the sanctuary of God enlightens every village, and the Bible every habitation?

With just conceptions of the rights of man and the true principles of a republican government, they will be under no temptation from any feelings of gratitude, from any sense of obligation, to warp from those principles, and involve themselves in entangling alliances with Russia or Austria. From them, from all the powers of the continent they have hitherto witnessed nothing, but unfeeling indifference or secret hostility. All that they now ask of them is—that they will let them alone. This, too, they may confidently expect; for the jealousies of Europe, which have long been the safety of Turkey, will now become the shield of Greece.

With a territory in Europe, occupied by three millions of people, and capable of sustaining twelve millions, will not the freedom of her government, the luxuriance of her soil, the deliciousness of her climate, the advantages of her commerce, and the enterprize of her people invite emigrants from the surrounding world? Will it be surprising if her population increases, for a series of years, in a ratio resembling our own?

The territory left in Europe to Turkey will be comparatively small, The pride of its government will be humbled, and the spirit of its people broken. Much of this remaining territory is occupied by the Moldavians, the Wallachians, and the Servians—tribes always ripe for revolt—professing the Greek religion and actually leading the way in the present revolution. The Turks and their govern ment are barbarian; the nations and governments around them are civilized. With Russia on the North, and Greece on the South, and the rumblings of a volcano underneath, the Turkish power in Europe will sink and be overwhelmed. In that case, the jealousies of the other powers will not improbably enable Greece, at no distant period, to extend her northern limits to the Danube. Should the Ottoman Porte withdraw to Asia Minor, hundreds of thousands of Greeks are already there; and the nation will hardly forget that Anatolia was a part of republican, and Caramania also of imperial, Greece. Should the Porte retreat to Damascus or Bagdad; even there it will hardly find a quiet habitation. Who can doubt that the Armenians and the Curds, the Chaldeans and the Syrians are steadfastly watching the issue of the present contest, and waiting only for the success of the Greeks to take their own place among the nations of the earth. If there be a passion found in every human bosom, kindled in a moment, and when kindled, absorbing every other, and spreading like the electric fire, from man to man and from nation to nation, it is the love of liberty; and if any thing can kindle it into inextinguishable flame, it is the recent example of a neighboring nation's successful struggle for independence. And what nations can have such powerful motives to follow this example, as those who are galled by a Turkish yoke. Their success would be the final overthrow of the Ottoman government; and Asia Minor, Armenia, and Curdistan, Mesopotamia and Syria, Arabia and Egypt, feeling their chains drop from around them, would rise up, shake themselves, and be free.

In proportion as Turkey, the bulwark of the Mohammedan faith, is humbled or subdued, will that faith be weakened or destroyed, Persia is already a nation of infidels; and Arabia and Egypt will easily renounce the religion of the Impostor, when there is no one of his family to wield his sword, or to fight his battles.

In Greece, also, Freedom will plant herself again behind intrenchments, from which she never will be driven. Here she will reign to enrich and enlighten, to reform and to bless. The eyes of Europe will be steadily turned on Greece; and, while they contrast her independence with their own subjugation, they will one by one imitate her example. Like a vast lighthouse throwing its strong and steady splendors on the surrounding darkness, she will point the tempest-beaten nations to the haven of security and peace.

How great will be the privilege to England and the Seven Republics of America, if they can find such an auxiliary in the south-eastern corner of Europe. What an advance will thus be made in behalf of the rights of man and the government of law.

What a field will here be opened for the triumphs of the Gospel. How delightful to overspread Greece with Bibles, and to furnish her the chosen heralds of salvation. What prayers will ascend for the influences of heaven, to fall upon her " like the rain upon the mown grass." Clinging, as she now does, to the great doctrines of our holy Religion, how early may we hope, that she will raise up and send forth her own evangelists to visit other climes.

The downfall of Turkey will remove that impassable barrier, which has hitherto shut out Christianity from Western Asia. The christian nations already there will open their eyes, at once, on the light of the Sun of righteousness. Missionaries loaded with Bibles will feel their way into the farthest retreats of Mohammedan darkness. In Egypt, Arabia and Persia, in Chaldea and Tartary, the tidings of salvation will be proclaimed; and the Gospel of peace, having gained admission, will begin to have free course, to run, and be glorified.

If this event takes place, Jerusalem will cease " to be trodden down of the Gentiles," and " the set time to favor her will come." God has promised by his prophet that, when he shall "set his hand a second time" to recover the remnant of his people, he will set up an ensign on the mountains of Israel, not only for the Jews, but for all the inhabitants of the earth to witness. What event can be so surprising, so calculated to fix the attention of both Jews and Christians, as the common downfal of Turkish and Mohammedan power, the recovery of Jerusalem, the liberation of the eastern churches, and the admission of the Gospel to Western Asia. What an instinctive and simultaneous movement will then take place of all the wandering tribes of Israel towards the land of Promise.

Thus we have glanced at the Country, which is the scene of this interesting Revolution; at the People who have revolted; at their present Prospects; and at the Consequences, which will follow both their failure, and their success.

With these things before you, My friends and countrymen, the solemn, the direct appeal is brought home to your hearts, WHAT FEELINGS WILL YOU CHERISH, WHAT CONDUCT WILL YOU PURSUE? This appeal sounds forth—not from this desk—not from the hall of your own Congress. It comes from the Peloponnesus—it issues from the Senate-house of Calamata. On the 25th of May, 1821, not two months after the declaration of Grecian independence, the Messenian Senate turned their eyes across the ocean: and remembered that this our native land, the glory of all lands, was the country which freedom had chosen as her favorite habitation. Not satisfied, therefore, with including us in the Manifesto addressed to Christendom in general, they made an individual appeal to the citizens of the United States. After announcing to us their fixed determination "to live or die for freedom," and to imitate the example which we have set to the nations of the earth; they call on us "to crown the glory we have thus acquired, by aiding them in purging Greece from the barbarians, who, for four hundred years, have polluted its soil; and in banishing ignorance and barbarism from the country of freedom and the arts." Conscious how little they had to expect from the cabinets of Europe, they look to our country as their last best hope, and bring their appeal directly to her door. "You will not, citizens of America," they say, "assuredly you will not imitate the culpable indifference, the long ingratitude, of some of the Europeans. No, the fellow-citizens of Penn, of Washington and of Franklin will not refuse their aid to the descendants of Thrasybulus and Phocion, of Philopœmen and Aratus."

This appeal, so honorable to our country, is made in the face of the world; and, in the face of the world we must answer it. What answer our Government should give, we leave exclusively to the deliberations of the Capitol. Yet, who that hears me does not rejoice, that the voice of this peninsula, speaking through her representative in the national councils, has already echoed through Europe; proclaiming her sympathy for Greece, and denouncing the machinations of tyranny. But the appeal thus made, is addressed—not to the government, but "to the citizens of the United States;" and, were I permitted for a moment to address my assembled countrymen, I would say to them—

"The voice, which now echoes from the cliffs of the Morea, is addressed to you, as Christians and as freemen. It calls on you, not for governmental aid, but for your personal sympathy, and your individual co-operation. Take care what answer it shall receive. What you do will not be done in a corner. You are not acting merely for yourselves. You have taken a lofty attitude among the nations of the earth. You are stationed on the very ramparts of freedom, and cannot escape their gaze. The question, whether a nation can safely govern itself; whether a great republic can be pre-eminently prosperous and happy; is no longer a matter of doubtful speculation. You furnish mankind the daily evidence of *fact*. Already your example, beaming like a rising sun, on the darkness of the eastern hemisphere—

> "*auspicious* twilight sheds
> On half the nations, and with fear of change
> Perplexes monarchs."——

Already has it rocked France as with an earthquake; swallowing up her throne, and convulsing the surrounding continent. Already has it drawn from the monarch of Prussia the offer of a high reward to the writer, who should most ably answer the question—"What is the best mode of stopping the progress of those dangerous principles, which were promulgated during the American revolution?" Already has it embolden the colonies of America, to burst their chains, and take their stations by your side, as free and independent republics. Already has it terrified the great sovereigns of the continent into the Holy Alliance. Already, in the face of that alliance, has it lit the torch of revolution in Portugal and Spain, in Piedmont and Naples.

Greece, too, has felt its power. Imitating your example, she has thrown down the gauntlet, and is breasting herself to the shock of war. Your wise and happy form of government, she has established; your laws and institutions, she is adopting. Will you perpetuate this salutary influence, if you are deaf to her calls, and discover no interest in her sufferings. Shall the taunting infidel, or the frowning despot, laugh at her overweening confidence in your attachment to religion and freedom. Will it redound to your honor, at last, that her sages and patriots have thus singled you out, and, in the hearing of the surrounding world, have said to you, 'We esteem you nearer to us than the nations on our frontiers, and we look to you as friends, fellow-citizens, and brethren,' if you suffer them to look to you in vain. Because you are free and safe yourselves, are those, who are struggling to break the chains of slavery, to have no hold on your hearts. Because you have weathered the storm, and reached the haven of peace; will you feel no sympathy for those who are still buffeting with the tempest, and in danger of being whelmed beneath the billows. Shall vassal France lend that aid to the freedom of America, which independent America will not lend to the liberties of Greece. Will you invite to your shores the Hero, who, in the hour of your extremity, fought by the side of Washington, and spent his treasures and his blood to set you free; and shall your sons when they hereafter visit Greece, be entitled to no kindness for the aid you furnished her in achieving her independence."

"Has then, oppression goaded on the Greeks to madness—Are they fighting, not merely for their fire-sides and their altars, but for the cause of freedom, and the cause of God—And do they look to you, my countrymen, for help? —Feel, then, for them as strongly, as deeply, as you would feel for yourselves, if you were fighting in their stead; or if you were called to fight over again the battles of your revolution. Let these feelings be universal—make their cause your own—and enlist in their favor the compassion, the sympathies of mankind.

"Are you a nation of Christians? Let these feelings lead you to fervent and unceasing prayer, in secret and in public, to Him who rules among the nations, that he will be "a wall of fire around about them, and the glory in the midst of them, and that on all the glory there may be a defence." Offer also your devout ascriptions of praise and thanksgiving, because, lending a gracious ear to their supplication,—"that he would afford them his Almighty protection,"—he has hitherto fought their battles, and been to them a shield and a buckler."

"Prove the sincerity of your feelings and your prayers by your works. God in his providence now presents you a happy opportunity to give vent to the feelings, with which Turkish barbarity and Grecian valor have inspired you. At this call, let every American, every Christian heart beat high, and every purse-string be broken; and an amount contributed for your suffering brethren, which will prove to the gazing nations your gratitude to God, your sympathy for the oppressed, your desires for the extension of Christianity, and your compassion for a world in chains. What you do, do quickly. The hour of trial has come. On the issue of this campaign, are the destinies of Greece suspended. Before its close, her sun will go down in darkness, and starless midnight brood for centuries over the fairest portion of the globe; or, ascending in unclouded splendor, will shed its warm influence on her hills and vallies, and throw its broad beams from the Baltic to the Niger, from the Tagus to the Caspian. O that Greece, O that Europe might see in the amount you send them, a spirit becoming the children of those, who invited Freedom, long banished from the world, to return, and take up her residence *here!*"

But, though not called to plead the cause of Greece, before my assembled countrymen; yet, at the request of your Committee, I am this evening, allowed, my friends and fellow-citizens, to urge her claims on you. But need

I *urge* them?—What heart does not throb, what bosom does not heave, at the very thought of Grecian Independence? Have you the feelings of a man, and do you not wish that the blood of Greece should cease to flow, and that the groans and sighs of centuries should be heard no more? Are you a scholar; and shall the land of the Muses ask your help in vain? With the eye of the enthusiast do you often gaze at the triumphs of the Arts; and will you do nothing to rescue their choicest relics from worse than Vandal barbarism? Are you a mother, rejoicing in all the charities of domestic life;—are you a daughter, rich and safe in conscious innocence and parental love; and shall thousands more, among the purest and loveliest of your sex, glut the shambles of Smyrna, and be doomed to a captivity inconceivably worse than death? Are you a Christian, and do you cheerfully contribute your property to christianize the heathen world?—what you give to Greece is to rescue *a nation of Christians* from extermination, to deliver the ancient churches, to overthrow the Mohammedan imposture, to raise up a standard for the wandering tribes of Israel, and to gather in the harvest of the world. Are you an American citizen, proud of the liberty and independence of your country? Greece, too, is struggling for these very blessings, which she taught your fathers to purchase with their blood. And when she asks your help, need I *urge* you to bestow it?—Where am I?—In the sanctuary of God, in the city of the Pilgrims, in the very birth-place of American Independence—hard by yonder HALL, and yonder WHARVES—and midway between the Heights of Dorchester and Bunker Hill. Here, then, I leave their cause.